Behavioral Group Therapy, 1981

An Annual Review

Dennis Upper
Steven M. Ross
Editors

Research Press Company
2612 N. Mattis Avenue
Champaign, Illinois 61820

RC 489. B4
B4357

Copyright © 1981 by Research Press Company

All rights reserved. Printed in the United States of America. No part
of this book may be reproduced by mimeograph or any other means
without the written permission of the publisher. Excerpts may be printed
in connection with published reviews in periodicals without express
permission.

Cover design by Jack Davis
Composition by Omegatype Typography, Inc.

Copies of this book may be ordered from the publisher at the address
given on the title page.

ISBN 0-87822-256-1 (book)

ISBN 0-87822-209-X (series)

ISSN 0191-5681

Library of Congress Catalog Card Number 80-642109

CONTENTS

Aims and Scope   v

Contributors   vii

Contents of *Behavioral Group Therapy, 1979*   xi

Contents of *Behavioral Group Therapy, 1980*   xiii

PART ONE: METHODOLOGICAL STUDIES   1

1   Group Training of Social Skills:
   Clinical Applications and Procedures   3
        Jeffrey A. Kelly

2   The Assessment of a Large Assertion Training Group:
   A Treatment and Evaluation Model for Community
   Mental Health Services   27
        John V. Flowers, Karen A. Hartman,
        Rochelle J. Mann, Susan W. Kidder,
        Curtis D. Booraem, and Bruce Tapper

3   Cognitive Behavior Therapy Groups:
   Methods and Comparative Research   41
        Joan R. Shapiro, Carolyn S. Shaffer,
        Lawrence I. Sank, and Donna J. Coghlan

4   Group Therapist Training: An Objective Assessment
   of Individuals' Leadership Ability   67
        John V. Flowers, Karen A. Hartman,
        and Curtis D. Booraem

PART TWO: BEHAVIORAL GROUP THERAPY WITH
COURT-ADJUDICATED CLIENTS   79

5   Social Skills Training for Juvenile Delinquents: Behavioral
   Skill Training and Cognitive Techniques   81
        Janice M. De Lange, Susan L. Lanham,
        and Judy A. Barton

6 **The Development and Evaluation of a Group Skills Training
Program for Court–Adjudicated Youths**   113
J. Stephen Hazel, Jean Bragg Schumaker,
James A. Sherman, and Jan Sheldon-Wildgen

7 **Analysis, Validation, and Training of Peer–Criticism
Skills With Delinquent Girls**   153
Neil Minkin, Bonnie L. Minkin, Richard S. Goldstein,
Marc W. Taylor, Curtis J. Braukmann,
Kathryn A. Kirigin, and Montrose M. Wolf

8 **Training Paraprofessionals to Do Assertion Training With
Mentally Disordered Sex Offenders**   167
Lou Ann Wieand, John V. Flowers, and
Karen A. Hartman

PART THREE: SPECIFIC POPULATIONS AND PROBLEMS   185

9 **Behavioral Group Therapy With Elderly Depressives:
An Experimental Study**   187
Dolores Gallagher

10 **The Effectiveness of Group–Administered
Relaxation Training as an Adjunctive
Therapy for Essential Hypertension**   225
D. Michael Rice and P. Scott Lawrence

11 **Behavioral Group Therapy With Psychiatric
Outpatients: A Controlled Study**   241
Ian R. H. Falloon

12 **Group Behavior Therapy for the Treatment of Obesity:
Issues and Suggestions**   279
Maxwell R. Knauss and D. Balfour Jeffrey

13 **Long-Term Follow–Up of Couples' Treatment of Obesity**   309
Carol Landau Heckerman and Robert E. Zitter

Subject Index   319

Author Index   325

Aims and Scope

Behavioral Group Therapy: An Annual Review is a multidisciplinary serial publication which is aimed at presenting significant research reports, clinical group studies, review articles, and other material related to the application of behavioral treatment procedures in group therapy settings. The primary purposes of this *Annual Review* are: (1) to serve as an up-to-date and central source of information about the important recent clinical work and research involving behavioral group therapy, (2) to indicate areas of needed research and to stimulate scientific inquiry in these areas, and (3) to provide a forum for communication among those doing clinical work and research of this type. In order to serve a desirable and needed training function, its articles include case material, detailed descriptions of therapeutic methods, and transcriptions of group therapy sessions in order to illustrate how target behaviors are identified, how treatment methods are selected and applied, how difficulties are handled, and how therapeutic progress is evaluated. Articles which critically analyze and discuss important theoretical, social, professional, and ethical issues involved in the practice of behavioral group therapy also are included.

This *Annual Review* has two major thrusts, one theoretical and one practical. The theoretical thrust is designed to answer the question: "Will research and case material using behavioral group approaches enable us to understand group psychotherapy in general as a lawful, predictable process?" The practical thrust is directed to the question: "Can analyzing group therapy from a learning point of view direct our attention to practical improvements in the practice of group therapy, whatever the theoretical persuasion of the therapist?" Even more specifically, this series addresses the question of which behavioral procedures have proven to be particularly amenable to implementation in group therapy situations and with what types of problematic behaviors and patient populations.

Included in this series will be articles describing behavioral group treatment in the following areas: (1) emotional and avoidance behaviors, (2) habitual and addictive behaviors, (3) children's behaviors and family interactions, (4) adolescent and delinquent behaviors, (5) adult social and sexual behaviors, (6) behaviors of institutionalized patients and inmates, (7) miscellaneous target behaviors and techniques (e.g., group treatment of stuttering, chronic pain, etc.), and (8) behavioral marital therapy. Although the scope of the *Annual Review* is broad enough to include a wide range of content and settings, two general limitations are observed. First, the *Annual Review*'s focus is on the application of behavioral procedures in group therapy settings, rather than on the more general area of behavior modification with a group of patients, such as through the use of hospital token economies or structured classroom programs. Second, although significant work is being done in the area of applying behavioral techniques in vocational counseling and training groups, this *Annual Review* concentrates on group work in which more "clinical" behavioral problems such as those enumerated above are the targets for change.

Contributors

Judy A. Barton

Sedro-Woolley School District, Special Services Department, Sedro-Woolley, Washington

Curtis D. Booraem

Booraem, Flowers and Associates, Newport Beach, California

Curtis J. Braukmann

Bureau of Child Research and Department of Human Development and Family Life, University of Kansas, Lawrence, Kansas

Donna J. Coghlan

Department of Health Care Sciences, George Washington University Medical Center, Washington, D. C.

Janice M. De Lange

School of Social Work, University of Washington, Seattle, Washington

Ian R. H. Falloon

Department of Psychiatry and the Behavioral Sciences, University of Southern California, Los Angeles, California

John V. Flowers

Booraem, Flowers and Associates, Newport Beach, California, and Fairview State Hospital, Costa Mesa, California

Dolores Gallagher

Ethel Percy Andrus Gerontology Center, University of Southern California, Los Angeles, California

Richard S. Goldstein

The Kansas Research Institute, Lawrence, Kansas

Karen A. Hartman

Department of Psychology, University of California at Riverside, Riverside, California

J. Stephen Hazel

Department of Human Development and Family Life, University of Kansas, Lawrence, Kansas

Carol Landau Heckerman

Section on Psychiatry and Human Behavior, Brown University, Providence, Rhode Island

D. Balfour Jeffrey

Department of Psychology, University of Montana, Missoula, Montana

Jeffrey A. Kelly

Department of Psychiatry and Human Behavior, University of Mississippi Medical Center, Jackson, Mississippi

Susan W. Kidder

Program in Social Ecology, University of California at Irvine, Irvine, California

Kathryn A. Kirigin

Bureau of Child Research and Department of Human Development and Family Life, University of Kansas, Lawrence, Kansas

Maxwell R. Knauss

Department of Psychology, University of Montana, Missoula, Montana

Susan L. Lanham

Issaquah School District, Special Evaluation Project, Issaquah, Washington

P. Scott Lawrence

Department of Psychology, University of North Carolina at Greensboro, Greensboro, North Carolina

Rochelle J. Mann

Program in Social Ecology, University of California at Irvine, Irvine, California

Bonnie L. Minkin

The Kansas Research Institute and Department of Human Development and Family Life, University of Kansas, Lawrence, Kansas

Neil Minkin

The Kansas Research Institute and Department of Human Development and Family Life, University of Kansas, Lawrence, Kansas

D. Michael Rice

Department of Psychology, University of North Carolina at Greensboro, Greensboro, North Carolina

Lawrence I. Sank

Department of Health Care Sciences, George Washington University Medical Center, Washington, D. C.

Jean Bragg Schumaker

Institute for Research in Learning Disabilities, University of Kansas, Lawrence, Kansas

Carolyn S. Shaffer

Department of Health Care Sciences, George Washington University Medical Center, Washington, D. C.

Joan R. Shapiro

Department of Health Care Sciences, George Washington University Medical Center, Washington, D. C.

Jan Sheldon-Wildgen

Department of Human Development and Family Life, University of Kansas, Lawrence, Kansas

James A. Sherman

Department of Human Development and Family Life, University of Kansas, Lawrence, Kansas

Bruce Tapper

Santa Ana Psychiatric Hospital, Santa Ana, California

Marc W. Taylor

Bureau of Child Research, University of Kansas, Lawrence, Kansas

Lou Ann Wieand

Department of Psychology, University of California at Riverside, Riverside, California

Montrose M. Wolf

Bureau of Child Research and Department of Human Development and Family Life, University of Kansas, Lawrence, Kansas

Robert E. Zitter

Section on Psychiatry and Human Behavior, Brown University, Providence, Rhode Island

Contents of
Behavioral Group Therapy, 1979

PART ONE: THE BEHAVIORAL GROUP THERAPY PROCESS

1 Behavioral Analysis of Group Therapy and a Model for Behavioral Group Therapy
John V. Flowers

2 The Role of the Group in Behavioral Group Therapy
David L. Sanbury

3 Process Analysis in Therapy Groups: A Behavior Sampling Technique with Many Potential Uses
William E. Piper, Ruta M. Montvila, and Anne L. McGihon

PART TWO: BEHAVIORAL GROUP THERAPY IN CLINICAL PRACTICE

4 An Analysis of Behavioral Group Treatment Programs Designed to Modify Sexual Dysfunction
Kevin B. McGovern

5 Group Treatment of Sexual Dysfunction: Coping Skill Training for Single Males
W. Charles Lobitz and Elgan L. Baker, Jr.

6 A Broad-Spectrum Behavioral Group Approach to Smoking Reduction
Steven P. Schinke, Betty J. Blythe, and Howard J. Doueck

7 Cognitive-Behavioral Group Therapy and Assertion Training
Arthur J. Lange

8 Behavioral Group Therapy with Adolescents: A Review and Pilot Program
Carl Schrader

PART THREE: MODELS FOR BEHAVIORAL GROUP THERAPY PROGRAMS

9 A Psycho-Educational Model for Skill Training: Therapist-Facilitated and Game-Facilitated Applications
Jeffrey R. Bedell and Lawrence R. Weathers

10 **A Proposed Model for Behavioral Group Therapy with Pain Patients**
Myles Genest and Dennis C. Turk
11 **A Proposed Behavioral Couples Group for Male Alcoholics and Their Wives**
Timothy J. O'Farrell and Henry S. G. Cutter
12 **Step Group Therapy: A Behavioral Group Approach for Short-Term Psychiatric Inpatients**
Kay Gustafson
13 **Behavioral Group Psychotherapy for Overweight Children and Adolescents**
Judith Coché, Leonard S. Levitz, and Henry A. Jordan

Contents of
Behavioral Group Therapy, 1980

PART ONE: SKILLS TRAINING APPROACHES

1 A Description and Evaluation of a Problem Solving
   Skills Training Program
        Jeffrey R. Bedell, Robert P. Archer, and Herbert
        A. Marlowe, Jr.

2 Heterosocial Skills Training: A Behavioral-Cognitive
   Approach
        Brian L. West, Katherine E. Goethe, and William
        M. Kallman

3 Changes in Assertiveness and Marital Satisfaction after
   Participation in an Assertiveness Training Group
        Judith S. Blau

4 Group Training of Problem Solving with Psychiatric
   Patients
        Barry A. Edelstein, Eugene Couture, Mary Cray,
        Pamela Dickens, and Nancy Lusebrink

PART TWO: DESCRIPTIONS OF INSTITUTIONAL PROGRAMS

5 Marital Therapy in an Educational Group Setting: The
   Communication Center in Leuven, Belgium
        Johan Verhulst and Cornelius B. Bakker

6 An Educational Approach to Psychiatric Day Care
        Hubert E. Armstrong, Jr.

7 Learning to Cope: Content and Context of an
   Educational Program
        Cornelius B. Bakker, Marianne K. Bakker-Rabdau,
        and Johan Verhulst

PART THREE: SPECIFIC POPULATIONS AND PROBLEMS

8 Multifactor Risk Reduction with Children and
   Adolescents: Taking Care of the Heart in Behavioral
   Group Therapy
        Thomas J. Coates and Cheryl Perry

9 Psychoeducational Skills Training for Individuals with
   Epilepsy
        Henne R. Queisser, Hubert E. Armstrong, Jr.,
        Wayne R. Smith, and Gay R. Davis

10 **Suggestions for Behavioral Group Therapy of Depression**
David Roth

11 **Behavioral Group Therapy with Chronic Day Hospital Patients: Problems, Pitfalls, and Recommendations**
Gary A. Williamson and Francisco X. Barrios

PART FOUR: PROCESS AND OUTCOME STUDIES

12 **Three Studies toward a Fuller Understanding of Behavioral Group Therapy: Cohesion, Client Flexibility, and Outcome Generalization**
John V. Flowers and Curtis D. Booraem

Study 1: The Components of Cohesion in Group Therapy
John V. Flowers, Mary J. Rotheram, Barbara Kenney, and Curtis D. Booraem

Study 2: The Effects of Group Cohesion and Client Flexibility on Therapy Outcome
John V. Flowers, Karen A. Hartman, Rochelle J. Mann, Susan Kidder, and Curtis D. Booraem

Study 3: Generalization and Maintenance of Client Outcome in Group Therapy
John V. Flowers, Bruce Tapper, Susan Kidder, Garrie Wein, and Curtis D. Booraem

13 **Methods of Increasing Self-Reinforcement in Group Therapy and the Effects on Therapy Outcome**
Nancy B. Cohn, Rochelle J. Mann, John V. Flowers, and Curtis D. Booraem

Part One

Methodological Studies

The four chapters included in Part One address a number of methodological issues pertaining to the implementation and evaluation of behavioral group therapy programs in applied settings, including the cost effectiveness of the interventions employed, the training and evaluation of group leaders, the generalization of newly acquired skills from the group to the natural environment, and potential improvements in the delivery of therapeutic services.

In Chapter 1 Jeffrey Kelly outlines a conceptual framework for social skills training approaches, presents a behavioral-clinical model for conducting skills training groups, and describes some empirical approaches to assessing the effectiveness of such group interventions. Since inadequate generalization of skills from the training setting to the natural environment is a problem frequently reported in the skills training literature, the discussion of specific techniques that can be used to facilitate such generalization may be particularly useful for group leaders.

John Flowers and his associates, in Chapter 2, present evidence that assertiveness training can be offered to a large number of participants simultaneously in a large group format ($N = 54$), and that it is both effective and cost efficient to do so. The authors point out some potential difficulties in attempting to evaluate the effectiveness of such interventions in the community mental health setting. Improvements in service delivery that could result from the use of larger skills training groups are discussed.

1

A cognitive behavior therapy approach to the group treatment of depressed and anxious outpatients is outlined in Chapter 3 by Joan Shapiro, Carolyn Shaffer, Lawrence Sank, and Donna Coghlan. Cognitive behavior therapy in a group format was found to be as effective as individual therapy in reducing depression and anxiety while increasing assertiveness, and here again the cost benefits of utilizing short-term, group-based interventions are emphasized, particularly for health maintenance organizations (HMOs) such as the one described in this chapter.

While the group therapy literature contains a number of articles that address the way in which group therapists should be trained, few have focused on the issue of how to assess individual leadership ability during or after training. In Chapter 4 John Flowers, Karen Hartman, and Curtis Booraem describe their attempts to identify objective criteria for evaluating the developing skills of group therapy leader trainees. The six objective measures they employed were found to correlate highly with experienced clinicians' judgments of the trainees' ability, and the authors suggest the potential usefulness in psychotherapy outcome research of assessing leadership ability in an ongoing way.

Chapter 1

Group Training of Social Skills: Clinical Applications and Procedures

Jeffrey A. Kelly

Abstract

This chapter outlines procedural issues in the conduct of group social skills training, particularly when treatment is carried out in an applied setting. Because many clients report, or are observed by therapists to exhibit, deficits in their handling of interpersonal interactions (such as situations requiring assertion, conversational skills, heterosocial or date-initiation skills, and job interview effectiveness), direct training of these behavioral competencies has been widely advocated. Following a brief review of some conceptual foundations for social skills training, procedures for the behavioral assessment of client social competency are considered. A component analysis approach to social skill definition is presented for various types of skills. Group skills training, because of its cost efficiency and the social environment it affords, appears to be a particularly useful method for increasing social competencies. Techniques such as instruction/coaching, modeling exposure, overt practice or rehearsal, and feedback or reinforcement can be incorporated in the skills training group session to increase the behavioral components of any type of social skill. Procedures to foster generalization of training and to evaluate applied group interventions are discussed.*

*The author extends appreciation to Ellen Berler and Mary Winford for their assistance. Requests for reprints should be sent to Jeffrey A. Kelly, Department of Psychiatry and Human Behavior, University of Mississippi Medical Center, 2500 North State Street, Jackson, Mississippi 39216.

Psychologists and personality theorists have long recognized the relationship between clients' interpersonal functioning and their psychological adjustment. For example, Sullivan, Adler, Horney, and George Kelly have all noted in their traditional theories that successful social interactions are both a consequence and a prerequisite of general adjustment and effective lifestyles. However, while the importance of client social competence has long been a descriptive element in traditional personality theories, it is only in the relatively recent past that clinicians have investigated empirically behavioral strategies for teaching social competencies directly to skills-deficient clients (Curran, 1977; Twentyman & Zimering, 1979). An even more recent development is the use of behavioral group-administered training to increase the ability of clients to handle interpersonal situations effectively in the naturalistic (criterion) environment. The purpose of this chapter is to: (a) briefly review the conceptual framework for social skills training interventions, (b) present a behavioral-clinical model for the procedural conduct of group-administered social skills training sessions, and (c) note several empirical approaches to assessment of the effectiveness of group social skills training, particularly when training is conducted in applied settings.

SOCIAL SKILLS ACQUISITION: A SOCIAL LEARNING FORMULATION

Social skills can be defined globally as those learned instrumental and interpersonal competencies that an individual uses to obtain or maintain levels of social reinforcement from his environment. Certain classes of social skills (such as conversational skills or heterosocial and dating-initiation skills) are useful because they serve to make the individual a more reinforcing agent to those with whom he interacts. Thus, such skills facilitate the establishment of social relationships. Other classes of social skills (such as refusal assertion) assist an individual in maintaining reinforcement when his goal-directed behavior is threatened unreasonably by other individuals. Still other types of skills are instrumental in a much more situationally specific manner, including the ability to present oneself effectively to a potential employer during job interviews or the ability of an alcoholic client to assert himself and refuse a drink offered by a friend.

Among some client groups, social skills deficits often appear to be quite pervasive and substantial. Bellack and Hersen (1978), for example, note that in spite of the diverse and contradictory theories that have been postulated to account for the development of schizophrenia, the visual image and interpersonal descriptors that come to almost all clinicians' minds when presented with the term "chronic schizophrenic" seem remarkably consistent: a picture of massive interpersonal deficits, blunted social responsiveness, and little spontaneity. Similarly, moderately retarded citizens who might otherwise adapt well in the community are often characterized by relatively pervasive, generalized social skills deficits (Kelly, Wildman, Urey, & Thurman, 1979). It appears that the behavior of many retarded persons and chronic psychiatric patients is characterized both by idiosyncratic social cues which accentuate their interpersonal "differentness" and by skill-deficient repertoires which make it difficult for them to establish social relationships across a variety of situations.

On the other hand, client groups functioning at a higher level can also exhibit severe interpersonal deficits, but in more isolated, situation-specific ways. Clients may handle most social interactions successfully but experience anxiety and diminished social performance when interacting with others on an informal basis in social situations, or even more specifically, only during interactions with members of the opposite sex. A number of investigations have suggested that such heterosocial or dating anxiety is problematic even for generally high-functioning college students (Curran, 1977; MacDonald, Lindquist, Kramer, McGrath, & Rhyne, 1975; Martinson & Zerface, 1970; Melnick, 1973). Similarly, assertive responses appear difficult for many persons to make, and assertive expression itself is quite situation-specific, depending on whether the antagonist is a friend or a stranger, on the gender of the client and the antagonist, and on the setting or circumstances surrounding the need for assertiveness (Bellack, Hersen, & Lamparski, 1979; Eisler, Hersen, Miller, & Blanchard, 1975). Other situations requiring specialized social skills, such as job interviews, are encountered infrequently by most individuals, who therefore may fail to acquire the skills that would enable them to handle that kind of situation effectively.

It appears that terms such as "social skills," "assertiveness," or "social competency" have often been used in a rather broad, trait-like sense. However, the social skills that an individual exhibits vary across situations, so an individual's social competence in one type of situation may be uncorrelated with her social competence in another type of situation (Mischel, 1968). Further, the utility value or appropriateness of specific social responses seems determined by the type of situation. Because "social skills" are not a uniform, generalized class of behavior, group skills training efforts must be closely tailored to the kind of situation being targeted for treatment (e.g., conversational skills when meeting an unfamiliar person, conflict-resolution skills when interacting with one's spouse, heterosocial or dating skills, assertive skills relevant to specific situations, or job interview skills) rather than being more general in focus.

Little research has been done to examine those variables that are responsible for the naturalistic development of social competencies in specific situations. However, social learning theory principles (see Bandura, 1969; Bandura & Walters, 1963) would suggest that several factors are principally responsible for the learning of social skills. *Instruction* or *direction* (from parents, peers, or others) in ways to handle certain social interactions probably serves as an initial, albeit weak, influence on naturalistic skills acquisition. *Observation of models* who exhibit socially skillful behavior during childhood, adolescence, and adult life provides an individual with a more potent vicarious source of interpersonal learning. *Opportunity for practice,* actually engaging in the relevant types of interaction, provides the individual with behavioral practice in the skills. Finally, *feedback from others and reinforcing consequences* following the specified interaction serve to shape further socially skillful responses and strengthen the probability that they will occur in the future. Presumably, if such influences are insufficient, the naturalistic learning of social competencies will be correspondingly limited. This result might occur if a client has little exposure to the behavior of socially skillful models, if the client has limited social interactions or opportunities to practice certain skills, if previous social initiations have been punished or nonreinforced, or if the client receives (or perceives) little feedback on her performance in social interactions to guide future learning. As will be elaborated more fully in the next section, the aim of group social skills training is to apply the same learning theory principles that account for naturalistic skills acquisition (instruction, modeling, rehearsal, feedback, and reinforcement) within the course of each treatment group session.

A final conceptual issue regarding the naturalistic learning of social competencies merits clinical attention. If, for whatever reason, a client has failed to acquire the skills to handle a given social interaction successfully, a "vicious cycle" pattern may develop that operates to maintain the deficiencies and preclude future *in vivo* learning. The individual who lacks the social-behavioral competencies to achieve successful outcomes in a particular situation is apt to encounter nonreinforcement or even punishment when in those situations, and the social responses will eventually extinguish. Thus, the heterosocially anxious person may come to avoid dating interactions, the unsuccessful job interviewee may stop going on job interviews, or the conversationally deficient client may become increasingly isolated. Moreover, when the client is confronted with interactions that she feels unequipped to handle successfully, anticipatory anxiety and anxiety-maintaining cognitions will further impair the probability of her making skillful responses. For example, Curran and his associates (Curran, 1977; Curran & Gilbert, 1975) have noted the deleterious effects of evaluative anxiety on skill performance in dating interactions among heterosocially anxious individuals. Under such conditions, it is extremely likely the individual will simply learn to avoid that class of social interaction. As a consequence of such avoidance, potential opportunities for naturalistic exposure to skillful models, as well as opportunities for practice and reinforcement, will be seriously limited. Thus, in the absence of clinical intervention, skill deficiencies can easily be perpetuated.

By teaching clients social skills directly, it is possible to interrupt this cycle and equip clients to handle successfully those situations that had been troublesome in the past. After learning new social skills during the group training intervention and then utilizing them with reinforcing consequences in the criterion environment, clients will be better able to seek out interpersonal situations previously avoided, and thus be exposed to naturalistic social learning opportunities. The dominant model in social skills training appears to assume that clients handle certain situations ineffectively, or avoid those situations altogether, because they do not have the skills to perform successfully in such situations. However, it also seems likely that many clients "know" cognitively how to behave in critical situations but inhibit their performance of appropriate skills due to evaluative anxiety or unrealistically low self-appraisals of their competence. Even when such factors inhibit social skill performance, direct training accompanied by external therapist feedback and cognitive modification procedures appears to be a useful treatment choice (see Lange, 1979).

GROUP SOCIAL SKILLS TRAINING: APPLIED CLINICAL CONSIDERATIONS

The preceding section briefly reviewed the conceptual rationale for interpersonal skills training among client populations. Attention will now be directed toward the actual implementation of behavioral group social skills training interventions, particularly those conducted in applied treatment settings. Five issues merit specific consideration: (a) elaboration of the purpose of a group skills training intervention, (b) behavioral definition of the target or goal social skills competency, (c) behavioral assessment of clients' pretreatment skills competency, (d) active treatment components incorporated within each group training session, and (e) procedural issues in the conduct of the skills training group.

Purpose and Aim of Group Social Skills Training

Traditional forms of group therapy attempt to establish a treatment environment promoting better interactions among clients within the group session itself; thus, a primary criterion or target environment for clients' behavior change is their interpersonal behavior *within the treatment session setting* (Frank, 1973; Yalom, 1975). In such a traditional framework, clinical attention is often focused on group process or dynamic factors (i.e., altering the manner in which clients interact with one another).

The group is viewed as a microcosm of the community. If client behavior is changed within the group, it may also be expected to change in the extra-therapy environment (Frank, 1973; Yalom, 1975). Often, the therapist role is relatively passive; she facilitates or interprets.

In contrast, group social skills training is highly structured, with the aim of the group to teach clients how to handle more effectively a clearly specified type of social interaction that they find problematic in the natural environment. While client behavior change does occur within the group session, it is structured (such as during behavior rehearsal or practice), it closely approximates the natural environment event that is being addressed (such as role-played job interviews if the purpose of the group is job interview training), and it has the clear aim of modifying client behavior within the *in vivo* environment, rather than focusing on within-group processes or dynamics per se. Results are accomplished by systematically applying learning principles to modify and shape each client's overt rehearsal or practice of the targeted skills in the group, and by then applying similar learning principles to bring about the generalization of this social behavior change from the group to the relevant *in vivo* social interaction. Clients in the skills training group interact extensively with one another in order to shape, prompt, reinforce, and provide feedback to each other on the behavioral practice that takes place in the session. The role of the therapist is active, educational, and often directive.

Behavioral Definition of the Target or Goal Social Skill Response

Before initiating any social skills training group, it is necessary to determine what type of social skill is being targeted for treatment and what constitutes effective behavioral exhibition of that goal skill. Previous research has demonstrated the use of training interventions for a wide variety of social skills and with a wide variety of client populations including: assertiveness among college students (McFall & Marston, 1970; McFall & Twentyman, 1973; Melnick & Stocker, 1977), schizophrenic patients (Edelstein & Eisler, 1976; Eisler, Hersen, & Miller, 1973; Hersen & Bellack, 1976), explosive personality-disordered individuals (Foy, Eisler, & Pinkston, 1975; Fredericksen, Jenkins, Foy, & Eisler, 1976), drug addicts (Callner & Ross, 1978), and children (Bornstein, Bellack, & Hersen, 1977); conversational skills among psychiatric patients (Kelly, Urey, & Patterson, 1980; Urey, Laughlin, & Kelly, 1979), retarded citizens (Kelly, Furman, Phillips, Hathorn, & Wilson, 1979; Kelly, Wildman, Urey, & Thurman, 1979), and students (Minkin, Braukmann, Minkin, Timbers, Timbers, Fixsen, Phillips, & Wolf, 1976); heterosocial or dating-initiation skills among students (Curran & Gilbert, 1975; MacDonald, et al., 1975; Melnick, 1973); and job interview skills (Furman, Geller, Simon, & Kelly, 1979;

Hollandsworth, Dressel, & Stevens, 1977; Hollandsworth, Glazeski, & Dressel, 1978; Kelly, Laughlin, Claiborne, & Patterson, 1979; Kelly, Urey, & Patterson, in press; Kelly, Wildman, & Berler, 1980). Implicit in this chapter's introductory section is the notion that "social skills training" is a very general treatment description term. When initiating a clinical group intervention, it is essential to specify exactly what class of social skill is being targeted.

A second and equally important issue is defining what specific behaviors or skill components constitute the desired goal response. For example, if the aim of the group is to develop clients' effective conversational skills, one must determine what particular verbal or nonverbal components make up effective conversational skills and should therefore be improved. If the goal of training is to increase the assertiveness of clients, one must define the constellation of behaviors that constitute an assertive response. If these component behaviors are not adequately defined, it will be impossible to assess the initial level of client skill, and it will be similarly impossible to know which specific component behaviors must be shaped to develop adequately the final skill goal response.

Table 1.1 summarizes those behavioral components that are presumed to constitute an end-product goal response for a number of social skills, based upon clinical research literature. For example, refusal assertion has often been defined by the presence of several behavioral components including reasonable eye contact, voice loudness, firm affect, verbal noncompliance with the antagonist, statement of the individual's own position, and requesting that the antagonist engage in more reasonable new behavior in the future (Eisler, Hersen, & Miller, 1973; Eisler, Miller, & Hersen, 1973). Presumably, if these components were present in an individual's response, that response would be judged as assertive; if these components were missing or poorly executed, the individual would be considered to have behaved unassertively in the interaction. The purpose of group training is to teach clients to include each of those behavioral components that together constitute an effective global skill (such as assertion) in their relevant responses.

Several cautionary comments are needed in this regard. First, a clinical model in which one defines a goal social skill by its behavioral components requires that the presence of those components actually be related to that skill. Several investigators (Kelly, Furman, Phillips, Hathorn, & Wilson, 1979; Minkin et al., 1976) have noted that many of the relationships between behavioral components and the goal skill they constitute are based upon intuitive speculation rather than carefully validated empirical demonstration. Minkin et al. (1976) have pointed out the need to "socially validate" those components that are presumably related to more global evaluations of social competency. This validation could be accomplished by

Table 1.1
Behaviors Identified As or Proposed to Be
Components of Several Types of Social Skills

Goal Skill	Source	Ratable, Identified, or Proposed Components
Assertion Skills (refusal)	Eisler, Miller, & Hersen (1973)	Speech characteristics (duration of reply, response latency, loudness, fluency); content/affect (noncompliance with antagonist, requests for new behavior, firm affect); nonverbal behavior (eye contact)
	Edelstein & Eisler (1976)	Eye contact, gestures, affect, loudness, presence/absence of information-seeking from antagonist, remarks in defense of client position
	Eisler, Hersen, & Miller (1973)	Eye contact duration, speech duration, response latency, loudness, verbal noncompliance, content requesting new behavior from antagonist, assertive affect, overall assertiveness
	Linehan, Goldfried, & Goldfried (1979)	Assertive verbal content (rated on 1–5 scale), speech fluency, loudness/affect, eye contact, frequency of assertive responses/interaction, subjective reports of reduced anxiety, guilt, or anger
Job Interview Skills	Hollandsworth, Glazeski, & Dressel (1978)	Eye contact, speech fluency, appropriateness of verbal content, composure, appearance (all rated on 1–4 scales)
	Kelly, Laughlin, Claiborne, & Patterson (1979); Kelly, Urey, & Patterson (in press)	Questions directed by client to interviewer, statements conveying favorable information about past experience, verbal expressions of job interest, reduced inappropriate or negative comments

Goal Skill	Source	Ratable, Identified, or Proposed Components
	Furman, Geller, Simon, & Kelly (1979)	Statements conveying favorable information about past job experience, gesturing, job-relevant questions directed to interviewer, favorable but non-job-relevant personal information statements
Conversational Skills	Minkin, Braukman, Minkin, Timbers, Timbers, Fixsen, Phillips, & Wolf (1976)	Conversational questions, positive conversational feedback, amount of time talking
	Kelly, Wildman, Urey, & Thurman (1979); Kelly, Urey, & Patterson (1980)	Statements eliciting information from other person, statements disclosing interests or personal information, reinforcing or complimentary comments
Heterosocial (Dating-Initiation) Skills	Arkowitz, Lichtenstein, McGovern, & Hines (1975)	Amount of time talking, infrequent silences, verbal reinforcers given to other person, head nods, smiles, eye contact, verbal content adding new substance to conversation, responsive verbal statements to other person's comments
	Glasgow & Arkowitz (1975)	Gazing (eye contact) time, eye contact when other person speaks, talking time during interaction, initiating conversation following silences, reducing frequency of silences

demonstrating that the presence of various component behaviors is associated with favorable global judgments of the goal skill (e.g., job interview effectiveness). Additional research is needed to confirm that clinical interventions actually target the most salient behavioral components for training.

Second, if group training is intended to modify the components of a social skill, it is essential that those components be defined in an objective manner. Both verbal and nonverbal components must be so clearly specified that the clients and the therapists can readily determine when they occur.

Finally, an issue that has as yet received little experimental attention involves the manner, style, or timing with which clients integrate behavioral components during a social interaction. It appears to be possible for a client to exhibit most or all of the components of a given goal skill (such as assertiveness or appropriate job interview behavior) but to time or pace those components in an ineffective manner, so that the final response appears stilted and unskillful. Stylistic aspects of socially skilled functioning probably involve the integration of discrete component behaviors, the ability of a client to modulate her responses depending upon cues from the other person in the interaction, and the "chaining" of sequential verbal statements so they are content-related to one another during a conversation. Little empirical attention has been given to the assessment and training of these more complex, stylistic aspects of socially skillful behavior. However, in clinical skills training interventions, it does appear important to recognize and attempt to shape not only the components of the goal skill but also the manner in which those components are integrated with one another.

Behavioral Assessment of Clients' Pretreatment Skill Competency

Following the identification of the goal social skill to be trained (a definition of the group's purpose) and those specific component behaviors that comprise the skill (components that will be taught in the group), the skill performance of each potential group member must be assessed. Pretreatment behavioral assessment of potential group members serves several clinical functions. First, it should be objectively determined whether clients are, in fact, skill-deficient in the goal skill prior to their participation in the group. Second, it appears useful for clients within a social skills training group to be relatively homogeneous or comparable in their initial skill performance. If some group members are highly deficient in the goal skill while others are quite proficient, it is difficult to pace group training sessions so that more deficient clients (who require more training) benefit and more proficient members are not bored. Therefore, initial skill comparability of group members is desirable, although more proficient group members can sometimes be used as assistant trainers to model component behaviors. Finally, pretreatment behavioral assessment of each client can provide an objective initial baseline against which to compare client performance later in the intervention, thereby generating data on the effectiveness of the group treatment.

Several assessment techniques have been used to evaluate client baseline social skills, as well as later response to the group training.

Client performance during structured role-played interactions that require use of the goal skill. Role-playing assessment approaches are useful when it is difficult or impractical to observe client skill behavior in the natural environment because situations requiring that skill occur at a low frequency or are inaccessible for observation. Assertiveness training interventions frequently utilize role-played approximations of troublesome interactions to assess client skill in handling these situations (e.g., Eisler et al., 1975). In this assessment paradigm, the client interacts with a partner who plays the role of the antagonist; the role-plays are of situations that require assertion of the client to the antagonist. While standardized role-play test scenes have been developed (e.g., the Behavioral Assertiveness Test, Eisler et al., 1975), it would appear clinically preferable to develop role-play scenes known to be relevant to the client population receiving the intervention. A similar role-play assessment approach has been used to assess job interview behavior (Furman et al., 1979; Kelly, Laughlin, Claiborne, & Patterson, 1979). Here, a therapist plays the part of an interviewer and the client behaves like an applicant during simulated interviews in which the partner directs a series of routine interview questions to the applicant. In any role-played assessment, client performance is specifically evaluated to determine the degree to which the client exhibits each component behavior of the skill.

Client performance during unstructured or minimally structured social interactions. In some cases, it is possible to assess client skill in a less structured manner than role-plays. Melnick (1973) observed minimally dating college student clients during their conversations with a female confederate before and after a program to teach them heterosocial (dating-initiation) skills. Similarly, conversational performance during 8-minute interactions between clients, or between a client and a confederate partner, has been rated and used to evaluate the behavioral deficits of clients later receiving conversational skill training (Kelly, Urey, & Patterson, 1980; Urey et al., 1979). When confederates are used as partners during interactions to assess client conversational skills, some general instructional constraints are usually placed on the confederate's behavior to ensure that responsibility for maintaining the interaction remains with the client. Once again, client performance is objectively rated to determine the extent to which the skill component behaviors are exhibited.

Naturalistic observation of client behavior during social interactions in the criterion environment. Role-plays or minimally structured but "staged" assessments are intended to approximate client performance in the natural environment. In certain circumstances, it may be possible to observe client social skill competency in the criterion environment itself. Observation is particularly feasible when the criterion environment is easily accessible and clients spend a substantial part of their time there (e.g., clients in residential facilities, partial hospital programs, or schools). If a training goal is to increase conversational skills during unstructured social periods in the setting, it might prove feasible to conduct observation periods of client behavior at such times before and after treatment.

Behavioral assessment procedures used to evaluate the presence of social skills components during any form of client sample social interaction or during *in vivo* observations require the careful definition of target components, the training of observers to rate the components reliably, and the development of appropriate rating forms to summarize or quantify observational data. The reader unfamiliar with the use of behavioral assessment methodology may wish to consult a more specialized text in this area (see Cone & Hawkins, 1977; Kazdin, 1980; Keefe, Kopel, & Gordon, 1978).

Paper-and-pencil self-report inventories of social skill. In most cases, client self-report inventories of social skill (such as assertiveness or social anxiety measures) yield only generalized information of limited utility for assessing pretreatment social competence in specific situations. Consequently, they provide little data on those areas or skill components that need to be targeted for group training. In addition, the correspondence between client *self-report* of skill competency and *actual behavioral* skill competency may be quite low (Mischel, 1968). Thus, these measures might best be used as a supplemental data source and not as a replacement for more specific observation of client behavior in real social interactions or role-plays.

By directly assessing the manner in which clients handle social interactions relevant to the purpose of the group, it is possible to determine quite specifically which component skill behaviors will require therapeutic attention in training. This careful assessment of each client should precede the implementation of the group training intervention.

Active Treatment Components of Group Social Skills Training

The group skills training procedure to be outlined here assumes that treatment will be conducted over multiple sessions with the same clients present in each group meeting. It further assumes that a clear goal skill has been defined as the purpose for group training and that all clients are relatively comparable to one another in their deficiency in performing that skill. Finally, as noted previously, it assumes that a component analysis has been used to determine those specific components that comprise the final goal skill and that the relevant components have been identified for training.

Based upon a social learning model of skills acquisition, a number of learning principles have been proposed for group sessions to shape clients' skill performance (Hollandsworth et al, 1977; Kelly, Laughlin, Claiborne, & Patterson, 1979). These principles include the provision of verbal instruction or rationales from the therapist, modeling exposure, behavior rehearsal or practice, feedback, and reinforcement. A review of several group skills training findings illustrates how these principles can be applied.

In recent studies, Urey et al. (1979) and Kelly, Urey, & Patterson (1980) reported the results of similar group interventions to teach conversational skills to formerly hospitalized psychiatric patients attending mental health aftercare programs. The targeted components of the goal conversational skill were identified, and included such behavior as: (a) eliciting information from one's conversational partner by asking the partner appropriate questions, (b) making self-disclosive statements to the partner concerning one's interests, hobbies, or activities, (c) making reinforcing comments or verbal acknowledgments to the partner so as to convey interest in the other person's comments, and (d) making no inappropriate self-disclosures (e.g., verbal statements about emotional problems or depression).

In both of these studies, training consisted of approximately three group sessions devoted to each of the identified component skills (e.g., the first three sessions targeted statements eliciting information and the next three sessions targeted appropriate self-disclosive statements). Group attention was thereby directed sequentially over each of the identified component behaviors. By the conclusion of the intervention, clients had received training on all components felt to define the goal skill.

All group sessions reported in the Urey et al. (1979) and Kelly, Urey, & Patterson (1980) studies followed a similar procedural format. At the beginning of the session, one of the two therapists identified for the group the component that was being targeted in that session and provided a rationale for its significance (such as the reasons that it is desirable to elicit information from another person during a conversation). Clients then observed a modeling videotape, which showed two persons skillfully conversing with one another and exhibiting all appropriate component behaviors. Clients were asked to note particularly how the models exhibited the component targeted for training in that day's session. At times the tape was halted when the target component occurred; at other times group members were asked to comment whenever they observed the component in the model's behavior. Following the showing of the modeling videotape, the therapists then led an in-group behavior rehearsal period. Clients were asked to overtly rehearse or practice using the component in conversations. For example, clients would practice asking questions they would use to elicit information from another person or would actually rehearse the kinds of self-disclosive information they would tell another person during a conversation.

This in-group rehearsal period served several functions. Clients actually verbalized the targeted responses (giving examples of actual questions they might ask or actual facts about themselves they would convey). This, in turn, required that clients cognitively organize and think about one aspect of their conversational performance that they wished to exhibit. As it became each client's turn to generate overt, personalized instances of the verbal target response, that client served as a live model for other clients in the group to observe. An in-group overt response rehearsal also provided specific behavior for the therapists and other clients to shape and reinforce.

Initially, the therapists can serve as observers of each client's in-group rehearsal and then provide feedback, suggestions, and verbal reinforcement for clients' appropriate exhibition of the targeted component. For lower functioning or less verbal clients, therapists may occasionally prompt client verbalization of the component behavior (such as by suggesting questions to ask in a conversation or the kinds of self-disclosive information the client might want to convey to others). However, as time progresses, other clients in the group can be shaped to take over effectively the functions of providing feedback, suggestions, and praise for one another.

As noted by both Urey et al. (1979) and Kelly, Urey, and Patterson (1980), efforts were made to prevent clients from merely imitating or "parroting" instances of the component behavior from the modeling film or from one another. It appears much more useful for clients to learn the general response class of the component skill rather than to attempt to memorize specific responses (e.g., to learn and practice general ways to elicit information from a conversational partner rather than to memorize specific questions to ask someone). Again, the group's therapists can prompt or suggest ways for clients to "personalize" the component behaviors.

In both of these studies each group session terminated following the in-group behavioral practice period with clients actually engaging in an 8-minute unstructured conversation with another person whom they did not know. Thus, additional behavioral practice of a realistic nature (an actual conversation) provided further opportunity for clients to use the targeted component. In this research, tape recordings were made of clients' postgroup conversations. Ratings of the taped conversations could demonstrate whether clients exhibited a particular component more often following the session that had targeted it for treatment.

In similar fashion, the learning principles of instruction/rationale, modeling, behavior rehearsal, feedback, and reinforcement have been incorporated in group training sessions to increase client job interview skills (Hollandsworth et al, 1977; Kelly, Laughlin, Claiborne, & Patterson, 1979) and assertiveness (Galassi, Galassi, & Litz, 1974; Nietzel, Martorano, & Melnick, 1977; Rathus, 1973). In the job interview training interventions, identified component behaviors were sequentially targeted across group sessions, with each group session focusing on a component through the therapist's description or examples of the component, as well as through modeling videotape exposure focusing attention on the component. In-group behavior rehearsal let each client practice what he would actually say in response to questions frequently asked by employment interviewers, exhibiting particularly the component trained that day. Therapists and other clients provided feedback, suggestions, and reinforcement after each member's rehearsal responses. Additionally, these studies had each client individually role-play a job interview after each group session. A staff member played the part of the interviewer and delivered a series of common interview questions during the simulated interactions. Clients were encouraged to practice exhibiting the component that had just been targeted in the group session.

It is also possible for clients to practice responses within a group session by role-playing with *one* other client or therapist, with the other members observing, critiquing, and reinforcing the client who is rehearsing his performance. This technique would appear useful for skills such as assertiveness or job interview training, where the behavior of the role-play partner can be relatively structured (e.g., a partner playing an antagonist making unreasonable comments that require the client's assertive response or a partner playing a personnel manager directing a series of interview questions for the client's response). During the rehearsal period of the group session, all clients can rotate having the opportunity to role-play responses to the problematic situations. This practice affords each member the opportunity to benefit from both peer-administered and therapist-administered feedback, as well as providing repeated modeling exposure to other clients' performance.

Procedural Issues in the Conduct of the Skills Training Group

While the aim of group skills training is to apply learning principles to enhance the interpersonal repertoire of clients, several procedural issues concerning the conduct of the group merit further discussion: the size of the group, duration and spacing of treatment sessions, and techniques for facilitating generalization of social behavior change to the criterion environment.

Size of the skills training group. There has been no research and therefore little basis for empirical comparison on the optimal size for skills training groups. However, procedures such as behavior rehearsal within group sessions require that each participant actively and repetitively rehearse social behaviors, either by performing observed role-plays within the group or by practicing verbalizations to be made during social interactions (such as a later conversation). Adequate time must be allocated for each client to practice her responses within each session to the point where they are performed successfully, so the size of the group must be limited. Most published reports of group skills training describe group sizes of from three to nine clients when an ongoing treatment session format is employed.

Duration and spacing of sessions. Once again, little empirical attention has been given to optimal session frequency or intervention duration for skills training groups. To a large degree, these issues may be determined by external factors, such as the type of applied setting (residential or outpatient) or the time availability of clients. Client groups functioning at a low level, including retarded or chronic psychiatric patients, may require more repetitive training, with several sessions devoted to even basic skill components such as eye contact or speech loudness. If the goal skill is relatively complex (i.e., comprised of a large number of components that will require sequential training and integration), the intervention duration will necessarily be increased. Interventions consisting of nine to sixteen 1-hour sessions spaced once weekly to three times weekly have been reported for the group training of conversational, heterosocial, and job interview skills among clinical populations.

Generalization of group social skills training. It was noted earlier that the aim of group skills training is to modify the way in which clients behave during specified social interactions in the natural environment. If training is to be successful, there must be generalization of behavior change from rehearsed or role-played responses during the group sessions to change in the corresponding interactions in the criterion environment. Research on the generalization of social skills training has suggested that skills demonstrated successfully in the training or group environment may not carry over adequately to situations requiring those skills in the natural setting. For example, several studies (Bellack et al., 1979; Bellack, Hersen, & Turner, 1978) have reported that patients who could effectively role-play assertive responses in a clinic setting performed less successfully when confronted with *in vivo* staged incidents that required assertive behaviors. Other investigators (Curran, 1977; Kelly, Fredericksen, Fitts, & Phillips, 1978; Twentyman & Zimering, 1979) have noted the need for research on factors that will enhance the generalization of skills training.

Several clinical techniques that may facilitate generalization should be incorporated in social skills training groups.

1. *Individualizing group training on interactions for each member of the client population.* When possible, the role-play interactions that clients practice during group sessions should be based upon situations that the client personally reports as problematic. If a client reports having difficulty asserting herself with co-workers at the office where she works, her practice interactions should be tailored to that setting. Ideally, practice or role-plays might be developed to approximate actual situations that the client has

encountered or expects to encounter. Since assertion deficits may be quite situation-specific (Eisler et al., 1975), training scenes must be equally specific and personally relevant to the client practicing them. Even when training is conducted in a group, it appears important to individualize the interactions that each group member practices.

2. *Explicitly asking clients to identify in vivo interactions where they utilize the acquired skill.* The therapists conducting the training group can make explicit the relationship between group training and client behavior in the natural environment by asking clients to identify situations in which they can apply the acquired skill. For conversational skills training, this might involve asking clients where they can initiate conversations with others to try out the skills they have learned. Similarly, instances of when clients intend to use assertive skills might be identified in the group session. Feedback from peers and therapists can assist clients in determining whether the identified situations indeed seem appropriate for use of the skills.

3. *Soliciting, encouraging, and reinforcing client reports of skill use in the natural environment.* A portion of each group session can be devoted to client reports of successful use of their skills during the interval since the previous session. A daily log or diary for each client to self-monitor interactions when skills were used (or could have been used) might further prompt the use of trained skills in the natural environment. Both the therapists and other group members can provide reinforcement for client reports of improved social functioning. Before encouraging any client to try out new skills in the natural environment, it is important for the therapists to feel confident that the client has progressed sufficiently in training to handle the problematic *in vivo* interaction successfully.

4. *Dealing with sources of behavioral skills inhibition (such as antici-pated punishment or rejection for social initiation).* An assumption apparently made in most social skills training interventions is that clients exhibit skill deficiencies because they have not learned appropriate responses. However, for some clients skillful responses may be present in their repertoire but become inhibited in the natural environment. Thus, clients may know how to behave assertively (and may do so in group training) but fail to behave in an appropriately assertive fashion in the criterion setting because they fear punitive consequences or dislike from other people. An individual who has recently received conversational skills training may continue to fear rejection from others and, therefore, may

not initiate social interactions even following training. These avoidances are probably a learned consequence of past punishment in the relevant situations and may be maintained by anticipatory anxiety and fear-related self-statements (Meichenbaum & Cameron, 1974). Discussion of these issues, the use of cognitive restructuring techniques, and modification of clients' maladaptive cognitive statements regarding the problematic interactions appear to be potentially useful areas for group attention. Repeated in-group practice and rehearsal or role-playing, accompanied by social reinforcement, should serve to increase client confidence in utilizing newly acquired skills and to desensitize clients to situations they have found troublesome in the past.

5. *Increasing clients' accurate self-appraisal of performance.* As noted earlier, some clients appear to experience social anxiety and behavioral inhibition because they are excessively and unjustifiably critical of their own performance in certain interpersonal situations. Thus, individuals may label their behavior as incompetent even when they are exhibiting appropriately skilled responses. Those who have not handled situations skillfully in the past may maintain excessively negative self-evaluations of performance though exhibiting objectively improved skills. Some clients have a history of inconsistent feedback or lack of social reinforcement for skilled behavior. Certain types of naturalistic social interactions rarely provide persons with the opportunity to receive *specific* feedback on their performance; these situations include job interviews, date-initiations, and similar interactions. If a client has not achieved success in these situations, perhaps even due to capricious factors unrelated to the quality of skills exhibited, the client may wrongly attribute negative evaluations to his performance. Similarly, recent data suggest that the interpersonal evaluation of appropriate expressions of assertion by females may be more negative than the evaluations of identical behavior exhibited by males (Kelly, Kern, Kirkley, Patterson, & Keane, 1980). Under these circumstances, one might predict that females would tend to self-evaluate their appropriate assertive behaviors more negatively than males.

The skills training group affords an opportunity for clients to learn more accurate self-appraisal of their skills when the therapist and, perhaps even more important, other clients provide positive specific feedback to a client's rehearsal performance. Initially, the therapist can ask members to comment specifically on desirable aspects of one another's skill behavior. Then, clients should be encouraged to verbalize positive aspects of *their own* handling of situations, both during practice rehearsals and in the natural environment. By helping clients focus on desirable elements of their skill behavior and actually verbalize the positive aspects, it should be possible to change excessively self-critical perceptions of performance.

EVALUATION OF GROUP SOCIAL SKILLS TRAINING IN THE APPLIED SETTING

Most behavioral clinicians who conduct social skills training groups will be interested in empirically evaluating the outcomes of their interventions. Certainly, the type of setting where the intervention is conducted may determine the form and rigor of any treatment evaluation. Traditional between-groups research designs are a desirable method for rigorously evaluating the pre- to postintervention skills performance change of clients receiving group skills training, if appropriate control group subjects can be found. For example, it would be possible to repeat the pretreatment behavioral assessment measures (role-plays, unstructured or minimally structured social interactions, or naturalistic observations) at the end of the intervention, both for all treatment group clients and for all control group clients. By determining change on all rated component behaviors, it is possible to evaluate the effect of the entire intervention on those components.

Unfortunately, there are practical limitations for between-groups evaluation designs in many applied settings. Relevant control group subjects in sufficient numbers may simply be unavailable. There may also be ethical or treatment policy priorities in applied service-oriented settings (such as mental health centers or residential facilities) that prevent assignment of clients to any non-maximum treatment condition. If such factors exist, alternative treatment evaluation choices may be necessary to measure the effect of a group skills training intervention.

One of the easiest but experimentally nonrigorous evaluation approaches is to repeat all clients' pretreatment behavioral assessment measures at the conclusion of the intervention but in the absence of any control groups. This one-group assessment determines change on those behavioral components that can be reliably rated. However, it fails to control for many internal and external validity threats, and posttest improvement cannot be conclusively attributed to the intervention (Campbell & Stanley, 1963). A "time series" modification of this design, which repeats several identical skills assessments before and again subsequent to the intervention for each client, can yield somewhat greater control but remains a relatively nonrigorous evaluation approach (Campbell & Stanley, 1963).

An alternative evaluation procedure for group training that does yield conclusive information on the intervention's effectiveness is a multiple baseline within the training group (Kelly, 1980). This evaluation technique is appropriate when (a) all clients in the group receive comparable training attention, (b) training is conducted over multiple treatment sessions, (c) the training group sequentially targets various component behaviors across sessions, and (d) it is possible to repeat the same skills assessment procedure (role-plays, etc.) for each client following each group training session. The rationale for this group training evaluation technique is identical to that of a multiple baseline across social skill component behaviors for an individually treated client (Hersen & Barlow, 1976), except that *each client* is evaluated on all component skills following each *group* training session. For example, in a study of group-administered job interview training (Kelly, Laughlin, Claiborne, & Patterson, 1979), clients individually role-played identical job interviews following each group training session. The tape-recorded role-plays were rated on components of job interview effectiveness (e.g., frequency of statements conveying favorable information of work experience and questions directed by the client to the interviewer). It was objectively determined that whenever group training had focused on a specific component, all clients exhibited the component more frequently during that day's role-played interviews, while other components were unaffected. Thus, over the course of the intervention, improvement on a given job interview component was always contingent upon specific group training for it. Using this method, in multiple baseline fashion and without the use of external control groups, a group treatment (as well as each client's individual response to it) can be closely scrutinized (Kelly, 1980).

SUMMARY

Behavioral group therapy provides a useful modality for teaching skills-deficient clients to handle troublesome social interactions. Learning principles that have been used to teach social skills to individually treated clients can be applied, with even greater effectiveness and cost efficiency, in a group-administered intervention. If clients participate in ongoing, multiple-session group training, it is possible to apply instructions, modeling exposure, behavioral rehearsal, feedback, and reinforcement successively to shape each of those component behaviors that together comprise the goal skill response. Consequently, by the conclusion of group training, all clients should be able to perform the goal skill more effectively. Attention given to those treatment factors that increase the generalization of skill use to the natural environment ensures the clinical benefit of group skills training to clients.

REFERENCES

Arkowitz, H., Lichtenstein, E., McGovern, K., & Hines, P. The behavioral assessment of social competence in males. *Behavior Therapy,* 1975, *6,* 3–13.

Bandura, A. *Principles of behavior modification.* New York: Holt, Rinehart & Winston, 1969.

Bandura, A., & Walters, R.H. *Social learning and personality development.* New York: Holt, Rinehart & Winston, 1963.

Bellack, A.S., & Hersen, M. Chronic psychiatric patients: Social skills training. In M. Hersen & A.S. Bellack (Eds.), *Behavior therapy in the psychiatric setting.* Baltimore: Williams & Wilkins, 1978.

Bellack, A.S., Hersen, M., & Lamparski, D. Role-play tests for assessing social skills: Are they useful? *Journal of Consulting and Clinical Psychology,* 1979, *47,* 335–342.

Bellack, A.S., Hersen, M., & Turner, S.M. Role-play tests for assessing social skills: Are they valid? *Behavior Therapy,* 1978, *9,* 448–461.

Bornstein, M.R., Bellack, A.S., & Hersen, M. Social skills training for unassertive children: A multiple baseline analysis. *Journal of Applied Behavior Analysis,* 1977, *10,* 183–195.

Callner, D.A., & Ross, S.M. The assessment and training of assertion skills with drug addicts: A preliminary study. *Journal of Addictions,* 1978, *13,* 227–239.

Campbell, D.T., & Stanley, J.C. *Experimental and quasi-experimental designs for research.* Chicago: Rand McNally, 1963.

Cone, J.D., & Hawkins, R.P. *Behavioral assessment: New directions in clinical psychology.* New York: Brunner/Mazel, 1977.

Curran, J.P. Skills training as an approach to the treatment of heterosexual social anxiety: A review. *Psychological Bulletin,* 1977, *84,* 140–157.

Curran, J.P., & Gilbert, F.S. A test of the relative effectiveness of a systematic desensitization program and an interpersonal skills training program with date anxious subjects. *Behavior Therapy,* 1975, *6,* 510–521.

Edelstein, B.A., & Eisler, R.M. Effects of modeling and modeling with instructions on the behavioral components of social skills. *Behavior Therapy,* 1976, *7,* 382–389.

Eisler, R.M., Hersen, M., & Miller, P.M. Effects of modeling on components of assertive behavior. *Journal of Behavior Therapy and Experimental Psychiatry,* 1973, *4,* 1–6.

Eisler, R.M., Hersen, M., Miller, P.M., & Blanchard, E.B. Situational determinants of assertive behaviors. *Journal of Consulting and Clinical Psychology,* 1975, *43,* 330–340.

Eisler, R.M., Miller, P.M., & Hersen, M. Components of assertive behavior. *Journal of Clinical Psychology,* 1973, *29,* 295–299.

Foy, D.W., Eisler, R.M., & Pinkston, S. Modeled assertion in a case of explosive rages. *Journal of Behavior Therapy and Experimental Psychiatry,* 1975, *6,* 135–137.

Frank, J.D. *Persuasion and healing.* New York: Schocken Books, 1973.

Fredericksen, L.W., Jenkins, J.O., Foy, D.W., & Eisler, R.M. Social skills training in the modification of abusive outbursts in adults. *Journal of Applied Behavior Analysis,* 1976, *9,* 117–125.

Furman, W., Geller, M.I., Simon, S.J., & Kelly, J.A. The use of a behavior rehearsal procedure for teaching job interviewing skills to psychiatric patients. *Behavior Therapy,* 1979, *10,* 157–167.

Galassi, J.P., Galassi, M.D., & Litz, M.C. Assertive training in groups using video feedback. *Journal of Counseling Psychology,* 1974, *21,* 390–394.

Glasgow, R.E., & Arkowitz, H. The behavioral assessment of male and female social competence in dyadic heterosexual interactions. *Behavior Therapy,* 1975, *6,* 488–498.

Hersen, M., & Barlow, D. *Single case experimental design.* New York: Pergamon Press, 1976.

Hersen, M., & Bellack, A.S. A multiple baseline analysis of social skills training in chronic schizophrenics. *Journal of Applied Behavior Analysis,* 1976, *9,* 239–245.

Hollandsworth, J.C., Dressel, M.E., & Stevens, J. Use of behavioral versus traditional procedures for increasing job interview skills. *Journal of Counseling Psychology,* 1977, *24,* 503–510.

Hollandsworth, J.G., Glazeski, R.C., & Dressel, M.E. Use of social skills training in the treatment of extreme anxiety and deficient verbal skills in the job interview setting. *Journal of Applied Behavior Analysis,* 1978, *11,* 259–269.

Kazdin, A.E. *Behavior modification in applied settings.* Homewood, Ill.: Dorsey Press, 1980.

Keefe, F.J., Kopel, S.A., & Gordon, S.B. *A practical guide to behavioral assessment.* New York: Springer, 1978.

Kelly, J.A. The simultaneous replication design: Use of a multiple baseline to establish experimental control in single group social skills treatment studies. *Journal of Behavior Therapy and Experimental Psychiatry,* 1980, *11,* 203–207.

Kelly, J.A., Fredericksen, L.W., Fitts, H., & Phillips, J. Training and generalization of commendatory assertiveness: A controlled single subject experiment. *Journal of Behavior Therapy and Experimental Psychiatry,* 1978, *9,* 17–21.

Kelly, J.A., Furman, W., Phillips, J., Hathorn, S., & Wilson, T. Teaching conversational skills to retarded adolescents. *Child Behavior Therapy,* 1979, *1,* 85–97.

Kelly, J.A., Kern, J.M., Kirkley, B.G., Patterson, J.N., & Keane, T.M. Reactions to assertive versus unassertive behavior: Differential effects for males and females, and implications for assertive training. *Behavior Therapy,* 1980, *11,* 670–682.

Kelly, J.A., Laughlin, C., Claiborne, M., & Patterson, J.T. A group procedure for teaching job interviewing skills to formerly hospitalized psychiatric patients. *Behavior Therapy,* 1979, *10,* 288–310.

Kelly, J.A., Urey, J.R., & Patterson, J.T. Improving heterosocial conversational skills of male psychiatric patients through a small group training procedure. *Behavior Therapy*, 1980, *11*, 179–188.

Kelly, J.A., Urey, J.R., & Patterson, J.T. Small group job interview training in the mental health center setting. *Behavioral Counseling Quarterly*, in press.

Kelly, J.A., Wildman, B.G., & Berler, E.S. Small group behavioral training to improve the job interview skills repertoire of mildly retarded adolescents. *Journal of Applied Behavior Analysis*, 1980, *13*, 461–471.

Kelly, J.A., Wildman, B.G., Urey, J., & Thurman, C. Group skills training to increase the conversational repertoire of retarded adolescents. *Child Behavior Therapy*, 1979, *1*, 323–336.

Lange, A.J. Cognitive-behavioral group therapy and assertion training. In D. Upper & S. Ross (Eds.), *Behavioral group therapy, 1979: An annual review*. Champaign, Ill.: Research Press, 1979.

Linehan, M.M., Goldfried, M.R., & Goldfried, A.P. Assertion therapy: Skills training or cognitive restructuring? *Behavior Therapy*, 1979, *10*, 372–388.

MacDonald, M.L., Lindquist, C.U., Kramer, J.A., McGrath, R.A., & Rhyne, L.D. Social skills training: Behavior rehearsal in groups and dating skills. *Journal of Counseling Psychology*, 1975, *22*, 224–230.

Martinson, W.D., & Zerface, J.P. Comparison of individual counseling and a social program with nondaters. *Journal of Counseling Psychology*, 1970, *17*, 36–40.

McFall, R.M., & Marston, A.R. An experimental investigation of behavior rehearsal in assertive training. *Journal of Abnormal Psychology*, 1970, *76*, 295–303.

McFall, R.M., & Twentyman, C.T. Four experiments on the relative contributions of rehearsal, modeling and coaching to assertion training. *Journal of Abnormal Psychology*, 1973, *81*, 199–218.

Meichenbaum, D., & Cameron, R. The clinical potential of modifying what clients say to themselves. In M.J. Mahoney & C.E. Thoresen (Eds.), *Self-control: Power to the person*. Monterey, Calif.: Brooks/Cole, 1974.

Melnick, J. A comparison of replication techniques in the modification of minimal dating behavior. *Journal of Abnormal Psychology*, 1973, *81*, 51–59.

Melnick, J., & Stocker, R.B. An experimental analysis of the behavior rehearsal with feedback technique in assertiveness training. *Behavior Therapy*, 1977, *8*, 222–228.

Minkin, N., Braukmann, C.J., Minkin, B.L., Timbers, G.D., Timbers, B.J., Fixsen, D.L., Phillips, E.L., & Wolf, M.M. The social validation and training of conversational skills. *Journal of Applied Behavior Analysis*, 1976, *9*, 127–139.

Mischel, W. *Personality and assessment*. New York: Wiley, 1968.

Nietzel, M. T., Martorano, R. D., & Melnick, J. The effects of covert modeling with and without reply training on the development and generalization of assertive responses. *Behavior Therapy*, 1977, *8*, 183–192.

Rathus, S.A. Instigation of assertive behavior through videotape-mediated assertive models and directed practice. *Behaviour Research and Therapy*, 1973, *11*, 57–65.

Twentyman, C.T., & Zimering, R.T. Behavioral training of social skills: A critical review. In R.M. Eisler & P.M. Miller (Eds.), *Progress in behavior modification* (Vol. 7). New York: Academic Press, 1979.

Urey, J.R., Laughlin, C., & Kelly, J.A. Teaching heterosocial conversational skills to male psychiatric patients. *Journal of Behavior Therapy and Experimental Psychiatry*, 1979, *10*, 323–328.

Yalom, I.D. *The theory and practice of group psychotherapy*. New York: Basic Books, 1975.

Chapter 2

The Assessment of a Large Assertion Training Group: A Treatment and Evaluation Model for Community Mental Health Services

John V. Flowers
Karen A. Hartman
Rochelle J. Mann
Susan W. Kidder
Curtis D. Booraem
Bruce Tapper

Abstract

A multi-level approach was employed to assess the effects of assertion training carried out in a large (N = 54) group. Results of self-reports, external reports, and observations all indicated that assertion skills had been learned. These same measures and the results of a behavioral task indicated that participants who voluntarily attended more behavioral rehearsal sessions improved more than participants who voluntarily attended fewer sessions. Within the behavioral rehearsal sessions, it was found that participants who role-played more frequently, who coached other participants more actively, and who had the clearest goals in their own role-plays improved the most. These results are discussed in relation to assertion training specifically and in relation to the assessment and delivery of other community mental health services via large-scale groups.

Historically, psychotherapeutic services have been delivered through two primary sources: the centralized mental hospital and the private practitioner. Traditionally, these services have focused on the treatment of exaggerated or protracted symptoms, as opposed to assuming a preventative stance. In accordance with the recommendations of the Joint Commission on Mental Illness and Health (Golann & Eisdorfer, 1972), decentralized mental health services are now being provided in communities in an attempt to be more responsive to local mental health needs. Decentralization involves more than a change in location and/or organization; decentralization also involves a broadening of objectives to include the prevention as well as the treatment of mental health problems (Zax & Cowen, 1972). This broadened focus has included innovations such as preventative consultation interventions (Beigel & Levenson, 1972), brief crisis interventions (Cowen, 1967), assertion training (Flowers & Guerra, 1974), and the use of paraprofessionals (Sechrest & Bryan, 1972). Nonetheless, the basic model of service delivery still includes the assumption that service begins only when the client seeks help (Cowen, 1967; Schwartz, 1972), and mental health services are still generally delivered individually or in small groups. In behavioral therapy, the use of even small groups has been very limited (Flowers, 1979).

In a recent review article, Flowers, Cooper, and Whiteley (1975) noted that assertion training is now being employed in larger group formats (i.e., from 15 to 100 people) for both prevention and intervention purposes. Assertion training focuses on the training of social skills that are important for the prevention of future mental health problems (Phillips, 1968) and is a proven method of treatment in community mental health centers (King, Liberman, & Roberts, Note 1).

There are three distinct advantages in providing assertion training in a large group format. First, paraprofessionals can be systematically integrated into the service delivery process and their performance can be monitored. Second, there is increased time and cost efficiency in terms of the use of professional services. Finally, the traditional client/helper roles are circumvented.

As Sechrest and Bryan (1972) have pointed out, the community mental health movement has increased the use of paraprofessionals to deliver services. However, as Chu and Trotter (1972) have indicated, the increased use of paraprofessionals has not always been accompanied by adequate professional supervision. To address this problem, large assertion training groups can employ paraprofessionals as aides in a treatment modality that is structured to provide continuous supervision automatically. This model both provides ongoing training for the paraprofessional and increases the quality of the service provided. The large group format also allows service delivery to a larger number of people without increased demands on professional time.

Since such programs can be advertised, the traditional passive-receptive stance of community mental health programs can be modified to an active-persuasional stance. In the passive-receptive stance, the service deliverers wait for the problem to become intense enough for the client to seek help; in the active-persuasional stance, the service deliverers sell the service to those who would not normally seek it, either because the problem is not severe enough to force the troubled person to seek help or because the troubled person would not label himself as a client under any circumstances. The active-persuasional stance is effective in the large group format because that format obscures the distinction between prevention and treatment. Participants are not labeled as clients, and the help given is not labeled as therapy or counseling but, rather, as training. The passive-receptive model of service delivery excludes many people who would be unwilling to label themselves as clients; but these same people are often willing to participate in large groups designed to improve their personal and interpersonal effectiveness.

This modification of the service delivery process is important only if large assertion training groups also achieve the desired outcome for the participants. To date, there has been no attempt to evaluate the effectiveness of such groups (Flowers, Cooper, & Whiteley, 1975). To evaluate any community mental health service adequately, the evaluation must assess both quantitative and qualitative variables. Traditionally, community mental health services have been primarily evaluated in terms of client-contact hours, which is solely a quantitative measure. Any large group obviously excels in such terms; however, to adopt this method of service delivery because of mere quantitative superiority would be unjustified.

The present study was undertaken to evaluate systematically the effectiveness of a large assertion training group. Two general hypotheses were tested: (a) that a large-scale community assertion training group, including both lecture-demonstration and behavioral rehearsal, would significantly increase the assertiveness of the participants, and (b) that subjects who voluntarily participated in more of the group behavioral rehearsal sessions would demonstrate the greatest improvement.

In an attempt to analyze the components of the large group intervention, five different process variables of behavioral rehearsal were measured: (a) duration of time spent role-playing as the asserter, (b) frequency of role-playing as the asserter, (c) degree of anxiety as the asserter, (d) level of activity as the coach of other asserters, and (e) goal clarity as the asserter. It was also hypothesized that, of the subjects who participated in two-thirds of the large group behavioral rehearsal sessions, those who role-played longer and more frequently, who were judged as experiencing lower levels of anxiety, who coached more actively, and who had the clearest goals would demonstrate the greatest improvement (Flowers & Goldman, 1976; Flowers & Guerra, 1974; McFall & Marston, 1970; McFall & Twentyman, 1973).

METHOD

Subjects

Seventy-five participants (23 males and 52 females), enrolled in a group in assertion training offered to the general public by a university, served as subjects. The assessment procedure (described later) was voluntary, and five participants chose not to participate in the assessment. Sixteen additional participants did not complete the training or the assessment procedures due to such complications as employment change, change in living location, or similar factors. The remaining 54 subjects (16 male and 38 female) ranged in age from 16 to 56 years, with a mean age of 33.6 years.

Teachers and Assistants

The large-group teachers were two psychologists with extensive experience in both assertion training and the training of assertion trainers. They were assisted by another psychologist and three graduate students who had had previous training in the techniques of assertion training.

Procedure

The group consisted of 13 weekly 3-hour sessions extending over a 3-month period. The first two sessions were devoted entirely to lecture and pretesting. The following nine sessions were each divided into two equal time spans. The first part of each session was devoted to lectures on various aspects of social skills by two psychologists. A detailed outline of the content can be found in Flowers and Booraem (1975). In the second half of each session, structured opportunities for behavioral rehearsal were provided. This behavioral rehearsal was voluntary, and was conducted in three separate rooms with a psychologist and a paraprofessional monitoring the rehearsals in each room. During these role-plays, groups of three participants each were formed to rehearse together (Flowers & Guerra, 1974). In each triad, the members alternated playing the roles of the asserter, other person, or coach while practicing ways to resolve effectively situations identified as problematic by the asserter. The psychologist and paraprofessional monitored the behavioral rehearsal and helped the triads with difficult situations. Additionally, the psychologist supervised the paraprofessional in her attempts to conduct the role-plays (all paraprofessionals were female).

Assessment

Pretraining assessment. During the second group session, all participants who had volunteered to participate in the assessment were administered the Rathus Assertiveness Schedule (Rathus, 1973), the Gambrill and Richey Assertion Scales (Gambrill & Richey, 1975), and the Azrin, Naster, and Jones Relationship Happiness Scale (Azrin, Naster, & Jones, 1973). The Rathus Assertiveness Schedule is a self-report measure of assertiveness in specified situations. The Gambrill and Richey Scales provide two distinct measures: (a) self-reported anxiety during assertive situations, and (b) self-reported probability of engaging in the designated assertive behaviors. The Azrin, Naster, and Jones Scale provides satisfaction ratings in 10 domains in the individual's current most significant relationship. Additionally, each participant was given another Rathus Assertiveness Schedule, which was to be completed by someone outside the group whom the participant considered able to judge accurately the participant's assertive skills. The participants were not to discuss this test with their external raters until after the sessions and the posttesting were completed. The externally rated Rathus Assertiveness Schedules were mailed to the experimenters by the raters.

Process assessment. At the completion of every role-playing session, each member of the triad filled out a process evaluation form. The form consisted of five questions:

Of the two other members of your triad,

1. who spent more time role-playing as the asserter?
2. who did more role-plays, either different ones or trials of the same one, as the asserter?
3. whose problem was more anxiety-producing?
4. who coached more actively?
5. which asserter's goals were clearer?

The member whose name was recorded in response to a question was scored as high on that variable, while the member whose name was not recorded was scored as low. Only participants attending two-thirds or more of the nine role-playing sessions were included in the analysis of the critical components of large assertion training groups. For each process variable, those participants who received a majority of high ratings were differentiated from those participants receiving a majority of low ratings. The two groups of subjects under each variable were then compared on all of their posttraining assessment scores to analyze the effects of qualitatively different participation in the behavioral rehearsal sections of the group.

Posttraining assessment. During Group Session 12, all of the participants were again administered the Rathus Assertiveness Schedule, the Gambrill and Richey Assertion Scales, and the Azrin, Naster, and Jones Relationship Happiness Scale. The participants also received a Rathus Schedule to be completed by the same outside rater who had completed the pretraining external Rathus Schedule. These Rathus Schedules were again mailed to the experimenters by the external raters. In addition, the participants were asked to record two personal assertion situations of similar intensity in the natural environment, one of which they had role-played in the behavioral rehearsal sections of the group and one of which they had not role-played. They were then asked to indicate an external rater who could assess improvement or deterioration in their ability to resolve these situations in the previous 3 months. Each external rater, blind as to whether or not the assertion problem had been role-played, rated the participant's improvement or deterioration in terms of dealing with the specified assertive situation on a Likert-type 5-point scale, with the midpoint (3) indicating no improvement.

The following assertion analogue task, the NASA game, was also employed to assess the assertive skills of the participants (Bodner, Booraem, & Flowers, 1978). A written examination was given at Session 13. On the day of this examination, participants were given a list of 12 possible final examination questions. Each participant independently selected four questions that she wished to answer, and she was then placed in a group of four participants, consisting of two who had attended at least two-thirds of the role-playing sessions and two who had attended fewer. The groups were instructed to reach a group consensus within 5 minutes as to which 4 of the 12 questions their group would have to answer on the written examination. If they did not reach agreement in the allotted time, they understood that they would get a final exam made up of the four questions that the instructors felt were the hardest. An assertion and a persuasion score were obtained for each participant. The assertion score consisted of the number of individually desired items that the group accepted for the final list. The persuasion score was derived from a weighted mean by which an individual received more points for items that the group selected that had not been chosen independently by other group members and fewer points for items that other group members had also preselected (Bodner, Booraem, & Flowers, 1978).

RESULTS

Table 2.1 indicates that group participants improved significantly from pre- to posttesting on all tests except the Azrin Communication rating. Subjects whose blind external ratings were returned ($N = 23$) demonstrated more improvement on situations they role-played (4.43) than on those they did not role-play (3.87), $t(44) = 2.95$, $p < .01$. Table 2.2 indicates that participants who role-played six or more times scored significantly higher on all eight posttests than participants who role-played fewer than six times.

Table 2.1
Pre- and Posttest Results of Participants Completing the Group ($N = 54$)

Test	Pre-workshop	Post-workshop	t	p
Rathus Assertiveness Schedule	0.16	20.33	4.49	.001
External Rathus Assertiveness Schedule	13.53	30.74	30.4	.01
Gambrill and Richey Assertion Scales				
Discomfort	92.71	77.67	4.14	.001
Assertion Probability	96.47	87.42	2.74	.01
Azrin, Naster, and Jones Relationship Happiness Scale				
Communication	6.02	6.79	1.44	.10
General Relationship Happiness	6.28	7.02	1.95	.05

Table 2.2
Comparison of Participants Who Voluntarily Attended Six or More Role-playing Sessions (32) With Those Who Attended Five or Less (22)

Test	Six or More	Five or Less	t	p
Rathus Assertiveness Schedule	24.69	12.50	3.06	.01
External Rathus Assertiveness Schedule	19.54	9.94	1.87	.05
Gambrill and Richey Assertion Scales				
Discomfort	20.52	−9.85	1.95	.05
Assertion Probability	13.74	−3.96	2.65	.01
Azrin, Naster, and Jones Relationship Happiness Scale				
Communication	1.62	−0.29	2.69	.01
General Relationship Happiness	1.78	0.02	3.14	.01
NASA Game				
Assertion Score	2.76	2.18	3.14	.01
Persuasion Score	7.04	4.22	2.87	.01

In terms of process variables, there was no difference between participants who spent more time as the asserter (16) and other participants (16) on any of the above variables. It should be remembered that only participants who attended six or more role-playing sessions were included in the process analysis.

In terms of goal clarity, those participants who were rated higher (18) by their fellow triad members also scored significantly higher on the following variables than participants rated lower (14) on goal clarity: (a) individual test items accepted by their test group (2.71 vs. 2.17, $t(30) = 1.95$, $p < .05$), (b) the persuasion score from the same task (6.59 vs. 3.58, $t(30) = 2.47$, $p < .01$), (c) the change in their external Rathus Schedule ratings (15.31 vs. 0.58, $t(30) = 3.17$, $p < .01$), and (d) the change in their Azrin General Relationship Happiness subscale ratings (1.78 vs. -1.00, $t(30) = 2.80$, $p < .01$).

The findings were identical for participants who coached more actively and who role-played more often. Participants who were judged as coaching more actively (18) scored higher on the number of test items selected by their test group (2.86 vs. 2.06, $t(30) = 3.12$, $p < .01$) and on their persuasion score on the same task (7.06 vs. 3.50, $t(30) = 2.70$, $p < .01$) than participants who were judged as coaching less actively (14). Similarly, participants judged as role-playing more times (17) scored higher on the number of test items selected by their group (2.86 vs. 2.06, $t(30) = 2.51$, $p < .05$) and on the persuasion score from the same task (7.00 vs. 3.25, $t(30) = 2.90$, $p < .01$) than participants judged as role-playing fewer times (15).

Finally, in terms of anxiety, those participants who were judged as being less anxious while they were role-playing (16) scored significantly higher on their change on the Azrin General Relationship Happiness subscale (2.31 vs. 0.81, $t(30) = 2.31$, $p < .05$) and on change on the Gambrill and Richey Discomfort subscale (-26.76 vs. -9.64, $t(30) = 3.10$, $p < .01$) than those participants who were judged as being more anxious while they were role-playing.

DISCUSSION

The most critical and difficult issue in a study of this type is the problem of appropriate control. A control group design would require that randomly assigned participants be tested with and without intervention. Such a form of experimental control would be inappropriate for the nature of the present project. In fact, emphasis on such control groups has severely limited the number and type of studies that can be done in community mental health settings, where service needs and ethical considerations often make random assignment and nonintervention impossible. Nevertheless, two potentially confounding elements require some form of control comparison.

First, it is essential to demonstrate that the intervention, not another factor such as maturation or regression toward the mean, caused the measured changes. In the present study, verification that the large group indeed caused the changes rests with the data produced by the blind external raters. The raters assessed changes made by the group participants in specific assertion situations. More important, solutions for some of the assertion situations had been practiced in group sessions, while solutions to others had not been practiced. Thus, if the data received from blind external raters discriminated significantly between problems worked on during the group sessions versus problems ignored, the observed changes could be attributed to the effect of the group. This method of assessment is actually a multiple baseline form of control. Results of this assessment procedure support the fact that the group produced the observed changes, since the external raters, unaware of which situations had been practiced and which had not, rated those in which assertive solutions had been practiced as significantly improved compared to similar situations that were not dealt with in the group.

A second potential confounding element involves the self-reports. The key issue is to ascertain whether any self-reported change is more than merely a function of experimenter demand. The traditional form of control is again the control group; however, as previously indicated, a control group is impractical in a large group intervention of this type. In the case of standardized self-reports, the multiple baseline design is also not helpful. Instead, the present study employed blind external ratings on one of the self-report scales, the Rathus Assertiveness Schedule, to control for experimenter demand. The two other self-report instruments, the Azrin, Naster, and Jones Relationship Happiness Scale and the Gambrill and Richey Assertion Scale, were not controlled for two reasons. First, when external raters are asked to do more, more data are usually lost due to noncompletion. Second, if one self-report test is not being unduly influenced by something other than the experimental intervention, it is unlikely that two other similar scales are being so influenced.

Conclusions, whether based on the two adequately controlled measures or on all four administered instruments, suggest that the large group format is effective in producing the desired outcome, i.e., increased assertive behavior in the participants. The importance of this result for community mental health programs is twofold. First, the large group format is an effective and obviously efficient method of delivering the service of assertion training. Second, while the present group employed only the intervention of assertion training, the success of this delivery method suggests that the large group could be employed to deliver any behavioral program that can be structured, such as stress management, weight control, sexual education and counseling, or fear control. The authors are presently testing the same format with sexual education and counseling content.

In terms of within-group comparisons, methodological problems of adequate scientific control also occur. The current study suggests that the more a participant voluntarily rehearsed, the more he improved. Given that rehearsal was voluntary, the present study cannot separate the motivation to rehearse from the act of rehearsing. While the assessment of these variables was impractical in the present group, this research question should be addressed. It is clear that rehearsal is important, since blind raters rate more improvement on problems rehearsed than on problems not rehearsed. In terms of more general improvement, however, it is not clear whether the crucial element is motivation or the activity itself. If motivation is a critical component, the groups might well be limited to people who will voluntarily rehearse. Since the service will probably always be limited, it makes sense to select as participants those who will gain the most from the service if the demand is greater than the supply.

While the first level of analysis dealt with the entire group and the second level compared those who had role-played six or more sessions with those who had role-played less frequently, the final level of analysis involved only participants who had role-played six sessions or more. The question addressed by such an analysis is that of which components of the intervention are more important for outcome. *Frequency* of role-playing in a session was positively associated with improved outcome, while *duration* of the role-play was not. This partially verifies the Flowers and Booraem (1975) contention that role-plays should be as short and frequent as possible, rather than the reverse. Simply put, assertion training should not be confused with psychodrama. The finding that coaching more actively was also associated with greater improvement supported the earlier findings (Flowers & Guerra, 1974) that assertion training participants gain by coaching as well as by role-playing.

With regard to anxiety, the current study did not find a relationship between anxiety and the measures of increased assertive performance. This finding differs from what might be expected, given the anxiety-reduction model of assertion proposed by Wolpe (1958). Flowers and Booraem (1975) have already questioned this model and have proposed that assertive behavior is not solely a reciprocal inhibitor of anxiety. In this regard, more research is needed since there are probably two distinct populations of participants, one of which requires anxiety reduction for improved performance and one of which does not.

The reader could interpret this finding to mean that the population tested here was made up primarily of people with a skills deficit, i.e., those who lacked the basic skills of assertion rather than those with a performance deficit whose assertive performance was interfered with by anxiety. While this interpretation could be true, the distinction between skills and performance deficits does not seem that clear in actual clinical practice. Participants who are not assertive because of anxiety tend to engage in assertive behavior much less frequently than those who are less anxious. Other participants who clearly have a basic skills deficit in the area of assertiveness may also be anxious about the lack of skills. It is our contention, especially in a less seriously disturbed population, that anxiety is neither the crucial variable nor the most responsive measure.

The process variable that seemed most clearly related to gains in assertive behavior was the group participant's goal clarity during the role-play. Goal clarity refers to the participant's statement of what she is trying to accomplish in the assertive interaction. A typical unclear and weak assertive goal would be "I want him to understand why I am upset." In this goal we do not know what message is to be transmitted or how the asserter would know if it had been received; even more crucial, the asserter has placed the success or failure of the interaction in the other person's control. A clear goal would be "I want to tell him that I am upset because he did not confer with me before making the dinner plans, and I want to ask him and get an answer as to whether he will consult with me in the future before making such plans." Here, what the asserter is to say and how she knows if she has been heard are clear, and the criterion of success is mainly in her control, i.e., has she performed the assertion to her own satisfaction? While Flowers and Goldman (1976) have demonstrated that goal clarification is an essential component of good assertion training skills, the present study is the first to demonstrate that goal clarity is a significant factor in assertion training outcome.

The present study has demonstrated that assertion training can be offered to a large number of participants simultaneously in a large group format and is an effective as well as efficient treatment. Beyond this immediate finding, the authors would argue that any systematic behavioral program can be so offered and that most, if not all, would also be effective. Clearly, traditional group therapy would be difficult to conduct in groups of 60 to 100 participants. However, behavioral group therapy with a focused goal is completely consistent with a large group format and could even be employed with a population with heterogeneous problems, if the leaders are willing to have smaller groups of varied sizes deal with different problems. It is our hope that other researchers will employ this efficient model with other programs and further test its effectiveness. The large group model solves more problems than it creates for behaviorally oriented practitioners interested in the improvement of community mental health service delivery.

REFERENCE NOTES

1. King, L. W., Liberman, R. P., & Roberts, J. *An evaluation of Personal Effectiveness Training (assertive training): A behavioral group therapy.* Paper presented at the Annual Conference of the American Group Psychotherapy Association, New York, 1974.

REFERENCES

Azrin, N. H., Naster, B. J., & Jones, R. Reciprocity counseling: A rapid learning-based procedure for marital counseling. *Behaviour Research and Therapy*, 1973, *11*, 365–382.

Beigel, A., & Levenson, A. I. (Eds.), *The community mental health center.* New York: Basic Books, 1972.

Bodner, G. E., Booraem, C. D., & Flowers, J. V. The assessment of assertion training. In J. M. Whiteley & J. V. Flowers (Eds.), *Approaches to assertion training.* Monterey, Calif.: Brooks/Cole, 1978.

Chu, F. D., & Trotter, S. *The mental health complex. Part I: Community mental health centers.* Washington, D.C.: Center for Study of Responsive Law, 1972.

Cowen, E. L. Emergent approaches to mental health problems: An overview and directions for future work. In E. L. Cowen, E. A. Gardner, & M. Zax (Eds.), *Emergent approaches to mental health problems.* New York: Appleton-Century-Crofts, 1967.

Flowers, J. V. Behavioral analysis of group therapy and a model for behavioral group therapy. In D. Upper & S. M. Ross (Eds.), *Behavioral group therapy, 1979: An annual review.* Champaign, Ill.: Research Press, 1979.

Flowers, J. V., & Booraem, C. D. Assertion training: The training of trainers. *The Counseling Psychologist*, 1975, *5*, 29–36.

Flowers, J. V., Cooper, C. G., & Whiteley, J. M. Approaches to assertion training. *The Counseling Psychologist*, 1975, *5*, 3–9.

Flowers, J. V., & Goldman, R. D. Assertion training for mental health paraprofessionals. *Journal of Counseling Psychology*, 1976, *23*, 147–150.

Flowers, J. V., & Guerra, J. The use of client-coaching in assertion training with large groups. *Community Mental Health Journal*, 1974, *10*, 414–417.

Gambrill, E. D., & Richey, C. A. An assertion inventory for use in assessment and research. *Behavior Therapy*, 1975, *6*, 550–561.

Golann, S. E., & Eisdorfer, C. *Handbook of community mental health.* New York: Appleton-Century-Crofts, 1972.

McFall, R. M., & Marston, A. R. An experimental investigation of behavior rehearsal in assertive training. *Journal of Abnormal Psychology*, 1970, *76*, 295–303.

McFall, R. M., & Twentyman, C. T. Four experiments on the contributions of rehearsal, modeling and coaching to assertion training. *Journal of Abnormal Psychology*, 1973, *81*, 199–218.

Phillips, E. L. Achievement Place: Token reinforcement procedures in a home-style rehabilitation setting for pre-delinquent boys. *Journal of Applied Behavior Analysis*, 1968, *1*, 213–223.

Rathus, S. A. A 30-item schedule for assessing assertive behavior. *Behavior Therapy*, 1973, *4*, 398–406.

Schwartz, D. A. Community mental health in 1972: An assessment. In H. H. Barten & L. Bellak (Eds.), *Progress in community mental health* (Vol. 2). New York: Grune & Stratton, 1972.

Sechrest, L., & Bryan, J. H. Astrologers as useful marriage counselors. In *Annual editions readings on psychology, 1972–1973*. Guilford, Conn.: Dushkin Publishing Group, 1972.

Wolpe, J. *Psychotherapy by reciprocal inhibition*. Stanford, Calif.: Stanford University Press, 1958.

Zax, M., & Cowen, E. L. *Abnormal psychology: Changing concepts*. New York: Holt, Rinehart & Winston, 1972.

Chapter 3

Cognitive Behavior Therapy Groups: Methods and Comparative Research

Joan R. Shapiro
Carolyn S. Shaffer
Lawrence I. Sank
Donna J. Coghlan

Abstract

A three-module cognitive behavior therapy (CBT) approach to group treatment of depressed and/or anxious outpatients is outlined. Each module is discussed in terms of content, length, format, typical problem areas alleviated by such treatment, utilization of skills, the role of the therapist, and homework assignments. Case examples are described to further elucidate this treatment approach. Research comparing the CBT approach in group vs. individual formats for depressed and/or anxious outpatients in a Health Maintenance Organization (HMO) is presented. Forty-four clients were randomly assigned to one of three treatment modalities: CBT-group, CBT-individual, or interpersonal group therapy. The Beck Depression Inventory, State-Trait Anxiety Inventory, and Adult Self-Expression Scale were administered prior to an evaluation and again pre- and posttreatment. The Hamilton Rating Scale for Depression and a clinician rating of client commitment to treatment were completed for clients as well. All treatments resulted in significant reductions in depression and anxiety as well as a significant increase in assertion. These results are discussed in terms of the effectiveness and cost benefits of group intervention. The chapter concludes with a discussion of future developments in both CBT treatment and research.*

*An additional description of the study described in this chapter can be found in Shaffer, Shapiro, Sank, & Coghlan (1981). This research was funded in part by NIH Grant No. 501-RR-5359-18.

In the evolutionary process of therapeutic treatment, increased attention is being given to Cognitive Behavior Therapy (CBT). This approach builds upon traditional behavior therapies rooted in learning theory and at the same time acknowledges the internal processes emphasized by more traditional psychoanalytic approaches. The CBT approach to understanding behavior focuses on the cognitive or internal processing of stimuli, i.e., the internal dialogue concerning a situation, as well as the stimuli themselves, i.e., the observable characteristics of a situation. Cognitive techniques (identifying and disputing irrational beliefs, changing illogical thinking patterns and irrational self-statements) and behavioral techniques (contracting, relaxation, desensitization, and behavior rehearsal) are both used to promote behavior change and modify thought patterns. Training in assertion and problem-solving skills are additional cognitive and behavioral change techniques that complement or round out this treatment approach.

Four variations of CBT have emerged in the past decade: (a) rational-emotive therapy (Ellis & Grieger, 1978), (b) cognitive therapy (Beck, 1976), (c) cognitive behavior modification (Meichenbaum, 1977), and (d) problem solving (D'Zurilla & Goldfried, 1971; Platt, Spivack, & Swift, Note 1). In the absence of data identifying any one of these variations as universally accepted or definitively appropriate for specific populations, we have incorporated elements of all of these, in addition to assertion and relaxation training (two of the more strictly behavioral interventions), into our approach to treating depression and anxiety in an outpatient population.

Anxiety and depression are the two most frequently reported clinical mental health problems. Individual and group psychotherapy since their inception have addressed these twin problems. Our version of CBT is a treatment approach in which clients are taught self-help techniques for use in the alleviation and prevention of depression and anxiety. Once clients are taught CBT skills and given ample practice in their use, they serve as their own therapists, altering their physical and intrapsychic responses to environmental events. In contrast to a historical perspective, which emphasizes pathogenesis, CBT is goal-oriented and focuses on both a topographic and a functional analysis of the problem behavior(s). CBT focuses on how, rather than why, symptoms develop. CBT is also consumer-oriented, in that the therapist accepts the client's goals and works with him in an allied, cooperative fashion, thus minimizing inequality in the therapist-client relationship.

CBT is a treatment approach that we hypothesize is appropriate in both short- and long-term intervention. The treatment plan that we follow in our facility (a prepaid health plan) and that we describe in this chapter involves using CBT as a short-term intervention (10-20 sessions) in both individual and group formats. It is our belief that short-term treatment can have a major impact on preventing and ameliorating problems of depression and anxiety. In addition, with the increased demand for services, the limited supply of providers, and the economic realities of health care facilities, short-term intervention is indeed warranted, and, in the case of health maintenance organizations (HMOs) such as ours, mandated.

In the first portion of this chapter, we describe in detail the three-module system of CBT used in our facility. Following a brief introduction of the three modules and basic information about client selection, each module will be discussed in terms of (a) content, (b) length, (c) format of session, (d) typical problems that are alleviated by such treatment, (e) utilization of skills, (f) role of the therapist, (g) homework assignments, and (h) case examples. We describe at length the group approach, followed by a description of the individual approach as it compares and contrasts to group CBT.

In the second portion of this chapter, we discuss our research comparing CBT in group versus individual formats for the treatment of depression and anxiety. The chapter concludes with a discussion of future developments in both CBT treatment and research, and with a description of additions to the original program.

THE THREE-MODULE SYSTEM

In our version of CBT, the following modules are employed (see Shaffer & Sank, Note 2):

1. *Relaxation Training.* Clients are taught to become aware of and to reduce the sensation and experience of stress and anxiety. In addition to musculo-skeletal tension reduction, this approach entails a quieting response that includes both sympathetic and parasympathetic nervous systems.

2. *Cognitive Restructuring.* Clients are taught how emotional responses to environmental events are mediated by their thoughts and how these emotions, particularly extremely negative emotions, can be altered by therapeutic intervention. Clients are also taught to identify their belief structures, to challenge irrational belief systems or automatic thoughts, and to replace these thoughts with more rational beliefs.

3. *Assertion Training.* Clients are taught to identify situations where assertive responses are appropriate but nonetheless lacking. They are instructed to be protagonists, acting decisively yet responsibly and considerately. Clients are taught to be direct and to stand up for their own rights in their dealings with others, without infringing on the rights of others.

The therapists in our program frequently use examples from their own lives to illustrate the skills taught in each module. Our version of CBT also employs the use of contracts, attendance performance records, personal logs, and homework assignments, as well as a buddy system (which entails calling a specified group member each week).

We have shown that these skills or techniques can be taught to all clients who are depressed or anxious, with the possible exception of clients who are severely depressed or actively suicidal, in a short time span (10 to 20 sessions) and in a group format. It is not our expectation that clients will emerge from therapy proficient in these skills, but rather that they will achieve sufficient understanding and practice to satisfactorily be able to implement and gradually improve upon these skills without additional professional intervention.

Justification of the Sequencing of the Modules

Implicit in the presentation of these skills is a belief that a reduced sensation of tension allows for enhanced learning of specific cognitive and behavioral skills. Consequently, we teach the relaxation module first. Moreover, relaxation is an easy skill to learn, provides for the immediate relief of some symptoms, and gives a sense of mastery over one's body. This module is also non-threatening and non-demanding for the client.

Cognitive restructuring follows the relaxation module and precedes the assertion module because of the underlying assumption that two components contribute to the successful performance of assertive behavior. These include (a) a belief system based on rationality or a reasonable appraisal of a situation and its potential consequences, and (b) the actual performance of interpersonal responses. Consequently, we teach cognitive restructuring as a prerequisite for assertion training, since it serves as a means of ferreting out irrational or unrealistic automatic thoughts that act as inhibitors to appropriate assertive behaviors. Only when the belief system has been appropriately modified do we work on behavioral skills. This stepwise progression of skills parallels traditional desensitization (relaxation, imagination, *in vivo* behavior) in that clients are first taught to relax their bodies so they can then work on their thinking, which in turn allows them to practice within and then outside the session. This order of presentation also parallels a gradual exposure to group participation; clients move from total passivity in the relaxation module, to disclosing their thoughts and negative emotions during the cognitive restructuring module, to interacting and role-playing problem situations and giving feedback to group members during the assertion module.

Selection of Clients for Treatment

Clients are considered appropriate for CBT treatment if they: (a) present problems of depression and/or anxiety, (b) are non-psychotic, (c) are not acutely suicidal, (d) demonstrate at least average intelligence, verbal skills, and psychological mindedness, (e) possess average social skills, (f) are committed to working on problems, and (g) are willing to comply with tasks and homework assignments.

Placement in Group versus Individual Treatment

Since our research (which is described in the Research section of this chapter) suggests that treatment outcome for individual and group formats is relatively equal, it is our practice to place clients in groups whenever possible. Clients who insist on individual treatment are placed with an individual therapist. While group CBT may be the treatment of choice, some people are predisposed to object to group therapy for various reasons: concern about confidentiality, fear of public speaking and self-disclosure among peers, unwillingness to listen to the problems of others, preference for the more expensive service, or bias that the individual attention of a therapist results in better, faster, and more substantial change. It is our practice to elicit the client's fears, address objections, and assure confidentiality prior to group placement. Fear of, or ambivalence about, group treatment are explained as normal reactions. The expertise and authority of the therapist, supported by the recommendation of the professional staff, are used to persuade the client to agree to be placed in the group.

Relaxation Module

Two types of relaxation are taught in this module. In the first session, following a brief introduction, Benson's relaxation response (Benson, 1975) is presented. In the second session, clients are taught deep muscle relaxation (DMR) (Jacobson, 1962), which is paired with pleasure and competency scenes. The Subjective Units of Discomfort Scale (SUDS) (Wolpe & Lazarus, 1966) is explained and pre- and postrelaxation SUDS-level measures are taken. Problems with the relaxation process are discussed, e.g., the presence of distracting thoughts, difficulty scheduling practice sessions, and difficulty relaxing certain muscle groups. Two handouts are then distributed: (a) a relaxation guide with cuing words for deep muscle relaxation and (b) a relaxation practice log. Clients are assigned the task of practicing relaxation regularly while gradually reducing the amount of tensing, the goal being to relax in a minimal amount of time through the use of cues.

Progressive muscle relaxation is used because the reduction in tension, preceded by the increase in tension through muscle flexing, helps the client learn the sensation of tension. This awareness of tension then serves as a cue for the practice of deep muscle relaxation. Relaxation is useful for the reduction of somatic problems such as chronic lower back pain and tension headaches, problems of reduced efficiency at work or anxiety in social situations, sleep problems, eating problems, and sexual dysfunction. Many of our clients are at some point inappropriately tense and seem to benefit from the mastery of relaxation skills. Clients can reduce their overall tension level during the day by appropriately timing their relaxation practice. They are also encouraged to use relaxation at bedtime to help themselves fall asleep. Our own clinical experience reflects that when sleep problems are alleviated, there is often an appreciable reduction in affective problems. We have learned from our experience with our clinical population that when clients fall asleep more easily and sleep longer, depression tends to lift. The successful use of relaxation can also lead to a reduction in the use of medication such as Valium, and the abuse of nonprescription drugs such as alcohol, marijuana, or other self-medicating substances.

During this module, one of the two therapists serves as a model illustrating the end result of DMR practice. The other therapist gives instructions for tensing and relaxing muscle areas. The therapists cite examples and anecdotes from their own lives to illustrate situations in which relaxation had been useful. The group members can suggest ways to remember to relax and to find opportunities for practice, and they can encourage one another through anecdotes. From our practice it seems to us that a group situation is very effective for teaching this skill, because clients seem less self-conscious about relaxing when others around them are doing it simultaneously. The buddy phone call system is used during the week to encourage the practice of relaxation. Two case examples of the use of relaxation skills follow:

J.M., a woman in her late 20s, was referred for daily cluster headaches of 5-years' duration, which were at times incapacitating and resulted in poor work attendance and inefficiency. She was taught Benson's relaxation response and practiced it religiously. She reported a reduction in headaches to the level of no headaches following her initial attempts at relaxation. She also reported no recurrence of the headaches throughout the course of treatment (2½ months). This case example is somewhat dramatic; more typically, patients experience a more gradual reduction of symptoms with occasional relapses in difficult situations.

V.J., a college-educated woman in her mid-50s working as a retail clerk, complained of an inability to do arithmetic calculations in the presence of others. Although she was taught relaxation techniques during the first two group sessions, not until the last group session was she able to report decreased subjective skeletal tension and enhanced ability to perform the arithmetic tasks. When pressed for an explanation for her success, she attributed it to her mastery of the relaxation exercises and her use of them prior to as well as during a retail transaction.

Cognitive Restructuring Module

During this module, which consists of four sessions, clients learn the concept of *cognitive restructuring* (CR) and practice it both within and outside the group. First, the therapists introduce the concept of CR and explain its utility in the alleviation of undesirable emotional reactions. Following this introduction CR is demonstrated, using both personal examples and examples likely to be common to all group members. The A-B-C-D-E paradigm of Ellis (1962) is presented and the 3 core and 11 corollary irrational beliefs are discussed. Rational alternatives for irrational beliefs (Lange & Jakubowski, 1976) are also presented. Clients are taught to recognize automatic thoughts or irrational beliefs contained in their self-talk, and are taught ways to dispute or challenge these beliefs. Clients are given standard "dispute handles" or "tabs," questions to ask themselves in order to challenge their beliefs (e.g., How do I know for certain? Is there any other explanation?). Homework tasks are assigned to both encourage and facilitate the practice of CR. Through the use of homework sheets, clients learn the written process of recording automatic thoughts and irrational beliefs, disputing these irrational thoughts, deriving rational alternatives, and noting positive changes in affect, cognitions, and behavior. The reading assignment for this module is the *New Guide for Rational Living* (Ellis & Harper 1975).

The format of the sessions during this module flows from didactic presentations to group participation and to repeated analyses of in-session demonstrations, homework assignments, and discussion of difficult problem areas for particular individuals. The therapists serve as teachers, role models, and facilitators. The group is used for public commitment, vicarious learning from peers, and role-playing. Once the skills are learned, group members act as therapists for one another, challenging assumptions and giving feedback on progress, further reinforcing a coping versus a mastery model (Kazdin, 1979). A coping model is one in which new skills are acquired gradually through the process of refinement of techniques, whereas a mastery model is one in which someone could perform the desired task without repeated practice. In a coping model, clients identify with the struggles of their peers. For a more detailed description of within-session procedures for this and other modules, see Shaffer and Sank (Note 2).

In our practice CR has been useful for dealing with sleeplessness, lack of concentration, work-related problems, public criticism, interpersonal or social embarrassment, achievement anxiety, perfectionism, need for constant social approval, and rigid expectations, among others. CR is utilized for the recognition of irrational beliefs and the substitution of rational beliefs that facilitate alternate, more productive modes of perception or behavior. A case example of the therapeutic effectiveness of cognitive restructuring follows:

> M.K., a woman in her late 20s, mother of four and full-time government worker, would return home from work to find her house always in disorder, her husband watching TV, and her instructions to her oldest daughter about dinner preparations not followed. This situation so frustrated her that she would either dissolve in tears or begin shouting at family members. She presented this problem to the group. Through discussion and group feedback she was able to identify her irrational beliefs; the resulting replies and rational beliefs of the others helped to modify her self-statements. She reported feeling better able to put disruptions into perspective, deal more calmly with family members, productively confront family members with her expectations, and develop more effective strategies for enlisting family support.

Assertion Module

This module consists of four sessions during which assertion is defined and distinguished from aggression and also from passivity or nonassertion. The components of assertive behavior (eye contact, voice tone, content of speech, etc.) are also outlined, and assertive behavior is practiced within and outside the group.

During the first session, clients are helped to formulate concrete goals, arranged according to level of difficulty. The format of the sessions consists of teaching, followed by role-playing of standardized situations (e.g., obtaining a diagnosis from an uncooperative physician), videotaping of these role-played situations, and, finally, videotaping of role-played situations specific to the personal lives of the group members. Clients are assigned the homework task of keeping behavioral logs in which they record details of situations for which assertion was or would have been appropriate. Their behavior, the reactions of others, and what they wish they had said are included in these logs. Clients are also encouraged to try out in their own daily situations the assertive behaviors that were role-played in the group, so as to facilitate the generalization of assertion skills. The reading assignment for this module is *When I Say No I Feel Guilty* (Smith, 1975).

Assertion training is useful for clients who want to deal more effectively with family, close friends, superiors, subordinates, and people in commerce, as well as in job-related and social situations. In this module, clients are helped to make positive, complimentary statements as well as to turn down requests and to offer constructive criticism. Through assertion training, clients learn to recognize cognitive and behavioral deficits and, following the application of CR techniques, to correct or alter any dysfunctional, inappropriate cognitions, and to use assertive techniques to implement behavior change. Clients are taught how to make their needs known responsibly and humanely while they are standing up for their rights.

During this module the therapists have numerous roles, which include: (a) defining assertion and describing and modeling assertive behavior, (b) role-playing assertive behavior with clients, (c) videotaping the role-plays, (d) helping clients define goals, (e) making suggestions for behavior change, and (f) encouraging feedback from group members. The group is very active during this module, role-playing various situations and then reversing roles, discussing the components of assertive behavior in the role-plays, critiquing one another's performance, suggesting alternate assertive responses, and reinforcing appropriate assertive behavior. The following are case examples of the successful use of the skills learned in the assertion module:

J.B., a secondary school teacher in his early 20s, had difficulty dealing with his supervisor (the school principal), who was reportedly insensitive to the subtle suggestions of J.B. and his fellow teachers for changes that would increase efficiency, boost morale, and generally improve the quality of the work environment. During the assertion module, J.B. learned to be more vocal in a tactful, assertive manner and to speak up in staff meetings, thus generating discussion of germane issues. J.B. reported feeling better about himself and his ability to make constructive suggestions. Unfortunately, he was discouraged by the lack of support from his older, more conservative colleagues, who perceived him as a "young upstart." As a result of this lack of support and a lack of receptivity on the part of the principal, J.B. sought and found more satisfying employment elsewhere.

C.W., a 38-year-old wife of an attorney and mother of two, complained of chronic depression, sexual dissatisfaction, and long-standing marital problems. Through the use of assertion skills, she was able, for the first time, to make requests of a sexual nature to her husband and, as a result, recognized other areas of her relationship with him in which speaking directly to him resulted in a positive response.

L.B., a 29-year-old woman working as a fund raiser for a nonprofit agency, was experiencing much stress in her work environment. Although she was mainly responsible for all grant proposals, her boss insisted upon reviewing each application. In addition, the boss never had the time to look at the proposals until shortly before they were due. The client experienced many somatic complaints at these times and also ended up working much unnecessary overtime.

Through the use of cognitive restructuring, role-playing, and feedback, the client was able to give her boss deadlines for reviewing materials. If the deadlines were not observed, the client sent out the proposals as they were. The boss never did meet the deadlines, but did offer the client a raise and eventually delegated to the client more and more responsibility.

Use of CBT in an Individual Format

In many ways the use of CBT in an individual format is similar to its use in a group format, although important differences do exist. Although the same CBT coping skills are taught, the techniques are tailored to the specific symptomatology and problem areas of the client. In contrast to the group sessions, which are 90 minutes in length, the individual sessions are 50 minutes in length and are less structured and less didactic than the group sessions. The therapists use examples directly related to the client's problems and, when appropriate, role-play particular situations directly with the client. Themes of a more personal nature may be discussed, and more sensitive personal problems are often disclosed in individual therapy than would be disclosed in a group. The same readings and homework tasks are assigned; but unlike the group, in which a sampling of assignments is selected for group discussion and feedback, all of the individual client's homework assignments are carefully reviewed.

COGNITIVE BEHAVIOR THERAPY RESEARCH

We have engaged in research within our agency in order to answer several questions about our clinical practice using CBT. The primary purpose of our study was to evaluate the relative efficacy of both group and individual CBT approaches in treating anxiety and depression. A secondary purpose was to compare these treatments to an interpersonal group therapy approach.

Several outcome studies have compared the effectiveness of CBT with waiting-list controls and other psychotherapy comparison groups. Subjects have included both depressed college student volunteers (Gioe, 1975; Shipley & Fazio, 1973; Taylor & Marshall, 1977) and depressed psychiatric clinic clients (Morris, 1975; Schmickley, 1976). Some investigators have employed a group format (Gioe, 1975; Morris, 1975; Shaw, 1977; Shipley & Fazio, 1973), while others used individual CBT (Rush, Beck, Kovacs, & Hollon, 1977; Schmickley, 1976; Taylor & Marshall, 1977). Generally, regardless of format, CBT has been found to be more effective than the various other treatments (Beck, Rush, Shaw, & Emery, 1978). To date, only two studies have examined the relationship between format (group or individual) and outcome of CBT treatment (Rush & Watkins,

1981; Shaw & Hollon, Note 3). Treatment outcomes for those two studies were similar in that individual CBT appeared to produce a greater reduction in depressive symptomatology than group CBT. However, both group and individual treatments were associated with significant remission of symptoms. These results are not considered conclusive, however, since in the Shaw and Hollon study, clients were not randomly assigned to treatments, and in the Rush and Watkins study, the group clients were not part of the same randomly assigned subject pool as the individual clients.

In the present study, which was a more rigorously controlled comparison of group and individual CBT, the group treatment was expected to be as effective or more effective than individual treatment, in that groups offer the opportunity for vicarious learning, role-playing with peers, and group feedback. The treatment techniques used in this study were similar to those of Beck and his associates (1978), with the addition of progressive relaxation (Jacobson, 1962) and assertion training (Lange & Jakubowski, 1976).

Two major hypotheses were studied:

1. Group CBT is as effective, or more effective, than individual CBT in producing significant changes in depression, anxiety, and assertiveness.
2. CBT, in an individual or group format, is significantly more effective than interpersonal group therapy in producing changes in depression, anxiety, and assertiveness.

METHOD

Subjects

The sample consisted of 44 subjects who sought relief from symptoms of anxiety and/or depression. All subjects were enrollees of a health maintenance organization (HMO) and were referred to the mental health unit by the primary medical care teams. Each subject was then screened by a mental health therapist and found to be appropriate for brief therapy. The typical diagnosis was adjustment disorder with depressed or anxious mood. Although some clients scored on the BDI and STAI in the mild range for depression/anxiety, they did request treatment and were referred by their physicians. Clients who were in need of immediate individual attention (e.g., suicidal, psychotic) were excluded from the study, as were clients who were on psychotropic medication, not primarily anxious/depressed, or unwilling to participate in the research. The demographic characteristics of these subjects are presented in Table 3.1.

Clients were assigned on a random basis to one of three treatment modalities: (a) the cognitive behavior therapy group (CBT-gp),

Table 3.1
Demographic Data For Subjects
(N = 44, Mean Age = 30, Age Range—21 to 41)

Sex		Marital Status					Education					Socio-economic Status*				
M	*F*	*Single*	*Engaged*	*Married*	*Separated*	*Divorced*	*Graduate*	*BA*	*Some college*	*HS*	*Some HS*	*I*	*II*	*III*	*IV*	*V*
36%	64%	48%	2%	37%	11%	2%	36%	46%	14%	2%	2%	18%	23%	54%	5%	0%

*Status was determined by the Hollingshead Two-Factor Index of Social Class (Myers & Bean, 1968).

(b) the interpersonal therapy group (IT-gp), or (c) the individual cognitive behavior therapy (CBT-ind).

Measures

Among the assessment instruments employed were the following:

1. *Beck Depression Inventory (BDI).* The BDI is a 21-item self-report measure that assesses numerous manifestations of depression. Each item is scored on a scale of 0 to 3, and the total possible score ranges from 0 to 63. The higher the score, the more severe the depression. The BDI was chosen because of its careful construction and validation (Beck, 1967; Beck, 1972; Beck & Beamesderfer, 1974) and its wide use in research on depression.

2. *State-Trait Anxiety Inventory (STAI).* The STAI is a 40-item self-report scale that measures two distinct anxiety concepts: (a) state anxiety (A-State scale) and (b) trait anxiety (A-Trait scale). The A-State scale is considered to be a sensitive indicator of the transitory anxiety experienced by clients in psychotherapy, and it has been demonstrated that scores on the A-State scale increase in response to various kinds of stress and decrease as a result of relaxation training (Spielberger, Gorsuch, & Lushene, 1970).

    The A-Trait scale measures relatively stable individual differences in anxiety proneness, i.e., the tendency to respond to situations perceived as threatening with elevations in state anxiety. The test-retest reliability of the A-Trait scale is relatively high, while the test-retest reliability for the A-State scale tends to be low, as it is designed to be influenced by situational factors. Both the A-Trait and the A-State scales have a high degree of internal consistency. The validity of the STAI has been reported elsewhere (Spielberger et al., 1970).

3. *Adult Self-Expression Scale (ASES).* The ASES is a 48-item self-report measure of assertiveness designed for use with adults. The scale has been found to have high test-retest reliability and moderate to high construct validity. Concurrent validity also has been established (Gay, Hollandsworth, & Galassi, 1975). The instrument was validated on a general adult population with an average age of 31 years.

4. *Rating of client's commitment to treatment.* Therapists were asked to rate each client's "commitment to treatment" on a scale from 1 to 5 (interrater reliability = .82, $z = 4.41, p < .0001$). Therapists based this rating on attendance, punctuality, completion of homework assignments, and participation of the client in the therapeutic process.

5. *Hamilton Rating Scale for Depression (HRS-D).* The HRS-D is a 17-item measure of depression designed for a clinician's rating. Hamilton (1960) reports an interrater reliability of .90 ($N = 60$) for the measure. Prusoff, Klerman, and Paykel (1972) report significant but moderate concordance (.17 − .64) between the HRS-D and a self-report inventory composed of items from the Inventory of Psychic and Somatic Complaints and Mood Scales.

Three self-report inventories were administered prior to an initial evaluation session (pre-1) and immediately before (pre-2) and after (post) treatment (10 sessions). The time between evaluation and treatment varied from 0 to 54 days, with a mean of 24 days. The HRS-D was administered to a subsample of 23 subjects immediately prior to treatment (pre-2) and following treatment (post). The measure was administered by experienced clinicians who were blind to the treatment groups.

Treatment Modalities

All treatments were conducted by two of the authors, both clinical psychologists with extensive experience with both individual and group CBT. These clinicians co-led the groups and also conducted the individual treatment. All three treatments consisted of 10 weekly sessions (1½-hour sessions for groups, 1-hour sessions for individuals). Due to holidays and snow days, treatment varied from 9 to 17 weeks, with a mean of 10 weeks.

The *CBT-group* treatment was composed of the three self-help modules described earlier: (a) progressive relaxation (Jacobson, 1962), (b) cognitive restructuring (Beck, 1967; Ellis, 1962), and (c) assertiveness training (Lange and Jakubowski, 1976). The *Interpersonal Therapy Group* treatment was a non-directive form of group therapy that attempted to elicit discussion of past and current problems, to encourage group interaction, and to reflect and clarify feelings in an empathic manner. The *CBT-individual* treatment consisted of teaching the same self-help modules included in the CBT-group where appropriate, according to the judgment of the therapists (i.e., relaxation, cognitive restructuring, and assertiveness training). While it would have allowed for greater comparability to have taught all three treatment skills to all individual therapy subjects, tailoring the treatment to the individual is more in keeping with our actual clinical practice. Cognitive restructuring was taught to 100% of the individual clients, assertion training to approximately 78%, and relaxation to 14%.

RESULTS

The total sample of 44 subjects excludes seven clients who declined to participate in the study and three clients who elected to terminate prematurely. These clients were evenly distributed across treatments. Of the subjects who participated in the study, nine did not fully complete all of the assessment measures.

One-way analyses of variance were calculated for the first and second assessments of each dependent measure (pre-1 and pre-2 scores) by treatment (CBT-gp, IT-gp, and CBT-ind). No significant differences were found among the three treatment groups. Mean scores and standard deviations for each self-report measure are reported in Table 3.2. One-way analyses of variance showed no significant differences in age, marital status, education, socio-economic status, commitment, or length of treatment among the three treatment groups.

Repeated measures analyses of variance were computed for clients with complete and valid data on all self-report measures ($N = 35$), adjusted for the following covariates: sex, marital status, socio-economic status, attendance, commitment, length of evaluation period, and length of treatment period. Main effects were found for each self-report measure

Table 3.2
Means and Standard Deviations on Four Self-Report Measures
Over Pre-1, Pre-2, and Post Scores
for Three Treatment Modalities ($N = 35$)

Measure	CBT-gp $N = 10$		IT-gp $N = 13$		CBT-ind $N = 12$	
	M	*SD*	*M*	*SD*	*M*	*SD*
BDI						
Pre-1	16.4	9.0	11.4	6.2	10.8	5.2
Pre-2	13.6	7.3	10.8	5.9	8.0	4.7
Post	8.3	6.3	6.5	4.9	4.5	4.3
STAI A-State						
Pre-1	54.0	9.2	50.3	12.0	47.7	8.6
Pre-2	47.0	8.2	48.1	12.4	46.0	10.6
Post	36.2	18.4	40.0	10.2	40.6	12.3
STAI A-Trait						
Pre-1	53.6	7.6	46.8	9.0	50.5	5.3
Pre-2	49.0	7.9	47.4	8.3	49.7	6.3
Post	41.8	9.6	42.8	10.8	43.3	7.3
ASES						
Pre-1	93.1	26.5	107.2	27.5	105.4	23.2
Pre-2	95.3	31.3	104.3	25.4	104.2	22.0
Post	115.2	21.5	118.1	25.0	112.8	16.3

(Depression F (2,64) = 22.23, p < .0001; State Anxiety F (2,64) = 13.73, p < .0001; Trait Anxiety F (2,64) = 16.35, p < .0001; and Assertiveness F (2,64) = 15.03, p < .0001). All treatments resulted in a significant reduction in depression, state anxiety, and trait anxiety, and a significant increase in assertion by the end of treatment. Neither main effects for treatments nor interactions between times of assessment and treatments were significant.

The means and standard deviations for the Hamilton ratings are reported in Table 3.3. These ratings are consistent with the BDI scores in that a significant reduction in the symptoms of depression was found between the pre-2 and post ratings (t (21) = 6.4, p < .0001). This significant reduction in depression was found for each treatment: for CBT-gp, t (5) = 2.91, p < .02; for IT-gp, t (7) = 3.22, p < .01; and for CBT-ind, t (5) = 8.09, p < .001. While each treatment modality resulted in significant symptom reduction, no significant differences among the three treatments were found in a repeated measures analysis of variance (F (2,19) = 1.40, p < .27).

Table 3.3
Means and Standard Deviations on
HRS-D Pre-2 and Post Ratings for Three
Treatment Modalities

Measure	CBT-gp N = 8		IT-gp N = 8		CBT-ind N = 7	
	M	SD	M	SD	M	SD
HRS-D Pre-2	14.4	9.4	13.8	5.9	18.8	4.7
HRS-D Post	5.1	4.6	4.4	5.3	7.2	4.2

Pearson product-moment correlations were calculated for the BDI and HRS-D scores. These two measures of depression were significantly correlated in both the pre-2 (r = .44, p < .03) and post (r = .54, p < .01) conditions.

Paired comparison t-tests were calculated for the pre-1—pre-2 difference scores for each self-report measure; these are reported in Table 3.4. A significant decrease in depression as measured by the BDI was found following the evaluation period. No significant differences between the pre-1—pre-2 mean scores were found for state anxiety (STAI, A-State), trait anxiety (STAI, A-Trait), or assertiveness (ASES).

Pearson product-moment correlations for the four pre-1, pre-2, and post self-report measures are reported in Table 3.5. Depression is positively and significantly correlated with state anxiety and trait anxiety.

Table 3.4
Paired Comparison t-Tests
Pre-1 with Pre-2

	t	df	Probability
BDI	2.93	38	$p < .01$
STAI, A-State	1.44	39	n.s.
STAI, A-Trait	1.76	38	n.s.
ASES	1.02	39	n.s.

Depression, state anxiety, and trait anxiety are all negatively and significantly correlated with assertiveness. These correlations are consistent across the three trials. While these correlations are significantly different from zero, their magnitudes are not high enough to suggest that only one dimension is being measured.

Table 3.5
Pearson Product Moment Correlations
Pre-1, Pre-2, and Post Scores

	Depression		State Anxiety		Trait Anxiety		Assertiveness
	N	r	N	r	N	r	r
Pre-1							
BDI		1.00					
STAI, A-State	38	.41**		1.00			
STAI, A-Trait	37	.73***	38	.35*		1.00	
ASES	39	−.53***	39	−.41**	38	−.49***	1.00
Pre-2							
BDI		1.00					
STAI, A-State	44	.53***		1.00			
STAI, A-Trait	44	.62***	44	.50***		1.00	
ASES	44	−.31*	44	−.30*	44	−.44***	1.00
Post							
BDI		1.00					
STAI, A-State	41	.62***		1.00			
STAI, A-Trait	40	.72***	40	.73***		1.00	
ASES	41	−.44**	41	−.33**	40	−.54***	1.00

*$p < .02$
**$p < .01$
***$p < .001$

DISCUSSION

The results of the present study support the hypothesis that CBT in a group format is as effective as individual CBT in reducing symptoms of depression and anxiety and in increasing assertiveness. For depression, this result held true for both the self-report ratings (BDI) and clinician ratings (HRS-D), lending concurrent validity to these conclusions. The equivalence of individual and group psychotherapeutic interventions with randomly assigned, moderately anxious and depressed clients is in contrast to the prior studies of Rush and Watkins (1981) and Shaw and Hollon (Note 3). There are important implications related to this finding. Since Health Maintenance Organizations (HMOs) provide care on a prepaid basis, economies such as are obtained from group versus individual interventions are of great importance. Such economies are reflected in decisions regarding premium rates and staffing patterns. An implication of the study findings is a recommendation for a treatment program emphasizing group intervention for clients with moderate anxiety and depression versus an individual intervention. Such a treatment program is likely to yield corresponding cost savings.

The hypothesis that CBT would result in greater significant positive change in the dependent measures than IT-gp was not supported. Two explanations are advanced to account for this lack of differential treatment effect. While the interpersonal group was clearly different from the CBT group, some elements of CBT were present in this therapy. The same CBT-oriented therapists co-led both the CBT and interpersonal groups, thus possibly confounding the results. In the interpersonal group, no relaxation training was given, coping skills were not taught directly in a structured way, and CBT language was avoided. However, rational thinking was encouraged, feedback was given for coping behaviors, and assertion was reinforced. Role-playing was not used, but examples of appropriate responses to situations were suggested or modeled by the group leaders.

The lack of difference between the CBT and interpersonal groups supports the findings of Zeiss, Lewinsohn, and Munoz (1979), who found that several treatment modalities significantly and nondifferentially alleviated depression; clients did not improve differentially on the dependent variables according to the kind of treatment received. One possible explanation is that all clients felt a sense of self-efficacy over their problems (Bandura, 1977).

A further finding relates to Lewinsohn's theory of depression. Lewinsohn (1975) postulated that a low rate of response-contingent positive reinforcement was likely to be associated with a depressed affect. Deficient social skills would be likely to yield such a low reinforcement rate and, thus, a dysphoric mood. Our findings of an inverse relationship

between clients' scores on the BDI and the measure of assertiveness provide indirect support for such a theoretical understanding of the etiology
and maintenance of depression. This relationship held constant for both
premeasures and postmeasures. Seligman's (1975) learned helplessness
theory of depression also contributes to an understanding of these findings. His theory states that depression is the result of the belief that one
is powerless and ineffectual and therefore unable to manipulate the
environment to advantage. An assertive stance would be incompatible
with the belief that one is helpless.

In addition, a similar inverse relationship existed between client
scores on the anxiety inventories and the assertiveness measures. This
has implications for an understanding of the etiology and maintenance
of anxiety. Social skills deficits and the attendant negative cognitive evaluations of the self and one's abilities can act as potent variables in the
subjective experience of anxiety. This parallels the findings of Glasgow
and Arkowitz (1975) and supports the theoretical understanding of
anxiety outlined by Curran (1977).

The depression (BDI) scores between the pre-1 and pre-2 measures
showed a significant decrement ($p < .01$) following a single evaluative
interview. Such a finding is related to the experience of Follette and
Cummings (1967) and that of Goldberg, Krantz, and Locke (1970),
who did not assess changes in depression following evaluation and treatment but did find that a single interview reduced future medical utilization (i.e., frequency of outpatient visits, hospitalizations, phone calls,
etc.) for up to 5 years and 1 year, respectively. Rosen and Wiens (1979)
found a similar significant reduction in medical utilization following
a single psychological evaluation interview. The findings of a reduced
level of depression and a reduction in medical utilization are probably
related in that reduced medical utilization is likely to follow a reduced
level of depression. In addition, many medical visits are in a major way
related to psychological dysfunction (Rosen & Wiens, 1979). Further
studies measuring both medical utilization and psychological dysfunction
are needed.

The current study is being extended to the collection of additional
data at 6 and 12 months following termination of treatment. Persistence
of treatment effects and differential effects of the three treatment conditions over time will be examined. This long-term consideration has not
been previously examined in those studies exploring differential effects
between group and individual CBT interventions.

FUTURE DEVELOPMENTS

Future studies in this area of research warrant some procedural and
design changes from the present study. These changes include (a) stan-

dardization of both the individual and group treatment procedures to enhance the comparability of the treatment content variable, (b) employment of a more severely depressed or anxious client sample to provide for a greater potential range for client improvement, (c) use of a more homogeneous client sample with respect to symptomatology (primarily depressed versus anxious subjects in separate groups), and (d) utilization of additional measures of outcome, including clinician ratings of clients, ratings by peers or significant others, measurement of client acquisition of the specific techniques taught in therapy, and specific changes sought, e.g., measures of adherence to irrational beliefs such as the Dysfunctional Attitude Scale (Weissman & Beck, Note 4). This last type of assessment would be included as a process measure which would help to determine whether improvement could be accounted for by the hypothesized effect of the treatment on the specific target behaviors. A related study investigating the effects of CBT intervention—more specifically, group versus individual intervention—on medical utilization is currently being conducted. A future study comparing a structured CBT group with a less structured, less direct CBT group is in the design stage.

ADDITIONS TO THE ORIGINAL PROGRAM

A Fourth Module: Problem Solving

Problem solving recently has been added as a fourth module for several reasons. It was the experience of the therapists that clients complained of problems outside the range of the three coping skills of relaxation, cognitive restructuring, and assertion. These additional problems would respond to problem-solving techniques. A problem-solving module also expands the behavioral component of CBT and provides a natural conclusion for treatment, since it incorporates and reinforces the three coping skills already learned during the course of therapy. In addition, problem-solving ability has been shown to be positively correlated with general social adjustment (Spivack, Note 5).

This module, based on the work of Goldfried and D'Zurilla (1979), presently consists of two sessions during which the components of problem-solving behavior are taught and practiced. Clients are initially taught to orient themselves to a problem, i.e., to place it in perspective, realizing that a problem is a normal, common occurrence which can respond to a calm, rational approach to finding and implementing solutions. This general orientation is emphasized throughout the module.

Following this general orientation, the remaining components of problem solving are presented sequentially: (a) problem definition or specification, (b) goal formulation, (c) generation of alternatives, (d) enumeration of positive and negative consequences of each alternative,

(e) decision making, (f) verification, and (g) implementation. The therapists present these components using standardized examples, help the group apply these components to a general problem, facilitate the formulation of personal goals for the module, model problem solving as a successful coping skill (using examples from their own experience), and encourage group participation in the generation and weighting of alternatives for specific problems of group members. During this module the role of the therapists is similar to that of group members, with the addition of keeping members on task and pressing for continued monitoring of orientation, i.e., keeping group members cognizant that a solution-oriented approach will assist in solving problems. The group is used to define a problem, to generate alternatives, to assess the reasonableness of these alternatives, and to suggest ways of implementing them. Once again the group also provides vicarious learning, encouragement from peers, and practice in giving and receiving feedback. Clients are assigned the homework task of implementing solutions discussed during the sessions to facilitate the behavioral transfer of skills learned in therapy. They are instructed to go through the written exercise of defining the problem, generating and assessing alternatives, and reporting on their implementation efforts.

Problem-solving skills are applicable to problems in such areas as job seeking, finding a date or mate, financial budgeting, making career decisions, and budgeting time for studies or other activities. Through the use of problem-solving skills, the client is able to recognize a problem as a normal part of living and to apply the components of problem solving sequentially until a solution is successfully implemented.

The following description is a case example of the successful use of problem-solving skills:

> J.F., an accountant in his late 20s, complained of an inability to meet women and a lack of a social life. He was able to define the problem as a need to meet people and increase social activities. With the help of the group, he generated 20 alternative ways to become socially active and to meet more like-minded women and men. (Incidentally, the women in the group found J.F. attractive and reinforced a positive self-image.) J.F. was surprised at the number of alternatives generated and the number of options available to him. Through the group he learned to be noncritical and nonjudgmental when generating alternatives, and he was able to implement some of the options, including giving his first party. J.F.'s mood improved, and he reported that the problem-solving techniques were the most helpful skills he had learned during therapy.

Pregroup Interview

In addition to the problem-solving module, a pregroup interview has also been added to CBT treatment. This interview has been included for several reasons. According to the literature on client expectancies, the course of treatment is facilitated by an accurate perception of what will take place in therapy (Goldfried & Davison, 1976). Several investigators (Cartwright, 1976; Goldstein, 1962; Yalom, 1970) suggest that not only do expectations affect group process and outcome, but that pretreatment preparation to clarify expectations is crucial. Through the pregroup interview the client gains a sense of being prepared for the group by learning what will happen, making personal contact with one of the therapists, asking questions about the group and/or therapy, and discussing fears and inhibitions. An enhanced understanding of the group and its specific components enables the client to determine whether this therapy seems appropriate, to define more clearly her own goals, and to make a commitment to follow through with the treatment recommendation and participate fully in the group. This interview provides the therapist with the opportunity to evaluate once again the appropriateness of group CBT for the client, to prepare the client to make full use of treatment, to enlist the client's commitment and active participation, and to impress upon the client the importance of confidentiality, attendance, compliance with ground rules, and homework assignments.

Prior to the interview, the therapist reviews the client's chart and the client is provided with a description of the group in general and each module specifically. The coping skills are outlined and typical problem areas are suggested. The client then meets with one of the co-leaders to discuss the group, ask questions, and formulate three or four goals for each module. During this session the therapist discusses the treatment recommendation, responds to any qualms the client may have, and clarifies misunderstandings or misgivings about any aspect of therapy.

SUMMARY

In this chapter we have presented a multimodule skill-building group intervention for the treatment of anxiety and depression. In contrast to many new treatment strategies, this therapeutic program has been clinically tested in comparison to two other interventions. While appropriate caution must be exercised in the application and overselling of new techniques, we feel optimistic about our modular version of CBT because of the rigorously controlled study described earlier. Refinements in clinical strategies and research design, as well as 6- and 12-month follow-ups, will be forthcoming.

REFERENCE NOTES

1. Platt, J. J., Spivack, G., & Swift, M. S. *Interpersonal problem-solving group therapy* (No. 31). Philadelphia: Hahnemann Medical College and Hospital, 1975.

2. Shaffer, C. S., & Sank, L. *A manual for cognitive behavior therapy in groups.* Unpublished manuscript, George Washington University Medical Center, 1980.
3. Shaw, B. F., & Hollon, S. D. *Cognitive therapy in a group format with depressed outpatients.* Unpublished manuscript, University of Western Ontario, 1978.
4. Weissman, A. N., & Beck, A. T. *Development and validation of the dysfunctional attitude scale.* Paper presented at the annual meeting of the Association for Advancement of Behavior Therapy, Chicago, 1978.
5. Spivack, G. *Problem solving approaches to therapy.* Paper presented at the Second Annual Conference on Cognitive Behavior Therapy Research, New York, October 1978.

REFERENCES

Bandura, A. Self-efficacy: Toward a unifying theory of behavioral change. *Psychological Review,* 1977, *84,* 191–215.

Beck, A. T. *Depression: Clinical, experimental and therapeutic aspects.* New York: Harper & Row, 1967.

Beck, A. T. *Depression: Causes and treatment.* Philadelphia: University of Pennsylvania Press, 1972.

Beck, A. T. *Cognitive therapy and emotional disorders.* New York: International Universities Press, 1976.

Beck, A. T., & Beamesderfer, A. Assessment of depression: The depression inventory. In P. Pinchot (Ed.), *Psychological measurements in psychopharmacology.* Basel: Karger, 1974.

Beck, A. T., Rush, A. J., Shaw, B. F., & Emery, G. *Cognitive therapy of depression: A treatment manual.* New York: Guilford Press, 1978.

Benson, H. *The relaxation response.* New York: Morrow, 1975.

Cartwright, M. H. A preparatory method for group counseling. *Journal of Counseling Psychology,* 1976, *23,* 75–77.

Curran, J. P. Social skills training as an approach to the treatment of heterosexual-social anxiety: A review. *Psychological Bulletin,* 1977, *84,* 140–157.

D'Zurilla, T. J., & Goldfried, M. R. Problem solving and behavior modification. *Journal of Abnormal Psychology,* 1971, *78,* 107–126.

Ellis, A. *Reason and emotion in psychotherapy.* New York: Lyle Stuart, 1962.

Ellis, A., & Grieger, R. *The handbook of rational-emotive therapy.* New York: Springer, 1978.

Ellis, A., & Harper, R. *A new guide to rational living.* North Hollywood, Calif.: Wilshire, 1975.

Follette, W., & Cummings, N. A. Psychiatric services and medical utilization in a pre-paid health plan setting. *Medical Care,* 1967, *5,* 25–35.

Gay, M., Hollandsworth, J., & Galassi, J. An assertiveness inventory for adults. *Journal of Counseling Psychology,* 1975, *22,* 340–344.

Gioe, V. J. Cognitive modification and positive group experience as a treatment for depression (Doctoral dissertation, Temple University, 1975). *Dissertation Abstracts International*, 1975, *36*, 3039B–3040B. (University Microfilms No. 75-28, 219)

Glasgow, R. E., & Arkowitz, H. The behavioral assessment of male and female social competence in dyadic heterosexual interactions. *Behavior Therapy*, 1975, *6*, 488–498.

Goldberg, I. D., Krantz, G., & Locke, B. Z. Effects of a short term out-patient psychiatric therapy benefit on the utilization of medical services in a pre-paid group practice medical program. *Medical Care*, 1970, *8*, 419–428.

Goldfried, M. R., & Davison, G. C. *Clinical behavior therapy*. New York: Holt, Rinehart & Winston, 1976.

Goldfried, M. R., & D'Zurilla, T. J. A behavioral-analytic model for assessing competence. In C. D. Spielberger (Ed.), *Current topics in clinical and community psychology* (Vol. 1). New York: Academic Press, 1979.

Goldstein, A. P. *Therapist/patient expectations in psychotherapy*. New York: Pergamon Press, 1962.

Hamilton, M. A rating scale for depression. *Journal of Neurology, Neurosurgery and Psychiatry*, 1960, *23*, 56–62.

Jacobson, E. *You must relax*. New York: McGraw-Hill, 1962.

Kazdin, A. E. Therapy outcome questions requiring control of credibility and treatment-generated expectancies. *Behavior Therapy*, 1979, *10*, 81–93.

Lange, A., & Jakubowski, P. *Responsible assertive behavior*. Champaign, Ill.: Research Press, 1976.

Lewinsohn, P. The behavioral study and treatment of depression. In M. Hersen, R. M. Eisler, & P. M. Miller (Eds.), *Progress in behavior modification* (Vol. 1). San Francisco: Academic Press, 1975.

Meichenbaum, D. H. *Cognitive-behavior modification: An integrative approach*. New York: Plenum, 1977.

Morris, N. E. *A group self-instruction method for the treatment of depressed outpatients*. Doctoral dissertation, University of Toronto, 1975. National Library of Canada, Canadian Theses Division, National No. 35272.

Myers, J. K., & Bean, L. L. *A decade later: A follow-up of social class and mental illness*. New York: Wiley, 1968.

Prusoff, B. A., Klerman, G. L., & Paykel, E. S. Pitfalls in the self-report assessment of depression. *Canadian Psychiatric Association Journal*, 1972, *17*, 101-107.

Rosen, J. C., & Wiens, A. N. Change in medical problems and use of medical services following psychological intervention. *American Psychologist*, 1979, *34*, 420–431.

Rush, A. J., Beck, A. T., Kovacs, M., & Hollon, S. D. Comparative efficacy of cognitive therapy and imipramine in the treatment of depressed outpatients. *Cognitive Therapy and Research*, 1977, *1*, 11–37.

Rush, A. J., & Watkins, J. T. Group versus individual cognitive therapy: A pilot study. *Cognitive Therapy and Research*, 1981, *5*, 95–103.

Schmickley, V. G. The effects of cognitive behavior modification upon depressed outpatients (Doctoral dissertation, Michigan State University, 1976). *Dissertation Abstracts International*, 1976, *37*, 987B–988B. (University Microfilms No. 76–18, 675)

Seligman, M. *Helplessness: On depression, development and death.* San Francisco: W. H. Freeman, 1975.

Shaffer, C. S., Shapiro, J., Sank, L. I., & Coghlan, D. J. Positive changes in depression, anxiety, and assertion following individual and group cognitive behavior therapy intervention. *Cognitive Therapy and Research*, 1981, *5*, 149–157.

Shaw, B. F. Comparison of cognitive therapy and behavior therapy in the treatment of depression. *Journal of Consulting and Clinical Psychology*, 1977, *45*, 543–555.

Shipley, C., & Fazio, A. Pilot study of a treatment for psychological depression. *Journal of Abnormal Psychology*, 1973, *83*, 372–376.

Smith, M. J. *When I say no I feel guilty.* New York: Dial Press, 1975.

Spielberger, C. D., Gorsuch, R. L., & Lushene, R. E. *State-trait anxiety inventory.* Palo Alto, Calif.: Consulting Psychologist Press, 1970.

Taylor, F. G., & Marshall, W. L. Experimental analysis of a cognitive behavioral therapy for depression. *Cognitive Therapy and Research*, 1977, *1*, 59–72.

Wolpe, J., & Lazarus, A. A. *Behavior therapy techniques.* New York: Pergamon Press, 1966.

Yalom, I. D. *The theory and practice of group psychotherapy.* New York: Basic Books, 1970.

Zeiss, A. M., Lewinsohn, P. M., & Munoz, R. F. Nonspecific improvement effects in depression using interpersonal skills training, pleasant activity schedules, or cognitive training. *Journal of Consulting and Clinical Psychology*, 1979, *47*, 427–439.

Chapter 4

Group Therapist Training: An Objective Assessment of Individuals' Leadership Ability

John V. Flowers
Karen A. Hartman
Curtis D. Booraem

Abstract

Group therapy leader trainees were trained in a behavior therapy technique and were assessed by both objective measures and expert ratings to determine if an objective method of rating leader trainees could be developed. Results indicated that the expert raters were in very high agreement as to which leaders were superior. Data derived from objective measures of sensitivity, a statement count, and a subjective measure of trust indicated that more highly rated trainees demonstrated the greatest increase of sensitivity to self and other group members when in the therapist role, the greatest overall sensitivity and sensitivity growth whether in the therapist or client role, and the least change in statement count in the therapist versus the client role. There was also a weaker finding that top-rated trainees were the most trusted by other group members. Results are discussed in relation to trainee assessment and group therapy in general.

While a number of investigators (Dies, 1974; Glatzer, 1971; Jarvis & Esty, 1968; Lakin, Lieberman, & Whitaker, 1969; Levin & Kanter, 1964; Limentain, Geller, & Day, 1960) have addressed the way in which group therapists should be trained, few have addressed the issue of how to assess individual leadership ability during or after training. Employing self-reports of the trainees, Wile (1973) assessed the differential effects of group leader training on leadership ability. Ebersole, Leiderman, and Yalom (1969) employed objective measures (ratings by experienced clinicians blind to the training assignment) of the effectiveness of group leader training, but only demonstrated that training was superior to no training rather than specifying differences among individual trainees' abilities.

The present study evaluated an objective method of assessing group leadership ability throughout training using the hypothesis that trainees' group leadership ability (evaluated on the basis of six objective comparisons) would significantly correlate with experienced clinical judgments of their ability. If so validated, such objective measures could both operationalize the clinical judgments and replace those judgments when they are not available.

The objective measures employed in the current study included: (a) the frequency of client-to-client interactions in the group (Matarazzo & Small, 1963), (b) group members' trust of the group leaders (Yalom, 1975), and (c) four different aspects of the leader's sensitivity to group process (Flowers & Booraem, 1980; Flowers, Booraem, & Seacat, 1974). This study also sought to determine if leadership ability, rated by two self-report measures, correlated with experienced clinical judgments of therapist ability.

METHOD

Subjects

The subjects were 16 university students with a mean age of 28.5 years who had enrolled in a graduate class on group psychotherapy. The subjects were divided into two groups containing three males and five females, and two males and six females, respectively. The subjects were naive to the experimental hypothesis.

Experimenters

The experimenters were two clinical psychologists employed as faculty members by the university, and who additionally served as the experienced clinical judges.

Therapists

During all training sessions, two therapists directed each group. During Sessions 1 and 2, the experimenters served as therapists for both groups. Thereafter, the subjects were randomly assigned to therapist pairs, four pairs for each group, and subsequently led two complete group sessions each. When not functioning in the therapist role, subjects and experimenters served as group members.

Procedure

The subjects were randomly assigned to one of two therapy training groups (A or B). Each group met in a 40-minute session once weekly for a period of 10 weeks. The training format required one group of subjects to meet for their group session while the other group of subjects observed the group session and recorded the objective data. Groups A and B alternated each session as to which group met first for therapy training.

In each session, the group members (including the leaders of that session) were given 20 red and 20 blue tokens (2 x 2-inch construction paper) and were instructed to give a blue token with each statement intended as positive and a red token with each statement intended as negative to the member to whom the statement was directed. Each subject deposited all tokens received in a separate container for a later count. Each subject's tokens were numbered so that after each group session a record was available of the total number of red and blue tokens each subject distributed, to whom they were given, how many of each type the subject received, and from whom they were received.

Subjective Ratings

After each 40-minute group session, and prior to counting tokens, all subjects rated themselves and all other members (including the leader pair of that session) on four variables:

1. Subject input plus output activity (high, medium, low)
2. Subject giver-receiver mode (giver, interactor, receiver)
3. Subject positive-negative input (supported, average, encountered)
4. Subject positive-negative output (supporting, average, encountering)

These variables were operationalized as follows:

1. *Activity.* Did the member give and receive a large number of tokens (high), an average number (medium), or a small number (low)?
2. *Mode.* Did the member primarily give tokens (giver), both give and get tokens (interactor), or primarily get tokens (receiver)?
3. *Input.* Of those tokens the member received, were they primarily positive (supported), both positive and negative (average), or primarily negative (encountered)?
4. *Output.* Of those tokens the member gave, were they primarily positive (supporting), both positive and negative (average), or primarily negative (encountering)?

At the end of each session, participating group members (excluding the experimenters) also anonymously listed the names of members they had trusted and members they had distrusted during that session, but did not list members who were neither trusted nor distrusted. Each member, including the therapist trainee, rated his satisfaction with that group session on a 5-point scale: (1) very unsatisfied, (2) unsatisfied, (3) average, (4) satisfied, and (5) very satisfied.

After these subjective evaluations were collected, the number of positive and negative tokens each subject had given and received was then determined. These data were used to determine the objective ratings of individual behavior.

Objective Ratings

The purpose of the objective ratings was to serve as the objective data source against which subjective ratings would be compared for accuracy. Subject input plus output activity was determined by a count of the total number of tokens, positive and negative, a subject gave and received. A subject whose total was 1 standard deviation above the group mean for that session was labeled *high* in activity, while a subject whose total was 1 standard deviation below the group mean was labeled *low* in activity. All other subjects were labeled *medium*.

Subject giver-receiver mode was determined by the percentage of tokens given to tokens given and received (positive and negative). A subject who gave more tokens than received (i.e., percentage of tokens given to total given and received was 1 standard deviation below the group mean) was labeled *a giver*, and one who received more tokens than he gave was labeled *a receiver*. All other subjects were labeled *interactors*.

Subject positive-negative input was determined by the percentage of positive tokens to total tokens received. A subject whose percentage of positive to total tokens received was 1 standard deviation above the group mean was labeled *supported*. This meant that the subject got proportionately more positive feedback than the average group member. A subject whose percentage of positive to total tokens received was 1 standard deviation below the group mean was labeled *encountered*. This meant that the subject got proportionately more negative feedback than the average group member. Subjects within 1 standard deviation of the group mean were labeled *average* during that session.

Subject positive-negative output was determined by the percentage of positive tokens to total tokens given, using the same method as for input.

Sensitivity

Sensitivity was defined as the percentage of the subjective evaluations that matched the objective ratings. Specifically, each subject's evaluation for every other group member on each variable was compared with the objective token count categorizations on the same variable. For example, in a session with nine members, each subject would evaluate the other eight members on each of the four variables, yielding 32 separate evaluations. To be correct on any single evaluation, the subject had to agree with the token count rating, e.g., evaluating another member as high in activity when the token count also rated the member as high. If a subject was correct on 24 of the 32 evaluations, his sensitivity to the group would have been 75% for that session. This measure was labeled as the subject's sensitivity to the group.

Subjects also evaluated themselves on the four variables each session. A subject's self-sensitivity was determined by the number of variables on which the subject correctly rated himself. Thus, if a subject agreed with two of the four ratings derived from the token count, his self-sensitivity would have been 50% for that session.

Observers

While one group was in session, two members of the other group recorded and kept a count of each member's statements. A statement was defined as two words or more that could be clearly heard. If a group member began a statement, was interrupted, and began again, it was counted as two statements for that person. The interrater reliability (percentage of agreement) for Group A ranged from 72% to 97% with a mean reliability of 84.3% over 10 sessions. The interrater reliability for Group B ranged from 78% to 96%, with a mean reliability of 87.9% over 10 sessions. These data were collected as a validity check to determine if the frequency of tokens exchanged accurately reflected the actual total frequency of verbal interactions in the group session.

Experienced Clinicians' Judgments of the Trainees' Ability

At the end of the 20 sessions, and prior to the calculation of the trainees' objective rankings, the two experimenters independently rank-ordered each trainee in terms of the trainee's effectiveness as a group leader. This ranking, consistent with the work of Ebersole, Leiderman, and Yalom (1969) was based on subjective evaluations by experienced clinicians (the experimenters) blind to the objective findings.

Objective Trainee Rankings

Six objective comparisons were used to rank-order the 16 subjects in the study. These were: (a) the increase in the subject's sensitivity when in the therapist role, as compared to when she was in the client role, (b) the subject's sensitivity to self when in the therapist role, (c) the subject's overall sensitivity to other group members over the eight training sessions, (d) the subject's change in sensitivity to other group members from the first four to the last four training sessions, (e) the number of other members who trusted the subject when she was in the therapist role, and (f) the difference in the subject's per session statement count when in the therapist role, as compared to when she was in the client role. Subjects in each group received scores ranging from 0 to 7 based on their points on each of the six objective ratings. For example, the subject in each group with the highest sensitivity over the eight training sessions received 7 points on that measure, the subject with the next highest sensitivity received 6 points, etc.

All objective ratings were scored likewise, with the maximum number of points assigned to the subject in each group with: (a) the greatest increase in sensitivity when in the therapist role as compared to the client role, (b) the highest self-sensitivity in the therapist role, (c) the highest sensitivity to other members over the last eight sessions, (d) the greatest growth in sensitivity from the first group to the last four training sessions, (e) the greatest number of other members trusting the subject when the subject was in the therapist role, and (f) the minimum increase or decrease in the number of statements the subject made in the therapist role as compared to the number the subject made in the client role. Thus, a subject could receive from 0 to 42 total points. The subjects were then rank-ordered from 1 to 16 on the basis of the total number of points received.

Self-Reported Trainee Rankings

Another rank order of the trainees was derived from the two self-report measures in which satisfaction with the group session was rated and trusted and distrusted members were listed. The subjects were assigned from 0 to 7 points based on: (a) their satisfaction with the group when they were in the therapist role, and (b) the number of other members they trusted when they were in the therapist role. For example, the trainee who was most satisfied with the two groups she led received 7 points, the next most satisfied leader received 6 points, etc. Thus, a subject could receive from 0 to 14 total points. The subjects were then rank-ordered on the basis of the total number of points they received.

RESULTS

Table 4.1 presents the trainees' scores on the six objective variables, the two self-report variables, the total points for each trainee's set of variables, the rank-order of the trainees on the basis of each set of scores, and the rank-order of the trainees as judged by the two experienced clinicians. The rank-order correlation of Clinical Judge 1 and the composite of the six variables was $r = .98$. The same rank-order correlation for Clinical Judge 2 was $r = .86$. The rank-order correlation of Clinical Judge 1 and the compos-

Table 4.1

Trainees' Individual Variable Scores and Trainees' Rank Orders According to Summaries of Objective Variables, Subjective Variables, and Expert Judgments

Objective Scores								Subjective Scores					
Sensitivity Increase in the Therapist Role	Self-Sensitivity in the Therapist Role	Overall Sensitivity	Sensitivity Growth	Number of People Trusting the Subject in the Therapist Role	Difference in Percentage of Statements Made in the Client and Therapist Roles	Objective Points	Rank Order Based on Objective Scores	Satisfaction When in the Therapist Role	Number of Other Members Trusted When in the Therapist Role	Subjective Points	Rank Order Based on Subjective Scores	Clinical Judge 1 Rank Order	Clinical Judge 2 Rank Order
14.4	75.0	65.2	8.8	12	22	36	1	4.0	15	8.0	6.5	1	2
13.7	87.5	63.5	11.2	9	8	34.5	2	4.0	15	8.0	6.5	3	1
4.4	87.5	71.2	11.5	10	29	34.0	3	4.5	14	6.5	10	2	3
1.3	62.5	62.6	6.9	12	−6	31.5	4	4.5	12	5.0	12	4	5
1.2	50.0	68.1	14.0	11	44	26.5	5	5.0	12	7.5	8	5	4
7.0	62.5	55.4	8.5	13	66	26	6	4.5	18	13.0	2	6	6
−0.5	37.5	58.6	1.2	12	42	21.5	7	4.0	10	2.0	14	9	10
11.5	75.0	55.6	2.7	8	41	21.0	8	5.0	17	10.0	4	7	7
4.7	62.5	55.0	5.0	11	71	17	9	3.5	12	3.5	13	8	8
−5.0	62.5	52.5	1.9	13	54	17	9	5.0	18	13.5	1	10	14
−4.9	87.5	55.4	4.6	10	77	16.0	11	3.5	18	7.0	9	13	15
4.9	50.0	48.4	5.4	9	52	15.0	12	3.0	5	6.0	11	11	11
1.9	62.5	51.1	7.6	11	73	14.5	13	3.5	14	1.5	15	12	12
2.2	50.0	46.1	−5.3	9	18	11.5	14	4.5	8	8.5	5	14	13
−3.3	37.5	62.4	6.8	5	64	12	15	3.0	18	1.0	16	15	16
−6.1	37.5	53.4	2.9	9	50	7.0	16	5.0		12.0	3	16	9

73

ite of the two self-report variables was .10. The same rank-order correlation for Clinical Judge 2 was .21.

Table 4.2 presents the correlations of trainees' rank-order based on each of the six objective measures with the rank-order of the two clinical judges. As the table indicates, all but one of these correlations was significant. The only exception was the correlation of Clinical Judge 2 and the variable of being trusted in the therapist role.

Table 4.2
Correlations of the Rank Order of Each of the
Six Objective Measures With the Rank Order of
Each Clinical Judge Over All Subjects

	Clinical Judge 1	p	Clinical Judge 2	p
Sensitivity Increase in the Therapist Role	.64	$<.01$	.65	$<.01$
Self-Sensitivity in the Therapist Role	.55	$<.01$	.41	$<.05$
Overall Sensitivity	.73	$<.01$	.65	$<.01$
Sensitivity Growth	.64	$<.01$	.69	$<.01$
Number of People Trusting the Subject in the Therapist Role	.41	$<.05$	.20	NS
Difference in Percentage of Statements Made in the Client and Therapist Roles	.52	$<.01$	.58	$<.01$

Finally, in a separate part of the study designed as a validity check on the sensitivity measures, the correlation of total tokens (those given and received) and the total number of statements made by each subject in each of the 16 sessions ranged from .76 to .97, with a mean correlation of .87.

DISCUSSION

Each of the objective measures employed to evaluate the trainees was designed to assess a different aspect of the trainees' leadership ability. While the variable of engendering trust in other group members is perhaps the clearest measure, it is also the weakest variable of the six in terms of correlation with the clinical judgments. The variable of minimum increase in the percentage of statements in the therapist role is even more complex. As

Matarazzo and Small (1963) noted, group therapy trainees tend to talk a lot and overly dominate their groups. When changed from a client to a leadership role, almost all trainees (15 of 16 in the present study) increase their statement count. While such an increase is expected, the greater the increase the more it decreases the opportunity for client participation. For this reason, the trainees making minimal increases in statement count while assuming the therapist role were evaluated as better. This decision of what makes a better leader is admittedly an assumption, whether it is made by a behaviorist or a non-behaviorist. The assumption of Matarazzo and Small (1963) (made from a non-behavioral perspective), which the present authors share (albeit from a behavioral perspective), is that group therapeutic process is more effective if done *by* the group rather than merely *in* a group (Flowers, 1979). While the behavioral leader would clearly employ different techniques (such as behavioral assessment, problem solving, self-control contracts, and behavioral rehearsal) than the non-behavioral leader and might have different goals (such as behavior change rather than insight or self-acceptance), good group leaders of any persuasion share, in our opinion, a common technique. Good group leaders conduct groups the way conductors lead orchestras: they control the process but they do not play the instruments.

The sensitivity variables are the most complex measures in the present study. Each sensitivity variable is calculated by the agreement of the individual's subjective judgment with an objective data source (frequencies of tokens exchanged). While the ability of the tokens to count positive and negative messages exchanged has been previously validated (Flowers & Booraem, 1980; Flowers, Booraem, Brown, & Harris, 1974; Flowers, Booraem, & Seacat, 1974), the present study is the first to demonstrate that the frequency of tokens exchanged also accurately measures the total group activity in terms of statement count. Thus, sensitivity to input plus output frequency can be either awareness of verbal activity or awareness of the exchange of positive and negative messages, since both co-vary.

Overall sensitivity assesses the trainee's ability to perceive correctly input plus output activity, the giver-receiver role, positive-negative input, and positive-negative output of all group members under all conditions, i.e., whether the trainee is in a client or therapist role, and whether he is disclosing, helpful, silent, or punishing. Change in sensitivity from the first half to the last half of training assesses a different ability—that of learning with feedback. Since trainees received feedback at the beginning of each session as to how accurate their subjective assessments of the group had been for the previous session, they could learn to become more sensitive over time. Fortunately, in the current study, no trainees were initially near any sensitivity ceiling; hence, overall sensitivity and change in sensitivity were not negatively correlated.

Sensitivity in the leader role compared to the client role assesses another distinct ability. It is our opinion, based on what trainees say, that almost all trainees responded to the leader role with increased arousal. For some leaders this arousal was positive, i.e., it produced approach behavior; for other leaders the arousal was more negative, i.e., it produced withdrawal behavior. In terms of the present data, some trainees were more sensitive in the therapist role, while others were less sensitive. Self-sensitivity in the therapist role is very much like sensitivity in the client role, but seems to assess a separate ability. Some trainees were able to remain self-reflective and objective in the therapist role, while other trainees lost their objectivity to the point that their awareness of their own behavior was impaired. Such loss of self-awareness was probably reflected in other therapeutic areas, but it was assessed in this study by self-sensitivity alone.

It should be emphasized that no single variable, nor any combination, correlated as well with the clinical judgments as did all six together. Each of the objective measures adds to the total assessment of the trainee's ability because each taps a somewhat different and important domain. The single best predictor of the clinical judgment is overall sensitivity, while the weakest predictor is the number of group members trusting the trainee in the leadership role. However, even if the weakest variable is removed from the calculation, the overall correlation with the experts' judgments is reduced. Thus, while still other variables remain to be identified as important measures of leadership ability, the six presently identified are all important.

In contrast to these six objective measures, the trainees' self-reported measures did not correlate significantly with the clinical judgments. While self-report measures are more frequently used than objective measures and far easier to employ, the conclusion from the present study (limited to the measures employed) is that self-reports by trainees do not aid in leadership skill assessment.

While the present methodology is somewhat complex, it has the advantage of yielding continual and individual assessments of trainees' group leadership ability. Future research must address the crucial issue of whether trainees evaluated as more skillful, no matter how the assessment was measured, actually achieve better client outcome with their own therapy groups than trainees evaluated as less skillful. It is the authors' hope that the present study is a step in that direction.

REFERENCES

Dies, R. D. Attitudes toward the training of group psychotherapists. *Small Group Behavior,* 1974, *5,* 65–79.

Ebersole, G. O., Leiderman, P. H., & Yalom, I. D. Training the nonprofessional group therapist. *Journal of Nervous and Mental Disease,* 1969, *149,* 294–302.

Flowers, J. V. Behavioral analysis of group therapy and a model for behavioral group therapy. In D. Upper & S. M. Ross (Eds.), *Behavioral group therapy, 1979: An annual review.* Champaign, Ill.: Research Press, 1979.

Flowers, J. V., & Booraem, C. D. Three studies toward a fuller understanding of behavioral group therapy: Cohesion, client flexibility, and outcome generalization. In D. Upper & S. M. Ross (Eds.), *Behavioral group therapy, 1980: An annual review.* Champaign, Ill.: Research Press, 1980.

Flowers, J. V., Booraem, C. D., Brown, T. R., & Harris, D. E. An investigation of a therapeutic technique for facilitating patient to patient therapeutic interactions in group therapy. *Journal of Community Psychology*, 1974, *2*, 39–42.

Flowers, J. V., Booraem, C. D., & Seacat, G. F. The effect of positive and negative feedback on members' sensitivity to other members in group therapy. *Psychotherapy: Theory, Research and Practice*, 1974, *11*, 346–350.

Glatzer, H. Analytic supervision in group psychotherapy. *International Journal of Group Psychotherapy*, 1971, *21*, 436–443.

Jarvis, P. E., & Esty, J. E. The alternate therapist-observer technique in group therapy training. *International Journal of Group Psychotherapy*, 1968, *18*, 95–99.

Lakin, M., Lieberman, M. A., & Whitaker, D. S. Issues in the training of group psychotherapists. *International Journal of Group Psychotherapy*, 1969, *3*, 307–325.

Levin, S., & Kanter, S. S. Some general considerations in the supervision of beginning group psychotherapists. *International Journal of Group Psychotherapy*, 1964, *14*, 318–331.

Limentain, D., Geller, M., & Day, M. Group leader-recorder relationship in a state hospital: A learning tool. *International Journal of Group Psychotherapy*, 1960, *10*, 333–345.

Matarazzo, J., & Small, I. An experiment in teaching group psychotherapy. *Journal of Nervous and Mental Disease*, 1963, *36*, 252–263.

Wile, D. B. What do trainees learn from a group therapy workshop? *International Journal of Group Psychotherapy*, 1973, *23*, 185–203.

Yalom, I. D. *The theory and practice of group psychotherapy.* New York: Basic Books, 1975.

Part Two

Behavioral Group Therapy With Court-Adjudicated Clients

The four chapters in Part Two appear to share a number of implicit assumptions despite clinical variations. Each of the authors assumes that social skills training is a necessary (but not always sufficient) therapeutic activity with clients involved with the criminal justice system. That is, clients often engage in illegal behavior because of inadequate repertoires for gaining pro-social reinforcers more appropriately. It may therefore be assumed that appropriate skill acquisition will contribute to lower recidivism rates (although gaining a skill does not mean that one will, in fact, use it). While it is yet to be determined exactly which court-adjudicated clients will benefit most from which types of skill training and how much recidivism variance will be accounted for in this way, these four chapters provide excellent overviews of behavioral group therapy methodologies developed thus far.

Chapter 5 by Janice De Lange, Susan Lanham, and Judy Barton begins by providing the reader with a review of factors that are thought to maintain delinquent behaviors. Next, development of a comprehensive treatment program, applicable to both males and females, is outlined. Finally, the results of the program are reported. While the results were equivocal, the authors provide a great deal of useful information on overcoming the obstacles to conducting such a program within an institutional setting.

In Chapter 6, J. Stephen Hazel, Jean Bragg Schumaker, James Sherman, and Jan Sheldon-Wildgen describe the development and evaluation of a group skills training program for youths on probation with a juvenile court. Of particular interest is the discussion of some of the common problems which arise in doing group therapy with such a population (e.g., inattentiveness, excessive off-task behavior, reluctance in role-playing, missed appointments), suggestions for minimizing such problems, and a description of specific techniques that can be used to promote generalization and maintenance of the acquired skills.

Chapter 7 by Neil Minkin, Bonnie Minkin, Richard Goldstein, Marc Taylor, Curtis Braukmann, Kathryn Kirigin, and Montrose Wolf focuses on a specific aspect of assertiveness training, namely, giving criticism to peers. Interestingly, no extrinsic rewards were used for participation. However, the participants were able to provide input into the training procedures, and their ongoing consent to participate was obtained along with their satisfaction with the procedures. These strategies probably enhanced the intrinsic rewards of the group and may have had other benefits as well. For example, participants probably felt more responsible for their own and other members' behavior because therapy was being conducted *with* them rather than being done *to* them. In addition, it probably was helpful in diminishing or preventing the staff-versus-resident factionalism that one often sees in residential treatment.

Chapter 8 by Lou Ann Wieand, John Flowers, and Karen Ann Hartman describes a study that was designed to assess the direct effects (on the behavior of institutionalized sex offenders) of teaching mental health workers to do assertiveness training. The authors note that research on the treatment of sex offenders has typically emphasized the elimination of deviant arousal patterns rather than training adaptive social skills. They argue convincingly for the desirability of including a specific social skills training component in the treatment of sex offenders. Of special interest in light of increasing shortages of mental health manpower are the results of the study, which indicate the positive effects of training paraprofessionals to engineer behavioral change.

Chapter 5

Social Skills Training for Juvenile Delinquents: Behavioral Skill Training and Cognitive Techniques

Janice M. De Lange
Susan L. Lanham
Judy A. Barton

Abstract

Youths adjudicated delinquent and incarcerated in a state residential center participated in one of two treatment approaches designed to improve interpersonal skills in problem situations elicited from and developed specifically for this population: a behavior skill training approach incorporating modeling, coaching, behavior rehearsal, self-evaluation, and feedback; and a cognitive-behavior approach adding problem-solving techniques and self-reinforcement to the behavioral program. Measures included the Behavior Role-play Test, anxiety and satisfaction ratings on role-played responses, the Piers-Harris Children's Self-Concept Scale, the Adolescent Self-Expression Scale, and the Nowicki-Strickland Locus of Control Scale. There is a discussion of the unique aspects of the development of the Behavior Role-play Test and of the program, in which videotapes of stimulus situations together with behavior and cognitive models were used. No statistically significant differences were found among treatment conditions and a no-treatment control. Problems inherent in a study within an institution and clinical implications of the program as developed are considered. *

*This study was conducted at Echo Glen Children's Center, Snoqualmie, Washington, under the auspices of the Department of Social and Health Services, State of Washington, and approved by Human Subjects Review Committees of that organization and the University of Washington. Appreciation is extended to James Giles, Superintendent; Bill Stark, Section Administrator; and staff at Echo Glen in making this study possible. Special thanks are due to Sue Anderson, Pat Arnesen, and Emily Titkin for their assistance in this study.

81

OVERVIEW OF THE PROBLEM

The problem of juvenile delinquency is an increasing challenge to our society, requiring effective approaches to prevention and treatment. The social learning model views delinquent behavior as a product of inadequate learning experiences (Phillips, Phillips, Fixsen, & Wolf, 1971; Sarason, 1968) and therefore subject to behavioral treatment methods. While the presenting problem of a youth may be delinquent behavior, the behavior therapist does not deal only with the referring problem. Treatment is "based on the premise that the youth does not have the requisite social, academic, or vocational skills to enable him to obtain in a socially appropriate fashion rewards as great as those he can obtain through criminal behavior" (O'Leary & Wilson, 1975, p. 214). One potential component of treatment is that of teaching socially acceptable behavior, as youthful offenders often have social skills deficits that underlie their interpersonal and legal difficulties (Freedman, Rosenthal, Donahoe, Schlundt, & McFall, 1978).

Social skills training has demonstrated potential as a vehicle by which the learning of appropriate behaviors can be accomplished. The literature reveals social skills training to be effective in changing behavior in a variety of populations including psychiatric inpatients (Goldsmith & McFall, 1975; Serber, 1972), college students (Rose, 1975; Twentyman & McFall, 1975), sexual offenders (Laws & Serber, 1975), children (Patterson, 1972), women (De Lange, 1977; Wolfe, 1975; Young, Rimm, & Kennedy, 1973), and juvenile delinquents (Sarason & Ganzer, 1973; Werder & Nickell, Note 1).

A lack of social skills is viewed by many behavior therapists as "faulty learning which has left the individual with certain behavioral deficits or maladaptive behaviors" (Wolfe, 1975, p. 9). This view suggests that a person's failure to manifest appropriate social behavior is due to never having learned the necessary interpersonal skills. Treatment, then, involves providing training in the specific skills lacking in an individual's response repertoire (Wolfe, 1975) and may include behavior rehearsal, modeling, coaching, feedback, and reinforcement. Research has identified these specific components as contributing to the acquisition of appropriate social behaviors (Lange & Jakubowski, 1976).

For individuals who have learned adequate social skills and continue to exhibit maladaptive behavior, the theoretical assumption is that appropriate interpersonal behavior is inhibited by anxiety (Brockway, 1976; McGovern & Burkhard, 1976) or by interfering cognitions (Ellis, 1962; Lange & Jakubowski, 1976; Meichenbaum, 1973). There is thought to be an interdependence between an individual's cognitions (i.e., internal dialogue) and his overt behavior (Meichenbaum, 1976). This view is held by cognitive-behavior therapists, who vary in their treatment approach to modifying an individual's inhibiting cognitions (Beck, 1970; D'Zurilla & Goldfried, 1971; Ellis, 1962; Meichenbaum, 1976).

Contributing Factors in Maintenance of
Maladaptive Behaviors in Delinquents

A review of the literature reveals that juvenile delinquents as a population show deficiencies in handling personal and social problems, as compared to their nondelinquent peers (Freedman et al., 1978). Explanations for the persistence of maladaptive behavior in this population vary. An *external locus of control* constitutes one factor that may contribute to the maintenance of maladaptive social behavior. Fodor (1972) asserts that delinquents tend to see what happens to them as "fate" or "bad luck." She found that delinquent girls in a training school viewed the control of their actions as in the hands of outsiders: "They (social workers, parents, the judge) put me in here and they will let me out" (p. 95). Such a view, in which the individual does not perceive a causal relationship between her own behavior and the consequences which follow it, has been labeled a belief in external control (Rotter, 1966) and learned helplessness (Seligman, 1975). Nowicki and Strickland (1973), authors of a locus of control scale for children, assert that this variable significantly influences children's behavior: "Particularly for males, an internal score on the Nowicki-Strickland measure of perceived locus of control is significantly related to academic competence and to social maturity, and appears to be a correlate of independent, striving, self-motivated behavior" (p. 153). Lefcourt's (1966) and Rotter's (1966) reviews of research findings indicate that if an individual possesses a general expectation that he can affect his consequences, that person will more likely exhibit coping behavior when situational problems occur. A delinquent who does not believe that his actions make any difference in what happens to him is unlikely to utilize assertive behaviors even if they are within his response repertoire.

A second, related factor that may inhibit appropriate social behavior is the *lack of impulse control* frequently encountered among juvenile delinquents (Fodor, 1972; Skrzypek, 1969; Stain & Sarbineta, 1968). Staff members in institutions for juvenile delinquents know the propensity of many residents to explode in rage at seemingly trivial provocation or to commit actions for which the undesirable consequences have been previously spelled out. While there is a paucity of investigations into the self-control processes of delinquents and adolescents in general, there is some research related to impulsiveness in schoolchildren and children labeled "emotionally disturbed." Kagan and his associates (Kagan, 1965; Kagan & Kogan, 1970; Kagan, Pearson, & Welch, 1966) found that when reflective children were faced with a situation in which the best solution was not immediately apparent, they responded only after they had considered available alternatives; impulsive children responded with less delay and without an evaluation of alternatives and were therefore more likely to make mistakes in judgment. Several researchers (Finch, Wilkinson,

Nelson, & Montgomery, 1975; Meichenbaum & Goodman, 1971) have reported a failure among impulsive children to utilize self-verbalizations in an instrumental way. The Russian psychologist Vygotsky (1962) has also asserted that the ability to produce covert self-commands is a crucial element in the development of self-control of one's behavior.

A third factor, theorized by Little and Kendall (1979), is that juvenile delinquents have *inadequate interpersonal problem-solving skills.* In comparing social-behavior skills in delinquent and nondelinquent adolescent boys, Freedman et al. (1978) found the delinquent group significantly less able to generate effective responses to interpersonal problem situations with a greater propensity to use incompetent solutions, thereby increasing the probability of involvement with the criminal justice system. A lack of an internalized problem-solving strategy with which to respond to various and new interpersonal situations may leave the delinquent at the mercy of habitual, impulsive behavior patterns.

A fourth factor, *low self-esteem,* may also inhibit assertive behavior among juvenile delinquents. Lefeber (1965) has found that delinquents' scores on self-concept measures tend to be lower than those of nondelinquent populations. Low self-concept has frequently been considered a correlate of low educational achievement and deficient social skills (Hauserman, Miller, & Bond, 1976).

Fifth, *environmental factors* may contribute to delinquents' persistence in inappropriate social behaviors even when alternate responses have been learned. Fodor (1972) suggests that institutionalized delinquents who cause the most trouble typically receive the most attention from staff. Consequences in the form of immediate peer reinforcement may also serve as a powerful factor in maintaining maladaptive behaviors (Beuhler, Patterson, & Furniss, 1966; Meichenbaum, Bowers, & Ross, 1968).

Intervention Approaches

For delinquents, it may be that both skill deficits and cognitive factors (including an external locus of control, lack of impulse control, deficits in problem-solving abilities, and low self-esteem) contribute to their lack of appropriate interpersonal behavior; adaptive social behavior might then be facilitated by both behavioral and cognitive techniques. Published research on the teaching of social skills to juvenile delinquents is limited and has been primarily aimed at correcting skill deficits. Sarason and Ganzer (1973) found modeling to be more effective than discussion in teaching appropriate interpersonal behavior to institutionalized delinquents. Werder and Nickell (Note 1) and Minkin, Braukmann, Minkin, Timbers, Timbers, Phillips, Fixsen, and Wolf (1976) effectively used procedures for instructing socially inadequate juvenile delinquents in conversational skills. Braukmann,

Maloney, Fixsen, Phillips, and Wolf (1974) trained predelinquents in prosocial job interview skills.

Recent published studies have reported the effectiveness of a variety of cognitive-behavioral techniques with nondelinquent children: training impulsive children to self-verbalize coping statements (Meichenbaum & Goodman, 1971), teaching social problem-solving skills to schoolchildren (Shure & Spivack, 1972), teaching problem-solving skills to hyperactive children by using a cuing technique (Schneider & Robin, 1974), teaching assertiveness using rational-emotive techniques to elementary-school children (Rashbaum-Selig, 1976), training learning-disabled children in social skills by teaching a specified set of problem-solving steps (Trupin, Gilchrist, Maiuro, & Fay, 1979), and training aggressive boys in verbal self-instruction in social interactions (Camp, Blom, Hebert, & Van Doorninck, 1977).

The specific effects of teaching cognitive strategies have not yet been adequately assessed with delinquent populations. Two investigations of social skills training with juvenile delinquents appear to include cognitive elements, although no systematic attempts at teaching a cognitive strategy are evident. Moser (1975) conducted a study of behavioral group treatment and role-playing with institutionalized delinquent boys which included the presentation of appropriate, alternative internally controlled behaviors and reinforcement for exhibiting such behaviors. Ostrom, Steele, Rosenblood, and Mirels (1971) employed a group-treatment strategy with noninstitutionalized delinquents on probation which focused on specific delinquent acts, the consequences of such acts, and alternative activities to achieve the participants' goals. Several other studies include problem-solving elements as part of an instruction program in negotiation skills with noninstitutionalized delinquents and their families (Alexander & Parsons, 1973; Kifer, Lewis, Green, & Phillips, 1974; Klein, Alexander, & Parsons, 1977; Stuart & Lott, 1972). None of these studies, however, evaluated the specific effects of the problem-solving component.

Group treatment is described by many clinicians as the preferred therapeutic approach with juvenile delinquents (Hersko, 1962; MacLennon, 1968; Yong, 1971). The effectiveness of social skills training in groups has been reported in the literature (Galassi, Galassi, & Litz, 1974).

The present study was designed to develop program materials specific to institutionalized juveniles, to develop a cognitive problem-solving strategy for use with this population, and then to assess the effects of a behavioral skills training program, as well as the additive effects of the cognitive component. The study was conducted at a Washington State institution for adjudicated delinquents. The effectiveness of the following treatment packages applied in small groups was compared to a no-treatment control group: (a) a social behavioral skill-training package (BEH) incorporating behavior rehearsal, modeling, coaching, self-evaluation, and feedback, and

(b) the skill-training package plus cognitive problem-solving techniques and self-reinforcement (COG/BEH).

DEVELOPMENT OF PROGRAM AND BEHAVIOR ROLE-PLAY TEST

An important goal in this research was to develop treatment packages with content relevant to juvenile delinquents as well as a behavior role-play test to be used in assessment. The investigators hoped the treatment/ assessment package could later be utilized by staff assertiveness trainers at the institution.

Following the model of Goldfried and D'Zurilla (1969), the investigators developed program content and a behavior role-play test through the following steps: (a) eliciting problematic interpersonal situations from institutionalized juvenile delinquents and selecting a sample of situations for use in treatment, (b) videotaping materials for use in treatment and the test, and (c) developing criteria for rating test responses.

Generation and Selection of Situations

Sixty residents (male and female) were interviewed prior to the beginning of the study, generating a total of 175 problematic interpersonal situations. The situations fell into 10 categories, according to the type of action needed to resolve the difficulty satisfactorily. The 6 categories with the largest number of situations were selected as themes for the treatment sessions. Session themes included: (a) talking to adults, (b) saying no, (c) handling peer aggravation, (d) expressing feelings of hurt and anger, (e) reacting to criticism, and (f) confronting adults and peers. The category of "saying no" included a disproportionately large number of situations, and a failure to say no to others' requests to engage in delinquent behavior seemed to be a frequent precipitating cause of incarceration among the interviewed residents. As a result, a decision was made to focus on this category during two of the seven treatment sessions. Within each of the above categories, the most frequently occurring situations were written into vignettes, along with modeling scripts of appropriate assertive responses for use in the treatment sessions.

Development of Modeling Videotapes

In the treatment groups, an important element was the modeling of behavior and cognitions. While there are conflicting results regarding the effects of the modeling component (Eisler, Hersen, & Miller, 1973; Friedman, 1971; McFall & Twentyman, 1973), there is research that suggests that modeling is an important variable among juvenile delinquents (Sarason & Ganzer, 1973). A critical question is the type of models to be used. The behavioral literature suggests that an effective model will be similar to the observer in competence, social status, age, sex, and racial status (Bandura, 1971). In addition, the cognitive-behavioral approach views an effective model as one who demonstrates coping cognitions by verbalizing her initial uncertainty and subsequent problem-solving strategy during an assertive encounter, and by self-reinforcing after an assertive response (Mahoney, 1974; Meichenbaum, 1975). Sarason and Ganzer (1973) found modeling to be effective in helping adolescents acquire social skills and, although they used college students as models, hypothesized that the best models for juvenile delinquents might be peers.

In this study, videotapes utilizing the vignettes described previously were developed for use in treatment sessions. The decision to use videotapes rather than audiotapes was based on the investigators' assumption that adolescents would be more attentive to a television monitor. Peer models who served as actors and actresses for the videotapes were chosen from the resident population by the cottage staff according to the following criteria: (a) ages 13-17, (b) frequent demonstration of appropriate social skills, (c) scheduled release from the institution prior to the beginning of the study, (d) high social status among other residents, since the literature indicates the importance of models' being of high social status for imitation to occur, and some subjects might know the models, having been at the center concurrently with them, (e) adequate reading skills to learn the scripts, and (f) willingness to be videotaped. Five female and four male residents of Black, Caucasian, and Indian heritage were selected and paid to be models. People unknown to the participants from outside the institution narrated the situations and gave the stimulus lines to which the youths responded.

A separate set of videotapes was prepared for each of the two treatment packages and the behavior role-play test. For each modeling sequence the Behavior Skill Training (BEH) tapes included: the narrator's description of the situation; the stimulus line, spoken by an adolescent or adult, to which the model and later the subject would be asked to respond; an appropriate assertive response demonstrated by one of the peer models; and the stimulus line repeated for the subject's practice. The Cognitive Behavioral Skill Training tapes were identical to the Behavioral Skill Training tapes with two additions: (a) after the presentation of the stimulus line, the model demonstrated the problem-solving techniques (described later) via a dubbed voice-over image, and (b) following the assertive response, the model, again in a dubbed voice, demonstrated covert self-reinforcement (e.g., "Hey, I did a good job!").

Development of the Behavior Role-Play Test

To create the Behavior Role-play Test (BRT) five items were selected from situations used in training during treatment, called *treatment items,* and five from situations not used in treatment, called *novel items*. The novel items permitted investigation of possible generalization effects of the treatment to situations not used in treatment.

Specific criteria for each BRT situation were developed to assess the effectiveness of audiotaped responses. Following the model of Goldfried and D'Zurilla (1969), the criteria took into account the social and situational context in which the behavior was to occur. Four staff assertiveness trainers (two female and two male) at the institution were selected as judges. Given a global description of assertiveness (De Lange, 1977), these judges were asked to state the goal and desired effect in each of the 10 situations. They also listed what an appropriate response would consist of and what it should not include. The information collected in this way was synthesized into a set of criteria which permitted the evaluation of youths' responses on a 5-point scale from most unassertive (1) to most assertive (5).

METHOD

Subject Selection

Because the nature of the treatment program at the institution allows little flexibility for participation in outside activities, numerous difficulties were encountered in obtaining an adequate sample population. An arrangement was made, however, whereby residents were permitted to miss their elective classes at school in order to participate in social skills training.

Prior to selection, each resident was evaluated according to the following criteria: (a) enrollment in elective courses at necessary time periods, (b) age 13-17, and (c) assurance from cottage social workers that the resident would not be discharged from the institution before completion of the study. Male adolescents to be included in the study were randomly selected from among all males meeting the criteria. Since treatment groups were to be conducted at two different time slots during the school day, a group of 12 males was selected from each of two different class periods, making a total of 24 males in the treatment groups. A control group of 12 males was selected from a third class period.

Special difficulties were encountered in obtaining a female sample because of the small number of young women in residence. At the time of the study, the female population of the institution had recently undergone a dramatic decrease due to a change in state law affecting status offenders. It was, therefore, impossible to obtain an adequate sample of females fitting the criteria and enrolled in elective courses by the random selection procedure used for males. Because it was considered important to have two girls in each of the treatment groups, it was necessary to include *all* females with elective courses in the two time periods, and an additional one who was randomly selected from a nonelective course. All remaining females in the institution who consented to participate were assigned to the control group. The female population thus consisted of 12 girls in the treatment groups and 3 girls in the control group.

Four boys and two girls were randomly assigned to each of three treatment groups in third period and three in sixth period, the school periods when social skills training groups were held. Each group was then randomly assigned a treatment condition (BEH or COG/BEH); thus, there were three groups of six residents within each of the two treatment conditions. The design was counterbalanced for therapists by randomly assigning each of the three therapists one group in each treatment condition. Treatment groups met on the same days for seven 1-hour sessions over a 3½-week period.

Subject Characteristics

All subjects voluntarily consented to participate in the project. After completing all pretests, one subject did not attend training sessions and was dropped from any further analysis. The final study population then consisted of 50 residents (35 males and 15 females). They ranged in age from 13-17 with a mean age of 14.49 years. School grade attended ranged from seventh through tenth grade, with a mean grade level of 8.1. The mean of math achievement scores for the population was 2.93 years behind grade level, and the mean of reading achievement scores was .82 years behind. Only 5 youths were at 1 year ahead of grade level in math; 10 were at grade level and 11 were ahead in reading.

Thirty-five of the youths were Caucasian, seven were Black, three Indian, one Chicano, and four were racially mixed. The mean length of current stay at the institution was 3.7 months, ranging from 1 to 11 months; however, the mean total number of months spent in institutions was 9.26, ranging from 2 to 22 months.

Prior to commitment to the institution, 12 youths were living with both of their natural parents, 15 lived with the mother and stepfather or mother alone, 9 lived with the father with or without a stepmother, 2 lived with other relatives, 9 were in group homes, and 2 in foster homes (data missing for one).

The Washington State Bureau of Juvenile Rehabilitation employs a system of classification for delinquents according to the duration, intensity, and frequency of delinquent activity. The categories range from A, most serious, through F, least serious. The study population included four subjects in A and one in F, with the rest fairly evenly distributed across categories.

Therapists

The treatment groups were conducted by three graduate students in social work, two of whom were the investigators. All therapists were

Caucasian females having had previous experience with delinquent adolescents and assertiveness training techniques.

The therapists completed 10 hours of training, including practice with a mock group of residents scheduled for release. During the study, the three therapists met together for six 1-hour periods between sessions to discuss the procedures and to standardize the way in which difficulties were to be handled. To standardize treatment, each therapist received a Therapist Manual[1] which outlined procedures for every session, standard introductory remarks, and coaching comments along with a transcript of the videotape for each session.

Measures

Two different classes of measures were utilized in assessing the effects of the treatment and control conditions. One consisted of a measure of overt behavioral responses to videotaped stimulus situations, the Behavior Role-play Test. The other included several self-report indices selected to assess: (a) situational anxiety and response satisfaction experienced during the BRT, (b) the degree to which the respondent perceived life events to be within her own control, (c) the participant's self-concept, and (d) the degree to which the youth asserted herself in a wide variety of situational contexts.

Paper-and-pencil measures, administered in small groups both before and after the treatment sessions, included the Piers-Harris Children's Self-Concept Scale, the Nowicki-Strickland Locus of Control Scale, and the Adolescent Self-Expression Scale. To control for possible test interaction and fatigue, the order in which two of the tests were administered to each group both before and after treatment was randomly determined so that one half of all participants first took the Piers-Harris Children's Self-Concept Scale followed by the Nowicki-Strickland Locus of Control Scale, while the remaining half took the tests in reversed order. The third paper-and-pencil measure, the Adolescent Self-Expression Scale, was administered 2 days later, after all participants had completed the BRT, since it was believed that this measure had the greatest chance of test interaction effects with the Behavior Role-play Test. Because the reading levels of subjects varied substantially, all paper-and-pencil tests were administered verbally.

Piers-Harris Children's Self-Concept Scale (PHCSCS). This scale (Piers & Harris, 1969) consists of 80 statements to which respondents answer yes

---

[1] The Therapist Manual can be obtained by writing the first author at the University of Washington, School of Social Work, Seattle, WA 98195.

or no, e.g., "I am a happy person." Items for this measure were developed from Jersild's (1952) collection of children's statements about what they liked and disliked about themselves and are appropriate for children over a wide age range. Normative data are reported for grades 4-12.

Nowicki-Strickland Locus of Control Scale (NSLCS). This 40-item test (Nowicki & Strickland, 1973) is designed as a measure of generalized expectancies for internal versus external control of reinforcement among children. Items for this measure were constructed on the basis of Rotter's (1966) definition of the internal-external control of reinforcement. The items describe reinforcement situations across interpersonal and motivational areas such as affiliation, achievement, and dependency. The measure is readable at the fifth-grade level, though the items are equally appropriate for older students. Norms have been established on Caucasian school-children, ranging from third to twelfth grade, with a tendency for responses to become more internal with age.

Adolescent Self-Expression Scale (ASES). This scale (Bellucci & McCarthy, Note 2) is a 50-item self-report inventory designed to measure adolescent assertiveness. Utilizing a 5-point Likert scale, the instrument identifies a dimension of assertiveness in a variety of interpersonal settings: with family members, teachers, friends, employers, and strangers. Items for the scale were obtained by interviewing a group of adolescents and by drawing from the work of other researchers in the area of assertiveness (Galassi, DeLo, Galassi, & Bastien, 1974; Lazarus, 1971; Wolpe, 1969; Wolpe & Lazarus, 1966). Normative data were collected on a group of 166 rural, parochial high-school students.

The Behavior Role-play Test (BRT). This measure, previously described, is composed of 10 items and was administered individually before and after treatment. Trained raters scored subjects' audiotaped responses to the 10 videotaped stimulus situations. Responses were rated from 1-5 using the criteria developed for each situation. Two raters independently rated all responses, one in reverse order to the other, and the mean of the two raters' scores was used for analysis. Interrater reliability was computed by using the mean of a second team of two raters who scored the responses of a randomly selected 32% of subjects, half from pretreatment and half from posttreatment responses. Pearson product-moment correlation coefficients ranged from .89 to .99 for eight of the items, and were .75 and .53 for one novel and one treatment item respectively, the latter being of questionable reliability.

Anxiety and satisfaction ratings for the BRT. Following each response to a BRT item, the juveniles rated their level of anxiety during response and satisfaction with their response on a scale of 0-10 (low to high anxiety or satisfaction).

Treatment Conditions

All groups using either treatment package worked with the same assertive situations in identical sequence. At the end of the group pretesting
session, each therapist met with her assigned group for 15 minutes of
get-acquainted conversation. Groups then met in seven 1-hour biweekly
sessions; both treatment conditions held sessions equal in length. The
juveniles in both treatment conditions viewed the same situations with
videotaped peer models demonstrating appropriate assertive responses.
Twenty minutes were allowed per situation, enabling each group member
to practice at least one situation during a session. While group procedures
were identical, the difference between treatment conditions consisted of
the addition of cognitive techniques for the COG/BEH groups.

Behavior skill training (BEH). In the first session, the therapist presented
a brief explanation of the modeling and behavior rehearsal procedures as
a means of learning appropriate assertive behavior. The group then began
work on the situations videotaped for that session. Unlike the remaining
vignettes, the first filmed situation included three different responses
(passive, aggressive, and assertive) as a means of demonstrating what was
and was not meant by assertive behavior. Three situations were worked
on by two youths apiece in each session, with the exception of the first
session, when only two situations were presented with three group members
responding to each (because of the time required for introductory remarks).
Throughout the training, therapists stressed both the verbal and nonverbal
components of assertiveness, including eye contact, body language, and
voice tone.

Following an introduction to the session topic, the treatment procedure
for each situation was as follows:

1. Videotaped presentation of the situation and stimulus line.
2. Elicitation of current level of functioning: the therapist asked,
   "How would you be likely to respond in this situation?"
3. Coaching: the therapist discussed the situation in terms of the
   task to be accomplished and gave general suggestions of how to
   handle it effectively.
4. Behavioral modeling: the videotaped stimulus line was followed by
   the response of a filmed peer model.
5. Group discussion of the model's response.
6. Recoaching: the therapist commented on factors that made the
   model's response effective, emphasizing that other responses
   might be equally appropriate.
7. Behavior rehearsal: a group member delivered the stimulus line
   and the designated youth responded.

8. Self-evaluation: the member was requested to give positive and negative aspects of his response.
9. Group and therapist feedback: group members gave positive comments about the respondent's performance and suggestions for improvement.
10. Repetition of steps 7-9 as necessary.
11. Repetition of steps 7-10 with second group member.

Each respondent was allowed to practice as many times as desired. It was sometimes necessary for the group leader to encourage a second trial with those group members who tended to give up after a single attempt. The leaders monitored group feedback carefully in order to prevent "cruel" comments which might result in hurt feelings and an unwillingness to try again. Group members were encouraged to make use of assertive responses outside the group sessions but no specific homework assignments were given.

Cognitive-behavioral skill training (COG/BEH). The procedures followed in this treatment condition were identical to those in the BEH condition with certain additions. The introductory comments in the first session included the presentation of a cognitive problem-solving process which group members were told would help them think through a problematic situation in order to arrive at an appropriate course of action. The process, consisting of five steps represented by the acronym WISER, was developed directly from D'Zurilla and Goldfried's (1971) proposals for applying problem-solving theory to behavior modification and from the techniques utilized by Trupin, Gilchrist, Maiuro, and Fay (1979). Each letter in WISER identified a step in the process: (a) use physiological arousal in a problematic situation as a cue to "wait" (Wait), (b) identify the problem from your own point of view and the points of view of others in the situation (Identify), (c) generate as many solutions as possible (Solutions), (d) evaluate each of the solutions on the basis of probable consequences and select a course of action (Evaluate), and (e) self-reinforce for attempting to put the chosen solution into action (Reinforce). Group members were told that applying the WISER Way would take some time at first but that, with repeated practice, they would probably be able to use it by simply repeating the word WISER to themselves. The importance of codes such as WISER in helping subjects improve their recall of modeled behavior is supported in the literature (Bandura, Grusec, & Menlove, 1966; Bandura & Jeffery, 1973; Gerst, 1971).

The treatment procedure was as follows:

1. Videotaped presentation of the situation and stimulus line.
2. Elicitation of current level of functioning: the therapist asked, "What would you be thinking in this situation?" and "How would

you be likely to respond?" and stressed the relationship between the thoughts and subsequent behaviors.

3. Practice of WISER Way: group members worked together to complete each of the steps in the problem-solving process.
4. Coaching (same as BEH).
5. Re-presentation of the videotaped stimulus line followed by a peer model covertly demonstrating use of the WISER Way (voice, indicating thought, dubbed over image), her overt response, and a demonstration of covert self-reinforcement (voice dubbed over image).
6. Group discussion of the model's use of the WISER Way and response.
7. Recoaching (same as BEH).
8. Self-verbalization: the member overtly practiced the WISER Way.
9. Behavior rehearsal (same as BEH).
10. Self-reinforcement: the member was encouraged to make a positive self-statement for having attempted an assertive response.
11. Self-evaluation (same as BEH).
12. Group feedback (same as BEH).
13. Repetition of steps 8-12, as necessary.
14. Repetition of steps 8-13, with second group member.

An example of a training situation sequence follows:

HERE'S THE SITUATION (narrated): You are at the local pool hall with a friend. It is 10:00 on a Friday night, and your parents have told you to be home by 11:00. If you're not home on time, you know there's likely to be a hassle with your parents and you'll probably get restricted. Besides, you're still on parole and you've got to be careful to play it straight. A couple of guys you know and like walk up and say, "We've got some really good dope. Why don't you come get high with us?" (stimulus line spoken by a videotaped youth).

COACHING: This is a difficult situation, because you would like to go out with your friends, but you also know the consequences if you do it. You don't want your friends to rank on you for your decision. If you don't say no clearly from the beginning, they are likely to keep trying to convince you to go. That will make it harder for you to stick to your no. After you say no, you can let your friends know that you're not telling them you don't want to be with them. Suggesting another time to see them would be one way to handle this situation.

HERE'S WHAT THE MODEL THOUGHT TO HERSELF BE-FORE SHE ANSWERED: Man, I've got a knot in my stomach. Wait! This is a real problem. I'd really like to go with them, but my parents will be pretty pissed off if I'm not home on time. These guys'll probably think I don't like them if I say no. What solutions have I got? I'd sure like to just go along and forget about what will happen when I get home. I oughta say no. How can I keep them from thinking I don't like them? I could just tell them that. Or, I could suggest they come over to my house tomorrow. OK, evaluate. If I go along I'll get hassled by my parents and my parole counselor. Sure don't want to end up back at the youth center. But what about my friends? Guess I'd better look out for myself this time. I'll ask them to come over tomorrow. I'll say no right away and maybe they won't hassle me too much.

HERE'S HOW THE MODEL ANSWERED: No, I'd like to but I can't. If I'm not home by 11:00, I'll get restricted. I'm still on parole, so I've got to keep clean. Why don't you guys come over to my house tomorrow afternoon?

AFTERWARDS, THE MODEL SAID TO HERSELF: That was pretty hard, but I did it. I feel pretty good about myself. If I can keep on doing this kind of stuff, I won't get stuck back at the center.

RECOACHING: She really knew from the beginning what she needed to do, but stopping and using her problem-solving skills helped her do it. She let her friends know that she still wanted to spend time with them, but that it wasn't possible tonight.

No-treatment control. Fifteen youths were randomly assigned to a control group as previously described and were tested at the beginning and end of the study. There was no additional contact with this group.

RESULTS

A one-way analysis of variance on background data and criterion variables revealed no pretreatment differences among treatment conditions. To analyze the effects of the treatment conditions, an analysis of variance with unequal call frequencies, a least-squares analysis with fixed effects, was performed on change scores for the dependent measures. The few instances of missing data were handled by excluding those cases for all analyses involving that variable.

An endeavor had been made to standardize each treatment method across therapists by both training therapists and controlling the program content through videotape presentation of the same situations in both treatments. In order to investigate whether any one therapist was more effective with any particular treatment, a two-way analysis of variance was performed on all dependent measures and revealed neither a main effect for therapists nor interaction effects of treatment with therapists.

Measures of Social Skill

Adolescent Self-Expression Scale. This instrument purportedly provides an indication of how likely an adolescent would be to respond assertively in several different categories of situations. A higher score indicates a higher probability of assertive responses. The pretreatment mean for the sample was 183.76 (SD = 21.61); for females, 186.21 (SD = 27.02), and for males, 182.77 (SD = 19.40). Normative data for 166 high-school students ranging in age from 14–18 were as follows: the mean for females was 124.96 (SD = 18.26); the mean for males was 122.34 (SD = 15.09). The mean reported for thirty 14-year-olds, comparable to the average age of our sample, was 121.88 and, for ninth graders, 121.54 (Bellucci & McCarthy, Note 2). It can be seen that the mean of the sample in this study was considerably higher, reflecting a higher probability of assertive responses. Reasons for this are discussed in the next section.

Pre- and posttreatment means for each treatment condition are presented in Table 5.1. Analysis of variance revealed no significant differences among treatment conditions from before to after treatment.

Behavior Role-play Test. Although all conditions showed improved scores (as can be seen in Table 5.1), analysis of variance revealed no significant differences among conditions. On the total BRT items, the BEH/COG scores improved the most, with the greatest increase apparent in the treatment items. In all groups there was less improvement on the novel items.

Anxiety and Satisfaction Scores on the BRT

No statistically significant differences were found for the anxiety and satisfaction self-report ratings to responses on the BRT. In both anxiety and satisfaction ratings, the greatest amount of change in the desired direction from before to after treatment occurred in the BEH/COG condition (Table 5.1).

Measure of Self-Concept

The Piers-Harris Children's Self-Concept Scale is intended to provide an overall measure of self-concept. The mean pretreatment score for the entire sample was 54.94 (SD = 13.98). This mean falls close to those presented in the Piers-Harris normative data collected from a sample of 1,183 public-school children (Piers & Harris, 1969). When compared to the Piers-Harris population, the subjects in this study ranged from the 45th to the 67th percentile on the pretest.

As presented in Table 5.1, change in a positive direction occurred from before to after treatment on this measure for the BEH and control groups only, while change was almost nonexistent for the BEH/COG group. Analysis revealed no statistically significant changes among treatment conditions.

Measure of Locus of Control

The Nowicki-Strickland Locus of Control Scale measures a youth's perceived locus of control on an internal-external dimension. Lower scores indicate that the youth has a greater tendency to perceive life events as within her control, internally rather than externally controlled. The pretreatment group mean was 12.82 (SD = 5.44), a comparable value to the means for eighth-graders in the Nowicki-Strickland data (for males, 14.73, SD = 4.35; for females 12.29, SD = 3.58) (Nowicki & Strickland, 1973). As Table 5.1 indicates, scores shifted toward more internal control for both treatment groups while remaining essentially the same for the control group; however, analysis of the variance revealed none of these differences to be statistically significant.

DISCUSSION

The results of this study do not argue for the efficacy of either treatment approach in improving the social skills of juvenile delinquents. However, conduct of the study was fraught with problems familiar to both researchers and clinicians in naturalistic settings which may have adversely affected study results. Some situational factors undoubtedly rendered both the BEH and COG/BEH treatment conditions less effective than they might have been under more ideal conditions; other factors more directly related to research methodology may also have reduced clinical effectiveness and obscured behavior changes.

One problematic factor was absenteeism from group sessions. Absences occurred for a variety of reasons, one being that not all teachers at the institution's school were convinced of the importance of residents' participation in the social skills program. Since residents are frequently absent from classes for a variety of reasons (including disciplinary action, medical and dental appointments, participation in other studies, home visits, and appointments with parole counselors), school personnel have understandably come to resist additional absences because of the resulting difficulty in maintaining continuity in the school program. Though arrangements had been made with administrative personnel for participants to be excused from their elective classes, it appeared that group members were sometimes discouraged from attending social skills groups. On some occasions, school field trips conflicted with group sessions, e.g., upon her arrival a leader once found her entire group gone to the circus along with other residents and therefore had to reschedule the group. Attendance was also denied on occasion by cottage staff for disciplinary reasons, e.g., when a resident was restricted to his cottage or to solitary confinement for misbehavior.

The voluntary nature of participation was probably an additional contributing factor to inconsistent attendance. Since participants were not required to attend social skills training, they sometimes chose other activities that appeared more pleasurable; for example, residents sometimes chose to stay in a physical education class with a boy- or girlfriend.

Table 5.1

Pre- and Posttreatment Means on Dependent Measures by Treatment Conditions

Measure	Behavioral M (SD)		Behavioral/Cognitive M (SD)		Control M (SD)	
	Pre	Post	Pre	Post	Pre	Post
Adolescent Self-Expression Scale	190.00 (21.07)	198.00 (28.67)	181.25 (21.28)	199.88 (18.93)	178.80 (22.16)	194.40 (23.29)
Piers-Harris Children's Self-Concept Scale	53.53 (16.09)	58.83 (13.04)	59.77 (8.98)	59.88 (14.26)	51.07 (15.35)	54.47 (16.39)
Nowicki-Strickland Locus of Control	13.06 (6.05)	10.67 (6.54)	13.00 (5.33)	11.35 (5.50)	12.33 (5.11)	12.20 (6.28)
Behavioral Role-play Test						
Total items	2.93 (.70)	3.13 (1.03)	2.77 (.66)	3.35 (.77)	2.55 (.47)	2.80 (.66)
Treatment items	3.06 (.63)	3.47 (1.09)	2.98 (.93)	3.82 (.78)	2.64 (.46)	2.99 (.66)
Novel items	2.80 (.94)	2.94 (1.04)	2.56 (.78)	2.86 (.92)	2.47 (.73)	2.61 (.75)

Anxiety Ratings						
Total items	4.46 (2.84)	3.82 (2.99)	5.65 (2.10)	4.57 (2.30)	5.11 (1.43)	4.97 (1.80)
Treatment items	4.38 (2.73)	3.74 (3.08)	5.57 (2.00)	4.46 (2.59)	5.11 (1.52)	4.93 (1.70)
Novel items	4.53 (3.13)	3.89 (3.06)	5.74 (2.55)	4.68 (2.26)	5.12 (1.91)	5.01 (2.16)
Satisfaction Ratings						
Total items	7.37 (1.55)	7.56 (2.24)	6.52 (2.15)	7.66 (1.36)	6.90 (1.47)	7.10 (1.66)
Treatment items	7.28 (1.71)	7.90 (2.15)	6.88 (1.94)	8.08 (1.25)	7.05 (1.46)	6.96 (1.86)
Novel items	7.46 (1.90)	7.21 (1.26)	6.15 (2.67)	7.24 (.88)	6.75 (1.98)	7.24 (.87)

As well as detracting from the overall clinical effectiveness of the program, absence may have affected research data, particularly on the Behavior Role-play Test. Absence from a session, of course, meant that those individuals were not trained in the treatment situations for that session. The effect would be to change the BRT items worked on in that session from the status of treatment items to novel items for those group members. The average number of sessions attended was 5.97, ranging from two to all seven sessions; however, since there was no significant difference between treatment groups for numbers of sessions not attended, the effect would be similar for both treatments.

The circumstances under which actual treatment sessions were conducted may also have had negative effects. Because of a space shortage at the school, it was necessary to conduct the groups in a vacant cottage at a considerable distance from the school building. Time spent assembling groups and walking to the cottage sometimes cut into time allotted for treatment. In addition, the cottage in which sessions were held was furnished with game equipment, and some group members were distracted by their desire to spend time playing pool rather than learning social skills. Group sessions, scheduled during the school periods immediately before lunch and at the end of the school day, were not conducted at optimal times of the day. The afternoon groups in particular were frequently restless and had difficulty maintaining focused attention.

Motivating reluctant clients to accept treatment is a problem frequently faced by staff members in residential treatment centers and one that was operative with some participants in this study. At this institution, prosocial behavior as defined by adults tended to be valued primarily as a means of gaining release from the institution, and the absence of authority figures could become a stimulus for relaxing behavioral constraints. Since residents had been told that their behavior in social skills training sessions would not be reported to the cottage staff, some tended to view social skills training as a pleasant diversion, not to be taken seriously if one did not feel so inclined. Some group members did not see any particular value in learning to be more assertive, believing neither that a lack of assertion had contributed to their present situation nor that becoming assertive would be useful and important to them in the future. The absence of support staff posed additional problems for group leaders, since they were required to expend effort attending to security issues such as preventing residents from running away and escorting restricted residents to and from their individual cottages. These responsibilities left less energy for focusing on treatment issues.

Another potentially important variable was previous exposure to assertiveness training. Assertiveness training was not new to this institution; some workers regularly incorporated it into their cottage program. The increasing popularity of such programs with an absence of treatment effectiveness data was part of the initial motivation for this study. Many youths had been required to take assertiveness classes in their cottages prior to the study, a factor which may have influenced pretest scores on all measures, particularly the BRT. Some residents expressed boredom at being asked to undergo a similar training procedure, even though their performance level left considerable room for improvement. It would have been useful to collect data on previous assertiveness training participation, since there may have been differential treatment effects for participants with prior experience and those for whom this study was an initial exposure. These data were not collected because of the anticipated difficulty in accurately quantifying the degree and nature of previous exposure.

Another factor involved the time frame in which social skills training was conducted. Because of constraints imposed by the group leaders' schedules, it was necessary to conduct all group sessions within a 3½-week time period. This may not have allowed sufficient time for participants to practice new skills between sessions and to experience reinforcement from their environment for more appropriate behavior. Conducting groups over a longer period of time might have increased the likelihood of greater attitudinal changes, as measured by the paper-and-pencil tests, since attitudes may change more slowly than overt behavior. Additionally, for youths whose disturbances are serious enough to have led to incarceration, it may be unreasonable to expect dramatic behavioral and attitudinal changes within a short period of time or as a result of a single component of the total treatment program.

While considered necessary for experimental purposes, the controlled content and time sequence of the training materials may have decreased the efficacy of both the BEH and COG/BEH. The necessity of focusing on the prepared materials did not allow for spontaneous discussion, which might have enhanced group cohesion and consolidated new skills. In addition, the situations selected for treatment, though elicited from the residents, may not have been equally relevant to all participants. Experimental considerations also necessitated that treatment sessions for the BEH and COG/BEH groups be of equal length. This factor posed problems in the COG/BEH groups, since the time spent on cognitive interventions allowed less time for practicing responses to the situations. The BRT was a measure of behavioral response and the COG/BEH participants, having spent less time in skills practice, may have been at a relative disadvantage.

None of the measures used specifically assessed the cognitive and problem-solving aspects of the program. One of the primary theoretical assumptions behind the development of the cognitive interventions was that teaching a problem-solving strategy would increase response latency and, therefore, decrease impulsive acting-out behavior. The BRT was not an adequate measure of impulse control since it was administered in an artificial setting that was unlikely to arouse strong emotions. *In vivo* behavioral observations, which might have revealed significant differences among the groups, were not considered feasible because of the difficulty of enlisting the help of already overburdened staff members and of obtaining comparable data from multiple observers.

Use of the Adolescent Self-Expression Scale with delinquent populations, or perhaps lower-class urban clientele, is questioned by the authors. The participants in this study had a considerably higher mean score on this measure than the norm group reported in the literature, so that the participants appeared more assertive than average. On the contrary, the authors hypothesize that this result was due to the difference between the population of rural, parochial high-school students on which norms were based and an incarcerated delinquent population, and the nature of the test items. The items ask if the respondent is able to express or discuss an incident or feeling with a person, e.g., "One of your teachers constantly criticizes you in front of the entire class. This bothers you immensely. Are you able to explain this to the teacher?" Often the youths in this study would say that they would express their feelings; however, the four-letter word response might have an effect opposite from the desired one. Many of the participants' responses would be considered aggressive and not assertive, a distinction that could not be made with this measure.

Contrary to the research data and in spite of the numerous problems reviewed above, anecdotal evidence suggests that both the BEH and the COG/BEH training programs were useful to many residents. With repeated behavioral rehearsal, participants were able to improve substantially on their initial attempts at responding to training situations during group sessions. Some group members spontaneously reported cottage interactions in which they had utilized new skills, stating that the training sessions had been valuable in helping them respond more appropriately when confronted with difficult situations. They sometimes expressed pleased surprise at the unexpected outcomes of situations in which they had attempted new behaviors. Members of the COG/BEH groups reported that they were frequently employing the WISER Way in their day-to-day cottage interactions and that they were finding it effective in reducing impulsive behavior. The following example is illustrative:

> One female participant reported that she had been mopping her cottage kitchen floor when another resident insulted her. She stated that her usual response would have been to throw the mop at the resident. This time, however, she stopped herself by using the WISER Way, considered the potential consequences of aggressive behavior, and gave an assertive response instead. She proudly related this incident to her group.

One COG/BEH group reported that they were reminding each other to use the WISER Way in potential conflict situations and had outlined the problem-solving steps to their cottage staff.

Several aspects of the treatment package seemed effective in gaining the interest and attention of many respondents. The modeling situations presented on videotape were acknowledged as relevant by group members, who frequently responded to the tapes with a comment such as, "Oh, that happened to me before." Group members were particularly enthusiastic about the videotaped modeling, especially since the actors were their peers. On an occasion when a video monitor broke down, the group members requested that the group be rescheduled so that they would not miss the session's tape. Though the participants' response to the efficacy of the models was not empirically assessed, utilizing "coping" rather than "mastery" models appeared valuable; in more than one instance, group members were able to suggest ways in which the model's response could have been made more effective, indicating the development of critical skills for evaluating behavior.

While not a part of the formal research, the residents who served as peer models seemed to accrue a particular benefit from their participation in the preparation of the training tapes. An interesting study could have been made by assessing the impact on behavior and self-esteem that resulted from their involvement in developing appropriate responses and practicing effective response delivery.

CLINICAL IMPLICATIONS

The Group as a Treatment Modality

A clinically relevant question that this research did not specifically address involves the appropriateness of group versus individual training in social skills. From the financial standpoint of the institution, group treatment provides the most efficient use of staff resources. For group members, it may also provide a useful arena for attempting new behaviors with the peers they must relate to outside of group sessions. This practice with peers may be particularly important for juvenile delinquents because of their frequent difficulty in resisting peer pressure and avoiding aggressive behavior with other youths. In the present study, group members were provided with many opportunities to rehearse appropriate behaviors with their peers in a structured setting in which constructive feedback was provided. Group members who were not participating in a particular role-play were also able to learn by observing their peers' behavior and were encouraged to evaluate critically what they observed. The leaders' emphasis

on communicating feedback in a supportive manner provided further training in appropriate social skills beyond the specific content of the training
situations. Though not utilized in this study, a buddy system outside of the
groups might also have facilitated peer support and positive reinforcement,
encouraging the use of newly acquired skills in real-life situations with peers.

If a group modality is considered the treatment of choice, an important
issue arises for the clinician: how to make group treatment sessions attractive
to participants. Group members are unlikely to learn new skills or to
utilize new behaviors in their own lives if they do not perceive treatment
as enjoyable or useful. Though no attempt was made to evaluate the various
components empirically, this study did attempt to build features into the
treatment package that would enhance group attractiveness for juvenile
delinquents. The participants were given highly valued smoking privileges
during group sessions, and drinks and cookies were available at the beginning
of each session. In addition, group leaders attempted to maintain a relaxed
and pleasant atmosphere that allowed for humor, but that was sufficiently
organized and controlled to permit attention to be focused on the task
at hand.

An additional clinical issue in group treatment of adolescents involves
the efficacy of same-sex versus mixed-sex group composition. In the present
study, the inclusion of girls in the predominantly male groups, a feature
infrequently reported in delinquency literature, seemed to provide valuable
opportunities for group members to become sensitized to the differing
perspective of the opposite sex. For example, a training situation in which
a girl turns down the sexual advances of a boy whom she likes but with
whom she does not wish to have intercourse was useful in this regard.
Though initially embarrassing, this situation sparked a discussion in some
of the groups about the girls' fears that turning down a boy would lead to
rejection or would be perceived by the boy as rejection.

Behavioral Control in Groups

In a group of delinquents, control issues become particularly salient,
and the leader must be prepared to deal with an established social hierarchy
among group members. In this respect, the use of a group modality had
both negative and positive aspects in the present study. At times, socially
aggressive group members who did not see value in social skills training
attempted to distract other group members or criticized and belittled their
efforts. In these situations, special encouragement was needed on the part
of the group leader to keep other residents involved. For the most part, it
was possible for leaders to maintain control of group interactions by staying
task-focused and by providing social reinforcement for appropriate behavior.
In some instances, however, socially powerful group members successfully
disrupted behavior rehearsal. In clinical settings, the occurrence of such

disruptions might be reduced by making reinforcements (such as access to smoking privileges and snacks) contingent on appropriate behavior and by making provision for mild punishment (such as time-outs) to be used when more desirable alternatives are unsuccessful. Establishing clear behavioral expectations, enforcing them in a straightforward, matter-of-fact manner, and securing the support of other staff members seem to be important factors in maintaining group control among juvenile delinquents. In addition, the experience of this study suggests the importance of scheduling group sessions at a time when participants are relaxed and rested and of choosing a setting that is relatively free of environmental distractions.

Anecdotal evidence from the current study indicates that peer pressure can also work in a positive direction. At times group members successfully banded together to resist attempts at disruption by ignoring negative comments or overtly expressing their displeasure. Whether or not this occurred appeared related to the member composition of the groups. On the one hand, group cohesion was facilitated by the presence of one or more high-status members who considered the skills training valuable. On the other hand, disruption seemed to occur most frequently in groups with two or more unmotivated members, or when a socially dominating member with a negative attitude toward skills training was included in a group of relatively low-status youths. Research that addresses the clinical issue of balancing group composition in terms of the participants' social status and motivation for treatment remains to be done.

Assessment of Social Skills Deficits

The wide range of scores on all dependent measures utilized in this study suggests a need for refined assessment techniques for determining the etiology of assertive difficulties in delinquent populations. Delinquents do not form a homogeneous group, and different factors such as anxiety, skill deficits, and poor impulse control may be of varying importance in contributing to behavioral problems for each individual delinquent. Adequate assessment techniques would provide the therapist with valuable information for determining which treatment approach or which combination of elements from different approaches to employ with specific individuals. For example, reinforcement by the therapist and training in self-reinforcement might be important for a delinquent whose difficulties stem primarily from low self-concept, while a youth with poor impulse control might benefit most from a cognitive intervention such as the WISER Way. Assessment techniques are also needed for determining the suitability of group versus individual treatment methods for specific individuals. More refined study linking etiology of social skills deficits to remediation approaches could prove helpful to the clinician who must devise treatment programs for individual adolescents.

CONCLUSION

This study provided a preliminary investigation of social skills training with a population for which there are few existing data in the current literature. In addition, it provided a model for the development of a treatment package utilizing behavioral and cognitive techniques. This model, which could be adapted for use with other clinical populations, contains a number of unique features, both in terms of treatment and assessment. Situations utilized for training and assessment of training effects were generated from the population to be studied. The selected situations included those applicable to both boys and girls, as well as those specific to residents of each sex. Videotapes were utilized as a way of holding group members' attention during the demonstration of appropriate responses to difficult interpersonal situations. The use of peer models personalized the tapes and provided group members with imperfect and therefore credible exemplars of assertive behavior. The Behavior Role-play Test rating manual, based on staff members' proposals of what would constitute appropriate and inappropriate responses to the test items, was specifically designed for the population under investigation.

This study was fraught with the very real problems one faces when doing research in an institution. However, the anecdotal information and the leaders' observations lead the authors to urge further use and investigation of social skills training incorporating a problem-solving approach for impulse control with juveniles in various settings, including schools and group homes as well as institutions.

REFERENCE NOTES

1. Werder, P., & Nickell, M. A. Teaching communication skills in Klickitat cottage. In Werder, P., Stenson, S., & Carlson, L., *A survival skills program at Echo Glen Children's Center.* Unpublished manuscript, 1976. (Available from Echo Glen Children's Center, 33010 S.E. 99th St., Snoqualmie, WA 98065).
2. Bellucci, J. E., & McCarthy, D. J. *The Adolescent Self-Expression Scale (ASES): Reliability and validity studies.* Unpublished manuscript, University of Cincinnati, 1976.

REFERENCES

Alexander, J. F., & Parsons, B. V. Short-term behavioral intervention with delinquent families: Impact on family process and recidivism. *Journal of Abnormal Psychology,* 1973, *81,* 219–225.
Bandura, A. (Ed.), *Psychological modeling.* Chicago: Aldine-Atherton, 1971.

Bandura, A., Grusec, J. E., & Menlove, F. L. Observational learning as a function of symbolization and incentive set. *Child Development*, 1966, *37*, 499–506.

Bandura, A., & Jeffery, R. W. Role of symbolic codes and rehearsal processes in observational learning. *Journal of Personality and Social Psychology*, 1973, *26*, 122–130.

Beck, A. T. Cognitive therapy: Nature and relation to behavior therapy. *Behavior Therapy*, 1970, *1*, 184–200.

Beuhler, R. E., Patterson, G. R., & Furniss, J. M. The reinforcement of behavior in institutional settings. *Behaviour Research and Therapy*, 1966, *4*, 157–167.

Braukmann, C. M., Maloney, D. M., Fixsen, D. L., Phillips, E. L., & Wolf, M. M. An analysis of a selection interview training package for pre-delinquents at Achievement Place. *Criminal Justice and Behavior*, 1974, *1*, 30–42.

Brockway, B. S. Assertive training for professional women. *Social Work*, 1976, *21*, 498–505.

Camp, B. W., Blom, G. E., Hebert, F., & Van Doorninck, W. J. "Think aloud": A program for developing self-control in young aggressive boys. *Journal of Abnormal Child Psychology*, 1977, *5*, 157–169.

De Lange, J. M. Relative effectiveness of assertive skill training and desensitization for high and low anxiety women. (Doctoral dissertation, University of Wisconsin, 1976). *Dissertation Abstracts International*, 1977, *38*, 351B–352B. (University Microfilms No. 77–8087)

D'Zurilla, T. J., & Goldfried, M. R. Problem solving and behavior modification. *Journal of Abnormal Psychology*, 1971, *78*, 107–126.

Eisler, R. M., Hersen, M., & Miller, P. M. Effects of modeling on components of assertive behavior. *Journal of Behavior Therapy and Experimental Psychiatry*, 1973, *4*, 1–6.

Ellis, A. *Reason and emotion in psychotherapy*. New York: Lyle Stuart, 1962.

Finch, A. J., Jr., Wilkinson, M. D., Nelson, W. M., III, & Montgomery, L. E. Modification of an impulsive cognitive tempo in emotionally disturbed boys. *Journal of Abnormal Child Psychology*, 1975, *3*, 47–51.

Fodor, I. E. The use of behavior modification techniques with female delinquents. *Child Welfare*, 1972, *2*, 93–101.

Freedman, B. J., Rosenthal, L., Donahoe, C. P., Jr., Schlundt, D. G., & McFall, R. M. A social-behavioral analysis of skill deficits in delinquent and nondelinquent adolescent boys. *Journal of Consulting and Clinical Psychology*, 1978, *46*, 1448–1462.

Friedman, P. H. The effects of modeling and roleplaying on assertive behavior. In R. D. Rubin, H. Fensterheim, A. A. Lazarus, & C. M. Franks (Eds.), *Advances in behavior therapy*. New York: Academic Press, 1971.

Galassi, J. P., DeLo, J. S., Galassi, M. D., & Bastien, S. The college self-expression scale: A measure of assertiveness. *Behavior Therapy*, 1974, *5*, 165–171.

Galassi, J. P., Galassi, M. D., & Litz, M. C. Assertive training in groups using video feedback. *Journal of Counseling Psychology,* 1974, *21,* 390–394.

Gerst, M. Symbolic coding processes in observational learning. *Journal of Personality and Social Psychology,* 1971, *19,* 7–17.

Goldfried, M. R., & D'Zurilla, T. J. A behavioral-analytic model for assessing competence. In C. D. Spielberger (Ed.), *Current topics in clinical and community psychology* (Vol. 1). New York: Academic Press, 1969.

Goldsmith, J. B., & McFall, R. M. Development and evaluation of an interpersonal skill training program for psychiatric inpatients. *Journal of Abnormal Psychology,* 1975, *84,* 51–58.

Hauserman, N., Miller, J. S., & Bond, F. T. A behavioral approach to changing self-concept in elementary school children. *The Psychological Record,* 1976, *26,* 111–116.

Hersko, M. Group psychotherapy with delinquent adolescent girls. *American Journal of Orthopsychiatry,* 1962, *32,* 169–175.

Jersild, A. *In search of self.* New York: Columbia University Bureau of Publications, 1952.

Kagan, J. Reflection-impulsivity and reading ability in primary grade children. *Child Development,* 1965, *36,* 609–628.

Kagan, J., & Kogan, N. Individuality and cognitive performance. In P. H. Mussen (Ed.), *Carmichael's manual of child psychology* (Vol. 1, 3rd ed.). New York: Wiley, 1970.

Kagan, J., Pearson, L., & Welch, L. Modifiability of an impulsive tempo. *Journal of Educational Psychology,* 1966, *57,* 359–365.

Kifer, R. E., Lewis, M. A., Green, D. R., & Phillips, E. L. Training predelinquent youths and their parents to negotiate conflict situations. *Journal of Applied Behavior Analysis,* 1974, *7,* 357–364.

Klein, N. C., Alexander, J. F., & Parsons, B. V. Impact of family systems intervention on recidivism and sibling delinquency: A model of primary prevention and program evaluation. *Journal of Consulting and Clinical Psychology,* 1977, *45,* 469–474.

Lange, A., & Jakubowski, P. *Responsible assertive behavior.* Champaign, Ill.: Research Press, 1976.

Laws, D. R., & Serber, M. Measurement and evaluation of assertive training with sexual offenders. In R. E. Hasford & C. S. Moss (Eds.), *The crumbling walls: Treatment and counseling of prisoners.* Champaign, Ill.: University of Illinois Press, 1975.

Lazarus, A. A. *Behavior therapy and beyond.* New York: McGraw-Hill, 1971.

Lefcourt, H. M. Internal versus external control of reinforcement: A review. *Psychological Bulletin,* 1966, *65,* 206–220.

Lefeber, J. A. The delinquent's self-concept (Doctoral dissertation, University of Southern California, 1965). *Dissertation Abstracts,* 1965, *26,* 2052–2053. (University Microfilms No. 65-10,094)

Little, V. L., & Kendall, P. C. Cognitive-behavioral interventions with delinquents: Problem solving, role-taking, and self-control. In P. C.

Kendall & S. D. Hollon (Eds.), *Cognitive-behavioral interventions.* New York: Academic Press, 1979.

MacLennon, B. W. Group approaches to the problems of socially deprived youth: The classical psychotherapeutic model. *International Journal of Group Psychotherapy,* 1968, *18,* 481–495.

Mahoney, M. *Cognition and behavior modification.* Cambridge, Mass.: Ballinger, 1974.

McFall, R. M., & Twentyman, C. T. Four experiments on the relative contributions of rehearsal, modeling, and coaching to assertive training. *Journal of Abnormal Psychology,* 1973, *81,* 199–218.

McGovern, K., & Burkhard, J. Initiating social contact with the opposite sex. In J. D. Krumboltz & C. E. Thoresen (Eds.), *Behavioral counseling methods.* New York: Holt, Rinehart & Winston, 1976.

Meichenbaum, D. H. Cognitive factors in behavior modification: Modifying what clients say to themselves. In C. M. Franks & G. T. Wilson (Eds.), *Annual review of behavior therapy: Theory and practice.* New York: Brunner/Mazel, 1973.

Meichenbaum, D. H. Self-instructional methods. In A. Goldstein and F. Kanfer (Eds.), *Helping people change.* New York: Pergamon Press, 1975.

Meichenbaum, D. H. A cognitive-behavior modification approach to assessment. In M. Hersen & A. Bellack (Eds.), *Behavioral assessment: A practical handbook.* New York: Pergamon Press, 1976.

Meichenbaum, D. H., Bowers, K. S., & Ross, R. R. Modification of classroom behavior of institutional female adolescent offenders. *Behaviour Research and Therapy,* 1968, *6,* 343–353.

Meichenbaum, D. H., & Goodman, J. Training impulsive children to talk to themselves. *Journal of Abnormal Psychology,* 1971, *77,* 115–126.

Minkin, N., Braukmann, C. J., Minkin, B. L., Timbers, G. D., Timbers, B. J., Phillips, E. L., Fixsen, D. L., & Wolf, M. M. The social validation and training of conversational skills. *Journal of Applied Behavior Analysis,* 1976, *9,* 127–140.

Moser, A. J. Structured group interaction: A psychotherapeutic approach for modifying locus of control. *Journal of Contemporary Psychotherapy,* 1975, *1,* 23–28.

Nowicki, S., Jr., & Strickland, B. R. A locus of control scale for children. *Journal of Consulting and Clinical Psychology,* 1973, *40,* 148–154.

O'Leary, K. D., & Wilson, G. T. *Behavior therapy, application and outcome.* Englewood Cliffs, N.J.: Prentice-Hall, 1975.

Ostrom, T. M., Steele, C. M., Rosenblood, L. K., & Mirels, H. L. Modification of delinquent behavior. *Journal of Applied Social Psychology,* 1971, *1,* 118–136.

Patterson, R. L. Time-out and assertive training for a dependent child. *Behavior Therapy,* 1972, *3,* 466–468.

Phillips, E. L., Phillips, E. A., Fixsen, D. L., & Wolf, M. M. Achievement Place: Modification of the behavior of pre-delinquent boys within a token economy. *Journal of Applied Behavior Analysis,* 1971, *4,* 45–59.

Piers, E. V., & Harris, D. B. *The Piers-Harris Children's Self-Concept Scale.* Nashville, Tenn.: Counselor Recordings and Tests, 1969.

Rashbaum-Selig, M. Assertive training for young people. *School Counselor,* November 1976, *24,* 115-122.

Rose, S. D. In pursuit of social competence. *Social Work,* 1975, *20,* 33-39.

Rotter, J. B. Generalized expectancies for internal versus external control of reinforcement. *Psychological Monographs,* 1966, *80* (1, Whole No. 609).

Sarason, I. G. Verbal learning, modeling, and juvenile delinquency. *American Psychologist,* 1968, *23,* 254-266.

Sarason, I. G., & Ganzer, V. J. Modeling and group discussion in the rehabilitation of juvenile delinquents. *Journal of Counseling Psychology,* 1973, *20,* 442-449.

Schneider, M., & Robin, A. The turtle technique: A method for the self-control of impulsive behavior. In J. D. Krumboltz & C. E. Thoresen (Eds.), *Counseling methods.* New York: Holt, Rinehart & Winston, 1974.

Seligman, M. E. P. *Helplessness.* San Francisco: W. H. Freeman, 1975.

Serber, M. Teaching the non-verbal components of assertive training. *Journal of Behavior Therapy and Experimental Psychiatry,* 1972, *3,* 179-183.

Shure, M., & Spivack, G. Means-end thinking, adjustment, and social-class among elementary-school-aged children. *Journal of Consulting and Clinical Psychology,* 1972, *38,* 348-353.

Skrzypek, G. J. Effect of perceptual isolation on anxiety, complexity preference, and novelty preference in psychopathic and neurotic delinquents. *Journal of Abnormal Psychology,* 1969, *74,* 321-329.

Stain, K. B., & Sarbineta, T. Future time perspective: Its relation to the socialization process and the delinquent role. *Journal of Consulting and Clinical Psychology,* 1968, *32,* 257-264.

Stuart, R. B., & Lott, L. A., Jr. Behavioral contracting with delinquents: A cautionary note. *Journal of Behavior Therapy and Experimental Psychiatry,* 1972, *3,* 161-169.

Trupin, E. L., Gilchrist, L., Maiuro, R. D., & Fay, G. Social skills training for learning disabled children. In L. A. Hamerlynck (Ed.), *Behavioral systems for the developmentally disabled.* New York: Brunner/Mazel, 1979.

Twentyman, C. T., & McFall, R. M. Behavioral training in social skills on shy males. *Journal of Consulting and Clinical Psychology,* 1975, *43,* 384-395.

Vygotsky, L. S. *Thought and language.* New York: Wiley, 1962.

Wolfe, J. Short-term effects of modeling/behavior rehearsal, modeling/behavior rehearsal-plus-rational therapy, placebo, and no treatment on assertive behavior (Doctoral dissertation, New York University, 1975). *Dissertation Abstracts International,* 1975, *36,* 1936B-1937B. (University Microfilms No. 75-22, 937)

Wolpe, J. *The practice of behavior therapy.* New York: Pergamon Press, 1969.

Wolpe, J., & Lazarus, A. A. *Behavior therapy techniques.* New York: Pergamon Press, 1966.

Yong, J. N. Advantages of group therapy in relation to individual therapy for juvenile delinquents. *Corrective Psychiatry and Journal of Social Therapy,* 1971, *17,* 34–39.

Young, E. R., Rimm, D. C., & Kennedy, T. D. An experimental investigation of modeling and verbal reinforcement in the modification of assertive behavior. *Behaviour Research and Therapy,* 1973, *11,* 317–319.

Chapter 6

The Development and Evaluation of a Group Skills Training Program for Court-Adjudicated Youths

J. Stephen Hazel
Jean Bragg Schumaker
James A. Sherman
Jan Sheldon-Wildgen

Abstract

A behavioral group training program that taught social and problem-solving skills was developed for court-adjudicated youths. The program was composed of seven social skills and one problem-solving skill. The skills were trained in a group format in a multiple-baseline design across skills using skill explanation and rationales, modeling, and behavioral rehearsal with feedback. The results showed that the youths' low pretraining skill levels increased substantially following training and that the increased skill levels were maintained throughout the program. Follow-up data on the number of court contacts showed a reduction in court contacts for trained youths compared to nontrained youths. Social validation measures generally showed a high level of satisfaction with the program. These results are discussed in terms of actual and potential problems, as well as application to other populations and settings.*

*The development of this program was supported by Training Grant 15200 from the National Institute of Mental Health to the Department of Human Development and Family Life, by Program Project Grant HD 00870 to the Bureau of Child Research, University of Kansas, and by a contract (#300-77-0494) between The University of Kansas Institute for Research in Learning Disabilities and the Bureau of Education for the Handicapped, through Title VI-G of Public Law 91-230. We wish to thank all those who were involved with this project including Frank Kuehn and the juvenile court staffs, the undergraduate student group leaders, and the judges involved in the assessment phase of the research.

Considerable attention has been directed in recent years to delinquent youths and their behaviors. However, delinquent behavior is difficult to observe directly and, consequently, is not often subject to direct modification. Methods designed to reduce the level of delinquent behavior have often employed behavior management techniques such as behavioral contracting and token economies. Another approach which has been less frequently used with delinquent youths is training in social-interactional and problem-solving skills. The logic behind this approach is that delinquent youths often lack the social and problem-solving skills necessary for achieving desired rewards and interacting with other people and, consequently, they engage in inappropriate or possibly illegal behaviors in their interactions with others.

Good social and interaction skills are important for delinquent adolescents. In many cases, the absence of these skills, particularly in interactions with authority figures such as parents, teachers, and police officers, has played a major role in a youth's referral to the juvenile court. A number of studies have shown that, although the type of offense is critical, the youth's interaction skills are a major determinant of police dispositional decisions (Black & Reiss, 1970; Goldman, 1963; Piliavin & Briar, 1964). Clark and Sykes (1974) state that the failure to accept alternatives offered by police during negotiations may lead to the youth's being arrested. In fact, a youth's interactions with police are seen to be so significant in apprehension decisions that Werner, Minkin, Minkin, Fixsen, Phillips, and Wolf (1975) developed a training package aimed specifically at teaching youths how to interact with police officers. Further research has shown that once a youth is labeled "delinquent," his or her ability to get along with police, probation officers, social workers, and judges often has a major bearing on whether the youth remains in the community, perhaps on probation, or is removed from the community and placed in some type of correctional facility (Cohn, 1963; Gross, 1967).

Social skills deficits may also be more directly related to delinquent behavior. For example, aggression in the form of fighting is a common problem among delinquent youths (Bandura & Walters, 1959). Toch (1969) has argued that individuals who get into fights are often deficient in the verbal and social skills necessary for resolving conflict situations. Bandura (1973) suggested that training in social skills may benefit assaultive individuals. A recent study has shown that social skills training may result in a reduction in aggressive behavior (Elder, Edelstein, & Narick, 1979).

Some social skills training programs have been developed for delinquent youths. Sarason and Ganzer (1973) described a group skills training program for institutionalized youths that taught a number of skills, including job interviewing and resisting peer pressure. Ollendick and Hersen (1979) also conducted a social skills training program for institutionalized delinquent youth. Individualized social skills training with court-adjudicated youths in group home placement has been conducted in conjunction with development of the Teaching-Family Model of group home treatment (Kifer, Lewis, Green, & Phillips, 1974; Werner et al., 1975). All of these programs, implemented with youths placed out of the home, involved either experimenter-trainers or professional therapists. The majority of court-adjudicated youths, however, are not in institutions or group homes, but are on probation with the juvenile court system (Carney, 1977). This is a large number of youths who, if deficient in social skills, could potentially benefit from social skills training. Because of the notoriously high caseloads and often inadequate training of probation officers, many times these youths do not receive needed treatment. The present research sought to develop a program that could effectively and efficiently provide services to these youths.

The group social skills training program described in this chapter is an attempt to overcome some of the limitations of earlier programs. One important concern in the development of this skills training program was that the areas targeted for training be those in which the youths were deficient. Many skills training programs did not include assessment of the skill deficits of the target population. The present program, beginning with a behavioral assessment of the population of youths to be served, was designed to validate the skills and skill components taught in the program.

The second concern in the development of the program was the use of the trainers' time in the most efficient and productive manner. A group program seemed to meet this need because it maximizes the number of individuals with whom the trainer can work in a relatively short period of time. Also, it is ideal for teaching social-interactional skills since it allows a variety of different people with different experiences to participate in training and discussion of the skills. Thus, in the group format, many opportunities for observational learning and peer reinforcement for appropriate behavior become available. Peer reinforcement is especially important for this population of adolescents, who seem to value peer opinion over adult opinion.

A third goal in the development of the program was to keep it as simple as possible to minimize the expertise required of the group leader. A skills approach was adopted that involved the teaching of specific skills that had been broken down into easily teachable component parts. Also, all leader behaviors were operationalized to facilitate the teaching of these skills.

A fourth goal was to develop a program that would allow evaluation of the youths' progress both during the course of the program and after completion of the program. For this purpose, the skills were trained successively in a multiple baseline design across skills to provide continuous feedback on the training program, and a comparison group of youths who did not participate in the program was included to evaluate the effectiveness of the program on future delinquent behaviors. In addition, social validation questionnaires were incorporated to provide information on the clients' satisfaction with the program.

The first section of this chapter describes the strategies used to validate the social skills and problem-solving skills included in the group social skills training program and to develop a reliable system of assessing those skills. The next section details the initial group program with resultant data. The third section describes later implementation of the program in which a home note procedure was evaluated. The fourth section outlines some of the problems a group leader might encounter and the solutions we have found to be useful. Finally, other applications of the program and future directions for research are discussed.

ASSESSMENT OF SOCIAL SKILLS DEFICITS OF DELINQUENT YOUTHS

Traditional clinical assessment has involved the evaluation of a person's personality characteristics, which are presumed to determine or affect that person's behavior in almost all life situations. Recently, however, behavioral approaches to assessment have focused more narrowly on a person's behavior in relationship to specific situations. Goldfried and D'Zurilla (1969), for example, proposed a definition of social competence as "the effective response of the individual to specific life situations" (p. 158). The emphasis on the importance of specific situations in influencing behavior suggests that a behavior assessment instrument used in group therapy has to be sensitive to or discriminate among different life situations or problems. Taken in its most restrictive form, this emphasis could lead to abandoning all attempts at any form of behavioral assessment. If, for example, a person's behavior is affected by the specific situation or problem that he or she faces, and if these situations differ, however slightly, prediction of behavior from one situation to the next becomes difficult or impossible. Taken in a less restrictive form, acknowledging the importance of life situations in behavioral assessment presents the problem of determining if there are classes of situations, each perhaps represented by an infinite number of specific examples, in which a person will behave similarly and in which similar behaviors have similar effects. If so, we need to describe what the salient characteristics of these situations are and to determine what characteristics of behavior are relevant in these situations. Consequently, in order to form a foundation for assessment of the social skills of delinquent youths, we need to determine what situations are representative of those faced by the youths, which of these are potentially important problem situations, and what behaviors (skills) should be displayed in these situations. Then we can begin to develop instruments to evaluate the presence or absence of those skills.

The analysis of representative and important problem situations and behaviors appropriate to those situations typically occurs at the same time: potential problem situations suggest appropriate behaviors that are missing, and vice versa. This section primarily describes how we selected problem situations and skills and how we began a preliminary evaluation of whether these were representative and important for youths. We need to note, however, that we made some arbitrary decisions about situations in which we would observe social skills and how we would evaluate the presence or absence of these skills.

It seemed evident that the most desirable place to observe the social skills of youths was in real-life situations, whether at home, at school, riding around in a car, or in the places where youths typically interact with other people; but for practical reasons, this was very difficult, if not impossible, to do. We needed to employ alternate strategies where we could obtain comparable data about the social skills of youths. We chose to use role-playing situations in which youths were presented with a particular problem, selected because it represented an example of a common problem for youths of that age, and in which they were asked to act out a possible solution to that problem with another person. Although this clearly was not the same as a real-life situation, we hoped that it offered a sample of the youth's behavior that corresponded to his or her behavior in real-life situations.

Another arbitrary decision was made about how the presence or absence of a skill would be evaluated. There are a variety of ways to do so. We chose to break each general skill down into a series of discrete components (to be described subsequently) that we hoped could be directly observed. As youths interacted with another person in the role-playing situations, the presence, absence, or partial presence of the component behaviors was scored. Thus, the social skill level of a youth on a particular skill was simply the percentage of discrete components that were appropriately displayed.

Initial Selection of Situations and Skills

The first step we took in developing a group skills training program for court-adjudicated youths (i.e., youths who have been formally classified as youth offenders by the juvenile court) was to determine common problem situations and areas of skill deficiency. Three sources of information were used for an initial determination of problem areas: a review of the literature, discussion with juvenile probation officers, and discussions among ourselves.

A review of the literature indicated that the literature on social skills deficits in delinquent youths is far from complete. One of the few studies that explicitly assessed skill deficits in delinquents was conducted by Freedman (1974). She followed Goldfried and D'Zurilla's (1969) behavior-analytic model, and, through situational analysis of youths' problems, found 16 categories of situation-skill deficits. These categories included:

controlling aggressive behavior, resisting peer pressure, interacting with authority figures, solving problems, getting out of bad moods, getting along with girls, planning ahead, and reducing boredom. Minkin, Braukmann, Minkin, Timbers, Timbers, Fixsen, Phillips, and Wolf (1976) showed conversational skill deficits in delinquent youths, while Kifer et al. (1974) trained delinquent youths and their families to negotiate conflict situations. These studies pointed to a number of possible areas in which youths may have social skills deficits.

The next step was an informal survey of probation officers, in which they were asked what problem areas and skill deficits they observed in the youths on their caseloads. The problem areas identified by the probation officers were inability to control aggression, poor self-image, low self-confidence, and little resistance to peer pressure.

These two sources, the literature search and the discussion with the probation officers, provided potential skill areas that could be included in the social skills assessment instrument. It was important, however, that the targeted skill areas be appropriate for diagnosis and training of observable behaviors. It was found that some of the problems reported by the literature seemed directly observable (e.g., resisting peer pressure), while others were not (e.g., low self-image and self-confidence). Thus, we used information from the literature search, the probation officers, and our own combined experience in working with juveniles to determine what skills could be behaviorally defined to allow their training in a group skills program. Since the research of Eitzen (1975) indicates that increases in appropriate behavioral skills may be correlated with positive changes in attitudes, no attempt was made to define or include the attitudes mentioned.

The eight observable skills that were judged to encompass the majority of problem situations reported by the probation officers and the literature were: (a) giving positive feedback, (b) giving negative feedback, (c) accepting negative feedback, (d) negotiating conflict situations, (e) resisting peer pressure, (f) following instructions, (g) carrying on a conversation, and (h) solving problems. Giving positive and negative feedback and carrying on a conversation all seemed related to Freedman's (1974) problem of "getting along with girls." These three skills, along with following instructions, accepting negative feedback, and negotiating conflicts, appeared helpful in situations with authority figures as well as peers. Resisting peer pressure to get involved in undesirable activities was one skill heavily emphasized by our sources, as was problem solving. The latter skill appeared to be valuable in helping the youths to plan ahead and to anticipate the consequences of their actions. By providing the youths with such skills as negotiation and receiving negative feedback, it was hoped that they would use these skills as alternatives to aggressive behavior. These skills were not intended to encompass *every* situation that could be encountered by a youth. Instead,

PROPERTY OF WASHINGTON
SCHOOL OF PSYCHIATRY
LIBRARY

an attempt was made to encompass a majority of the situations while at the same time limiting the list to a practical number of skills that could be taught in a relatively short period of time (8 to 10 weeks were suggested as an appropriate period for youths on probation).

Social validation of the importance of the skills. The next step was to have interested persons indicate their opinions of the relative importance of each skill (Wolf, 1978). The persons chosen for this part of the study were a chief probation officer, 5 probation officers, 41 parents of youths on formal probation, and 39 court-adjudicated youths on probation. Each person was asked to rate each of the eight skills according to how important it is for a youth to have the skill in his or her repertoire. A 5-point scale ranging from "very important" to "very unimportant" was used. The chief probation officer for a large metropolitan juvenile division reviewed the skills and judged all of the skills as very important for youths on probation. Probation officers from the same juvenile court, asked to rated the importance of the skills for the youths on their caseloads, rated all of the skills as important or very important for the youths.

The results of the 41 parents' ratings showed that across the eight skill areas, 97% of the responses were in the important or very important categories for their son or daughter. The results of the youths' ratings show that of the 39 youths surveyed, the majority (78%) believed that it was important or very important for them to have the skills.

Another way to determine the importance of teaching certain skills to a specific population is to evaluate whether persons view that population as having deficits in those skills. Forty-one parents of youths on probation were asked to rate how well their son or daughter performed each of the eight skills. A 5-point rating scale ranging from "very good" to "very poor" was used. The results showed that the youths were rated as "poor" or "very poor" on the eight skills an average of 52% of the time. The results show that a large number of delinquent youths were viewed as deficient in these skills by their parents. These data indicate not only that the training skills are viewed as important for the youths, but that adjudicated youths are believed to be deficient in these skills.

The final method of determining the importance of the skills was through a parent checklist which asked the parents to rate how well their son or daughter performed in various situations or on various components of each of the skills. A checklist was developed which had approximately 12 questions per skill. The questions included, for example, "Does your son/daughter easily resolve conflicts with other persons?" and "Does your son/daughter remain calm when he/she receives criticism?" The parents were asked to rate their child's performance on a 5-point rating scale ranging from "never" to "always." Twelve parents of court-adjudicated youths completed the questionnaires. The results showed that 71% of the responses were in the "never," "seldom," or "sometimes" categories with 36% being in the first two categories. This indicates that parents of court-adjudicated youths view their children as often performing poorly in situations requiring the targeted skills.

Social validation of the representativeness of the skills. The representativeness of the skills as ones needed by delinquent youths was assessed in two ways. Five probation officers and one child psychologist were asked to rate the representativeness of the eight skills on a 5-point scale ranging from "very representative" to "very unrepresentative." The results of this survey showed that all of the probation officers and the child psychologist rated the skills as either representative or very representative of the problems encountered by youths.

Another method of assessing the representativeness and completeness of the skills was through reports of problem situations by delinquent youths and their parents. Forty parents of delinquent youths were asked to list problem behaviors of their child. Eighteen youths on probation were asked to list problem situations that they had experienced. The parents reported 148 problems and the youths reported 181 problems. These problems were reviewed to determine if the training skills encompassed these problems.

The reported problems were grouped into four categories by two independent observers. The first type of problem specifically named one of the skill areas (e.g., resisting peer pressure or inability to accept criticism) or one of the skill components (e.g., doesn't listen). The percentage of problems that fell into this category equalled 8%. The second category included problem situations that were directly related to the assessed skills (i.e., would be affected by the youths' learning these skills). Examples of such problems included wanting more allowance (which could be affected by negotiation skills) or "getting high" in school (which could be affected by problem-solving and resisting-peer-pressure skills). This category contained 82% of the problems mentioned by the respondents. The third category, containing 7% of the problems, included attitudinal statements such as poor self-image and lack of respect, which might be related to poor or inadequate social skills. The final category, which contained 3% of the problems, included all items apparently not encompassed by the program. Examples of these items were smoking cigarettes or not completing homework.

This survey showed that the skills appeared to be directly related to a large percentage (90%) of the problem situations encountered by youths and perhaps indirectly related to an additional 7% (for a total of 97%) of the problems reported by youths and their parents. Point-by-point reliability was calculated on the assignment of problems to categories by comparing the observers' assignments for each problem listed by the youths and parents. The observers agreed on 300 out of 329 assignments for a percentage agreement of 91%.

Social validation of the skill components. Following initial validation of the skill list, behavioral descriptions were developed for each skill. These descriptions included verbal and nonverbal components that were thought to be important for each skill. The skill components for one skill, giving negative feedback, are presented in Figure 6.1 as an example. The skill components for all eight skills were validated through two methods. As a first step, court-adjudicated youths were asked to provide feedback on

Figure 6.1. Skill components for giving negative feedback.

GIVING NEGATIVE FEEDBACK

1. Face the person.
2. Keep eye contact.
3. Keep a serious facial expression.
4. Keep a straight posture.
5. *Ask* if you could talk to the person for a moment.
6. First say something *positive* about the person.
7. *Tell* the person how you feel or what you think he/she did wrong.
8. Give the person a *reason* for changing.
9. *Ask* if the person understood what you said.
10. If the person did not understand, *explain again.*
11. *Ask* how the person feels.
12. *Give* the person *suggestions* for changing.
13. *Thank* the person for listening to you.
14. *Change the topic* to something else.
15. Use a serious voice tone.
16. Throughout, be sure to tell the person that you are concerned about him/her or you understand how he/she feels.
17. Throughout, do not "put down" the other person.

the adequacy and appropriateness of the skill components in a discussion format. This was done to insure that the language and actions required by the components were appropriate for adolescents. The skill components were modified according to the youths' feedback.

The second method of validating the skill steps was to obtain ratings of the importance of each component by knowledgeable people. These included four probation officers, a child psychologist, and the counselor in a residential facility for delinquent youths. These individuals were asked to rate the importance of each step in the descriptions using the same 5-point scale that had been previously used in the rating of the importance of the eight skills. For the eight skills, the percentage of component steps rated as important or very important ranged from 93% to 100%. These results show that people who work with delinquent youths rate a large majority of the skill steps as important for each skill.

Reliability of Assessment

Once the importance of the skills had been validated, it was necessary to determine whether performance of the skills could be reliably measured. Checklists were developed for assessing the performance of each youth on each skill.[1] The checklists organized the skill components into three sections for scoring convenience. The first section of each checklist contained all of the nonverbal components, the second section contained the specific verbal steps in the skill, and the third section contained the general verbal components of the skill. An example of a checklist is presented in Figure 6.2. A 3-point rating scale was used for scoring the adequacy of the performance of each skill component. The observer scored a 2 if the skill component was

Figure 6.2. Checklist for giving negative feedback.

GIVING NEGATIVE FEEDBACK

Does the youth:

_____ 1. Face the person when giving feedback?
_____ 2. Maintain eye contact with the person?
_____ 3. Keep a serious facial expression?
_____ 4. Keep a straight posture?
_____ 5. Ask to talk to the other person for a moment?
_____ 6. Initially give a positive statement or compliment?
_____ 7. Tell how he/she feels or what he/she thinks that the other person has done wrong?
_____ 8. Give the other person a reason for changing?
_____ 9. Ask if the other person understood what he/she said?
_____ 10. Clarify the feedback if necessary?
_____ 11. Ask how the other person feels (what is the other person's side)?
_____ 12. Give the other person suggestions for changing or improving?
_____ 13. Thank the other person for listening?
_____ 14. Change the topic to something else?
_____ 15. Use a serious tone of voice?
_____ 16. Make a statement of concern or understanding?
_____ 17. Not "put down" the other person?

---

[1] Descriptions of the skill sheets, the checklists, and the role-playing situations are available from the authors, Department of Human Development and Family Life, University of Kansas, Lawrence, Kansas 66045.

performed appropriately, a *1* if the performance included an approximation to the skill component, or a *0* if the skill component was not included in the performance. Pilot research indicated that this 3-point rating scale yielded higher reliability than a 2-point rating scale.

The eight checklists were used to assess youths' levels of the eight skills during role-play situations. The staff member who acted the role of the other person in the role-play situation with the youth completed the checklist for the skill immediately after each role-play. Role plays were conducted with individual group members before, during, and after the program. Thus, performance of trained skills, as well as skills to be trained, was evaluated. Two different types of reliability were evaluated for the inventory, interobserver reliability and alternate-form reliability:

1. *Interobserver reliability.* This form of reliability refers to the consistency of scores obtained by two independent observers using the same instrument at the same time while observing the same event(s). Interobserver reliability was assessed by having a second observer independently score the checklists during 375 role-play situations with court-adjudicated adolescents. After each situation ended, the observers' scores were compared on each skill component. Each skill step in which both observers scored the same rating (0 and 0, 1 and 1, 2 and 2) was scored as an agreement. Each step in which the observers were within 1 point of each other (0 and 1, or 1 and 2) was scored as one-half agreement. When the observers' scores were 2 points apart (0 and 2), a disagreement was scored. The total number of agreements was divided by the total number of skill components on the checklists and multiplied by 100 to obtain the percentage of agreement. This type of reliability calculation allowed for a measure of amount of agreement over a training period that started with high nonoccurrence and changed to high occurrence. The results of the reliability evaluation showed that for pairs of observers over 375 role-play situations, they agreed on 4382 skill components out of 5025 possible agreements, for a total percent agreement of 87%. Interobserver reliability on individual skill checklists ranged from 81% to 92% agreement. These results indicate that the inventory can be used reliably to assess the level of skill performance in juveniles.

2. *Alternate-form reliability.* When an assessment instrument is to be used repeatedly, alternate forms of the assessment instrument are usually developed to avoid the error that might accrue through repeated administrations of the same test. The consistency of the measures obtained on the alternate forms of the test must then be evaluated.

Alternate situations to be used with the checklists were developed by producing a pool of situations in which each of the eight skills might be used. Thus, for each skill, about 15 situations were derived from parent and youth surveys of problem situations (three example situations and lead-in lines for the resisting-peer-pressure skill appear in Table 6.1). Nineteen youths were presented with novel test situations (or alternate forms of the same test) which were randomly chosen from the pools of situations.

Table 6.1
Three Situations Used for Resisting Peer Pressure

1. I'll play a friend and let's act out the following situation. "_____, there's a big party this weekend. Let's tell our parents that we are staying at each other's house and go all night to the party."

2. You are at a party with a bunch of your friends. A friend lights up a joint. You are on probation and worried about getting busted so you really don't want to smoke. We will pretend to be in that situation and I'll be your friend. "_____, here's a joint" (pretend to hand a joint to the youth).

3. You are walking down the street with a good friend and you see a car with the keys in it and nobody is around. I'll be your friend and let's act out the situation. "_____, look, the keys are in that convertible. Let's take it for a spin!"

In order to calculate alternate form reliability, the scores for each skill from different sessions during baseline were correlated using the Pearson product-moment coefficient. A youth's score for a session was calculated by adding up the observer's scores for all the skill components of a given skill, dividing that sum by the total number of points available (2 × the number of skill components), and multiplying by 100. This procedure produced the percentage of appropriately performed skill components for each skill for a youth. Correlations were performed between a youth's percentage score on the first and second test administrations for each skill. The test administrations were 2 to 3 weeks apart. The resulting correlation coefficient was .51, which was significant at the .01 level.

Since the youths may not have been functioning at the best of their ability during their first experience in the role-playing situation (the first test administration), a second evaluation of alternate-form reliability was conducted. This time, correlations were calculated between the last two test administrations for each skill prior to training on that skill. The correlation coefficient produced was .67, which also was significant at the .01 level.

Social Validation of Changes in Skill Levels

To determine whether changes in the social skills levels of youths after training would be detected by others and judged as desirable, audiotapes were made of the youths' performances in role-play simulations prior to and after group skills training (to be described later). Thirty-two performances, 16 before and 16 after training, representing all eight skills, were randomly chosen for this evaluation and randomly ordered for presentation to the judges. The judges were a probation officer, a professor who teaches courses in juvenile delinquency, a former teaching-parent in a group home for delinquents, a staff member of Boys Town, and an expert in communication skills. None of these judges had been previously associated in any way with our research. The judges were asked to listen to 16 of the tapes (8 pre- and 8 posttraining tapes which had been randomly ordered) and to rate how satisfied they were with the youth's performance on a 5-point scale ranging from "very satisfied" to "very unsatisfied." The judges' ratings for pre- and posttest sessions are shown in Table 6.2. These results indicate that, on the pretests, 57% of the ratings were "dissatisfied" or "very dissatisfied."

Table 6.2
Pre- and Posttest Ratings of Youth Skill Changes by Five Judges

	Very Satisfied	Satisfied	Neither Satisfied nor Dissatisfied	Dissatisfied	Very Dissatisfied
Pretest	0	8	9	15	8
Posttest	21	14	5	0	0

In contrast, on the posttests, 87% of the ratings were "satisfied" or "very satisfied." In addition, median judges' ratings for each test-situation performance were correlated, using the Pearson product-moment correlation coefficient, with the observer ratings obtained on the skill checklists for the same performance. The correlation was .81, which was significant at the .01 level. These results show that observers using the skill checklists discriminate social skills deficits that are also discriminated by persons who have experience working with adolescents.

INITIAL EVALUATION OF THE PROGRAM

The assessment strategy we have described served to validate the eight skills as necessary and important skills for court-adjudicated youths. The specific components of each skill were validated as necessary for the performance of the skills. Checklists were developed that could be reliably used to assess skill performance and were valid in detecting changes in skill levels. This assessment package formed the foundation for a group training program which could be aimed at teaching necessary and important social skills to court-adjudicated adolescents. This section describes a pilot study designed to evaluate the group training procedures with five of the skills.

Method

Subjects. The subjects were court-adjudicated youths on probation in a large suburban family court. They had been referred by their probation officers as youths whom the officers judged deficient in social-interactional skills. These youths and their parents were mailed a letter which briefly explained the program and stated that they would be telephoned concerning the program. The parents were contacted by telephone and, if they were interested, an interview with the parents and the youth was scheduled. During the interview, the program was fully described and the parents and youths were asked if they wished to participate. If so, they were asked to sign informed consent forms.

Twenty-eight youths were referred to the program and six of these youths agreed to participate. One of the six youths attended only two group meetings, and his data are compiled with the remaining 22 youths.

The five youths who participated fully in the treatment group were three males and two females with ages ranging from 13 years, 11 months, to 17 years, 0 months, with a mean age of 15 years, 6 months. The youths' number of prior offenses ranged from 1 to 4, with a mean number of prior offenses of 2.2. The offenses ranged in seriousness from truancy and running away to burglary and assault.

The remaining 23 youths were placed in comparison group A. These youths did not participate in the program for a variety of reasons including: our inability to contact the youths, the youths' refusal to participate, scheduling conflicts with other activities, or the youths' receiving counseling services currently. These youths' ages ranged from 12 years, 7 months, to 16 years, 11 months, with a mean age of 15 years, 3 months. The number of prior offenses ranged from 1 to 9 with a mean of 3.3 prior offenses; the range of seriousness of offenses was the same as for the five treatment youths. A second comparison group, B, was developed from within this initial comparison group A because of the difference in number of prior offenses between the treatment group and comparison group A. Comparison group B consisted of seven youths who were matched on the number of prior offenses and sex with the youths in the treatment group. If more than one youth in comparison group A could be matched with a youth in the treatment group, they were both included in comparison group B. The mean age of the youths in comparison group B was 15 years, 8 months, with a mean number of prior offenses of 1.7. Comparisons were made between the youths in the treatment group and the total 23 youths in comparison group A, and between the treatment group and the subset of comparison youths placed in comparison group B.

Measures. The checklists described were used to evaluate the youths' performance of the skills. In addition, social validity questionnaires were developed which asked the youths, their parents, and their probation officers to rate their satisfaction with the program. A 7-point rating scale was used which ranged from "very satisfied" to "very dissatisfied." The youth questionnaire was composed of 25 questions asking the youths to rate their satisfaction with the effectiveness of the program in teaching each of the skills, with the benefits of the program, with the group leaders, with the type of program, and with the overall group program. The parent questionnaire contained three questions which asked the parents to rate their satisfaction with changes they had observed in their son or daughter and with the cooperativeness of the group leaders. The questionnaire for the probation officers asked four questions concerning their satisfaction with the changes that they had observed in the youths, the relevance of the program to their own needs, and the cooperation of the group leaders. All three questionnaires were administered to the respondents at the end of the program. The youths responded during the last meeting, and the parents and probation officers received their questionnaires in the week following the last meeting. These measures were used to evaluate the satisfaction of the major consumers of the program.

Measures of recidivism during and after the program were also taken. Court records provided information regarding the number of court contacts for each of the youths. A court contact was defined as a referral to the juvenile court that resulted in a juvenile court journal entry in the official court records. These data were collected 1 year after the last group meeting.

Skills training procedures. Each hour-long group meeting was devoted to learning one skill. Once the group had gathered, the group leader began the meeting by briefly describing the skill to be learned. For example, the skill of negotiation was described as "a skill that is used when two people are having a conflict or disagreement and each person wants something that is incompatible with what the other person wants. By negotiating, the two people can tell their sides and come to some agreement that satisfies both of them." The group leader checked the group members' understanding by asking particular youths to define words used in the description.

When the group members appeared to understand what skill they would be learning, the second training step, a discussion of rationales for learning the skill, began. Rationales are statements of how a skill will benefit the youths. For example, one rationale for knowing how to negotiate is "If you know how to negotiate reasonably when you're having a disagreement with someone, you will be more likely to get at least some of what you want." Other benefits that might result from negotiation are: "The other person will understand your side of the issue"; "The other person will be more likely to think of you as a mature, rational person"; and "The other person will be less likely to get angry with you." These types of rationales were facilitated by the group leader's giving a few of them as models and prompting others from each of the group members. Thus, each youth had a turn in giving a rationale. The group leader asked questions like, "John, can you think of how you would feel if you settled a disagreement in a calm, rational way?" or, "Sally, can you guess what an adult would think of you if you could discuss a disagreement calmly?" Each time the youths participated throughout the group, the group leader complimented them for their contribution by saying something like, "That's a very good reason" or, "You're really thinking tonight!" or, "Nice idea." This rationale training is an important training component because it teaches the youths to connect consequences with their behavior and it can serve to motivate the youths to apply the skill in situations outside the group meetings.

The third training step involved a discussion of representative situations in which the youths could use the skill. This step is important in teaching the youths to discriminate the situations where the skill can be appropriately applied. In this step, the group leader first shared a concrete situation from her life where the skill could have been used. For example, for the negotiation skill, the leader might have described a situation where her employer had asked her to get a job done by a particular date but, because of other work he'd given her, she couldn't get it all done on time. Then each youth was asked to share a personal situation with the group. For example, the group leader said, "John, can you think of an example situation where you could use negotiation?" and prompted as necessary with such questions as, "With whom have you recently disagreed on some issue?" An example mentioned by the group members for the negotiation skill was the situation where a youth wants a later curfew than his or her parents typically allow in order to go to a special concert.

The fourth training step involved distribution of the skill sheets to the youths, followed by an explanation and rationale for each step. Usually, each member of the group had a turn at reading a step aloud and thinking of a rationale for that step. The group leader read the first step and gave a rationale as a model. For example, for the step "Face the other person," the rationale offered might be, "In this way the other person will know you are talking to him or her." In addition, concrete examples might be offered by the group leader or group members to illustrate the more abstract steps. For example, for the step "Say something positive," such examples as "I really like you" or "You're a good friend of mine" would be given. Thus, this training step provided instruction in the necessary components of the skill as well as reasons for including each component.

The fifth training step involved modeling of the skill by the group leader and served to translate the written skill into an actual performance. The group members were asked to choose a situation, perhaps one of the examples previously discussed. The group leader then chose a partner with whom the situation would be role-played. In a quickly whispered interaction, the leader instructed the partner in how to play the role. Then, the leader acted the youth role with this partner. For example, in the situation of a curfew disagreement, the leader would play the youth and the partner would play the youth's father. The leader incorporated all but one or two steps of the skill in her performance. The steps that were left out were not crucial steps and provided a basis for the group members to give the leader critical feedback on her performance. They were asked to identify which steps she had included and which steps she had omitted. For this purpose the skill sheet was used, and each group member took a turn at evaluating a skill step as it appeared on the list. If necessary, the group leader remodeled the skill, incorporating the youths' suggestions.

The sixth training step involved behavioral rehearsal of the skill by the youths, with feedback from the other group members and the group leader. In this step each group member practiced the skill using the skill sheet at least two times, once performing the skill and once playing the opposite role. Each youth was asked to choose a different situation each time he or she performed the skill. This practice insured that the situations a youth practiced pertained to his or her own life situation, and provided the group with many examples of how the skill could be applied. After each role-play, the group leaders asked one of the group members to give feedback to the youth who had practiced the skill. The youths did not know in advance who would be asked to give the feedback, so the need to be prepared served to focus each youth's attention on all role-plays and to increase the amount of observational learning. After all group members had practiced the skill once, the skill sheets were collected, and each youth was required to practice the skill in a new situation without utilizing extraneous prompts.

A number of group leader behaviors seem to be important when teaching the skills. One of these behaviors is facilitating constant youth involvement, which consists of asking the youths to provide examples, give rationales, explain steps, and give feedback. Involvement serves to keep the youths interested in the group and is a particularly good technique for controlling off-task behaviors. Group leaders were instructed to make no more than two or three statements between opportunities for youth participation. Another important leader behavior is the use of praise, both to reinforce appropriate behavior and to encourage involvement. Correct pacing of the group is also important to maintain each youth's interest and to complete the required skill training during the allotted time. Appropriate pacing includes keeping the discussion on target, speaking at a brisk pace, allowing little lag time between youth contributions, and being prepared and knowledgeable about the material.

There are a number of other group leader behaviors that are difficult to define behaviorally, but that also appear to be important in leading a group. These behaviors are enthusiasm, humor, empathy, and sincerity. Enthusiasm is important in "selling" the skill to the youths and contributes to appropriate pacing. Enthusiasm appears to involve elements such as having a bright facial expression, smiling, speaking in a lively voice, and making use of inflections. Whenever possible, humor in the form of jokes and laughter should be incorporated to make the group a pleasant experience. This can be done by giving funny examples of situations, laughing with the youths when they share funny experiences, and laughing at oneself when one makes a mistake. Empathy involves the use of statements of concern or understanding like, "I can see how that was a tough situation" or, "Something like that happened to me, too, and I felt badly." Sincerity includes making eye contact when speaking to the youths, being consistent in expectations of them, and following through with any promises made to them (e.g., calling them to find out how something went, or following through on promises to do something special with them in the future).

The group leaders in this training program were undergraduate practicum students under the supervision of the authors. The students were required to take courses in juvenile problems, juvenile justice, and an introductory probation and counseling course. They met with the authors in the practicum class to learn these group leader skills. The skills were trained using readings, skill explanations, rationales, modeling, and behavioral rehearsal with feedback. One of the authors was present during each of the group meetings to observe the group leaders and provide feedback to them.

Testing procedure. When a youth arrived at the group meeting, he or she was individually tested. This testing took place in an office (adjoining the meeting room) containing at least two chairs and a tape recorder. During the testing session each youth's skills were measured by using several role-playing situations. Generally, the skill learned in the previous meeting was tested along with other skills (e.g., one skill that had not been trained and one skill that had been previously trained). This practice allowed for measures of (a) application of the new skill to novel situations (a type of generalization), (b) baseline stability in skills not trained, and (c) maintenance of previously learned skills. Thus, each youth's testing results formed a multiple-baseline across-skills design.

Each testing session involved a series of novel situations never encountered by the youth in previous training or testing sessions. The situations were randomly chosen from a pool of situations derived from parent and youth reports. The adult tester read the situation description to the youth and instructed the youth to act as he or she normally would in the situation. For example, the youth was told that he or she was walking through the hall at school between classes and a good friend was approaching. The adult tester then turned on the tape recorder, stood up with the youth, and played the role of the "good friend."

The youth being tested was not told which skill was required for the situation, so each role-play test not only assessed the youth's ability to perform the skill in a novel situation but also his or her ability to discriminate which situation required which skill. After a situation had been enacted, the tester turned off the tape recorder and scored the performance on the appropriate checklist. Then a new situation was presented, and the same procedure followed for that and all other scheduled test situations.

These testing procedures were followed in the initial interview with the youths to obtain initial baseline measures on all of the skills. The youths were also tested using these procedures 2 months after the last meeting in order to obtain a maintenance measure.

Results

Interobserver reliability was assessed on 76% of the role-play test sessions by having a second observer present during testing to score the youth's performance. The two observers' checklists were compared item-by-item. Reliability results showed that for pairs of observers of 177 role-play sessions, there was agreement on 1798 items out of 2135 possible agreements, for a total percent agreement of 84%. Interobserver reliability on the individual skills ranged from 81% to 87%.

Five skills were trained in this pilot study. The results of the behavioral role-play tests are presented in Figure 6.3. The figure shows the percentage of skill components correctly performed for each skill during test sessions, averaged over the group members. The data indicate that skill levels increased immediately after the onset of training in four of the five skills trained. Problem solving did not show an increase above baseline levels until the third testing session after training. The increases in skill levels were maintained throughout the training program for three of the five skills, with some decrease at the follow-up testing 2 months later in four of the five skills. The results for individual youths closely parallel these group data except in two instances: one youth showed an immediate increase in problem-solving

Figure 6.3. Percent of skill components performed correctly across five skills during baseline, after training, and at follow-up testing, averaged across group members.

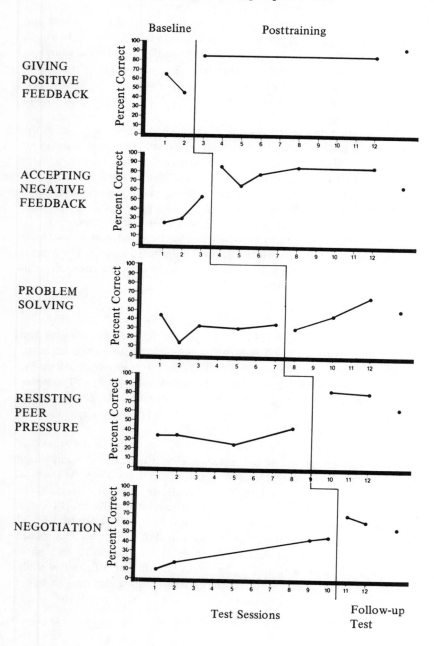

skills following training, and a second youth did not show an increase in the negotiation skill level until the second testing.

The results of the social validation measures generally showed a high level of satisfaction with the program. All of the probation officers indicated on a 7-point scale that they were either satisfied or completely satisfied with the outcome of the program. The results of the parent evaluation showed that, of the four parents who returned the questionnaire, one parent was completely satisfied, one parent was slightly satisfied, and two parents were neither satisfied nor dissatisfied. The results of the youth satisfaction evaluation showed that, over 25 questions, 78% of the youths' responses were in the completely satisfied, satisfied, or slightly satisfied categories, with 70% of the responses in the first two categories. These results show that the program was judged satisfactory by both the youths and their probation officers, with only moderate satisfaction being indicated by the parents.

Recidivism data were collected for all youths referred to the program at a 1-year follow-up point. Recidivism data were available for all five of the youths who participated in the program. None of them had had any further contacts with the juvenile court. Of the 23 youths in comparison group A, data were available for 22 youths. Nine (or 41%) of the comparison youths had at least one further court contact. However, this comparison group had a mean number of prior court contacts of 3.3, as compared to 2.2 for the treated youths. Since this difference might account for some of the difference in recidivism, the treated youths were compared to comparison group B, which consisted of seven youths matched to the treated youths on number of prior court contacts and sex. Court records showed that three (or 43%) of these seven youths had at least one further juvenile court contact at the 1-year follow-up point. These results showed that, while the treated youths had no further court contacts, there was a higher rate of court contacts for the comparison youths, who received normal court services.

Discussion

The results demonstrated that court-adjudicated youths could learn social and problem-solving skills in a group program and that the youths and their probation officers were generally satisfied with the program. Finally, compared to the comparison groups in which at least 41% of the youths committed further offenses, none of the treated youths had any further court contacts. Nevertheless, we were concerned about a number of issues. First, the behavioral role-play data did not show the clear changes that we would like to have seen. Part of the reason for this was that some of the baselines appeared to be rising (e.g., accepting negative feedback and negotiation) just before training was implemented. This effect occurred because the youths were tested at the beginning of the group meetings, thus not allowing sufficient time to calculate the results and plot the data before a new skill was chosen for training. In addition, we found the youths to be much more difficult to "settle down" after these initial testing sessions than if we had started the group immediately. Another concern focused on the magnitude of the changes obtained and the maintenance of these changes. Although the youths were generalizing their application of the skills to some extent, they did not perform two of the five skills at very high levels (i.e., above the 80% correct level) even after repeated training sessions. For some of the skills, their performance was declining even during the training program. A final concern was the generality of the procedures. We wondered whether other group leaders in another juvenile court setting could use the procedures effectively. To resolve these problems, we changed the training and testing procedures slightly and conducted a further evaluation, a report of which follows.

FURTHER EVALUATION OF THE PROGRAM

Method

Subjects. The subjects were 41 court-adjudicated youths on probation in two separate juvenile court districts (one of the youths was court-referred but had not been formally adjudicated). The youths were referred by their probation officers as youths who might benefit from a training program in social skills. In Court District A, 24 youths were referred to the program and 11 of these youths agreed to participate. Of these 11 youths, 8 youths completed the entire program with the other 3 youths attending half of the group meetings.

In Court District B, 17 youths were referred to the program. Nine of these youths agreed to participate, but one of these youths did not attend any group meetings. The data for this youth were compiled with the other comparison youths. The demographic data for all youths are presented in Table 6.3, which shows that the trained youths and the youths in the comparison group, comparison group A, were comparable in terms of

Table 6.3
Demographic Data for All Youths

Group	N	Mean Age	Age Range	Mean Number of Prior Offences
Trained	19	15 years, 8 months	14 years, 5 months 16 years, 10 months	1.79
Comparison	22	15 years, 5 months	12 years, 11 months 17 years, 11 months	2.95

age. However, comparison group A had a higher number of prior court contacts. Therefore, a second comparison group, comparison group B, was developed from the original group for comparison of recidivism rates. Because individual matching was not possible, this group was composed of youths from the original comparison group who had four or fewer prior court contacts. There were 15 youths in this group with a mean number of prior court contacts equal to 1.40, which was comparable to the number of prior contacts for the group of trained youths.

Measures. The same materials were used as in the first study. These included the skills checklists and the social validation scales. In addition, two self-report measures were developed. A self-report delinquency scale was adapted from the one used by Zimmerman and Broder (Note 1) and was composed of questions asking the youths how often they had engaged in each of 28 offenses in the past 2 months. These offenses ranged in seriousness from cheating on an exam in school and staying away from school to using a weapon in a fight and using force to get money. Another self-report scale was developed asking the youths to rate their ability on each of the skills targeted by the training program. For each skill, a 5-point, Likert-type rating scale was used which ranged from "very good" to "very poor."

Finally, a home note was devised that included four parts: a note to the parent about the skills to be practiced at home that week, a place for the parent to record the three situations used to practice the new skill and the one situation used to practice a previously learned skill, a place for the parent to rate the youth's performance in each practice situation, and a place for the parent's signature. Attached to the home note was a skill sheet which listed the component steps of the new skill to be practiced.

Procedures. The same procedures were used as in the previously described study, with the following exceptions. First, the youths were required to practice a skill until they reached a criterion of 100% correct in a new situation without using written or oral prompts. As each youth reached the criterion, he or she was allowed to leave the group for testing. Thus, testing took place at the end of the training sessions. This procedure motivated the youths to learn the skill quickly, since they could leave once the testing was completed. It also allowed the group leader to spend concentrated time with the youths who were having the most difficulty learning the skill. Finally, it insured that each youth performed the skill at a certain level.

Second, an arbitrary criterion—an average of 80% of the components performed by the entire group in a testing—was set. The youths, as a group, had to reach this level of generalization before a new skill was taught to the group.

Third, a review procedure was instituted. At the beginning of each meeting, all previously learned skills were reviewed before a new skill was introduced. The review took the form of the group leader's presenting a youth with a situation that required him or her to use one of the previously learned skills. The other youths were asked to provide feedback. This procedure was followed until all of the previously learned skills had been practiced once more.

Fourth, in an effort to promote further maintenance of the skills, a home note procedure was added. We reasoned that one way to enhance generalization would be to increase the youths' practice of the skills outside of the training situation. The home was targeted as the best place to have the youths practice the skills because the practice could be monitored by the parents. The home note procedure required the youths to practice the new skill three times during the next week with their parents and to practice an old skill one time. At the end of each meeting, each youth received a home note to take to his or her parents. At the beginning of the next meeting, the home notes were given to the group leader, who then led a discussion of the situations practiced by the youths with their parents during the previous week. Each youth was asked to describe the situations chosen and how the practice session had fared. The group leader delivered praise throughout this discussion. In order to further encourage the youths to complete their assignments, points were awarded each week for the returned home notes. These points were recorded on a visual "thermometer" display for each youth, and the youths were told that they would complete the program when they had returned all of their home notes.

Since the home note procedure was relatively time-consuming, it seemed necessary to evaluate its effectiveness by utilizing a comparison design. In each court system, there was a group of treated youths who participated in the home note procedure, a group of treated youths who did not participate in the home note procedure, and a group of comparison youths who did not receive training or testing. Two pairs of group leaders conducted sessions, one pair in each court setting. Thus, the comparable training groups in each court district had the same group leaders.

The youths who received training but who did not have the home note procedure were encouraged to use the skills outside of the group meetings. At the beginning of each meeting, the youths were asked to describe situations in which they had used the skills.

The two self-report scales were filled out by all the youths in the training program during the first and last meetings.

Results

Behavioral role-play test results. Interobserver reliability was assessed on 43% of the role-play tests. The results showed that for pairs of observers over 400 role-play tests, there was agreement on 4601 items out of 5295 possible agreements. This is a total percentage agreement of 86%, ranging for individual checklists from 83% to 95%.

The results of the behavioral role-play tests for the trained group of youths in Court District A with the home note procedure are shown in Figure 6.4, which shows the percentage correct for each skill at each test session, averaged over group members. Six skills were trained in 8 weeks, the time allotted for the program. The two skills that were not trained (i.e., conversation and following instructions) were performed at relatively high levels throughout the program. The figure shows that for each trained skill, levels of performance increased substantially following training. This increased level of performance was maintained throughout training at consistently high levels.

The results of the behavioral role-play tests for the trained group without the home note procedure in the same court district (A) are shown in Figure 6.5, which shows generally the same results as achieved by the group of youths with the home note procedure.

The results of the two trained groups in the second court system were the same as in the first court system. Stable baseline levels were followed by performance increases after training in each skill. There were no consistent differences between the home note and no home note groups in terms of the rate of acquisition or maintenance levels of the skills. Data from individual youths are similar to the group results with increased variability for some youths.

Questionnaire results. The results of the questionnaires were calculated over all trained youths in both court districts. The youths were asked to rate their performance on each of the skills before and after the group program. The results for nine youths who completed both sets of questionnaires showed that before training 17% of the skill ratings were in the very good category, 26% were in the good category, 42% were in the fair category, 11% were in the poor category, and 4% were in the very poor category. The posttraining ratings for these youths showed 44% of the ratings were very good, 41% were good, 11% were fair, 4% were poor, and none were very poor. The results serve to confirm the behavioral data showing increases in skill levels.

The results of the social-validation measure for the youths showed that over 25 questions which asked them to rate their satisfaction with various aspects of the program, 13 youths rated the program in the following way: 39% of the responses were completely satisfied, 44% were satisfied, 8% were slightly satisfied, 7% were neither satisfied nor dissatisfied, and 2% were slightly dissatisfied. There were no responses in the dissatisfied or completely dissatisfied categories. The eight completed forms from the juvenile court officers showed that, on the four questions concerning the

Figure 6.4. Percent of skill components performed correctly across
eight skills during baseline and after training, averaged
across the home note group members in Court District A.

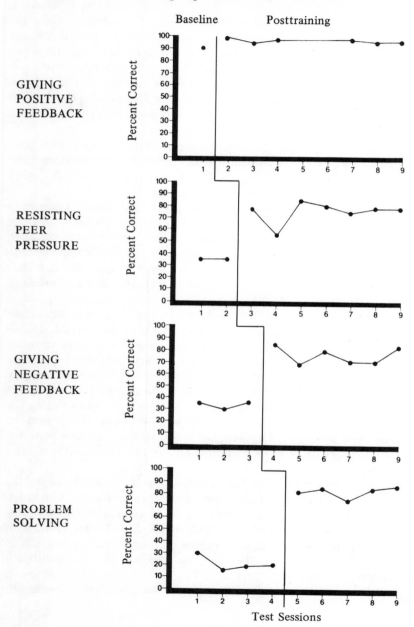

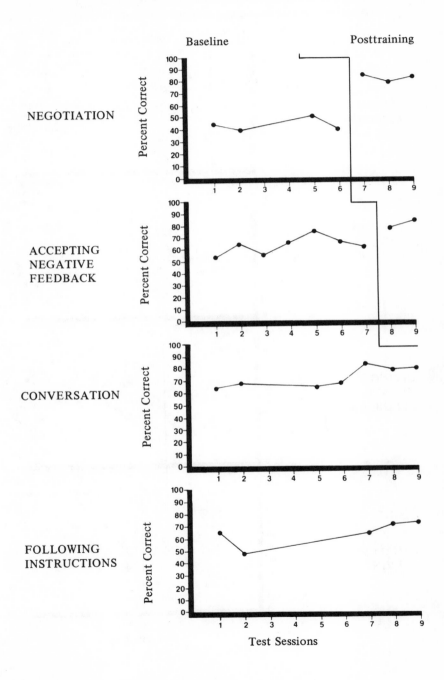

NEGOTIATION

ACCEPTING
NEGATIVE
FEEDBACK

CONVERSATION

FOLLOWING
INSTRUCTIONS

Test Sessions

Figure 6.5. Percent of skill components performed correctly across eight skills during baseline and after training, averaged across the no home note group members in Court District A.

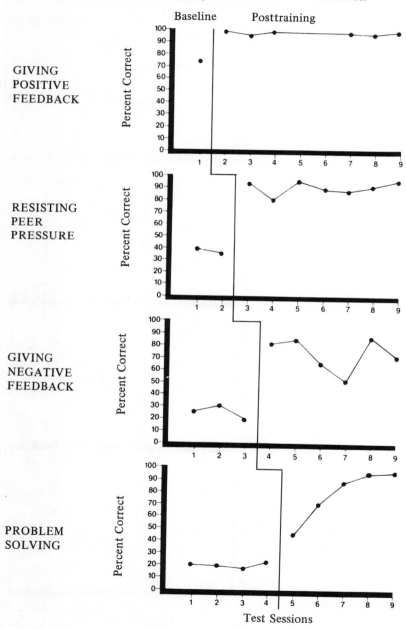

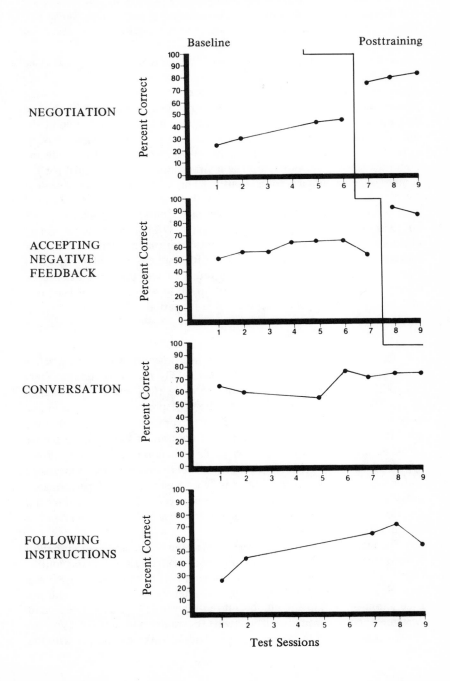

program, 31% were completely satisfied, 60% were satisfied, 3% slightly satisfied, 6% neither satisfied nor dissatisfied, and no responses were in the slightly dissatisfied, dissatisfied, or completely dissatisfied categories. Too few parents returned the satisfaction questionnaire for the results to be representative.

The effect of the program on future delinquent activity was assessed through two measures: a pre- and posttraining self-report delinquency scale administered to the youths and a comparison of court contacts for the trained and untrained youths. The self-report delinquency results showed that for 14 youths who completed the questionnaire prior to and at the end of the program, the youths checked an average of 9.07 illegal behaviors in the 2 months prior to the program, as compared to 6.71 items in the 2 months during the program. The court records were examined for the number of court contacts for all youths 10 months after the completion of the program. Of the 19 trained youths in the four groups, four (or 21%) of these youths had an additional court contact. Court records were available for 19 comparison group A youths; seven (or 37%) of these youths had an additional court contact. In order to control for the number of prior court contacts, recidivism rates were calculated for a subgroup of this comparison group, comparison group B, who had four or fewer prior court contacts. Fifteen youths were in this group; six (or 40%) of them had at least one additional court contact during the follow-up period.

Discussion

The results of the behavioral role-play assessment showed stable baseline levels of responding that increased substantially following training. Only one skill in each court district required more than one training session to reach criterion. All skills reached the 80% performance criterion and were maintained at this level throughout the program. It appears that the combination of the review procedures and criterion procedure was effective in maintaining levels of performance. The home note procedure did not appear to have any effect on skill acquisition or maintenance as measured within group sessions. Because there were no measures of skill performance outside of the group meetings, the home note effects in this regard remain unclear. Further, the training program was effective in different communities with different group leaders.

The results of the questionnaire showed the youths and their probation officers were satisfied with the program and the effects it had on the youths. One assessment of the effects of the program on delinquent behavior was through self-report inventories before and after the program which showed a reduction of 26% in the number of self-reported illegal acts. The second assessment, comparison of court contacts for trained and untrained youths, showed that 21% of the trained youths had at least one contact with the juvenile court within 10 months as compared to 37% and 40% for the two comparison groups of untrained youths. These recidivism results as well as those from the first study must be interpreted with some caution because of the non-random assignment of the subjects to the treatment and control groups.

GENERAL DISCUSSION

The results of the reported studies indicate that the behavioral group training program can be an effective and efficient method of teaching social and problem-solving skills to court-adjudicated youths. The usefulness of this procedure, however, depends on how well the groups are conducted and the performance level required of the youths. Although a specified format designed to discourage problems is followed when conducting the groups, a number of problems may arise that affect how smoothly the group sessions are conducted, and, consequently, how well the youths learn the skills. It is critical to recognize these problems and attempt to solve them immediately. The following is a discussion of common problems that may arise while conducting a group.

General Problem Behaviors Exhibited by Youths

Inattentiveness and excessive off-task behavior. Two of the most common problems exhibited by the youths are inattentiveness and off-task behavior. It is not unusual at initial meetings to see several youths looking at the table, the floor, or off into space for prolonged periods. Often when called on, the youths will answer, "What? Uh, I didn't hear what you just said." Another common response is asking, "Could you say that again?" After the first couple of sessions, when the youths begin to know one another, the leader may see off-task behavior in the form of talking to one another, flipping a pencil, leaning back in a tilted chair, writing notes, or playing with paper.

One of the procedures that we have found to be helpful in eliminating these problems is to specify at the initial meeting that there are certain rules to which the group must adhere. For example, smoking may occur before and after the meetings but not during the meeting; during the meetings, group members may not have personal belongings on the table; and group members may not talk while someone else is talking. It is important not to have too many rules (probably there should be no more than five). The rules may be presented after a general description of the group meetings and in a manner which is not authoritarian (e.g., "By the way, there are a few rules that we will all need to follow . . . "). Rationales are given for each rule (e.g., "Members will not have personal belongings such as pens, pencils, or notebooks on the table since they can be distracting. If we get distracted, it will take us longer to finish the meeting and we obviously won't get out as early"). Thus, from the first meeting there is no question about certain behaviors being inappropriate. The establishment of rules alone may not control all inappropriate behavior. If a rule is broken, the group leader should point out an inappropriate behavior as a rule violation (e.g., "Remember, one of our group rules is that we don't talk while another person is talking. Do you remember why this is a rule? Right—because it means that it will probably disrupt the group and slow us down, and it will take longer for us to finish"). This reminder may help control future inappropriate behavior.

Another method that a group leader should employ when these types of problem behaviors occur is to examine how the group meetings are functioning as a whole. It may be that the group meetings are not paced quickly enough to maintain the youths' attention. Another possibility is that the group leader is not enthusiastic enough, or is not rewarding appropriate behavior. A common occurrence is that the group members reinforce each other's inappropriate behavior through attention. After examining these possibilities, the group leader can respond accordingly by "picking up" the pace of the meeting, by being more enthusiastic and reinforcing, or by attempting to limit the amount of attention given to a youth who is behaving inappropriately. The general strategy in dealing with these problems is to reinforce appropriate behavior through praise and attention and to extinguish inappropriate behaviors through ignoring.

One procedure the group leader can follow if an inappropriate behavior continues is to give the youth an instruction in a pleasant voice tone (e.g., "Mary, please stop tapping your finger"). If the youth continues, the group leader can discuss the inappropriate behavior as a group problem, with the group deciding on the best solution.

Another useful technique can be used during any session after the skill of accepting negative feedback has been taught. If a youth is engaging in an off-task behavior or being inattentive, the group leader can stop the group and give very descriptive negative feedback in an exaggerated voice: "Okay, John, I've had it! I'm tired of the way you never pay attention, the way you lean back in your chair, the way you talk when others are talking. You're slowing us down, and I, for one, AM SICK OF IT!!!!" John will usually look at the group leader in astonishment, since the leader normally tries to be extremely positive and supportive. At this point, the leader quietly prompts by saying, "Now remember, John, what are the skills in accepting negative feedback?" John normally "straightens up" and then is required to go through the steps of accepting negative feedback. Once he finishes accepting the feedback appropriately, the leader should praise him on performing the skill well. We have found this technique to be quite successful because it emphasizes the inappropriate behavior, requires the performance of one of the skills, and requires John to state that he will change in the future. It has the nice feature of drawing attention to the inappropriate behavior in front of the entire group, yet allowing John to save face by practicing a skill.

If an inappropriate behavior continues despite these techniques, it may be necessary to talk with the youth privately. It is inadvisable to stop in the middle of a group to talk with an individual youth. When talking with the youth, the group leader may directly address the problem of the behavior in the group and then problem solve (a skill that is taught in the program) with him or her to determine an acceptable solution. For example, the youth might be taught a behavior that is incompatible with the problem behavior, such as folding his or her hands instead of tapping on the table. Another approach when handling a particularly difficult youth is to talk to him or her privately and ask him or her to "help" during group meetings. Giving youths responsibility in the group will often provide sufficient reinforcement to maintain appropriate behavior.

Other behaviors may occur that are not rule violations but are, nonetheless, inappropriate. The following are specific examples of these problems and solutions for handling them. If a youth appears to be daydreaming or off in his or her own world and not paying attention (but not disrupting the group), the group leader may call on the youth by name and ask the youth a question requiring a response. If Sally responds with, "I don't know" and it is clear that she does not know because she was not paying attention, it may be necessary to provide a rationale for paying attention, e.g., "Sally, it is important to pay attention so that all of us can learn the skill and then go get refreshments." Sally is then filled in on what has happened and required to answer the question. Therefore, she cannot get out of participating by not paying attention, and it may be that the rest of the group will exert some peer pressure to get her to pay attention.

Another example of inappropriate behavior is when a youth monopolizes the group by relating all of his or her personal experiences and not allowing other youths to talk. The group leader can praise the youth for providing examples and then state a rationale for allowing all group members to speak. The group leader must take the initiative of calling on the other youths and allowing the talkative one a level of participation equal to the others.

One of the best ways to minimize inappropriate behavior (including both inattentiveness and off-task behavior) is to prevent it from occurring by keeping each of the youths involved in thinking of rationales, role-playing situations, and providing corrective feedback. If the youths are involved and the group meetings are properly paced, behavior problems should occur infrequently.

Nonresponsive behavior. Some youths, rather than exhibiting disruptive or off-task behavior, will simply be nonresponsive. When asked a question they will say, "I don't know." These youths are often overlooked because the more responsive ones tend to dominate the group. It is important with non-responsive youths that the group leader attempt to prompt more desirable responses and reinforce them when they occur. The use of a questioning or evocative approach is often sufficient to produce responses, e.g., "Alice, why do you think it is important to be able to give people criticism?" Alice should be highly praised for any approximation toward a correct response until her level of responding increases sufficiently to match that of the other group members. Otherwise, she will fail to learn the skills to the necessary criterion and may not receive the benefits derived from learning the skills.

Reluctance in role-playing. When asked to role-play, some youths may make statements like, "This is stupid," "I don't want to do it," "I can't do that," or, "Have somebody else do it." These responses are natural since few people like to get up in front of a group and perform. This reluctance usually decreases over time, and we have never had anyone who consistently refused to role-play. Until the reluctance fades, however, the group leader will need to encourage the youths to engage in role-playing. First, the group leader should never expect a youth to role-play something that has not yet been modeled before the group. The group leader can encourage a reluctant youth by role-playing with him or her. This way, the group leader can control the first role-play situations the youth encounters so that they are not too difficult. If the youth needs help during the role-play, the group leader can give prompts on what to do. Primarily, however, the group leader should provide a great deal of enthusiastic praise, tell the youth how well he or she did, and comment on how easy he or she made the skill look. Thus, the youth should be prompted and praised through a whole role-play situation until it is successfully completed. In the future, he or she should be more willing to role-play.

Failure to learn the skills. Sometimes the youths will not learn the skill in one session and may require an additional training session. If this happens repeatedly, the group leader should examine his or her own behavior in leading and conducting the group. The youths' failure to learn may be the result of the group leader's providing poor or ambiguous explanations and examples, or non-specific feedback, or of not requiring the youths to learn to criterion. Additionally, if the youths are engaging in excessive off-task behavior, the amount that is learned will be reduced.

Failure to return home assignments. The group leaders should give a rationale for the importance of completing home assignments and reinforce the youths for returning home assignments. Some youths may, however, fail to return the home assignments. There are a number of ways to deal with this problem. The first approach is to talk with the youths and further emphasize, through rationales, the importance of the home notes. Another technique is to implement a point system to motivate the youths to complete and return home assignments. The group leader can also talk to the parents and solicit their help in getting the youths to complete the assignments.

Missing meetings. Youths sometimes miss meetings, and the best procedure to deal with this problem is to try to prevent it from occurring. This can be done by contacting (i.e., telephoning) the youths the night before a meeting to remind them of the meeting. The group leaders should also make the meetings as pleasant as possible to encourage attendance. Providing a refreshment and conversation period following each group meeting may increase the attractiveness of the meetings.

If the youths are on probation with the juvenile court, one procedure is to contract with them that every meeting they attend reduces their time on probation. Another procedure is to have the probation officer agree to review the youth's probationary status if the youth successfully completes the group program. Thus, a youth may be dismissed from probation soon after completing the program.

Youths who miss a group meeting could be required to come 30 minutes early to the next meeting to learn the skill that they missed by not attending. This insures that each youth learns each skill and that all youths are at the same point in learning the skills.

Outcome Considerations

The group skills training program presented in this chapter appears to be an effective approach to teaching social and problem-solving skills to court-adjudicated adolescents. There are, however, a number of concerns that need to be addressed in future work in this area.

One concern is that, although all of the youths who participated in the program showed marked improvements in the various skills, there were some individual differences in posttraining skill levels. Two general classes of problems may account for these differences. One type may be problems of individual youths. For example, some youths may have learning problems and be unable to acquire the skills at the same levels as others in the relatively short period of time allotted for group meetings. The other general class of problems concerns the effectiveness of training procedures. For example, some rationales may not be credible to certain youths, or there may be insufficient reinforcement when the youths perform the skills. Determination of these factors may lead to greater control over these individual differences and increase the efficiency of the training program.

A second area of concern is the generalization of the skills to settings outside the group meetings. Even though the behavioral role-play data resulted from presentation of novel situations in a somewhat different setting, research has shown that role-plays do not always accurately reflect performance in the actual environment. Measures of generalization to the natural environment would provide information on the effectiveness of such procedures as the home note procedure. Although the recidivism data, the self-report delinquency results, and the social validation measures indicate that the program has positive effects that extend into the natural environment, we have not been able to assess such effects directly. There are various methods to assess generalization, including direct in-home or in-school observation, parent or teacher report, or youth self-report. The home note procedure was a form of self-report assessment validated by parents' signatures. More extensive use of such measures might determine the extent of response generalization.

A second issue regarding generalization is the development of methods to promote rather than simply to measure generalization. The home note procedure was developed to promote generalization of the skills by requiring the youths to practice each newly learned skill three times with their parents during the week. Another technique to promote generalization that we attempted in one group was to have the youths play a game where they surprised each other with situations requiring them to use one of the skills. For example, at the end of the group meeting, one youth might try to talk another into some inappropriate activity. If the other one was persuaded, the initiator would say "Gotcha" and receive a point bonus. This procedure was designed to create unexpected situations to test the youths' skills. Other possible approaches include the use of a buddy system in which youths contact each other during the week to check on progress (Rose, 1977) or the use of peers as confederates to test the youths. Parent training in the skills that are reciprocal to those the youths learn may be another technique for promoting generalization. The issue of response generalization is central to skill training. Only if the youths use the skills in their everyday lives can they benefit from skills training programs.

Another concern is the maintenance of the trained skills. Although testing during the program shows high skill levels, there is no guarantee that these skill levels will be maintained. There have been one direct and two indirect long-term measurements of the maintenance levels of the skills. In one study (Hazel, Schumaker, Kuehn, Sherman, & Sheldon-Wildgen, Note 2), youths were tested in behavioral role-plays 8 months after completion of the group programs. The results showed good retention of the skills, with an average 9.7% decrease in skill levels from posttesting to follow-up. These results indicate that the youths do retain the trained skills up to 8 months later. One indirect measure of skill maintenance has been the 1-year follow-up of juvenile court contacts. The trained youths have fewer court contacts, an indication that the youths may be using the skills. Another indirect measure of generalization has been the verbal reports by parents and probation officers of the youths' use of skills in everyday situations. Although these data are difficult to quantify, they do indicate that the youths are generalizing the skills to home and court settings.

A second issue regarding maintenance of the skills is the development of procedures to enhance maintenance. The central issue in maintenance is reinforcement of the performance of the skills. There are a number of considerations to this issue. The first consideration concerns whether the skills have been designed properly to maximize the potential for reinforcement. Improperly designed skills may engender punishing consequences which would decrease future performance of the skills. The second consideration is whether the youths not only are able to perform the skills correctly, but also are able to discriminate which situations are likely to provide reinforcement. Some situations have a low probability of reinforcement and may not be conducive to maintaining skill performance. For example, a youth has a low probability of success when negotiating with his or her parents to allow him or her to perform an illegal act. A third consideration of this issue is whether persons in the youths' environment are likely to provide reinforcement for the performance of these new skills. If the youths' skill performances do not result in reinforcement, the youths will be unlikely to continue performing the skills. Some possible approaches to increasing maintenance of the skills include involving parents, teaching the youths how to obtain reinforcement from others (Stokes and Baer, 1977), teaching the youths self-reinforcement procedures, and teaching the youths to provide reinforcement to each other for appropriate behavior.

A further concern regarding the present group program is the variability in the decrease in recidivism for the trained youths. In the first study, none of the trained youths had any further court contacts, whereas in the second study 4 of the 19 youths had another court contact. In work with delinquents, an important criterion of success has been subsequent court contacts. Although this measure has numerous difficulties, it is generally accepted by juvenile court personnel as the necessary measure of success of a program. The present program appears to reduce delinquent behavior, but it would be useful to determine if performance in the group is related to subsequent delinquent behavior for individual youths. Youths who have continuing court contacts may require additional services.

A final concern in developing, implementing, and evaluating a group training program with court-adjudicated youths is obtaining the cooperation of the youths and their parents as well as the cooperation of the juvenile court. Youths who come into contact with the juvenile court are often unwilling participants in any treatment program. Often the court's powers are necessary to obtain the youths' initial cooperation. Programs for delinquent youths must be designed not only to deal with the initial reluctance to participate, but must provide sufficient reinforcement for continued participation. The present program used prompting and reinforcement to teach new behaviors and avoided the use of punishment. This practice may have helped increase the attractiveness of the group for the participants. In the present program, we found that once youths attended one or two group sessions, they were more than willing to continue the program. In the same manner, the program must be designed to reinforce the parents' participation and consent for their child's participation. The description of the program and the initial contacts with the parents appear to be important determinants of parent involvement. However, we have experienced continuing difficulty in persuading parents to complete and return questionnaires.

The consent of the court for conducting such a program depends on a number of factors. Undoubtedly, the use of appropriate skills in introducing and explaining the program to court personnel plays an important role in initial court participation in the form of youth referrals. Demonstration of the effectiveness of the program is important in maintaining juvenile court support as is adequate communication between the group leaders and the youths' probation officers.

Generality of Approach

The present group training approach was initially developed for court-adjudicated youths on probation with the juvenile court. Since the studies reported here were completed, the program has been conducted in different settings, with different populations, and by different types of group leaders. One early extension of the program to a different setting was to court-adjudicated youths in a group home. That setting had an excellent potential for more naturalistic observation of skill performances, as well as reinforcement for correct skill use. Another setting in which we conducted the program was a juvenile diversion program designed to provide services to adolescents referred from the court system. A group training program provided an ideal vehicle for treatment in this setting. The program has also been conducted in an alternative school (Hazel, Schumaker, & Sheldon-Wildgen, Note 3).

In the alternative school, we worked with a different population of youths, the learning disabled. Learning-disabled youths are more highly represented among the delinquent populations than among the population at large (Keilitz, Zaremba, & Broder, 1979). Social skills training may be important in helping these youths avoid court contact. We have also conducted the program with adolescents labeled "personal-social adjustment problems" in a school district's counseling center. We have extended the approach to group training of parents in skills complementary to the skills that their children are learning (Serna, Hazel, Schumaker, & Sheldon-Wildgen, Note 4). For example, when their children learn to give negative feedback, the parents learn to accept negative feedback. The preliminary results indicate that parents can be trained using a group format in social and problem-solving skills. The indirect effect of this parent training on the youths is not yet known.

The program has also been conducted with different types of group leaders. The group leaders for the groups discussed in this chapter were undergraduate practicum students. The program has also been implemented by probation officers with youths on their caseloads. Implementation by the probation officers not only provides benefits to the youths, but also serves as a vehicle by which these persons can offer treatment. Staff members of a youth diversion program, as well as social workers and counselors in various schools, also have been trained to lead the groups. The results of the training programs in different settings, with different types of group members and group leaders, have all shown skill level increases comparable to those reported in the second study in this chapter.

REFERENCE NOTES

1. Zimmerman, J., & Broder, P. K. Deriving measures of delinquency from self-report data. Washington, D.C.: National Center for State Courts, 1978.
2. Hazel, J. S., Schumaker, J. B., Kuehn, F., Sherman, J. A., & Sheldon-Wildgen, J. Group training of social skills with delinquent youths. Paper presented at the 67th annual convention of the American Psychological Association, New York City, September 1979.
3. Hazel, J. S., Schumaker, J. B., & Sheldon-Wildgen, J. Application of a social skill and problem-solving group training program to learning disabled and non-learning disabled youth (Research Report No. 30). Lawrence, Kans.: University of Kansas Institute for Research in Learning Disabilities, 1981.
4. Serna, L., Hazel, J. S., Schumaker, J. B., & Sheldon-Wildgen, J. Parent and youth training of reciprocal social skills. Article in preparation, 1981.

REFERENCES

Bandura, A. *Aggression: A social learning analysis.* Englewood Cliffs, N.J.: Prentice-Hall, 1973.

Bandura, A., & Walters, R. H. *Adolescent aggression.* New York: Ronald, 1959.

Black, D., & Reiss, A. Police control of juveniles. *American Sociological Review,* 1970, *35,* 63–77.

Carney, L. P. *Probation and parole: Legal and social dimensions.* New York: McGraw-Hill, 1977.

Clark, J. P., & Sykes, R. E. Some determinants of police organization and practice in a modern industrial democracy. In D. Glaser (Ed.), *Handbook of criminology.* Chicago: Rand-McNally, 1974.

Cohn, Y. Criteria for the probation officer's recommendation to the juvenile court. *Crime and Delinquency,* 1963, *9,* 262–275.

Eitzen, D. A. The effects of behavior modification on the attitude of delinquents. *Behaviour Research and Therapy*, 1975, *13*, 295–299.

Elder, J. P., Edelstein, B. A., & Narick, M. M. Adolescent psychiatric patients: Modifying aggressive behavior with social skills training. *Behavior Modification*, 1979, *3*, 161–178.

Freedman, B. J. *An analysis of social-behavioral skill deficits in delinquent and nondelinquent adolescent boys.* Unpublished doctoral dissertation, University of Wisconsin, 1974.

Goldfried, M. R., & D'Zurilla, T. J. A behavioral-analytic model for assessing competence. In C. D. Spielberger (Ed.), *Current topics in clinical and community psychology.* New York: Academic Press, 1969.

Goldman, N. *The differential selection of juvenile offenders for court appearance.* New York: National Council on Crime and Delinquency, 1963.

Gross, S. Z. The prehearing juvenile report: Probation officer's conception. *Journal of Research in Crime and Delinquency*, 1967, *4*, 212–217.

Keilitz, I., Zaremba, B. A., & Broder, P. K. The link between learning disabilities and juvenile delinquency: Some issues and answers. *Learning Disability Quarterly*, 1979, *2*, 2–11.

Kifer, R. E., Lewis, M. A., Green, D. R., & Phillips, E. L. Training predelinquent youths and their parents to negotiate conflict situations. *Journal of Applied Behavior Analysis*, 1974, *7*, 357–364.

Minkin, N., Braukmann, C. J., Minkin, B. L., Timbers, G. D., Timbers, B. J., Fixsen, D. L., Phillips, E. L., & Wolf, M. M. The social validation and training of conversational skills. *Journal of Applied Behavior Analysis*, 1976, *9*, 127–139.

Ollendick, T. H., & Hersen, M. Social skill training for juvenile delinquents. *Behaviour Research and Therapy*, 1979, *17*, 547–554.

Piliavin, I., & Briar, S. Police encounters with juveniles. *American Journal of Sociology*, 1964, *70*, 206–214.

Rose, S. D. *Group therapy: A behavioral approach.* Englewood Cliffs, N.J.: Prentice-Hall, 1977.

Sarason, A. G., & Ganzer, V. J. Modeling and group discussion in the rehabilitation of juvenile delinquents. *Journal of Counseling Psychology*, 1973, *20*, 442–449.

Stokes, T. F., & Baer, D. M. An implicit technology of generalization. *Journal of Applied Behavior Analysis*, 1977, *10*, 349–367.

Toch, H. *Violent men.* Chicago: Aldine, 1969.

Werner, J. S., Minkin, N., Minkin, B. L., Fixsen, D. L., Phillips, E. L., & Wolf, M. M. "Intervention package": An analysis to prepare juvenile delinquents for encounters with police officers. *Criminal Justice and Behavior*, 1975, *2*, 55–84.

Wolf, M. M. Social validity: The case for subjective measurement or how applied behavior analysis is finding its heart. *Journal of Applied Behavior Analysis*, 1978, *11*, 203–214.

Chapter 7

Analysis, Validation, and Training of Peer-Criticism Skills With Delinquent Girls

Neil Minkin
Bonnie L. Minkin
Richard S. Goldstein
Marc W. Taylor
Curtis J. Braukmann
Kathryn A. Kirigin
Montrose M. Wolf

Abstract

Many contemporary models for the treatment of delinquency consider peer participation in criticism-giving to be an important means by which delinquents can help each other solve their problems. This experiment investigated peer criticism within the context of self-government meetings at a group home. Five delinquent girls were interviewed to obtain descriptions of behaviors that they believed would make criticism more positive and more effective. The behaviors generated by the youths were reliably defined and included praise, a statement of understanding, and a request for acknowledgement. A group training procedure employing a multiple-baseline design and consisting of instructions, rationales, and practice with feedback was used to teach the behaviors to the five girls. After each training session, a questionnaire was given to each girl to assess her ongoing satisfaction with the training procedures and to obtain her continuing consent to participate. Generalization of the trained behaviors was assessed by recording the frequency of each behavior from videotapes of self-government meetings that occurred prior to and after training. The training resulted in an increased use of the behaviors. In order to socially validate the benefits of the behavior change, samples of each girl's pretraining and posttraining criticism-giving behaviors were randomly selected from the videotapes, recorded on audiotapes, and rated by groups of youth and adult judges. The judges' ratings indicated that the girls' posttraining samples were considered to be significantly better along relevant dimensions. The results suggest that permitting group members input into the design and implementation of their own treatment program may result in more positive procedures and perhaps increased chances of achieving rehabilitation goals.

Interpersonal feedback is considered to be an important component of human interaction (Patton & Giffin, 1974). One form of interpersonal feedback—criticism-giving—involves the expression of negative evaluative judgements (Bennis, Schein, Steele, & Berlew, 1968; Levine & Bunker, 1975). In interpersonal relationships, the nature and frequency of criticism-giving can be an important determinant of the extent to which the relationship is rewarding. In relationships between peers, the ability to give criticism in a manner that is likely to be acceptable to the recipient and is functional in effecting behavior change has been suggested as an important source of harmony (Bach & Deutsch, 1970; Bach & Goldberg, 1974; Bach & Wyden, 1970; Whittaker, 1979). It has been noted, however, that few empirical studies have dealt with the behaviors involved in the delivery of functional criticism (Jacobs, Jacobs, Feldman, & Cavior, 1973).

Peer-group feedback, often involving criticism-giving, has been used as a behavior-change strategy in several contemporary models for the treatment of delinquency (Whittaker, 1979). Models using "guided group interaction" and "positive peer culture" consider group participation in criticism-giving to be an important method of providing motivation for delinquents to help each other solve their problems (Empey & Lubeck, 1971; Keller & Alper, 1970; Vorrath & Brendtro, 1974). Some group criticism-giving styles are considered to be positive and to show concern. Youths who receive this type of criticism have been referred to as "being on the help seat" (Vorrath & Brendtro, 1974). However, other group criticism-giving styles are considered punitive and have been termed "attack therapy" (Walder, 1965). Youths who receive this type of criticism have been referred to as "being on the hot seat" (Vorrath & Brendtro, 1974; Walder, 1965).

Another way delinquent youths can give each other feedback is through group participation in self-government systems, which are becoming more prevalent in juvenile treatment programs (Fixsen, Phillips,

& Wolf, 1973; Moos, 1975). Self-government gives youth direct involvement in the direction of their treatment program, and has been seen as possibly increasing their commitment to participation in the treatment process and their chances for success (Empey & Rabow, 1961).

Peer-group feedback in the context of self-government is an important component of the Achievement Place (Teaching-Family) delinquency treatment approach. This approach is designed to provide family-style treatment for five to eight youths in group home settings directed by trained teaching-parents (Phillips, Phillips, Fixsen, & Wolf, 1974). Self-government is considered to be a critical part of this treatment program and occurs at daily meetings called family conferences, which are structured to encourage group participation in all aspects of the treatment program. The group decides on consequences for each other's behavior and makes and changes rules. From a behavioral perspective, the family conference procedure includes parameters that are important in promoting behavior change. For example, several behavioral investigators have found that providing reinforcing or punishing consequences for one client in a group situation can lead to systematic behavior change in other clients whose behavior has not been directly reinforced (Kazdin, 1977).

One major component of family conferences is called "peer reporting." During the daily meetings, youths report on issues that they feel are important to the group. They are encouraged to specify what they consider to be appropriate or inappropriate behavior of peers and what they consider to be unjust rules.

The purpose of this research was to investigate peer participation in criticism-giving within a group-home family conference context. Specifically, this involved (a) interviewing the youths to obtain descriptions of behavior they believed would make peer criticism more positive and effective, (b) intensive training of the criticism-giving behaviors identified by the youths, (c) assessment of youth satisfaction with the training procedures and desire to continue participation, (d) measurement of the follow-up generalization effects of training, and (e) social validation of the benefits of training by having other youths, as well as adults, compare the criticism-giving behaviors of the group before and after training.

Peer criticism was targeted both because it is an integral skill in preferred and effective group therapeutic activities (Phillips et al., 1974), and because one of the treatment goals of the group-home program was to teach appropriately assertive but nonaggressive ways of expressing disapproval. Adolescents with delinquent histories have been observed to employ aggressive or otherwise inappropriate criticism behaviors that can result in undesirable outcomes for them (Goldstein, Sherman, Gershaw, Sprafkin, & Glick, 1978).

INTERVIEWS AND BEHAVIORAL DEFINITIONS

Research Participation Interview

Girls in an Achievement Place treatment program were interviewed by the experimenters, and each was asked if she wished to participate in a group research project in which the goal was to learn how to give more positive and effective criticism. The girls were informed that the research would involve some of their after-school free time, that they would receive no compensation, and that other people would listen to recorded segments of their family conferences. They were also informed that, if they chose to participate initially, they could withdraw later at any time without having to give a reason to the experimenters or the teaching-parents.

Participants and Setting

Five girls chose to participate. They ranged in age from 13 to 16 and were in the seventh through eleventh grades in school. Each of the girls had been adjudicated by the juvenile court, and each had numerous reported instances of unsuccessful family and peer group interactions. The setting was a family room in the group home.

Behavior Specification Interview

The girls were interviewed as a group by the experimenters and asked to describe behaviors they believed would make their criticism-giving more positive and effective. During each of the interview sessions, the girls were instructed to describe and to arrive at a consensus about one behavior they felt would improve their criticism-giving. They were instructed to give oral examples of the selected behavior and to provide rationales explaining the importance of each behavior in giving positive and effective criticism. (Immediately following this procedure the girls practiced the skills, as described in the next section.) The behaviors described by the girls were later defined by the experimenters to the point where they could be reliably measured, and included:

1. *Praise.* A phrase or statement that expresses a favorable judgement of another person, another person's behavior, or a rule, such as "I like the way you. . ." or "It's a good thing that we have a rule that. . . ."
2. *Statement of understanding.* A phrase or statement that shows an understanding of another person's feelings, ideas, and/or behavior, or shows an understanding of why a rule exists, such as "I have felt that way myself," "I know what you mean," "I've done that before," or "I can understand."

3. *Request for acknowledgement.* A phrase or question that asks whether another individual or a group understands the discussed issue, such as "Do you understand. . . ?" or "You know what I mean?" This type of query usually appears at the end of an individual's discussion.

INTENSIVE TRAINING PROCEDURE

The intensive training procedure for the three behaviors was a group experience that occurred over a 4-day period. Each daily training session lasted approximately 1 hour and had three components: *instructions, rationales,* and *practice with feedback.* The first two components comprised the behavior specification interview already described. That is, in each session, the group was asked to agree upon, describe, and provide reasons for a behavior that would make criticism-giving more positive and more effective. In the third component, practice with feedback, the girls were given filled-in sample family conference report cards (see Figure 7.1) and asked to practice giving peer reports using the selected behavior. The practice sessions were videotaped, and the tapes were played back so that the girls could get feedback on their criticism behavior and comment on each other's behavior. When all the girls stated that they had "mastered" a new behavior, the training session ended.

A multiple-baseline design (Baer, Wolf, & Risley, 1968) across the three behaviors of criticism-giving was used to assess the effectiveness of the intensive training procedure. Use of this design permitted simultaneous recording of baseline rates of the specified behaviors prior to successive introduction of training for each of the behaviors.

During baseline and posttraining conditions, each girl was videotaped alone giving several peer reports involving criticism. She was given a family conference report card that described either an instance of inappropriate behavior by another girl or a rule in the home that she was asked to consider unfair. These sample peer reports were selected by the teaching-parents as being representative of those "commonly reported" and "relevant." Upon receiving the family conference report card, each girl was given one of two instructions, depending upon whether the peer report was of an inappropriate behavior or an unfair rule.

For an *inappropriate behavior,* the instructions were:

Here is a family conference report card on which you are bringing up a report about (name of experimenter). We would like you to pretend that you are concerned with this problem and think her behavior was inappropriate. Read the card and, when ready, bring up the report as you normally would at a family conference.

Figure 7.1. Family Conference Report Card.

FAMILY CONFERENCE REPORT CARD

Number of Youths Present _____ Date _____

Problem behavior ☐ Rule problem ☐ Other ☐ _____

_____

What was the problem? _____

_____

Who brought it up (or reported it)? _____

Did the teaching-parents deliver any decision before the family conference?

_____

If a problem behavior was discussed did:
☐ Youth admit guilt? ☐ Peers vote on guilt? ☐ T-P determine guilt?
☐ Not guilty.

What was the outcome (rule change or consequence) of the conference?

_____

_____

☐ T-P decision. ☐ Peer decision. ☐ Both. ☐ Youths accepted responsibility.

Indicate all consequences delivered to any or all youths. _____

_____

_____

Did you discuss the issue of:
☐ Fairness? ☐ Effectiveness? ☐ Happiness? ☐ Concern? ☐ Pleasantness?
☐ Helping youth to become a better person?

For an *unfair rule,* the instructions were:

> Here is a family conference report card on which you are bringing
> up a report about a rule. We would like you to pretend that you
> think the rule is unfair and would like to change it. Read the card
> and, when ready, bring up the report as you normally would at
> a family conference.

After having been read the instructions, and having read the peer
report, the girl was asked if she understood the instructions and if she

had any questions. She was then requested to state when she was ready to begin, and upon her signal the videotape unit was turned on and her peer report was recorded.

The occurrence or nonoccurrence of each of the three behaviors (i.e., praise, understanding, and acknowledgement) during each sample report was recorded during the videotaped baseline and posttraining peer reports. Three types of reliability computations were used: point-by-point, occurrence, and nonoccurrence. Mean agreement in all cases averaged over 90%.

Figure 7.2 shows the mean effects of the intensive training procedure for all five girls. The data indicate that, with each successive implementation of training, the girls' behavior demonstrated a substantial increase over baseline levels.

Following each daily session, a questionnaire consisting of three questions was given to each girl in order to assess her level of satisfaction

Figure 7.2. Mean effects of the intensive training procedures for all five girls across the three criticism behaviors.

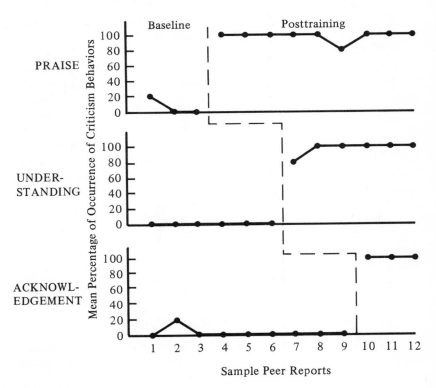

Sample Peer Reports

with the intensive training procedures and to assure her ongoing consent. The first two questions asked each girl to rate the daily experimental procedures on the dimensions of fun and interest, using a 7-point, Likert-type scale. The third question asked each girl if she wished to continue her participation in the experiment and was to be checked yes or no. The questionnaires were not seen by the experimenters until the conclusion of the intensive training procedure. However, the girls' teaching-parents checked them daily to see if any girl was dissatisfied with the procedures or wished to discontinue her participation.

Results of the satisfaction questionnaire showed that the girls agreed that the procedures were fun and interesting, and all girls indicated daily that they wanted to continue their participation.

To determine the generalization effects of training, routine daily family conferences were videotaped for 8 sessions prior to the intensive training procedure and for 18 sessions thereafter. The frequency of the specified criticism behaviors used during peer reports were gathered from these videotaped sessions. For the first 7 sessions after intensive training, the teaching-parents prompted the girls to use the trained components during peer reports. The prompts were in the form of a "reminder" to use the trained behaviors and were given once at the beginning of each family conference. The prompts were withdrawn for the next 11 family conferences, which occurred over 5 weeks, in order to observe if the trained behaviors had generalized.

Use of the trained behaviors was recorded in two ways: percent of the occurrence of criticism behaviors used by all girls during a complete discussion of each peer report, and percent of the occurrence of criticism behaviors used by each girl who initiated a peer report. Figure 7.3 shows that during the 33 peer reports in the 8 baseline family conferences prior to training, 4% of the time the group used the criticism behaviors. However, for the 45 peer reports that occurred in the 11 family conferences during the follow-up generalization period, the group's average use of the criticism behaviors rose to 34%.

Figure 7.4 illustrates the percent of trained criticism behaviors used by each girl each time she initiated peer reports. The variable number of pretraining and posttraining points across girls is due to variations in the number of reports initiated by each of the girls during those periods. The data show that the girls used the trained behaviors at a higher level during the follow-up generalization period.

SOCIAL VALIDATION AND BENEFITS OF CHANGE

While the data indicated that the girls' use of the trained criticism behaviors increased during peer reports at family conferences, the social

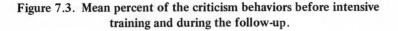

**Figure 7.3. Mean percent of the criticism behaviors before intensive
training and during the follow-up.**

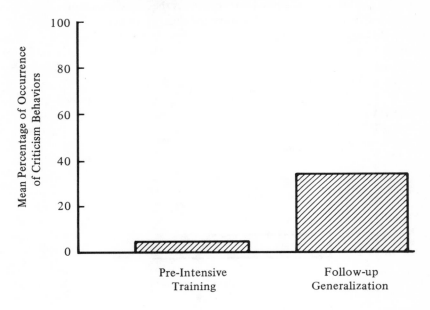

and practical value of the training remained unknown. Thus, a social
validation procedure (Minkin, Braukmann, Minkin, Timbers, Timbers,
Fixsen, Phillips, & Wolf, 1976) employing two groups of relevant judges
was used to determine if the training produced effects judged beneficial. One group of judges consisted of nine youths who lived in other
Achievement Place-style group homes. The other group consisted of 15
adults from the local community. The judges rated 10 peer reports that
were randomly selected from the videotaped family conferences. These
included one sample of each girl's peer-reporting behavior prior to the
intensive training procedures and one sample during the follow-up generalization period. The peer reports were randomly ordered and transcribed
onto audiotapes.

The rating procedures were identical for both groups of judges.
Initially, the operation and goals of the Achievement Place program were
briefly described. The judges were then informed that they would be
listening to and rating short audiotape samples of criticism-giving from
actual family conferences, and were instructed to concentrate on the
form of the criticism and the *manner* in which it was delivered and not
to form an opinion about the content of the criticism. They were told
to rate independently, and were allowed to go back at any time and

**Figure 7.4. Percent of trained criticism behaviors when initiating peer
reports prior to intensive training and during the follow-up.
The vertical dashed line represents the introduction of
intensive training.**

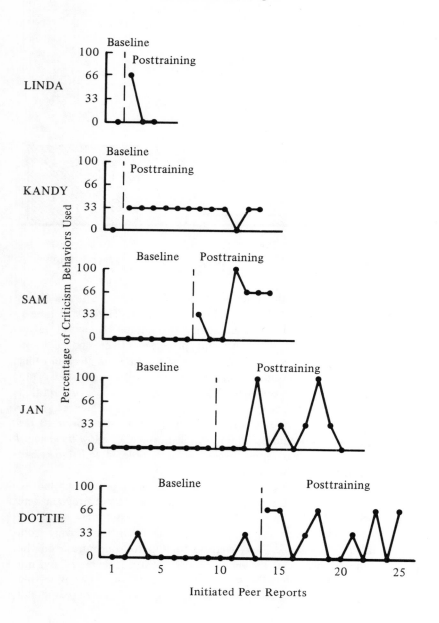

change ratings. A practice tape was played and rated, and then questions about the procedure were answered.

The judges rated each sample peer report on nine questions using a Likert-type scale ("strongly agree" to "strongly disagree"). The questions consisted of four categories: (a) questions on whether that type of criticism would make family conferences more positive and more effective; (b) questions on the quality of the criticism; (c) questions on the naturalness of the criticism; and (d) a question on how positive the criticism would have been if it had been given to the judge.

The results of the social validation procedure showed that, before intensive training, the mean rating by all judges on all dimensions was 4.9. During the follow-up generalization period this rating rose to 5.9. The average rating by the youth judges on all dimensions for all girls was 5.1 prior to intensive training and 6.1 during follow-up generalization, while ratings by the adult judges averaged 4.7 and 5.9, respectively. These differences, presented in Figure 7.5, were found to be statistically significant ($p < .005$) for the two periods using the t test for matched groups.

Figure 7.5. Judges' mean ratings of all the girls' criticism-giving behavior prior to intensive training and during the follow-up. N for all judges is 24, for youth judges is 9, and for adult judges is 15.

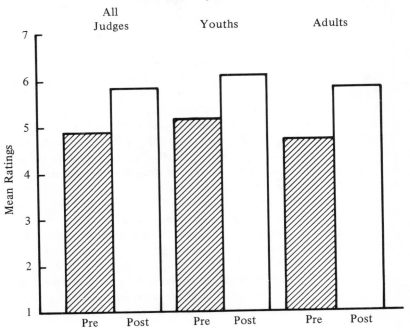

DISCUSSION

The results of this study suggested that preferred criticism-giving behaviors could be generated by a group involved in a therapeutic program and could be objectively specified and trained. The trained behaviors were found to generalize to the youths' natural environment, and the benefits of the behavioral change were observable by relevant judges.

The behaviors generated by the youths have been considered important by others. Hogan, Fisher, and Morrison (1974) suggested that the use of praise increases group cooperation. Keefe (1976) suggested that statements that show understanding of others' feelings are critical behaviors in affecting the outcome of the helping process. Golembiewski and Blumberg (1970) suggested that requests for acknowledgement to insure accurate reception are important components of a helping relationship.

Ongoing satisfaction with the intensive training procedure was assessed by each girl after each session, and each girl's continuing consent to participate was also assessed. The results indicated that the girls were satisfied with, and wished to continue, their training experience. At times, external rewards such as tokens, points, or money are used to encourage research participation. In this experiment, participation was voluntary and no extrinsic reinforcement was used.

The reported generalization effects showed that the group emitted the trained behaviors at a substantially higher level after training. However, the value of the prompt to use the trained behaviors during the initial posttraining family conference meetings was not determined. Thus, it was not possible to determine at what level the behaviors would have generalized if the prompted generalization condition had not occurred.

Social validation by relevant judges of the benefits of the behavioral change indicated significant improvements in the girls' criticism behavior when making a peer report. The judges' ratings indicated that, following training, the girls' peer-reporting behavior was more likely to contain the type of criticism that would make family conferences more positive and more effective, and that it would be positively received if the judges were the recipients. While the judges rated the posttraining peer reports as more natural, the changes on this dimension were not statistically significant.

The identification and modification of socially valid styles of peer-group feedback would seem to have implications for other models of group treatment of delinquents. Peer-group feedback is often considered to be an important element in various approaches to behavior change with delinquents (Whittaker, 1979). Unlike the approach described in this research, group feedback in delinquency treatment programs is frequently associated with punitive styles. Future research might directly investigate the effects of positive styles compared to more punitive styles. It may be found that delivering criticism that is positive and effective enhances both meaningful participation in group treatment approaches and social interaction in general.

Active involvement of participants in applied behavior analysis research and treatment is emerging as an important issue. Behavioral studies concerning youth input in juvenile treatment programs have produced some interesting results. For example, Fixsen et al. (1973) found that when youths were permitted to determine consequences for appropriate and inappropriate behaviors of peers, participation in the self-government program tended to increase. Increased participation in self-government has been found to be related to increased satisfaction with the fairness and pleasantness of a treatment program (Kifer, Ayala, Fixsen, Phillips, & Wolf, Note 1). Such increased satisfaction ratings may have important treatment implications. Braukmann, Kirigin, and Wolf (Note 2) found that satisfaction ratings by youths concerning their treatment program were related to other measures of outcome. Specifically, Braukmann et al. reported that youth ratings of their satisfaction with professional care staff on dimensions of fairness, pleasantness, concern, and effectiveness were significantly and inversely correlated with police and court contacts: the higher the youths' satisfaction ratings, the less their officially recorded delinquency. Thus, development of treatment models that encourage group participation in determining and evaluating treatment processes and objectives may well increase treatment satisfaction, as well as resulting in increased likelihood of achieving treatment goals.

REFERENCE NOTES

1. Kifer, R. E., Ayala, H. E., Fixsen, D. L., Phillips, E. L., & Wolf, M. M. *The teaching-family model: An analysis of self-government systems.* Paper presented at the Annual Convention of the American Psychological Association, New Orleans, September 1974.
2. Braukmann, C. J., Kirigin, K. A., & Wolf, M. M. *Achievement Place: The researchers' perspective.* Paper presented at the Annual Convention of the American Psychological Association, Washington, D. C., September 1976.

REFERENCES

Bach, G. R., & Deutsch, R. M. *Pairing.* New York: Avon, 1970.
Bach, G. R., & Goldberg, H. *Creative aggression.* New York: Avon, 1974.
Bach, G. R., & Wyden, P. *The intimate enemy.* New York: Avon, 1970.
Baer, D. M., Wolf, M. M., & Risley, T. R. Some current dimensions in applied behavior analysis. *Journal of Applied Behavior Analysis*, 1968, *1*, 91–97.

Bennis, W. G., Schein, E. H., Steele, F. I., & Berlew, D. E. *Interpersonal dynamics.* Homewood, Ill.: Dorsey Press, 1968.

Empey, L. T., & Lubeck, S. G. *The Silverlake experiment: Testing delinquency theory and community intervention.* Chicago: Aldine, 1971.

Empey, L. T., & Rabow, J. The Provo experiment on delinquency rehabilitation. *American Sociological Review,* 1961, *26,* 679–697.

Fixsen, D. L., Phillips, E. L., & Wolf, M. M. Achievement Place: Experiments in self-government with pre-delinquents. *Journal of Applied Behavior Analysis,* 1973, *6,* 31–47.

Goldstein, A. P., Sherman, M., Gershaw, H. J., Sprafkin, R. P., & Glick, B. Training aggressive adolescents in prosocial behavior. *Journal of Youth and Adolescence,* 1978, *7,* 73–92.

Golembiewski, R. T., & Blumberg, A. *Sensitivity training and the laboratory approach.* Itasca, Ill.: Peacock, 1970.

Hogan, J. L., Fisher, R. H., & Morrison, B. J. Social feedback and cooperative game behavior. *Psychological Reports,* 1974, *34,* 1075–1082.

Jacobs, M., Jacobs, A., Feldman, G., & Cavior, N. Feedback II–The credibility gap: Delivery of positive and negative and emotional and behavioral feedback in groups. *Journal of Consulting and Clinical Psychology,* 1973, *41,* 215–223.

Kazdin, A. E. The application of operant techniques in treatment, rehabilitation, and education. In S. L. Garfield & A. E. Bergin (Eds.), *Handbook of psychotherapy and behavior change* (2nd ed.). New York: Wiley, 1977.

Keefe, T. Empathy: The critical skill. *Social Work,* 1976, *21,* 10–14.

Keller, O. J., & Alper, B. S. *Halfway houses: Community-centered correction and treatment.* Lexington, Mass.: Heath (Lexington Books), 1970.

Levine, M., & Bunker, B. B. *Mutual criticism.* Syracuse, N. Y.: Syracuse University Press, 1975.

Minkin, N., Braukmann, C. J., Minkin, B. L., Timbers, G. D., Timbers, B. J., Fixsen, D. L., Phillips, E. L., & Wolf, M. M. The social validation and training of conversational skills. *Journal of Applied Behavior Analysis,* 1976, *9,* 127–139.

Moos, R. H. *Evaluating correctional and community settings.* New York: Wiley, 1975.

Patton, B. R., & Giffin, K. *Interpersonal communication.* New York: Harper & Row, 1974.

Phillips, E. L., Phillips, E. A., Fixsen, D. L., & Wolf, M. M. *The teaching-family handbook.* Lawrence, Kans.: University of Kansas Printing Service, 1974.

Vorrath, H. H., & Brendtro, L. K. *Positive peer culture.* Chicago: Aldine, 1974.

Walder, E. Synanon and the learning process: A critique of attack therapy. *Corrective Psychiatry and Journal of Social Therapy,* 1965, *II,* 299–304.

Whittaker, J. K. *Caring for troubled children.* San Francisco: Jossey-Bass, 1979.

Chapter 8

Training Paraprofessionals to Do Assertion Training With Mentally Disordered Sex Offenders

Lou Ann Wieand
John V. Flowers
Karen A. Hartman

Abstract

The present client outcome study was designed to assess the effects of a group assertion training model first administered to paraprofessionals in a mental hospital setting, who then conducted patient groups using the same model. It was hypothesized that the training with mentally disordered sex offenders would result in significant change on 18 posttreatment variables and 2 follow-up variables. Randomly assigned patients who received the training scored significantly different from before to after training on both behavioral and self-report measures, when compared with the control group of patients. Two-year follow-up indicated the experimental subjects also differed from controls in hospital release ratings and subsequent court dispositions. The findings suggest the importance of a specific social skills approach for sex offenders and serve to clarify issues regarding the effects of staff training and development on client outcome.

Although research in training psychotherapeutic skills has proliferated in the past decade, attempts to evaluate those techniques have often fallen short of the Truax and Carkhuff (1967) maxim that, in addition to measurement of trainee improvement, measurement of patient improvement as a function of that training is also a necessary variable. Matarazzo (1978) reiterated the importance of using client feedback and client change as ultimate criteria of the efficacy of training when she stated, "Patient satisfaction, patient rating of therapist qualities, and patient outcome remain the final proof of the pudding" (pp. 962–963).

Client-centered clinicians and researchers, following models by Rogers and his early collaborators, first developed training workshops and measured their effectiveness (Blocksma & Porter, 1947). The training emphasis centered on the importance of learning to establish a facilitative environment with a client. Specifically, the research measured the relationship between therapist variables, such as accurate empathy and positive regard, and client variables, such as depth of self-exploration (Anderson, 1968; Piaget, Berenson, & Carkhuff, 1967; Rogers & Truax (cited in Matarazzo, 1978)). However, the judgment procedure of evaluating these highly subjective constructs has been questioned (Matarazzo, 1978). Much of the research cited has appeared to confound training variables with initial therapist selection, and dependent measures have seemed to focus on qualities involved in "being a good client" rather than on some external criterion of mental health. Thus, none of these studies actually attempted to train therapists, to assign them clients, and to measure client outcome in terms of more effective coping skills or more healthy functioning.

The more contemporary client-centered orientation, using didactic-experimental training, has accentuated the importance of conducting quasi-group and individual therapy sessions in which the trainee can explore her own role as therapist rather than exclusively studying theory. Several studies have combined training procedures and subsequently taped interviews with actual clients (Carkhuff & Truax, 1965; Truax & Carkhuff, 1967). Naive judges focusing on brief audiotaped excerpts from interviews attempted to assess therapist qualities such as empathy, warmth, and respect. The literature has suggested the helpfulness of this feedback for training, but client outcome correlates of these ratings have been low (Matarazzo, 1978).

Behavioral programs, combining systematic methods of training with direct modification of specific client behaviors, have had more success in assessing client improvement. Due perhaps to the specificity of both training procedures and target behaviors in the client, many studies have related training techniques and client follow-up. Critiques of these studies have suggested that much of this research has involved single case studies, such as the parent-trainee, child-client literature (Reisinger, Ora, & Frangia, 1976). Assessment of client improvement has generally been measured by the trainee with checklists or rating scales of behavior change. Again, few studies have been located in which the trainees worked with groups of "live" clients and objective data were collected on patient change.

Thus, it appears that in the two major training modalities of psychotherapy, client-centered and behavioral, little research has related training procedures to client outcome, and no studies have used the client's mental health as the ultimate criterion of effective training.

One may ask why there have been so few attempts to research the relationship between training model and client change, when the primacy of such research has been indicated by scholars in this field. Matarazzo (1978) suggested that a multiplicity of problems face the researcher. Variables are poorly defined. The training situation is often a combination of conceptual, experiential, and behavioral stimuli and responses that are continually shifting. The Ns are small for the time-consuming nature of the product, and the measuring instruments are inadequate, involve subjective judgments, and are often non-comparable across modalities.

The following study was designed to assess the direct effects of the training of mental health workers on client change in an institutional setting. Its purpose was to study change and to document those changes that were a direct function of the applied treatment (Nunnally, 1975). A group training model was chosen, acknowledging that paraprofessionals were already required to spend most of the treatment time with groups of patients, and that treatment in groups was the most efficacious way of treating the largest number of clients in this facility. Incorporated within the study was the goal of avoiding as many methodological errors as possible while maintaining ethical standards within the natural setting of a state mental hospital. The following steps were taken: (a) an experimental and a control group were randomly selected from a population of identically labeled patients who volunteered for the project; (b) the treatment (the independent variable) was specific, well-documented in the literature (and therefore replicable), and administered by trained personnel; (c) multivariate analyses were performed on gain scores (post minus pre) (Campbell & Stanley, 1966) to apply the most rigorous error rate to those data in order to achieve a better conceptual understanding of the results (Eber, 1975; Kaplan & Litrownik, 1977); (d) while one of the measures was purely experimental in nature, most were chosen for their known reliability estimates and for normative and factor analytic data available; (e) observers were trained to judge nonverbal behaviors, and interrater reliability was calculated; and (f) follow-up data were collected 20 months after the conclusion of treatment.

Assertion training has been specified as a treatment modality of choice for various classes of behavior problems, including passivity (Wolpe & Lazarus, 1966), lack of social skills (Flowers & Booraem, 1975), depression (Tapper, 1978), and communication problems among geriatric populations (Corby, 1978). Although individual case studies have reported significant behavior change in the sex offender as a result of assertion training (Edwards, 1972; Laws & Serber, 1975; Stevenson & Wolpe, 1960), no research has evaluated the effectiveness of assertion training with groups of institutionalized sex offenders under experimentally controlled conditions, to date.

One reason for this lack of research on the effects of assertion training on mentally disordered sex offenders may be that, despite the case studies cited above, it is not immediately apparent that assertion training is a treatment of choice for such a population. The mentally disordered sex offender is defined by California state law (Welfare and Institutions Code #6300, 1972) as:

> any person who, by reason of mental defect, disease or disorder, is predisposed to the commission of sexual offenses to such a degree that he is dangerous to the health and safety of others. (p. 331)

Although dangerousness and aggressiveness are not synonymous terms, this definition seems to indicate that there is a uniform personality characteristic that identifies this population, and that the basic treatment should involve the removal of the aggressive threat to others. Such an assumption may explain why research on the treatment of sex offenders has generally emphasized the elimination of deviant arousal patterns rather than training in adaptive social skills (Wilson & Davison, 1974).

The work of Cohen, Seghorn, and Calmas (1969) indicates that the sex offender category is not as homogeneous as is commonly presumed. While some offenders display antecedent aggressive behavior, others display passive antecedent and even passive consequent behavior in terms of sexual arousal. For sex offenders who do not display aggressive antecedent behavior, treatments other than response suppression may be more effective.

One response acquisition method that has been demonstrated to be highly effective with various populations is assertion training (Rich & Schroeder, 1976). Since Ellis and Brancale (1956) and Serber and Wolpe (1972) have indicated that sex offenders display deficits in the same interpersonal skills that assertion training attempts to train—sexual communication (Liss-Levinson, Coleman, & Brown, 1976), requesting and refusing (Flowers & Booraem, 1975), conversational skills (Cotler & Guerra, 1976), and job interview skills (McGovern, Tinsley, Liss-Levinson, Laventure, & Britton, 1975)—assertion training may be a treatment of choice for sex offenders when elimination of deviant arousal patterns is not the indicated treatment.

The present study was designed to test the hypothesis that a specified assertion training procedure, administered by trained paraprofessionals, would result in significant change on 18 posttreatment variables and 2 follow-up variables when experimental subjects were compared to control subjects.

METHOD

Leaders and Subjects

Six mental health staff members (three co-leader pairs) were trained in assertion training, following the procedures reported in a previous article (Flowers & Booraem, 1975). Forty-eight patient volunteers from one hospital unit were randomly assigned to treatment and non-treatment conditions. Six subjects (three from each condition) were lost due to discharge procedures prior to completion of treatment, leaving an intact population of 42. Subjects ranged in age from 18 to 55, and all were labeled mentally disordered sexual offenders according to the legal definition (24 having committed rape and 18 having participated in child molestation).

Measures

Assertion Inventory (AI). This 40-item self-report inventory (Gambrill & Richey, 1975) assesses the subject's self-report on the probability of an assertive or passive response in specific situations (GRF). In addition, the self-reported degree of discomfort is assessed for each situation (GRA). This instrument was selected because of its ability to verify or discredit the negative correlation of anxiety arousal and overt assertive behavior suggested in the literature (McFall & Marston, 1970; Wolpe, 1958).

Rathus Assertiveness Schedule (RAS). This 30-item self-rating scale (Rathus, 1973) assesses the subject's attitudes toward assertiveness in certain specific situations. This measure was selected because it is popular in current assertion research where a global self-report of assertion is indicated, and because it is the most standardized of the assertion-testing instruments (Rathus & Nivid, 1977).

Pleasant Events Schedule (PES). This 320-item list (MacPhillamy & Lewinsohn, Note 1) yields a self-report of the frequency and pleasurableness of events commonly found to be pleasurable in our society. Three scores are obtained: (a) an assessment of how frequently the subject engages in the activity on a 3-point scale (none, some, frequently) (PES-F), (b) an assessment of how pleasurable the event is on a 3-point scale (unpleasant or not pleasant, somewhat pleasant, pleasant) (PES-P), and (c) a summation of the product of item scores on (a) and (b) as an indication of obtained pleasures (PES-FP). In the past, this test has been employed to demonstrate the relationship between depression and activity level. It was employed in the present study on the basis of a suggestion by Tapper (Note 2) linking nonassertion and depression. Specifically, he cited evidence (Libet & Lewinsohn, 1973) that depressed individuals typically emit low rates of interpersonal behaviors, such as positive statements to others, and fail to initiate positively reinforcing interpersonal activities, thus appearing behaviorally similar to the "nonassertive" client described in the assertion training literature.

NASA game. This behavioral analogue task (Bodner, Booraem, & Flowers, 1978) requires four participants (two experimental and two controls) to come to a consensus about four recording artists, from a list of 15, in order to receive a selection of record albums for the ward. Each subject privately rank-orders his first four choices and then a debate ensues among the group members. At its conclusion, two scores are obtained for each subject: (a) the number of initial four selections that the subject convinces the group to include on the final list (NASA), and (b) a persuasion score based on the difficulty of getting the group to accept the individual's selected item(s) (Nper). The latter score is based on the assumption that it is easier to get an item on the final list when more of the other members have also independently selected the same item, and more difficult when fewer of the others have selected that item.

Behavioral Assertion Test (BAT). The BAT (Eisler, Hersen, & Miller, 1973) required each subject to be placed in three role-playing situations—one assessing refusals, one assessing requests, and one assessing the ability to initiate and maintain conversation before and after treatment. Each role-play was videotaped for later analysis. On the refusal and request role-plays, a male played the role with the client and different situations were used pre- and posttreatment. On the conversation role-play, a female counterpart was used, and the same situation was used pre- and posttreatment.

The introduction was given each subject *verbatim* (adapted from Eisler, Hersen, & Miller, 1973):

> We are going to ask you to play a role for us, to be an actor for a short while. The purpose is to find out how you can handle certain situations both inside and outside the hospital. The idea is for you to respond to the situation in the way we tell you and also the most normal and comfortable way for you. The television camera is in the room so that we can observe you on the screen here. Most people find that they can relax in front of the camera in a short time. When I describe a scene to you I want you to imagine that you are really there. Mr. (Ms.) X will play the part of the other person I will tell you about. (p. 297)

The following standard situations were used with every subject.

REFUSAL ROLE-PLAY(S)
Description: Mr. X often borrows cigarettes from you and other people. He is going to ask you for a cigarette. You *do* have some but do not want to loan him one. Your task is to refuse no matter how many times or what ways he asks.
On tape:

Actor:	Can I bum a cigarette?
Client:	(Answer)

Actor:	Come on, all I want is one. You can spare just one.
Client:	(Answer)
Actor:	I would loan you one if I had them and *you* were out. I mean, what is one cigarette between friends?
Client:	(Answer)

Description: Mr. X often borrows radios from you and other people. He is going to ask you to borrow your radio but you do not want to loan it. Your task is to refuse no matter how many times or in what ways he asks.

On tape:

Actor:	Can I borrow your radio?
Client:	(Answer)
Actor:	Come on, I only need it for a little while.
Client:	(Answer)
Actor:	If I had a radio, I'd loan it to you. I thought we were friends.
Client:	(Answer)

REQUEST ROLE-PLAY(S)

Description: You are out of cigarettes and you want to borrow one from Mr. X, a fellow ward member who has some. Your task is to ask him for one, and to keep it up until he says yes.

On tape:

Client:	(Request)
Actor:	No, I've decided not to loan out cigarettes anymore.
Client:	(Request)
Actor:	No, I'm tired of people bumming cigarettes from me. I'm going to buy my own and they're going to buy their own.
Client:	(Request)
Actor:	(If third request is made, actor says yes and hands him one.)

Description: You don't have a radio and you want to borrow one from Mr. X, a fellow ward member who has one. Your task is to ask him to borrow it, and to keep it up until he says yes.

On tape:

Client:	(Request)
Actor:	No, I decided not to loan out my radio anymore.
Client:	(Request)
Actor:	I'm tired of people bumming my radio. If you want to listen to the radio, you'll just have to get your own.
Client:	(Request)
Actor:	(Says yes if client requests this third time.)

FREE INFORMATION ROLE-PLAY
    Description: You are at a party and you see a young woman across the room you would like to get to know. The situation is one in which it is O.K. for you to talk to her. You walk over to her and try to get to know who she is and what she is like.
    On tape:

Client:	(Initial comments ending with question)
Actor (female):	Responds with a closed answer.
Client:	(Comments and question)
Actor (female):	Responds as she wants with more open information.
Client:	(Comments and question)
Actor (female):	Responds as she wishes.

Nonverbal Assessment

At the conclusion of the posttraining assessment session, all video-tapes of the BAT (Eisler et al., 1973) were spliced into individual segments and randomly reassembled to control for order and pre-post bias effects. Two pairs of raters, blind to the experimental and pre-post conditions, timed the latency and duration of the responses for each role-play. Given the findings of McFall and Marston (1970) that refusals and requests are different domains of behavior, the score for each role-play was treated as a separate dependent variable. Thus, each subject received a refusal, request, and conversation latency score (Refl, Reql, FI1) and a refusal, request, and conversation duration score (Refd, Reqd, FId). The raters also recorded the number of times the subject broke eye contact during the role-play. Interrater reliability (agree/agree + disagree) was 93.6% for refusals, 91.6% for requests, and 91.0% for conversations. Each subject received a "lookaway per unit time" score (calculated as the number of times he broke eye contact divided by the duration of speaking time for that situation) for refusals, requests, and conversation (Reflo, Reqlo, FIlo). Additionally, after the first several rating sessions, it became evident that the subjects' interruptions of the actor were interfering with the scoring of latency of response time. Therefore, the raters recorded the number of times the subject interrupted in the role-plays. Because of the low frequency of interruptions, these data were summed over all three role-plays, thus giving the subjects an interruption score.

Procedure

All subjects were tested prior to and on completion of treatment on the various measures described. Twenty-one of the original volunteers (11 child molesters and 10 rapists) received 16 sessions of assertion training from one of the three co-leader pairs, in addition to their ongoing unit treatment program. The 21 control subjects (13 child molesters and 8 rapists) received no assertion training, but did receive the ongoing unit treatment procedures identical to those of the experimental group.

Patient Follow-up

Twenty months following posttesting, patient follow-up data were collected in an interview with three staff members. All three were blind to the experimental condition of each patient discussed, as well as to the original training procedures. These staff members had 100% agreement on the final staffing recommendation for 41 of the 42 patients in the original sample. An "A" staffing recommendation means that the patient has received maximum benefit from hospitalization and is no longer a danger to the health and safety of others, while a "B" recommendation means that the patient has not recovered and is still a danger (Welfare & Institutions Code #6325, 1972, p. 278). The third recommendation possible, "R/T," retains the patient in the hospital for further treatment and postpones the release date. Such recommendations are made in a meeting of the entire ward staff just prior to a patient's leaving the hospital to return to court.

In addition, the three staff members were aware of the subsequent court decisions and final dispositions of 29 of the 32 patients who had been released from the hospital. Patients on whom the staff did not agree (one staffing decision) or of whom they had no subsequent knowledge (three court decisions) were excluded from the analysis.

RESULTS

On all pretests, the experimental and control groups were not significantly different, indicating that even with this sample size the random assignment was effective in distributing pretraining skills equally (see Table 8.1).

A discriminant function analysis was performed on the change scores of 17 variables for the two groups. Of all cases, 96% (21/21 of the experimental and 20/21 of the control) were correctly classified; $\chi^2 = 38.18$, $p < .001$. The multivariate F for the analysis was $F(17,24) = 4.22$, $p < .001$. Thus, the results verified that the intervention was effective with the experimental group.

Table 8.1 contains the pretest raw scores, the group gain (mean change) scores, standard deviations, univariate F values, and discriminant function coefficients for each variable. Experimental subjects changed significantly more in the predicted direction on the Gambrill and Richey anxiety and frequency tests, the Rathus Schedule, the Pleasant Events Schedule, and on lookaways in the refusal and free-information behavioral assertion tests. Of these significant changes, neither the Rathus Schedule nor the Pleasant Events Schedule discriminated well between the groups; however, two variables that approach significance, the NASA persuasion change score and the refusal duration change score, are among the top half of group discriminators.

Intraclass correlations were also examined to determine which significant correlations existed between variables that contributed to the discriminant function. Table 8.2 contains these correlations. Variables with intraclass correlation coefficients above .42 ($p <.01$) fall into three groups. The correlations of the Rathus Schedule score and the two scores of the Gambrill and Richey Inventory indicate that all are measuring some common element of self-reported assertiveness. The correlation of the Pleasant Events Schedule frequency, pleasurability, and frequency times pleasurability scores indicates that all scores from this test tap some common dimensions of activity. The correlation of the NASA items and persuasion scores indicates that both analogue game scores measure a common behavior. No other correlations were significant at the .01 level.

Data on another variable, interruptions during the behavioral assertion tests, were too sparse to be included in the multivariate analysis, but were analyzed with a separate chi-square test. The experimental group interrupted 10 times prior to the intervention and 4 times after, while the control group interrupted 6 and 13 times, respectively, $\chi^2 = 5.12$, $p <.02$.

Follow-up data collected 20 months after the completion of the intervention indicated that of the 21 control subjects, 6 had been released from the hospital with an A rating, 6 released with a B rating, 5 were still institutionalized at the hospital, 1 had escaped, and 2 had been released on legal grounds without any rating. (One other had been released but the staff did not agree on what the decision had been.) Of the 21 experimental subjects, 14 had been released with an A rating, 1 with a B rating, 4 were still institutionalized, and 2 had been released on legal grounds without a rating. In order to perform a chi-square analysis, the subjects who either escaped or were released with no rating were included within the "B" decision category since the staff had not made a decision that they were ready for release. A chi square for the hospital staffing decision, $\chi^2 = 6.296$, $p <.05$, indicates that experimental subjects received significantly different decisions than did the controls.

In addition, the known court decisions on 30 subjects were analyzed. Fourteen experimental subjects were paroled and three went to prison, while seven control subjects were paroled and six went to prison. The chi square approached significance, $\chi^2 = 2.84, p < .10$.

Finally, a correlation was performed on the two decisions made for each subject to analyze the amount of agreement between the hospital staff and the court and yielded $\phi = .31$, which was not significant.

Table 8.1

Pretest Raw Scores, Group Gain Scores, Standard Deviations, *F* Values for Univariate Group Comparisons, and Discriminant Function Coefficients

Variable	EXPERIMENTAL			CONTROL				Discriminant Function Coefficient
	Pretest Scores M	Gain Scores M	SD	Pretest Scores M	Gain Scores M	SD	F	
1. GRA	84.95	−21.28[a]	29.09	84.95	−6.04[a]	17.88	4.18*	−0.185
2. GRF	97.67	20.47	24.93	97.76	7.66	14.85	4.09*	0.236
3. RAS	−1.71	30.80	35.93	−1.10	10.09	27.67	4.38*	−0.032
4. PES-F	222.67	21.95	33.16	245.38	−13.09	49.17	7.33**	−0.414
5. PES-P	322.57	18.14	65.14	337.57	−30.52	64.73	5.89***	−0.081
6. PES-FP	318.29	44.33	93.26	346.29	2.47	87.71	2.24	0.005
7. NASA	2.38	0.09	1.48	2.19	−0.57	1.24	2.49	−0.113
8. Nper	6.76	2.90	8.59	4.57	−1.00	6.09	2.88	−0.135
9. Refl	.866	−0.10	0.51	.666	0.05	0.40	0.13	−0.110
10. Refd	4.54	−1.25	2.17	3.30	0.15	3.30	2.68	0.428
11. Reflo	.557	−0.14	0.24	.464	0.32	0.37	22.99***	0.715
12. Reql	1.04	−0.39	1.50	.731	−0.29	0.43	0.09	0.122
13. Reqd	3.87	1.65	3.17	3.98	1.67	2.81	0.00	−0.010
14. Reqlo	.376	−0.21	0.16	.385	−0.12	0.21	2.57	0.006
15. FIl	.623	0.02	0.48	.518	0.01	0.37	0.00	−0.133
16. FId	4.42	0.36	1.76	3.74	0.56	2.76	0.08	0.086
17. FIlo	.494	−0.20	0.18	.475	−0.07	0.23	4.32*	0.131

[a] A negative score indicates anxiety level decrease.

*p < .05
**p < .01
***p < .001

Table 8.2

Intraclass Correlation Coefficients for Variables Included in the Discriminant-function Analysis

Variable	GRA	GRF	RAS	PES-F	PES-P	PES-FP	NASA	Nper	Refl	Refd	Reflo	Reql	Reqd	Reqlo	FIl	FId	FIlo
GRA	1.00																
GRF	−.80	1.00															
RAS	−.87	.79	1.00														
PES-F	−.12	.09	.04	1.00													
PES-P	−.16	.26	.15	.51	1.00												
PES-FP	−.20	.28	.11	.62	.80	1.00											
NASA	−.19	.11	.14	.00	−.21	.04	1.00										
Nper	−.11	−.01	.04	.10	−.08	.03	.55	1.00									
Refl	−.25	.41	.25	.20	.17	.30	−.12	−.22	1.00								
Refd	.13	.09	−.05	.26	.15	.23	−.26	−.08	.04	1.00							
Reflo	−.10	.06	.05	.19	.28	.33	.12	.33	.04	.11	1.00						
Reql	.07	−.01	−.12	−.11	−.23	−.24	−.15	.01	−.09	.35	−.12	1.00					
Reqd	.25	−.19	−.30	.01	−.04	.05	−.15	−.22	.01	.04	.35	.04	1.00				
Reqlo	.03	.07	.00	.05	.09	.21	.00	−.13	.10	.38	−.11	.09	−.07	1.00			
FIl	−.14	.09	.05	.34	.12	.29	.30	.17	.09	−.38	.10	−.36	−.01	−.25	1.00		
FId	−.18	.25	.36	.10	−.24	−.10	.14	−.21	.37	−.06	−.03	−.24	.05	−.02	.35	1.00	
FIlo	.14	−.06	−.20	.00	−.05	−.14	−.21	−.20	−.05	−.06	−.06	.09	.27	−.38	.04	−.11	1.00

DISCUSSION

An important conclusion that can be drawn from this study is the demonstrable effectiveness of assertion training with mentally disordered sex offenders. The overall differences between treated and untreated groups were significant. In addition, one can draw conclusions as to the relative importance of individual measures in terms of their ability to discriminate differentially treated groups. Finally, it appears that an assertion-trained subject fares better in the staff decision process regarding his release classification, as well as in the court decision following his hospitalization.

The general findings of this study point very clearly to the importance of a specific social skills training approach for sex offenders in comparison to a general milieu therapy that is frequently offered in the mental hospital setting. In this particular situation, all patients were actively involved in small groups, had individual therapy assignments, went to sex education classes, and were encouraged to discuss their "problems" in one-to-one sessions with the staff. With such encouragement for social interaction, one might expect that the inclusion of an additional therapeutic modality would increase the explained variance in behavior only slightly. Instead, both measured and informally assessed gains were noticeable. The staff reported that subjects in training at this time were offering their experience as coaches in behavioral rehearsal with other nonexperimental patients, some of whom were control subjects. With this much enthusiasm, the chances for experimental drift were greatly increased, yet significant effects were still noted.

In addition, one can infer a generalized effect over time on the behaviors of the experimental group in terms of the subsequent release ratings and court depositions. It is possible that the subsequent patient ratings upon release might have been influenced by the staff's knowledge of the patient's participation in the specialized program, rather than any behavior change brought about by the program. However, this possibility is unlikely for two reasons. First, the final rating was made by the entire psychiatric staff long after the training had terminated. Second, given the number of specialized treatments occurring during the patient's hospital stay, it is unlikely that knowledge of a patient's involvement in any one treatment would particularly influence the final rating. Furthermore, rater bias cannot explain the subsequent court decision on each patient since the brief summary from the hospital to the court includes nothing regarding treatment procedures. Given that the staffing decision and the court decision do not significantly differ from each other, it appears that the court decision may rest on judgments of clients' behaviors that parallel those used by the hospital to classify patients as either "A" or "B" and that this court decision may have been somehow influenced by the intervention.

Since the body of literature on the assessment of assertion training procedures is growing, it seems important to note those measures that significantly discriminated between treatment and control groups in this study. Although both the Gambrill and Richey Inventory subtests and the Rathus Schedule have significant univariate F tests, they are highly correlated, indicating that they supply redundant information. Since both subtests of the Gambrill and Richey Inventory are better discriminators of the groups than is the Rathus Schedule, and since they measure both frequency of behavior and its accompanying anxiety level, rather than a generalized situational response, the utility of this measure as a self-report scale in future research is indicated.

The Pleasant Events Schedule and the NASA game assess different results of the intervention: self-report of actual activity and an assessment of assertive performance. Both significantly add to the ability to discriminate trained from non-trained clients. Thus each measure is potentially important for assertion research; however, the high correlations of the subscales indicate that the separate scores are redundant. The NASA measure is important because it assesses actual performance instead of self-report. The PES measure is important for a different reason. While each of the measures above directly assesses assertion, the PES assesses the result of being assertive. The highly significant change in the trained clients' frequency of pleasant events engaged in while they were still confined to the hospital grounds demonstrates the power of the intervention, even within a confined environment.

The nonverbal measures are more difficult to assess in terms of future research. The eye contact measure clearly adds to the ability to discriminate trained from nontrained clients; however, the latency and duration measures are not clearly important assessment devices. Given previous research (Eisler et al., 1973), this lack of assessment capability may be due to one of two reasons. Research in which these nonverbal measures were shown to be part of the assertive response employed subjects who were described as solely passive. The present research employs subjects who are classified as passive, aggressive, and passive-aggressive. Thus, the previous findings may not hold for the present population, and future research may have to look for a curvilinear relationship (Eisler, Note 3) of duration and latency to assess if these variables discriminate trained from non-trained clients. A second possible reason for the lack of latency and duration discrimination may be the methodology employed in the present study. In previous research, latency and duration measures were only assessed in the initial interaction, while in the present research latency and duration were assessed in a continuous three-line interaction. While this three-line interaction is more like naturally occurring interactions, this methodology may not yield the same results as that used by Eisler et al. (1973). In any case, measures of latency and duration as presently employed in this study do not seem to add important information to the interpretation of outcome results.

All assessments in this study except the staff judgments and the imprisonment rates may be considered as intermediate measures. The purpose of such intermediate measures is to provide the therapist and clients with information with which to improve the intervention. The ultimate outcome result is improved client functioning in the natural environment. One desired result is reduced recidivism. Another is reduced imprisonment after treatment termination. Intermediate assessment is only worthwhile if it predicts the ultimate outcome and/or if it allows the intervention to be modified to help attain the goals.

While the major assessment of this study had to do with client variables, a larger question was actually posed: can client change be brought about by training paraprofessionals in therapy techniques? Given both the lack of research in this area and the pessimism with which mental health professionals and paraprofessionals alike view the ability of the paraprofessional to engineer change, this study serves more than one function. It not only serves as a verification of a method of therapy in relation to improved client outcome, but also speaks to the issue of how trainable paraprofessionals are in delivering that therapy. Paraprofessionals often lack confidence as to the amount of impact they have on their own clientele. They have not generally been reassured either by professionals in the field or by accurate information regarding follow-up of their clients. Evidence from this study serves as documentation of the impact that training has on on-line staff in a mental hospital and on their ability to engender change in their clients. The impact that such a study may have on the future of research in staff training and subsequent patient change can only be anticipated.

REFERENCE NOTES

1. MacPhillamy, D. J., & Lewinsohn, P. M. *A scale for the measurement of positive reinforcement.* Unpublished manuscript, University of Oregon, 1973.
2. Tapper, B. Personal communication, February 10, 1976.
3. Eisler, R. Personal communication, July 25, 1977.

REFERENCES

Anderson, S. C. Effects of confrontation by high- and low-functioning therapists. *Journal of Counseling Psychology,* 1968, *15,* 411–416.
Blocksma, D. D., & Porter, E. H., Jr. A short-term training program in client-centered counseling. *Journal of Counseling Psychology,* 1947, *11,* 55-60.

Bodner, G., Booraem, C., & Flowers, J. V. The assessment of assertion training: Past, present, and future trends. In J. M. Whiteley & J. V. Flowers (Eds.), *Approaches to assertion training.* Monterey, Calif.: Brooks/Cole, 1978.

Campbell, D., & Stanley, J. *Experimental and quasi-experimental designs for research.* Chicago: Rand McNally, 1966.

Carkhuff, R. R., & Truax, C. B. Training in counseling and psychotherapy: An evaluation of an integrated didactic and experiential approach. *Journal of Consulting Psychology,* 1965, *29,* 333–336.

Cohen, M., Seghorn, T., & Calmas, W. Sociometric study of the sex offender. *Journal of Abnormal Psychology,* 1969, *74,* 249-255.

Corby, N. Assertiveness and the elderly. In J. Whiteley & J. Flowers (Eds.), *Approaches to assertion training.* Monterey, Calif.: Brooks/Cole, 1978.

Cotler, S., & Guerra, J. *Assertion training.* Champaign, Ill.: Research Press, 1976.

Eber, H. Multivariate methodologies for evaluation research. In E. Struening & M. Guttentag (Eds.), *Handbook of evaluation research* (Vol. 1). Beverly Hills, Calif.: Sage, 1975.

Edwards, N. Case conference: Assertive training in a case of homosexual pedophilia. *Journal of Behavior Therapy and Experimental Psychiatry,* 1972, *3,* 55–63.

Eisler, R., Hersen, M., & Miller, P. Components of assertive behavior. *Journal of Clinical Psychology,* 1973, *29,* 295-299.

Ellis, A., & Brancale, R. *The psychology of sex offenders.* Springfield, Ill.: Charles C. Thomas, 1956.

Flowers, J., & Booraem, C. Assertion training: The training of trainers. *The Counseling Psychologist,* 1975, *5*(4), 29-36.

Gambrill, E., & Richey, C. An assertion inventory for use in assessment and research. *Behavior Therapy,* 1975, *6,* 550-561.

Kaplan, R. M., & Litrownik, A. J. Some statistical methods for the assessment of multiple outcome criteria in behavioral research. *Behavior Therapy,* 1977, *8,* 383–392.

Laws, D. R., & Serber, M. Measurement and evaluation of assertive training with sexual offenders. In R. E. Hosford & C. S. Moss (Eds.), *The crumbling walls: Treatment and counseling of prisoners.* Champaign, Ill.: University of Illinois Press, 1975.

Libet, J., & Lewinsohn, P. The concept of social skill with special references to the behavior of depressed persons. *Journal of Consulting and Clinical Psychology,* 1973, *40,* 304-312.

Liss-Levinson, N., Coleman, E., & Brown, L. A program of sexual assertiveness training for women. *The Counseling Psychologist,* 1976, *5*(4), 74–78.

Matarazzo, R. G. Research on the teaching and learning of psychotherapeutic skills. In S. L. Garfield & A. C. Bergin (Eds.), *Handbook of psychotherapy and behavior change* (2nd ed.). New York: Wiley, 1978.

McFall, R. M., & Marston, A. R. An experimental investigation of behavior rehearsal in assertive training. *Journal of Abnormal Psychology,* 1970, *76,* 295-303.

McGovern, T., Tinsley, D., Liss-Levinson, N., Laventure, R., & Britton, G. Assertion training for job interviews. *The Counseling Psychologist,* 1975, *5*(4), 65-68.

Nunnally, J. C. The study of change in evaluation research: Principles concerning measurement, experimental design and analysis. In E. Struening & M. Guttentag (Eds.), *Handbook of evaluation research* (Vol. 1). Beverly Hills, Calif.: Sage Publications, 1975.

Piaget, G. W., Berenson, B. G., & Carkhuff, R. R. Differential effects of the manipulation of therapeutic conditions by high- and moderate-functioning therapists upon high- and low-functioning clients. *Journal of Consulting Psychology,* 1967, *31,* 481-486.

Rathus, S. A. A 30-item schedule for assessing assertive behavior. *Behavior Therapy,* 1973, *4,* 398-406.

Rathus, S., & Nivid, J. Concurrent validity of the 30-item Assertiveness Schedule with a psychiatric population. *Behavior Therapy,* 1977, *83,* 393-397.

Reisinger, J. J., Ora, J. P., & Frangia, G. W. Parents as change agents for their children: A review. *Journal of Community Psychology,* 1976, *4,* 103-123.

Rich, A. R., & Schroeder, H. E. Research issues in assertiveness training. *Psychological Bulletin,* 1976, *83,* 1081-1096.

Serber, M., & Wolpe, J. Behavior therapy techniques. In H. Resnick & M. Wolfgang (Eds.), *Treatment of the sex offender.* Boston: Little, Brown & Co., 1972.

Stevenson, I., & Wolpe, J. Recovery from sexual deviation through overcoming of non-sexual neurotic responses. *American Journal of Psychiatry,* 1960, *116,* 737-742.

Tapper, B. Assertion training with suicidal and depressed clients. In J. Whiteley & J. Flowers (Eds.), *Approaches to assertion training.* Monterey, Calif.: Brooks/Cole, 1978.

Truax, C. B., & Carkhuff, R. R. *Toward effective counseling and psychotherapy: Training and practice.* Chicago: Aldine, 1967.

Welfare and Institutions Code, #6300 Definition. In *West's Annotated California Codes.* St. Paul, Minn.: West Publishing Co., 1972.

Welfare and Institutions Code, #6325 Commitment Classification. In *West's Annotated California Codes.* St. Paul, Minn.: West Publishing Co., 1972.

Wilson, G. T., & Davison, G. Behavior therapy and homosexuality: A critical perspective. *Behavior Therapy,* 1974, *5,* 16-28.

Wolpe, J. *Psychotherapy by reciprocal inhibition.* Stanford, Calif.: Stanford University Press, 1958.

Wolpe, J., & Lazarus, A. *Behavior therapy techniques.* Oxford: Pergamon Press, 1966.

Part Three

Specific Populations and Problems

The five chapters in this final part focus on several prevalent clinical problems. Dolores Gallagher, in Chapter 9, addresses the problem of depression in the elderly. She asks if elderly outpatients will respond differently to a behavioral group therapy approach compared to a more traditional supportive group approach, and whether or not individual differences in such areas as physical health and cognitive ability are related to outcome. This work marks one of the first attempts to investigate these variables with the elderly, despite the high priority assigned to this population for research and services by various agencies. Encouraged by her findings, Gallagher provides a number of excellent suggestions for both clinical work and outcome evaluation with this population.

D. Michael Rice and P. Scott Lawrence bring us into the area of behavioral medicine with their work on essential hypertension in Chapter 10. These authors were careful to use a variety of dependent variables, as well as generalization tasks, for subjects whose hypertension had not been brought completely within normal limits with medication. Diastolic blood pressure proved to be the best measure of change and held across generalization tasks as well as posttreatment.

In Chapter 11, Ian Falloon reports the results of an ambitious study of the components of many behavioral group therapy programs—modeling with rehearsal, structured group discussion, and homework assignments. Several aspects of this research are noteworthy, namely, the variety of clinical diagnoses within each group and the use of significant others to assist

185

patients with their homework assignments. While only half the patients completed their homework assignments, those who did so with the help of a significant other showed superior outcomes on their target behaviors. This chapter will be of special interest, then, to those who work with patients having a variety of diagnoses within the same group.

Chapters 12 and 13, the final two chapters in this volume, deal with group behavior therapy of obesity. In Chapter 12, Maxwell Knauss and D. Balfour Jeffrey discuss several issues of importance that are often omitted from the literature. These include the therapist's own attitudes toward obesity, the use of group interaction as a facilitative tool, attrition, therapist preparation, and common questions asked by obese clients. Both the neophyte and the experienced weight control therapist will find the discussion of these issues useful and interesting.

Carol Heckerman and Robert Zitter discuss spouse involvement in the treatment of obesity in Chapter 13. In addition, they report the results of a 3-year follow-up to a study in which the amount of spouse involvement was systematically varied. The chapter also includes a discussion of relevant but often overlooked variables as well as recommendations for future research and treatment, e.g., what is the role of marital satisfaction in weight loss, and what should be the precise nature of spouse involvement?

Chapter 9

Behavioral Group Therapy with
Elderly Depressives:
An Experimental Study

Dolores Gallagher

Abstract

This study was designed to investigate three questions relevant to psychotherapeutic research with elderly individuals: (a) are elderly clients with moderate to severe depression capable of responding positively to outpatient psychological intervention?; (b) would differential treatment effects result from structured behavioral therapy as compared to supportive psychotherapy, when carried out in a group format with the elderly?; and (c) are individual difference factors (e.g., health and cognitive status) related to outcome?

The sample was drawn from a clinical population of elderly depressed individuals applying for outpatient services. Twenty-eight elderly depressed outpatients were randomly assigned to either behavioral or supportive group psychotherapy. Each group participated in biweekly sessions for 5 weeks. Two experienced psychotherapists led one group in each condition. Assessment occurred before treatment, immediately upon completion, and after a 5-week follow-up period. Multivariate analyses of variance indicated that clients in both conditions improved considerably over time on self-report measures of depression and social behaviors and on observer ratings of interpersonal skills (both social and cognitive). No differential treatment effects on self-report measures of depression or interpersonal behavior were obtained. Trends on these measures were comparable in both groups. However, observer ratings of in-group verbal interaction patterns indicated significantly greater improvement for behavioral subjects over time. In addition, at posttreatment interviews, behavioral subjects reported greater satisfaction with treatment and improved overall functioning. Various subject variables (e.g., demographics such as sex and education) were not significantly related to outcome for this sample; however, self-perceived health status did show a significant association with reduction in depression over time.

Future research should focus on refinement of measures so that qualitative (as well as quantitative) change can be assessed. Treatment efficacy may be enhanced by creatively adapting behavior therapy procedures to address specific concerns of older persons, and by careful selection of appropriate reinforcers on an individual basis. The effect of group process variables and social interaction on the outcome of therapy should also be investigated further. *

INTRODUCTION

Little systematic attention has been given to the evaluation of psychological interventions for improving the mental health status of the elderly. Professional psychotherapists seem to hold tacit beliefs that older persons are more rigid, less "psychologically minded," and more likely to have concomitant organic pathology than younger patients, and therefore are poor therapeutic risks (Butler & Lewis, 1977). These attitudes may contribute to the discrepancy noted in the literature between estimates of need for mental health services and their actual use in this age group. Although persons over 60 comprised 9.9% of the population in 1970, only 2 to 4% actually utilized outpatient mental health facilities (Kramer, Taube, & Redick, 1973). Yet the mental health needs of this population are a serious issue in light of recent studies that point to the prevalence of psychiatric disorders in the aged. Pfeiffer (1977), for example, reviewed prevalence data and concluded that "approximately 15 percent of the elderly in the

---

*This chapter is based on a dissertation submitted in partial fulfillment of the requirements for the PhD degree at the University of Southern California. The author would like to express her appreciation to L. W. Thompson, dissertation chairman, and to the other committee members, A. S. Frankel, M. Hartford, and K. Rowland, as well as to P. Lewinsohn (University of Oregon) for his helpful consultation and interest in this work. Also acknowledged are the contributions of the therapists (A. Alkire and E. Levitt) and raters (B. McKee and S. Costello) involved in this research, along with the UCLA Neuropsychiatric Institute faculty, particularly Dr. Ivan Mensh. Finally, the author wishes to thank the Goldenera Society of the University of Southern California for their financial support. This work was also supported in part by National Institute of Mental Health Grants #1 RO1 MH32157-01 and #1 RO1 AG01959-01.

United States suffer from significant, substantial, or at least moderate psychopathology" (p. 652).

Blumenthal (Note 1) recommended to the President's Commission on Mental Health that research efforts be directed specifically to the study of depressive disorders, since the incidence of depressive symptomatology in older age groups is extremely widespread. Although definitive data are lacking at this time, in several community surveys (see Gaitz, 1977; Lowenthal & Berkman, 1967) the *majority* of elderly respondents reported symptoms of depression. Prevalence of clinically diagnosed depression in the elderly has been variously estimated at between 2 and 6% (Gurland, 1976); however, in surveys of psychiatrically hospitalized elderly and those seeking outpatient psychiatric treatment, depression is diagnosed 40-50% of the time as the primary problem (Pfeiffer, 1977). It is thus regarded as the most common functional disorder in this age group (Butler & Lewis, 1977).

Despite the fact that depression is a frequent problem for older adults, its treatment has received little attention in the literature. In fact, there are only a few scattered reports on the results of psychotherapy completed specifically with elderly depressives, and these have primarily been case studies, or studies on institutional samples (these will be reviewed subsequently). Far more common in the literature are descriptive studies that use samples with mixed diagnoses. Eisdorfer and Stotsky (1977), Gottesman, Quarterman, and Cohn (1973), and Rechtschaffen (1959) have reviewed such studies and their findings are encouraging. Apparently many forms of counseling and/or psychotherapy practiced with the elderly have been perceived as beneficial, and at least short-term gains in psychological functioning have been associated with most of the interventions reviewed. However, as pointed out earlier, these studies have tended to be case reports describing general positive benefit from "treatment." Little attempt has been made to date to specify diagnostic status, techniques utilized, or levels of therapist skill. Therefore, general conclusions are premature as to the efficacy of psychotherapy with older adults having a variety of diagnoses. These conclusions rest largely on descriptive data and not on well-controlled experimental studies. The field needs more careful, controlled experimental research, so that information can systematically be collected to shed light on this issue.

The present study attempts to address this problem. It carefully evaluates the effectiveness of behavioral and supportive group psychotherapies, and it suggests a number of issues to be considered in future research with elderly depressed individuals. Before discussing the rationale and specific questions addressed, it would be helpful to review briefly several areas of prior research: (a) behavior therapy with younger depressed persons; (b) behavior therapy with the elderly; (c) effectiveness of a variety of group therapies; and (d) relationship factors and treatment outcome.

Behavior Therapy with Younger Depressed Persons

There is a fairly extensive amount of literature on the effectiveness of behavioral interventions for short-term treatment of depression in adults under the age of 50, developed primarily by Lewinsohn and his colleagues at the University of Oregon. Lewinsohn worked within an extinction model that views depression as the result of an interruption in positive reinforcement received by the individual. This means that a large number of behaviors in the person's repertoire, notably those involved in social interaction, are on an extinction schedule. More specifically, Lewinsohn's model is based on three hypotheses (Lewinsohn, 1974):

1. A low rate of response-contingent positive reinforcement functions as a discriminative stimulus for certain depressive behaviors, such as sad affect and fatigue.
2. This minimal reinforcement is responsible for the low rate of behavior that results from the person being on extinction.
3. The total amount of response-contingent positive reinforcement received by a person is a joint function of three factors: (a) the number of activities and events that are reinforcing, (b) their availability in the environment, and (c) the person's ability to obtain these reinforcers, i.e., his or her skill in emitting the behaviors that will elicit a positive response.

Lewinsohn's major research findings can be summarized as follows:

1. There is a significant relationship between mood and the number and kinds of pleasant activities engaged in (Lewinsohn & Graf, 1973; Lewinsohn & Libet, 1972).
2. Depressed individuals find fewer activities pleasant, engage in pleasant activities less frequently, and therefore obtain less positive reinforcement than either normals or individuals with other psychiatric problems (MacPhillamy & Lewinsohn, 1974).
3. Depressed persons exhibit less skill socially and thus elicit less positive reinforcement from others (Libet & Lewinsohn, 1973; Shaffer & Lewinsohn, Note 2). For example, Libet and Lewinsohn (1973) found that in small group interactions, depressed subjects elicited fewer responses from others, emitted fewer positive reactions, and evidenced a longer latency of response to others' behaviors.

Thus, in general, these findings have been consistent with the assumptions of the model. Blaney (1977) recently reviewed the data supporting the model and found them basically correlational, so that the relevance of these factors in the causation of depression is unclear. Work by other researchers (notably Coyne, 1976, and Prkachin, Craig, Papageorgis, & Reith, 1977) tends to support the idea of a social skills deficit in depressives' behavior; however, a study by Hammen and Glass (1975) on moderately depressed college students failed to find the predicted effect that increase in frequency of pleasant activities would result in reduction of depression.

Several studies have shown that modules on social skills, pleasant activities, and cognitive modification all lead to improvement of depression in younger individuals (e.g., Lewinsohn, Weinstein, & Alper, 1970; Lewinsohn, Weinstein, & Shaw, 1969; Munoz, 1977; Robinson & Lewinsohn, 1973; Youngren, 1977; Zeiss, 1977). Comparative outcome studies with depressed clients using one or the other of these modules have found them beneficial, although not necessarily superior to other techniques (Campbell, 1974; Padfield, 1976; Shaw, 1977; Taylor & Marshall, 1977).

The above studies of the efficacy of behavioral therapy with younger depressed samples suggest that it is as effective as cognitive and nondirective therapy, though it may not be superior to them; further, specific focus on pleasant events or social skills does not seem to create differential impact on reduction of depression.

The present study was based on Lewinsohn's model, rather than the cognitive-behavioral model of Beck (1967, 1976), the learned helplessness model of Seligman (1974, 1975), or Rehm's self-control model (1977), because of our interest in specifying the roles of activity levels and social skills in depression among the elderly. The other models noted emphasize the centrality of cognitive factors to the depressive syndrome. They contend that depression is secondary to a dysfunctional interpretation of reality and emphasize various disorders of thinking that seem salient. For example, Beck (1967, 1976) describes several faulty cognitive mechanisms that typify the thinking of depressives, such as overgeneralization and magnification. Seligman (1974, 1975) argues that depression occurs when an individual perceives a lack of control over obtaining rewards or punishments from the environment. Rehm (1977) views depression in terms of dysfunctional self-control processes, including such factors as infrequent self-rewards and frequent self-punishments. The interested reader is referred to the primary sources cited for a more comprehensive exposition of each of these cognitively oriented systems; for our purposes, it is sufficient to note that these models of depression emphasize the contribution of more "internal" processes to the origin of this disorder, in contrast to Lewinsohn's focus on external, observable behaviors. Future research will, no doubt, shed more light on how these perspectives can interact and mutually contribute to the improved understanding and relief of affective distress.

Behavior Therapy with the Elderly

Most controlled behaviorally oriented studies with the elderly have been done with institutionalized samples. Richards and Thorpe (1978) recently reviewed this literature and reported a number of studies that have successfully used operant procedures to modify a variety of target behaviors in their samples (e.g., walking, eating, or prosocial activity). Berger and Rose (1977) were the first to attempt to modify more complex social interaction patterns in nursing home residents. They developed a brief individualized social skills training program and reported moderate success. However, in these studies, diagnostic classifications are typically mixed and the sample may include persons with serious cognitive impairment who would not be expected to respond as well as older persons with normal cognitive functioning.

Many clinical gerontologists have argued for the utility of behavioral interventions with noninstitutionalized elderly clients. Rebok and Hoyer (1977), for example, suggest that behavioral approaches offer a way to evaluate the adaptability of the elderly individual, since they assume that any human behavior can be modified through learning. Knight (1979) concurs with this in his review and encourages thoughtful clinical experimentation to actualize the promise of behavioral approaches for a variety of common problems in older adults (e.g., anxiety and depression). Cautela and Mansfield (1977) suggest that the whole range of techniques developed by behavioral therapists could be used with aged clients, including: relaxation training, desensitization, assertiveness training, thought stopping, and operant techniques.

Several recent papers reviewed in Richards and Thorpe (1978) suggest that behavior modification techniques can be appropriately used to treat affective disorders of the elderly, although they are not typically used. The closest application of behavior therapy to depression in older outpatients can be found in two case studies, Flannery (1974) and Gauthier and Marshall (1977), in which individuals experiencing grief reactions were effectively treated using behavioral contracting and extensive social reinforcement. It appears that behavioral interventions with elderly depressed persons may be promising, although their effectiveness has not been studied in a controlled manner.

Effectiveness of a Variety of Group Therapies

Bednar and Kaul (1978) reviewed the literature on outpatient group therapy and concluded that here also controlled studies are few, regardless of the age of the client population of interest. The many case reports they reviewed do indicate that participation in group therapy can be beneficial; however, firm conclusions as to its efficacy are premature. Samples need to be more clearly delineated, techniques specified, and controlled studies done before conclusions can be drawn as to when group psychotherapy (of any type) can be considered effective.

All of the preceding clearly applies to group work with the elderly, where case reports predominate. Larson (1970), for example, reported beneficial effects for an outpatient group of persons in their 70s that met for 4 years. Liederman, Green, and Liederman (1967), working with persons who were apparently both organically impaired and depressed, reported reduction in somatic complaints, increased socialization, and lack of significant deterioration over time. Berger and Berger (1973) obtained similar findings in what they called a "holistic group approach."

Recently, several analogue studies have appeared in the literature (e.g., Haber, Murphy, & Taylor, 1977; Ingersoll & Silverman, 1978) in which short-term group counseling methods were compared for their ability to improve self-esteem. Both studies were done on nonclinical samples of older persons; they each reported little statistical evidence of change as a result of the interventions. However, descriptive data obtained from participants suggested improvement, regardless of the type of intervention. These authors concluded that group therapy has value for the aged, but specific methods used may be inappropriate for certain clients. For example, clients with hearing impairment seem less able to benefit from group-oriented techniques. Both studies also point to the lack of clarity as to what factors are really responsible for improvement. This may be partially due to the fact that no diagnostic homogeneity was attempted, nor were standard psychotherapeutic methods employed. It is also possible that self-esteem would be increased by participating in an experience in which a positive helping relationship occurred; in fact, many clinicians who practice group therapy from a variety of theoretical perspectives argue that it is precisely the quality of the relationship formed that affects outcome.

Behavioral group psychotherapists, in contrast, emphasize the importance of utilizing both a problem-solving approach and specific techniques to facilitate change. They argue that relationship factors are insufficient in themselves to create positive change; new learning must occur in order for change to occur. Although behaviorally oriented group therapy has not been applied to the problems of older persons, its potential usefulness should be evident. We have already noted that older persons respond well to individually applied behavioral therapy, as well as to supportive group therapies; therefore, there is reason to assume that presenting behavioral techniques in a group format would provide a therapeutic experience.

Relationship Factors and Treatment Outcome

A number of studies on psychotherapy have called attention to conceptual and methodological difficulties inherent in doing good outcome research. Adequate justice cannot be done to all these issues here; rather, we will review some basic conclusions. First, it is difficult to demonstrate significant differences between two or more types of psychotherapy statistically. For the most part, well-designed outcome studies have not shown significant differences due to the therapeutic method used. Luborsky, Singer, and Luborsky (1975) carefully reviewed 124 outcome studies, including both individual and group modalities, and found that when two or more treatments were compared, the proportions of clients who benefited were roughly equivalent. This result was also noted in a subgroup of 19 studies that contrasted behavioral therapies with psychotherapy; in 13 cases, ties occurred in terms of outcome.

Second, it may be that failure to find greater differences between specific types of psychotherapy occurs because treatments are not potent enough to produce a significant advantage over the beneficial forces generated by nonspecific factors (Frank, 1961, 1979). This kind of finding has a long clinical tradition, beginning with the work of Frank (1961) on the role of influence, faith, hope, and persuasion in accounting for change in psychotherapy. Frank (1979) discussed how such nonspecific factors as reliance on the therapist as an expert who will relieve distress might be facilitative of change in themselves, regardless of what particular strategy of psychotherapy is used.

A well-designed comparative study of the differential effects of psychotherapy and behavior therapy conducted by Sloane, Staples, Cristol, Yorkston, and Whipple (1975) clearly illustrates this point. Similar findings were obtained in both conditions, as compared to a waiting list control. Experienced therapists were used, multimodal assessment of outcome occurred, and the sample size was large enough to permit statistical sensitivity to change. These kinds of findings led Bergin and Lambert (1978) to conclude that the interpersonal relationship between therapist and client is a crucial determinant of change, and to state: "This is not to say that techniques are irrelevant but that their power for change pales when compared with that of personal influence" (p. 180). This suggests the tremendous importance of the therapeutic relationship, whose study should not be dismissed as merely reflective of nonspecific or placebo effects; it may be the relationship that is the active ingredient, so its components must be carefully studied, specified, and measured.

The tradition of client-centered psychotherapy provides a backdrop for specification and measurement of these factors. According to Rogers (1951, 1967), clients grow and change if a relationship can be established in which the client experiences acceptance and understanding. It is the therapist's responsibility to create an atmosphere marked by accurate empathy, genuineness or congruence, and warm positive regard. Rogers believes that these are necessary conditions for the possibility of change. Client-centered therapy has also provided methods to measure these therapist variables. A number of outpatient studies that reported adequate levels of therapist nonspecific factors (using both individual and group formats) have been reviewed by Truax and Mitchell (1971), leading to their conclusion that "therapists who are accurately empathic, nonpossessively warm in attitude, and genuine, are indeed effective" (p. 310). Unfortunately, these variables have not been manipulated in controlled studies, so that their independent contribution to outcome has not yet been determined.

Marshall (1977) reviewed problems with scaling and measurement of these variables and found that their reliabilities were highly variable. Carefully done studies using the Truax and Carkhuff scales to measure therapist factors found that client self-exploration was related to therapist empathy and congruence; also, clients who did more self-exploration were more successful. With regard to individual therapy, Marshall (1977) concluded that there is "limited but promising evidence that genuineness and accurate empathy may influence individual therapy with schizophrenics" (p. 57). However, regarding group therapy, Marshall concludes that the data are incomplete, and further research is required to determine the relationship between therapist factors and outcome in the group situation.

In order to show, as clearly as possible, any differences in results between the use of behavioral group therapy as opposed to the more traditional supportive group approach, this study focused on the relationship factors noted. The decision was made to develop two therapeutic conditions with similar optimal levels of the nonspecific factors discussed. One would operate primarily as a supportive psychotherapy experience, using minimal therapist directiveness and minimal structure. The relationship variables would become the primary agents of change. The other would be a more structured behavioral group, using a problem-solving approach and specific methods for change. This would allow comparison between a treatment that made systematic use of behavioral principles and techniques and one that did not, while also permitting comparison between therapists' levels on relationship factors across the two treatment conditions. If therapist relationship factors were found to be essentially similar across conditions, then any significantly greater change observed in behavioral group therapy participants could be more confidently attributed to the behavioral approach per se, and not to the common relationship factors present in both group therapies.

RATIONALE AND RESEARCH QUESTIONS

These various bodies of literature, taken together, suggest that elderly persons may benefit from outpatient psychological treatment in general and, more specifically, from behavioral group-oriented approaches. Behavioral group therapy for elderly depressives seems particularly appropriate in light of the fact that deficient social skills and reduction in pleasant activities tend to be common in this age group. Positive reinforcement may also be diminished due to the numerous losses that accompany aging for most persons (e.g., spouse, job, physical integrity). According to several theories in social gerontology (Cumming & Henry, 1961; Kuypers & Bengston, 1973), self-esteem diminishes as older individuals are removed from many roles that have been critical to the maintenance of positive self-evaluation; this may in turn lead to atrophy of the very social skills necessary to obtain rewards from the social system. Therefore, behavioral group therapy was selected as the primary treatment of interest, and a supportive group condition was selected to control for relationship factors known to influence outcome across a variety of psychotherapeutic approaches (Parloff, Waskow, & Wolfe, 1978).

The present research was designed to address three questions pertinent to the study of psychotherapy with the elderly. First, would elderly outpatients with moderate to severe depression be capable of change over time as a result of outpatient psychological treatment? It was hypothesized that most persons would show improvement (rather than stability or deterioration) on the specific battery of outcome measures utilized. Second, would depressed subjects in behavioral group treatment show greater improvement over time than those who participated in the supportive group experience? It was hypothesized that differential treatment effects would occur on self-report measures of depression and specific behaviors such as assertiveness, as well as on observer ratings of in-group verbal interaction and interpersonal style, with greater improvement in the behavioral condition. Third, what is the contribution of various individual difference variables (e.g., health status and cognitive functioning) to change over time? Exploration of these variables was expected to provide information as to which form of treatment was superior for subjects with given characteristics at the start of treatment.

METHOD

Subjects

Selection. The sample was drawn from a clinical population of elderly depressed individuals applying for service at the Psychosocial Clinic for Persons over 65 at the Neuropsychiatric Institute of the University of California at Los Angeles (NPI). Subjects were selected according to several criteria: (a) assessment by an independent evaluator that depression was in fact the chief complaint, (b) attainment of a significantly elevated score on a self-report depression measure, (c) absence of major organic impairments, and (d) recommendation by the clinic team that group psychotherapy would be an appropriate treatment modality.

Client flow was increased prior to the start of this study by several newspaper feature articles describing the clinic's activities in general. Interested persons called in for an intake appointment (usually conducted by someone other than this investigator). At that time the presenting problem was assessed by means of a standard clinical interview and, if depression was the major issue, then the Mental Status Questionnaire (Kahn, Goldfarb, Pollack, & Peck, 1960) and Face-Hand Test (Fink, Green, & Bender, 1952) were administered to rule out organic pathology. The MMPI Depression Scale (D) (Hathaway & McKinley, 1967) was also completed by subjects to index the severity of their depression. Only those subjects whose D-scale scores were at least 2 standard deviations above the mean were considered for inclusion in this study. This cutoff has been used as a criterion in a number of other outpatient studies of depression (e.g., Lewinsohn, Biglan, & Zeiss, 1976).

All subjects who met the criteria up to this point were then reviewed at the weekly clinic multidisciplinary team meeting to discuss appropriate treatment assignment. If group psychotherapy was judged likely to be beneficial for the particular client, then an additional screening appointment was scheduled with the investigator. At this time, the study was outlined and written informed consent was obtained. Subjects were also given the packet of pretest measures to complete and return prior to the first therapy session. All subjects were registered as outpatients of the NPI. Complete medical records were maintained on them in the same manner as other outpatients. The Psychosocial Clinic team psychiatrist assumed medical responsibility and was available for emergency consultation and medication evaluation throughout this project.

Twenty-eight clients were accepted for inclusion in this study; of these, five dropped out prior to completion, so that the total N was 23. Three others were randomly dropped to provide equal cell size for statistical analysis.

Sample characteristics. Salient characteristics of the sample are described in Table 9.1. It is apparent that this was a fairly intelligent, healthy, somewhat well-educated group of older individuals who reported psychological distress along a number of convergent dimensions and who were motivated to seek psychiatric help for their problems. They were reliable in attendance; fewer than two absences (out of the total 10 sessions) occurred for each member. These clients were highly motivated for treatment and cooperative in completing a variety of paper-and-pencil measures at the three evaluation intervals. Seven of the 20 continued in additional psychotherapy following completion of the follow-up period (four from the supportive groups and three from the behavioral groups).

Table 9.1
Sample Characteristics: Demographic Data and Primary Depression Measures

	Age	Education	Sex M	Sex F	Vocabulary[a]	Health Status[b]	Mean MMPI D-scale Score	Mean Zung SDS Score	Mean BDI Score
Behavioral									
Therapist 1	67.8	11.2	3	2	37.0	2.2	76.2	61.2	20.4
Therapist 2	68.8	13.6	2	3	45.2	2.4	84.4	60.8	23.6
Supportive									
Therapist 1	68.0	12.4	2	3	46.2	2.2	80.2	61.4	18.4
Therapist 2	66.0	13.8	2	3	48.0	2.0	78.4	60.4	20.0

[a] The vocabulary subtest was taken from the Primary Mental Abilities Test (PMA) (Thurstone & Thurstone, 1948).

[b] Health Status is the subject's self-rating of physical health on a 1–4 scale where 1 = "I feel well most of the time" and 4 = "I am doing poorly most of the time and usually don't feel well."

Measures

Six distinct sets of measures were obtained in this study. These can be summarized as follows: participants gave self-ratings of depression and various interpersonal events; observers rated therapists' effectiveness as well as clients' verbal interaction patterns and interpersonal style; and clients gave interview data on treatment change. Each of the measures used in these sets will be reviewed briefly.

Self-ratings of depression. Clients were given six different measures to assess severity of depression: the MMPI Depression Scale (D), Zung Self-Rating Depression Scale (SDS) (Zung, 1965), Beck Depression Inventory (BDI) (Beck, Ward, Mendelson, Mock, & Erbaugh, 1961), depression scale of the Hopkins Symptom Checklist (SCL-90) (Derogatis, Lipman, & Covi, 1973), Dysfunctional Attitude Scale (Weissman & Beck, Note 3), and Cognitive Distortion Vignette series (Gallagher & Thompson, Note 4).

The D scale of the MMPI is a 60-item multidimensional true-false measure that taps a variety of common symptoms of depression, such as low self-esteem, negative affect, and somatic complaints including sleep and appetite problems. The Zung SDS is a 20-item multidimensional scale widely used to measure depression in the elderly (McNair, 1979), despite the fact that its reliability is not fully adequate in the older age ranges (Gallagher, McGarvey, Zelinski, & Thompson, Note 5). The Beck Depression Inventory (BDI) is a similar 21-item multidimensional scale; in contrast, the depression scale of the SCL-90 contains nine items that primarily evaluate depression as a mood disorder (e.g., feeling lonely, blue, or helpless). Both the Dysfunctional Attitude Scale (DAS) and Cognitive Distortion Vignettes (CDV) were included to explore the role of distorted cognitions in maintenance of depression. High scores on the DAS reflect very negative attitudes toward oneself, and frequent depressed/distorted responses to the vignettes are likely to be related to high levels of depression. The CDV's were developed from the work of Hammen and Krantz (1976), who found that depressed college students more frequently selected depressed, distorted responses on a similar measure.

Research has not been reported on the use of the BDI, SCL-90, or CDV with elderly depressives, so these were included to explore their utility with this population. The D scale, Zung SDS, and SCL-90 are converted to standardized scores. The BDI, DAS, and CDV scores are simply totaled. For all six measures, higher scores mean greater depression and lower scores signify improvement.

Self-ratings of interpersonal behaviors. Clients completed the 63-item Interpersonal Events Schedule (IES) designed by Youngren, Zeiss, and Lewinsohn (Note 6). This scale contains statements about various interpersonal behaviors, like talking with a friend; each is rated for frequency and enjoyability. There are five rationally derived subscales: Social Activity, Give

Positive, Assertion, Receive Positive, and Interpersonal Cognitions. Mean rate, impact, and cross-product scores are assumed to provide an approximate measure of response-contingent positive reinforcement obtained during the interval rated. This scale has been found to be sensitive to change in depression status over time with younger persons (Youngren & Lewinsohn, Note 7), but it had not been used previously with elderly persons.

Observer ratings: Therapist effectiveness. Therapists were rated on four dimensions that reflect the "nonspecific" factors hypothesized to be present in effective psychotherapy. These dimensions were: accurate empathy, congruence, directive competence, and enthusiasm. *Accurate empathy* refers to the therapist's ability to communicate an accurate understanding of the client's feelings; optimally, the therapist is "tuned in" to the client's wavelength and encourages him to explore previously unexplored material (Truax, 1967). *Congruence* (or genuineness) refers to the therapist's communication of his true responses to the client; optimally, the therapist responds spontaneously and employs his own genuine responses in a constructive manner (Kiesler, 1967). *Directive competence* is a construct developed to measure the therapist's flexible goal orientation or sense of what needs to be accomplished throughout the session. *Enthusiasm* refers to the therapist's energy level, involvement, and interest in the interaction. The latter two constructs were developed in pilot work prior to this study. They appeared relevant to effectiveness in other outpatient groups for the elderly that were observed and rated during the pilot phase. All four factors were rated on 5-point scales; for each, level 3 was considered the anchor point, or minimally acceptable level, necessary for effective therapist functioning.

In addition, to measure the extent to which therapists were following the specific treatment protocols, observers counted such behaviors as: clarifications, statements of approval or support, suggestions, and specific instructions. This count provided a "manipulation check" on the procedures and verified that, in fact, the two treatment conditions could be distinguished from each other.

Clients also rated their therapist at the conclusion of treatment on the Barrett-Lennard Relationship Inventory (Barrett-Lennard, 1963), which assesses factors similar to those the observers were rating. This 92-item questionnaire contains statements such as: "He understands my words but not the way I feel." There are five subscales: empathy, congruence, regard, warmth, and willingness to be known. Scores for each subscale were compared across treatments to determine whether there were significant differences between the two therapists on any of these dimensions.

Observer ratings: Client verbal interaction patterns. This was done using the verbal interaction coding schema of Lewinsohn, Munoz, Youngren, Zeiss, & Talkington (Note 8). However, rather than coding verbalizations in terms of "action" and "reaction" as Lewinsohn did (because of his interest in cross-diagnostic comparisons), the focus here was on the quality of interaction as being "positive" or "negative." Lewinsohn's descriptive categories were maintained (e.g., psychological complaint, somatic complaint, criticism, praise, self-approval, agreement with others, etc.). Ratings were obtained in a time-sampling procedure on half of the total number of sessions for each of the four groups. Proportions of subjects' positive and negative verbalizations were compared across groups. All subjects were coded by number and prepared coding sheets were used to facilitate accuracy in record keeping.

Observer ratings: Client interpersonal style. Youngren and Lewinsohn (Note 7) found that interpersonal style was problematic in depressives, yet sensitive to improvement in clinical status. Style was rated using their 21 suggested descriptive adjectives, evaluated on 7-point scales from "extremely characteristic" to "not at all characteristic." Fifteen adjectives reflected social skills like "interested in what others say" and six reflected cognitive skills like "has positive outlook." These same adjectives can be classified as reflecting "positive" as compared to "negative" attributes. Both types of classification were used in data analyses.

Patient interview data. At both postassessment and follow-up, participants were asked a series of questions designed to obtain their perception of change in several specific areas. They were asked, for example, if the group helped; if there had been any change since therapy began; if feelings of depression and life satisfaction had changed; and if there were any changes in activities, interpersonal skill, and overall level of functioning. Responses were compared between the two treatment conditions to evaluate any differential perceptions of change.

Procedure

Assignment of subjects to groups. Once subjects were screened, they were randomly assigned to one of the two treatment conditions: behavioral or supportive group psychotherapy. An effort was made to maintain a comparable male-female ratio in each group. The four treatment groups initially consisted of seven clients each. The five persons who dropped out (two males and three females) did so for a variety of reasons including: inability to commit to the schedule, mild organic impairment, hospitalization, and inability to adapt to the group format. Three dropouts were in the supportive condition.

Therapists. Groups were conducted by two experienced therapists who led one group in each condition. They were selected out of a pool of 30 NPI staff interested in the treatment of age-related depression. Both were males over the age of 40; they had been practicing clinical psychologists for over 10 years, described themselves as competent to lead both types of groups, and had the requisite time available to complete the project.

Schedule. Two treatment groups were run in each condition. Each condition consisted of 10 sessions of 1½ hours' duration, held twice weekly for 5 weeks. Posttesting consisted of readministration of the same self-report measures used in the pretesting with an additional interview conducted by independent observers to obtain clients' evaluation of the therapy experience. At that time, each client's case was reviewed to determine if additional treatment was required. These subjects then went through a 5-week no-treatment follow-up period, after which they were given the same measures and interview for the final assessment.

Treatment. Behavioral treatment followed the structure outlined in two therapy manuals (developed by Lewinsohn and his associates and excerpted with permission) which aimed to improve social skills and increase the frequency of engagement in pleasant activities. These manuals were integrated to provide a strong sequence of social learning opportunities for these clients; this sequence resulted in development of a specific treatment manual for this project. Its final version was reviewed in detail with each therapist before the groups began. This insured maximum familiarity with the model and elicited cooperation in following the structure, within the limits of clinical exigencies.

In the first four sessions, extensive use was made of role-playing and modeling to teach listening skills and to focus on each client's social stimulus value. Group feedback was used to sensitize each individual as to how he was coming across to others in the group in terms of ability to elicit positive reinforcement. From the beginning, individualized homework assignments were made to encourage practice of skills in everyday life situations whenever possible.

Sessions 5 and 6 focused on monitoring the level of pleasant activities currently engaged in, and identifying obstacles to greater activity and/or enjoyment. Realistic obstacles (e.g., decreased mobility due to poor health or transportation problems) necessarily place some limits on older individuals; therefore, clients had to be helped to specify carefully changes they were really capable of carrying out (however small they might have been). The aim was to get across the notion that greater participation in pleasurable activities would assist in reducing depression. As clients learned this from experience, they became more motivated to continue the trend, at least during treatment.

Session 7 introduced the concept that personal effectiveness training (emphasizing appropriate assertive responses) could help to increase both one's social reinforcement value and one's activity level. For example, many depressed older persons fear rejection if they express themselves (particularly to their adult children) and can be quite timid about articulating their emotional and social needs, thereby setting themselves up for continued dysphoria. One 75-year-old female client was estranged from her family because of this but, through role-playing and learning some basic assertion techniques, was able to reestablish satisfying relationships.

Sessions 8 and 9 continued the themes of personal effectiveness: how to increase pleasant activities and how to evaluate one's impact on others. Group members also continued to do homework assignments agreed upon in sessions. The last appointment was viewed as a wrap-up session to review behavioral principles, assess progress, and encourage development of individual plans for continued improvement.

In contrast, supportive treatment was quite unstructured; plans for what to cover were not established in advance, therapists did not emphasize learning skills to modify depression, and no specific homework assignments were made. In fact, because of the very nature of a nondirective, supportive approach, it was not possible to give a session-by-session outline to follow, as in the behavioral condition. Such detailed structure would have violated the assumptions of the model, in that the therapeutic facilitative conditions occured partially in response to the material provided then and there by the clients. Treatment intervention centered on helping clients to clarify their statements about their feelings and what influenced their moods, to express their feelings, and to develop an atmosphere of group support. General goals were developed (e.g., to facilitate personal growth and increased self-understanding). The only therapist structuring was a specific attempt to have every client talk in each session.

Both of these treatment modalities were adapted for use in a group format, and some modifications were made on the basis of the investigator's prior clinical experience with an elderly depressive population. For example, therapists indicated early on that *all* persons would have an opportunity to talk and that, if discussion occured that seemed to wander off the topic at hand, the therapist would interrupt and refocus. Other ground rules, such as how to handle between-session phone calls, were dealt with by group decision-making. For example, it was agreed that phone calls to obtain extra counseling time from therapists were inappropriate; whatever needed to be discussed would be "held" for the actual group meeting.

In the behavioral treatments, therapists periodically sought consultation from other experts on mental health and aging when they needed clarification on how to present didactic material or skills training techniques in ways to enhance learning for the older individual. For example, a multimodal presentation of the behavioral rationale for depression helped a great deal to facilitate comprehension and cooperation. Blackboards and specific written materials were used to reinforce therapists' points, and frequent references to outside readings were made so as to demystify the experience of depression.

Finally, the therapists requested periodic support from other project staff because rates of change seemed slower to them than when working with younger depressives. In some instances, their expectations had to be lowered and smaller increments recognized as signs of improvement. The opportunity for the staff to discuss *their* feelings about these groups seemed extremely beneficial in their maintaining appropriate optimism and energy levels in subsequent sessions.

Observers. Two undergraduate students were recruited, trained, and paid to rate various aspects of therapist and client in-group behaviors (as previously outlined). Training consisted of 5 hours of didactic orientation to the measures, followed by 15 additional hours of actual practice observing and coding several outpatient groups at NPI. Raters were trained to a mean level of 80% accuracy on each dimension rated, as computed by item-for-item agreement with predetermined criteria. They remained blind to the hypotheses throughout this project.

RESULTS

Therapist Differences

Mean observer ratings on the four nonspecific therapist factors are shown in Table 9.2. Overall means that summarize observations of both raters on each factor are reported; factors were sampled twice per session and then collapsed over the five sessions observed for each group. Computation of interrater reliability yielded a Spearman rank order correlation coefficient of $r = .63$ ($p < .01$). Wilcoxon signed-rank tests (Siegel, 1956) were completed on the observer ratings to determine if each therapist was rated significantly differently when he carried out each of the two treatments. Mann-Whitney U tests (Siegel, 1956) were also done to further compare the two therapists with each other. The results indicate that the two therapists were perceived both as consistent across conditions and as similar to each other within conditions.

Clients' perceptions of similar therapist factors were measured by scale scores on the Barrett-Lennard Relationship Inventory (Barrett-Lennard, 1963). Separate two-factor analyses of variance on each of the five dimensions measured by this scale found no significant differences by therapist or condition, and no significant Therapist × Treatment interactions.

Taken together, these data support the position that any treatment differences present in this sample can be attributed to the treatment manipulations themselves, rather than to differences between the individual therapists. The data were then collapsed across the therapist factor in subsequent analyses.

Table 9.2
Mean Observer Ratings of Therapists on Nonspecific Factors
During Behavioral and Supportive Therapy[a,b]

Factor	Therapist 1		Therapist 2	
	Behavioral	*Supportive*	*Behavioral*	*Supportive*
Empathy	2.96	3.12	3.06	2.90
Congruence	3.36	3.30	3.32	3.02
Enthusiasm	3.26	2.84	2.96	2.96
Directive Competence	3.66	3.22	3.30	3.30

[a]Therapists were rated during five sessions in each condition by two trained observers, blind to experimental conditions and hypotheses.

[b]No comparisons were statistically significant.

Self-Report Measures of Depression and Interpersonal Events, and Observer Ratings of Interpersonal Style

These three data sets were analyzed by separate repeated-measures multivariate analyses of variance (MANOVA) tests, and these sets are reported in Table 9.3. The "depression set" includes scores from all six depression measures utilized; the "interpersonal events set" includes the total crossproduct score and cross-product scores for each of the five IES subscales; the "interpersonal style set" contains mean observer ratings on the four dimensions of style described earlier. The MANOVA statistical procedure yields a multivariate or maximized F obtained for a linear combination of the dependent variable set, as well as a univariate F for each measure separately. It was used because it is the preferred method of analysis when dependent measures are correlated with each other, which is clearly the case with these data. Computing serial F tests on such measures raises the alpha level considerably and can lead to spurious rejections of null hypotheses (McCall & Appelbaum, 1973).

Changes in pre to post and pre to follow-up depression measures were highly significant using MANOVA ($p < .001$ for both). This indicates that a reliable decline in depression over time occurred by the end of treatment and continued through the follow-up period. However, there were no significant main effects for Group and no significant Group X Time interactions. This same pattern is observed in analyzing the univariate F tests; five of the six were significant but no main Group effect or interaction occurred for any of the set.

Table 9.3

Repeated-Measures Multivariate Analyses of Variance on Self-Report Measures of Depression and Interpersonal Events, and Observer Ratings of Interpersonal Style

	F for Group Main Effect	F Pre-Post Linear Trend	F Pre to Follow-up Linear Trend	F: Group × Time (Pre-Post) Interaction	F: Group × Time (Pre to Follow-up) Interaction
Multivariate F:					
Depression Set	.140	8.22***	14.48***	.30	.34
Univariate F's (1, 18 df):					
D Scale	.421	42.99****	54.41****	.23	.03
Zung	.003	14.30****	15.06****	.01	.75
Beck BDI	.132	17.80****	30.23****	.82	.27
Vignettes (D-D)	.086	2.90	4.20	1.38	.19
DAS	.209	21.90****	7.77**	.05	.002
SCL–90 Depression	.191	11.84**	14.43***	.97	.04
Multivariate F:					
Interpersonal Events Set (Frequency × Enjoyability)	1.258	6.52**	.49	.29	.42

Univariate *F*'s (1, 18 df):					
Social Activity	.00	34.19***	.18	.19	.07
Give Positive	1.26	.03	.13	.89	.01
Assertion	.577	1.24	.63	.10	.03
Receive Positive	1.30	1.23	.00	.49	1.04
Interpersonal Cognitions	3.69	1.35	1.64	.38	.75
Multivariate *F*:					
Interpersonal Style Set	3.22*	3.47*	NA	.54	Not administered at follow-up
Univariate *F*'s (1, 18 df):					
Social Skills	1.37	5.22*	NA	.43	
Cognitive Skills	.014	.98	NA	.003	
Positive Attitude	.617	1.29	NA	.057	
Negative Attitude	.064	.66	NA	.003	

*p < .05
**p < .01
***p < .001

Figure 9.1 graphically presents change in the three major depression measures (BDI, Zung SDS, and D scale) for the two treatment groups over time. It is clear that significant change occurred in the predicted direction of less reported symptom distress, and that the degree of change is not significantly different in the two groups over time.

For the interpersonal events set, Table 9.3 shows a significant pre to post linear trend ($p < .01$), but this was not apparent in the pre to follow-up comparison. No significant main effect for Group and no Group × Time interaction occurred. On the univariate F's in this set, only one of the five subscales showed a significant change by the end of treatment. This was the computed amount of positive reinforcement obtained from Social Activity ($p < .001$).

Observer ratings of interpersonal style (85% agreement between raters) yielded a main effect for Group ($p < .05$). Inspection of these means indicated that the behavioral group subjects scored higher (i.e., adjectives used to describe positive interpersonal behavior were perceived as more characteristic of the behavioral subjects). Although there was also a significant main effect for Time (pretest-posttest), there was no significant Group × Time interaction. Therefore, it cannot be concluded that behavioral subjects changed to a significantly greater degree. Only one univariate in this set, social skills, showed significant pretest-posttest change, and this was not differentially affected by group membership. Observer ratings were not obtained at follow-up.

In summary, both Table 9.3 and Figure 9.1 indicate that self-reports of depression were significantly reduced at posttest and 5-weeks' follow-up evaluation for all subjects. The entire sample also showed a significant improvement on the Interpersonal Events Schedule, with the major change located in the Social Activity subscale. Subjects' interpersonal style improved over time, with social skills showing most significant gain. However, none of the Group × Time interactions were significant, indicating that subjects in both conditions showed similar patterns of change with treatment.

Observer Ratings of Verbal Interaction

As noted earlier, five therapy sessions were observed and rated for each of the four treatment groups. Interrater reliability here was also $r = .63$ ($p < .01$). Lewinsohn's schema for coding the "positive" and "negative" interaction patterns of each group member was used. Each subject's mean proportion of positive responses was calculated (relative to her total number of responses per session). These data were then combined across subjects within each of the treatment conditions. A BMDP repeated measures univariate analysis of variance was done for the five times of measurement, using Group Membership as the independent variable. A significant main

Figure 9.1. Mean scores on BDI, Zung SDS, and MMPI D scale
before, immediately after, and 5 weeks following treatment
for behavioral and supportive group therapy participants.

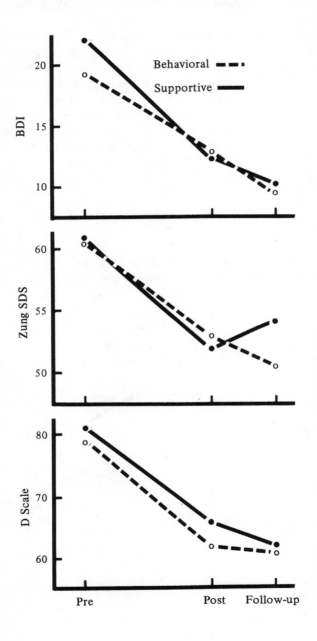

effect for Group (F (1, 18) = 4.53, p <.047), and a significant Group X Linear Trend interaction (F (1, 18) = 8.42, p <.01) was found.

Inspection of Figure 9.2 shows that the proportion of positive responses in both behavioral groups increased over the five sessions observed, while positive responses in the two supportive groups leveled off early and maintained that level for the duration of treatment.

It is apparent that by the final session, positive verbal interaction between members occurred approximately 56% of the time in both behavioral groups, compared to about 40% in the supportive groups. Thus, elderly depressed clients who participated in the structured behavioral intervention program were significantly more likely to give and receive positive feedback, to assert themselves appropriately, to emit fewer psychological and somatic complaints, and to respond in a noncritical manner to the problems of others. In contrast, those in supportive group psychotherapy averaged these kinds of responses to a significantly lower degree per session and did not show significant change over time on these variables.

Figure 9.2. Change in observed ratings of positive verbal interaction over time for behavioral and supportive group therapy participants.

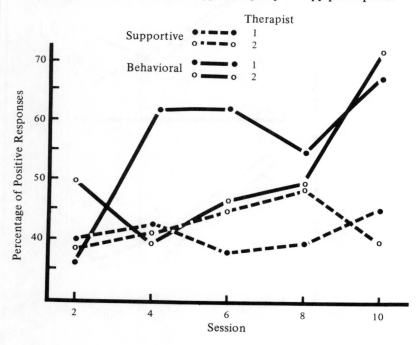

Interview Measures

After completion of therapy and again after the 5-week no-treatment follow-up period, clients were asked several specific questions designed to evaluate their perception of change. These interviews were conducted by the two observers utilized in the project. Responses were coded into three categories: yes, positive change; yes, negative change; no, no change. For some questions, only the first and third categories contained data and in those cases, Fisher's exact test of probability was computed; χ^2 analyses were used for the other questions. Table 9.4 presents the interview results.

At the posttest evaluation, 65% of the sample reported that the group experience helped them, 60% reported change since therapy began, and 65% reported feeling less depressed. There were no group differences on these questions. In contrast, 7 out of 10 behavioral subjects reported improvement in *life satisfaction,* whereas 8 out of 10 supportive subjects reported no change on this question (χ^2 (1) = 3.23, $p < .05$). Similarly, 8 out of 10 behavioral subjects reported improved *overall functioning,* in contrast to 7 out of 10 supportive subjects who said their overall functioning was the same as or worse than when treatment began (χ^2 (1) = 3.23, $p < .05$).

These two specific group differences were no longer significant at follow-up; no other group differences emerged. Cell proportions were roughly equal on the other questions, suggesting that although behavioral subjects perceived themselves as better in some respects at the end of treat-

Table 9.4
Posttest and Follow-up Interview Data:
Comparison of Behavioral vs. Supportive Clients' Responses

Question	Posttest			Follow-up		
	χ^2	df	p	χ^2	df	p
1. Did group therapy help?	2.27	2	.32	Not asked		
2. Change since treatment?	2.67	2	.26	2.09	3	.55
3. Change in feelings of depression?	1.08	2	.58	3.47	2	.18
4. Change in interpersonal ability?			.50[a]			1.00[a]
5. Change in activities?	1.88	1	.10			1.00[a]
6. Change in life satisfaction?	3.23	1	.04[b]			1.00[a]
7. Change in overall level of functioning?	3.23	1	.04[b]			.31[a]

[a]This was computed using Fisher's Exact Probability Test.
[b]On the two significant findings, behavioral subjects more often reported improvement.

ment, this perception did not continue when group therapy was no longer available. About half the sample reported continued change after therapy stopped, and 60% reported continued improvement in their mood level.

Individual Difference Measures

Further exploratory analyses were done to see if any specific subject variables were associated with positive outcome in this sample. The large number of dependent and independent measures were combined into logically grouped sets and composite scores were derived by summing measures within each set. Five dependent measures and six independent measures were formed. A multiple regression analysis was then performed for each dependent measure.

Only one of these sets of independent variables was significantly related to outcome. The regression of health factors (i.e., subjective health rating and number and duration of symptoms reported) was significant with respect to the composite depression score $(F (4, 15) = 3.73, p < .05)$. The multiple R for this set was .70. Inspection of the simple correlations indicated that subjective rating of current health status correlated most highly with improved affective status $(r = .62)$. This "health factors" set was not significantly related to any of the other four composite outcome scores.

On a second set of more specific health-related variables (medication, chronic pain, insomnia, and health before treatment), the F value approached significance $(F (5, 14) = 2.23, p < .10)$ in predicting the composite depression change score. The multiple R for this set was .66. The single measure of this set that contributed most to the explained variance was health rating for the year prior to treatment, with $r = .62$.

None of the remaining F's for other variable sets approached statistical significance. Given the number of regression analyses performed, the two significant findings reported must be interpreted cautiously. They do suggest that health status warrants further investigation in future therapy research, since health status appears to be related to the ability of older depressed persons to respond effectively in time-limited psychotherapy.

DISCUSSION

The present study was designed to address three questions relevant to psychotherapy with elderly individuals. First, would elderly clients with moderate to severe depression be capable of responding positively to outpatient psychological intervention? Second, what techniques might produce differential treatment effects? Specifically, would a structured, behavioral intervention produce greater benefit than a supportive, relational approach? Third, what is the contribution of various individual difference variables in accounting for change in depression and other behaviors?

Response of Depressed Elderly to Treatment

With regard to the first question, the data clearly indicate that most of the depressed clients who participated in this study responded well to the treatment. They reported significantly reduced levels of depression after 10 sessions, and this change was maintained through the follow-up period. They also reported significant change in social behaviors outside of treatment (notably, increased frequency and enjoyability of social activities). Observers rated significant improvement in clients' interpersonal style over time, as reflected in actual in-session behaviors. Finally, posttreatment and follow-up interviews indicated satisfaction with treatment and improvement in affective status, life satisfaction, and overall level of functioning.

At the very least, these data point out that the total package of an individual's seeking help, participating in short-term treatment, and cooperating with multiple evaluation procedures has a measurable impact on depression. Furthermore, older depressives seem capable of responding appropriately to both structured and nondirective approaches in a group context. These findings are consistent with other studies that note improvement in both individual psychotherapy (reviews by Eisdorfer & Stotsky, 1977; Gottesman et al., 1973) and group psychotherapy with the elderly (Burnside, 1971; Larson, 1970; Liederman et al., 1967). They do not agree with those of Haber et al. (1977), who found lack of significant change over time on self-report measures of depression following a brief group intervention with a retirement home sample.

Thus, the majority of this literature suggests that brief psychological interventions warrant further application in clinical work with the elderly. Future research may even indicate that they offer viable alternatives to more standard treatments for depression in this age group. For example, older depressives cannot always be treated with psychotropic medications; problems frequently arise when such prescriptions are attempted (Salzman & Shader, 1979). Therefore, it may prove to be extremely useful not only to continue to carefully research the psychosocial therapies themselves, but to evaluate them as compared to pharmacological interventions for depression in the elderly.

Behavioral Approach vs. Supportive Approach

The data are mixed with regard to differential treatment effectiveness. On the one hand, there are no statistically significant differential effects between groups on self-reports of depression; in clients' self-reports of certain behaviors (e.g., assertiveness, or ability to give and receive positive attention); in observers' ratings of interpersonal style (e.g., friendliness, ability to understand others); or in responses to most post and follow-up interview evaluation questions. On all of these variables, similar change in a positive direction occurred in both groups over time. On the other hand, observer ratings of constructive verbal interaction patterns did indicate significant differential treatment effects. Behavioral group participants were rated as proportionately higher in expression of positive statements in the group. They also reported greater improvement in life satisfaction and overall level of functioning immediately after treatment, although these differences did not persist through the follow-up period.

These mixed results are not inconsistent with the bulk of the psychotherapy outcome literature reported on younger clients that has, by and large, obtained similar findings. In the Sloane et al. (1975) study, for example, there were no significant differences between behavior therapy and psychodynamically oriented psychotherapy on target symptoms, improved overall functioning, or a number of self-report measures, although the behaviorally treated clients were judged more improved on global adjustment than the psychotherapy clients.

Specifically with depressed patients, Zeiss, Lewinsohn, and Munoz (1979) found no differences among three types of behavioral treatment compared in their recent outcome study. They suggest that common factors present in all behavioral treatments may be more responsible for improvement than the specific technique. For example, all behavioral therapies present a treatment rationale, emphasize training in skills of some significance to the client, and encourage their use outside the therapy context. These common factors reflect Bandura's concept of self-efficacy (1977), which says that any approach that reduces demoralization and increases self-perceived ability to function should alter psychological distress.

The present findings are also consistent with those of Shaw (1977), who found that following brief psychotherapy, behavioral and nondirective treatments were equally effective in reducing depression. Shaw (1977) suggests that behavioral and nondirective programs may have had distinct but essentially equivalent effects, and encourages further exploration of their similarities and differences.

Finally, the fact that a differential effect for behavioral treatment was found on ratings of clients' verbal behavior and on some interview response data, but was not observed on self-report rating scale measures of depression, is similar to a finding of Berger and Rose (1977). Their study of institutionalized elderly people found a similar discrepancy; they suggested that this discrepancy may be due to "attitudinal lag," which refers to the fact that changes in self-evaluation tend to lag behind performance change. It may be that enhanced self-evaluation is a consequence of improved performance and therefore requires more time to become manifest. Other studies of behavioral treatments, such as Schinke and Rose (1976), have reported similar discrepancies. Had observer ratings been obtained at follow-up in the present study and again compared to self-report measures, some light might have been shed on this issue.

At this point, several other factors need to be considered that might provide constraints in interpretations one can make from these data. It has been observed that change does occur, but this change takes place in the context of a number of other factors that may influence results. One must keep in mind the total situations of these clients: they came to a psychiatric outpatient clinic acknowledging their need for professional assistance; they were carefully evaluated and then invited to join a research program with positive expectancies for change; they were retested a number of times; and they also were participants in one or the other of the treatments of interest here. Unfortunately, the appropriate control groups needed to evaluate the impact of each of these various components to the overall change observed were not included in the present study (e.g., a delayed treatment condition or a minimally interactive control group). Their absence was a function of the research policies at the agency under whose auspices the study was done. However, some psychotherapy researchers, such as O'Leary and Borkovec (1978), have argued against the use of no-treatment and "placebo" control conditions with clinically depressed samples.

Given the problems of establishing suitable control conditions and the overall context of the research as described, it cannot be concluded that change was due to treatment per se; it is therefore necessary to explore some other factors that are likely to have contributed to the change over time observed in the present study. There seem to be at least three plausible explanations for the finding that, regardless of type of treatment, subjects significantly improved on self-report measures of depression and interpersonal behavior. First, a factor that certainly seems to be operating in this study is the presence of a helping relationship, which was noted by both clients and observers to be equivalently present in both treatment conditions. As the literature has repeatedly pointed out (Luborsky et al., 1975; Sloane et al., 1975), this may be the major factor accountable for change in psychotherapy. The present study suggests that involvement in a helping relationship may be related to positive outcome with elderly depressives; however, it is unclear to what extent this is responsible for change, given the research design.

A second plausible explanation for essentially equivalent change across time in both treatment groups focuses on the relevance of factors outside the therapy situation itself. A factor often thought to be critical (particularly with respect to depressives) is spontaneous remission, although the extent of this phenomenon is not known with accuracy. This was examined in post hoc analyses by computing the percentage of change in the sample (divided into initial high vs. low depressives) and correlating this change in depression with other outcome measures. If spontaneous remission were operating, those clients who were less severe to begin with would be expected to show most change as a function of the passage of time, while the more severe would be less likely to improve when retested after a short interval. The post hoc analyses found that this was not in fact the case; therefore, this factor may not be exerting a major influence on these results.

Another extra-therapy factor to consider is the issue of reactivity of measurement (Webb, Campbell, Schwartz, & Sechrest, 1966). This issue refers to the observation of change following measurement alone (without intervention) as a result of the nature of the measures used. It has frequently been noted that the very process of discussing, observing, or recording one's behavior may be associated with behavior change. Rowland and Haynes (1978), for example, noted the significance of this factor in their study of a sexual enhancement program designed for elderly couples. They found significant improvement in the pretreatment phase following initial measurement. A similar finding was reported by Zeiss (1977) and Zeiss et al. (1979), who noted that positive change occurred as a function of extensive and/or repeated testing in their depressed samples. The factor of staff attention is likely to amplify reactivity of measurement effects; but it can be present independently as well (e.g., scheduling appointments, inquiries as to status, and general monitoring behavior). It may be that staff attention itself is a significant factor in reduction of depression, especially for elderly persons whose social world may be narrow. The effects of the passage of time, the intrusiveness of measures, and the presence of staff attention all need to be evaluated in future research to determine their relative contribution to change.

A third possible explanation for equivalent change across conditions in the present study involves the socialization effects of group process. There is an ample literature to suggest that group process variables can interact with treatment methods in such a manner as to either amplify or obscure treatment efficacy (Bednar & Kaul, 1978). Shaw (1977) observed that lack of differences in his group treatment study may have been due to the value of discussion with interested persons. This factor may operate quite independently of any specific treatment effect. Others suggest that it may be important to regard the group as an entity in itself and to measure such process variables as cohesion and stages of the group's development (Hartford, 1971, 1976). Although no such measures were taken, it would appear from inspection of therapists' progress notes recorded after each session and from the observer ratings that the groups in the study were cohesive and progressive in development. The groups did differ, however, in that more "negative" verbal interaction occurred in the two supportive groups. Perhaps by virtue of lack of structure, a greater degree of "depressive" content (e.g., verbalization of somatic and psychological complaints and discussion of other people's problems) may have been necessary for clients to attain self-understanding, even though such talk tends to produce negative reactions in others. For example, Coyne (1976) found that "depressive talk" reduced the likelihood of further interpersonal interaction with nondepressed individuals. In the current study, low interpersonal attraction among the supportive group participants may account to some extent for the specific treatment differences obtained.

Future research should consider inclusion of an appropriate control group, such as a "rap" group, that would be nonpsychotherapeutic in orientation but would control for such factors as activity, social interaction, and experience of a helping relationship. Such control conditions may be difficult to formulate with a depressed sample for the ethical reasons discussed and because of the problem in creating equal expectancies for change across conditions. Nevertheless, inclusion of such conditions needs to be considered in designing future studies, particularly when the psychotherapy is done in a group rather than an individual format (see Roth, 1980, for expanded discussion of this point).

The Role of Subject Variables

The third question this research was designed to investigate was the role of individual differences in relationship to outcome. A number of individual difference variables were expected to relate significantly to outcome; these were investigated through post hoc analyses, but very few significant relationships were found. For example, demographic factors such as age, sex, and marital status did not significantly relate to outcome. This finding is somewhat unexpected in light of the numerous changes in the lives of older individuals relative to such items as socio-economic status and living conditions that might be expected to relate to mood changes. Similarly, the Sloane et al. (1975) study reported that no personality characteristics, demographic variables, or severity indices were significantly related to successful outcome in younger depressed individuals.

One variable, however, did significantly relate to change in depression: subjective ratings of physical health status. Evaluation of health status in relation to outcome in studies of depression has not previously been reported in the literature. From the present study, it appears that those elderly clients who report that they are in good physical health at the outset of therapy show significantly greater improvement in mood than those in poor health. This raises an issue as to the significance of health status as a parameter influencing responsiveness to psychotherapy in this age group. The correlation between change in depression and perceived wellness suggests that subjective health rating may be a sensitive predictor of the client's ability to respond to behavioral treatment. Those who perceive themselves to be in poor health may not be able to participate as fully in treatment and thus will not receive its full benefits.

CONCLUSIONS

In conclusion, this study has raised a number of issues that deserve attention in future psychotherapy research with older adults. First, older depressed persons can gain much benefit from participation in behaviorally oriented groups, but not all of these benefits are reflected in numerical data. For example, two of the older women were able to move to better living quarters shortly after their therapy ended, an issue they had worked on in the group in terms of their ability to develop new social relationships. Several of the men resumed relationships with family members that had decreased over time and that were a source of distress during treatment. Others sought and obtained volunteer jobs, thereby increasing their sense of competence. These findings suggest that follow-up inquiries be worded so as to permit older respondents to give qualitative information that really indicates their ability to translate what was learned in treatment into their everyday life situations. Most of our current measures are not sensitive in this regard, so important information will be lost unless the researcher is aware of the limitations of paper-and-pencil measures with the elderly and specifically asks for more qualitative data.

Second, future research on the effectiveness of behavioral treatment may need to adapt procedures creatively, so as to better address the specific complaints of this age group. Careful consideration must be given to participants' health status in designing interventions and homework. For example, goals and treatment techniques need to be implemented flexibly so that older individuals can make maximum use of them in their daily lives. Relaxation training procedures, for instance, have to be adapted for older persons with arthritis and heart conditions, and specific homework assignments must take into account realistic limitations such as transportation and economic difficulties. In addition, an effort should be made to determine appropriate reinforcers prior to treatment, since there is wide interindividual variability in the type and adequacy of reinforcers reported. For example, some elderly individuals may respond better to "concrete" than to "interpersonal" reinforcers; this area remains to be explored, possibly through utilization of such measures as the Cautela and Kastenbaum (1967) Reinforcement Survey Schedule.

Finally, future research on behavioral group psychotherapy needs to look more carefully at group process variables themselves and at the value of social interaction per se. These may be especially powerful variables with the elderly, because problems of loneliness are usually amplified in this population. It is hoped that this chapter will stimulate such research and thus lead to development of more effective psychosocial interventions for this segment of our population.

REFERENCE NOTES

1. Blumenthal, M. D. *Research problems in mental health and illness of the elderly.* Report to the research task force of the President's Commission on Mental Health, 1978.
2. Shaffer, M., & Lewinsohn, P. M. *Interpersonal behaviors in the home of depressed versus nondepressed psychiatric and normal controls.* Unpublished manuscript, University of Oregon, 1971.
3. Weissman, A., & Beck, A. T. *A preliminary investigation of the relationship between dysfunctional attitudes and depression.* Unpublished manuscript, University of Pennsylvania, 1977.
4. Gallagher, D., & Thompson, L. W. *Cognitive distortion vignettes: Preliminary report on development of a measure to assess cognitive factors in depression in the elderly.* Unpublished manuscript, University of Southern California, 1978.
5. Gallagher, D., McGarvey, W., Zelinski, E., & Thompson, L. W. *Age and factor structure of the Zung depression scale.* Paper presented at the 31st Annual Meeting of the Gerontological Society, Dallas, November 1978.
6. Youngren, M., Zeiss, A., & Lewinsohn, P. *Interpersonal Events Schedule.* Unpublished manuscript, University of Oregon, 1975.
7. Youngren, M., & Lewinsohn, P. *The functional relationship between depression and problematic interpersonal behavior.* Unpublished manuscript, University of Oregon, 1977.
8. Lewinsohn, P., Munoz, R., Youngren, M., Zeiss, A., & Talkington, J. *Depression project research coder's manual* (Rev. ed.). Unpublished manuscript, University of Oregon, 1975.

REFERENCES

Bandura, A. Self-efficacy: Toward a unifying theory of behavioral change. *Psychological Review*, 1977, *84*, 191–215.

Barrett-Lennard, G. T. Dimensions of therapist response as causal factors in therapeutic change. *Psychological Monographs*, 1963, *76* (1, Whole No. 562).

Beck, A. T. *Depression: Clinical, experimental, and theoretical aspects.* New York: Harper & Row, 1967.

Beck, A. T. *Cognitive therapy and the emotional disorders.* New York: International Universities Press, 1976.

Beck, A. T., Ward, C. H., Mendelson, M., Mock, J. E., & Erbaugh, J. An inventory for measuring depression. *Archives of General Psychiatry,* 1961, *4,* 561–571.

Bednar, R. L., & Kaul, T. J. Experiential group research: Current perspectives. In S. Garfield & A. Bergin (Eds.), *Handbook of psychotherapy and behavior change* (2nd ed.). New York: Wiley, 1978.

Berger, L., & Berger, M. A holistic approach to psychogeriatric outpatients. *International Journal of Group Psychotherapy,* 1973, *23,* 432–444.

Berger, R. M., & Rose, S. D. Interpersonal skill training with institutionalized elderly patients. *Journal of Gerontology,* 1977, *32,* 346–353.

Bergin, A., & Lambert, M. The evaluation of therapeutic outcomes. In S. Garfield & A. Bergin (Eds.), *Handbook of psychotherapy and behavior change* (2nd ed.). New York: Wiley, 1978.

Blaney, P. Contemporary theories of depression: Critique and comparison. *Journal of Abnormal Psychology,* 1977, *86,* 203–223.

Burnside, I. Long-term group work with hospitalized aged. *Gerontologist,* 1971, *11,* 213–218.

Butler R., & Lewis, M. *Aging and mental health* (2nd ed.). St. Louis: Mosby, 1977.

Campbell, D. *Short-term psychotherapy for depression: A second controlled study.* Unpublished doctoral dissertation, University of Connecticut, 1974.

Cautela, J. R., & Kastenbaum, R. A Reinforcement Survey Schedule for use in therapy, training and research. *Psychological Reports,* 1967, *20,* 1115–1130.

Cautela, J. R., & Mansfield, L. A behavioral approach to geriatrics. In W. D. Gentry (Ed.), *Geropsychology: A model of training and clinical service.* Cambridge, Mass.: Ballinger, 1977.

Coyne, J. C. Depression and the response of others. *Journal of Abnormal Psychology,* 1976, *85,* 186–193.

Cumming, E., & Henry, W. *Growing old.* New York: Basic Books, 1961.

Derogatis, L. R., Lipman, R. S., & Covi, L. The SCL-90: An outpatient psychiatric rating scale. *Psychopharmacology Bulletin,* 1973, *9,* 13–28.

Eisdorfer, C., & Stotsky, B. Intervention, treatment and rehabilitation of psychiatric disorders. In J. E. Birren & K. W. Schaie (Eds.), *Handbook of the psychology of aging.* New York: Van Nostrand Reinhold, 1977.

Fink, M., Green, M. A., & Bender, M. The Face-Hand Test. *Neurology,* 1952, *48,* 2–5.

Flannery, R. B. Behavior modification of geriatric grief: A transactional perspective. *International Journal of Aging and Human Development,* 1974, *5,* 197–203.

Frank, J. D. *Persuasion and healing: A comparative study of psychotherapy.* Baltimore: Johns Hopkins Press, 1961.

Frank, J. D. The present status of outcome studies. *Journal of Consulting and Clinical Psychology,* 1979, *47,* 310–316.

Gaitz, C. M. Depression in the elderly. In W. Fann, I. Karacan, A. Pokorny, & R. Williams (Eds.), *Phenomenology and treatment of depression.* New York: Spectrum, 1977.

Gauthier, J., & Marshall, W. L. Grief: A cognitive-behavioral analysis. *Cognitive Therapy and Research,* 1977, *1,* 39–44.

Gottesman, L. E., Quarterman, E. E., & Cohn, G. M. Psychosocial treatment of the aged. In C. Eisdorfer & M. P. Lawton (Eds.), *The psychology of adult development and aging.* Washington, D. C.: American Psychological Association, 1973.

Gurland, B. The comparative frequency of depression in various adult age groups. *Journal of Gerontology,* 1976, *31,* 283–292.

Haber, L., Murphy, P., & Taylor, S. The effect of short-term group psychotherapy on the elderly. *Canadian Journal of Psychiatric Nursing,* 1977, *18,* 8–11.

Hammen, C., & Glass, D. Depression, activity, and evaluation of reinforcement. *Journal of Abnormal Psychology,* 1975, *84,* 718–721.

Hammen, C., & Krantz, S. Effect of success and failure on depressive cognitions. *Journal of Abnormal Psychology,* 1976, *85,* 577–586.

Hartford, M. *Groups in social work.* New York: Columbia University Press, 1971.

Hartford, M. Group methods and generic practice. In R. Roberts & H. Northen (Eds.), *Theories of social work with groups.* New York: Columbia University Press, 1976.

Hathaway, S. R., & McKinley, J. C. *Minnesota Multiphasic Personality Inventory manual* (Rev. ed.). New York: Psychological Corp., 1967.

Ingersoll, B., & Silverman, A. Comparative group psychotherapy for the aged. *Gerontologist,* 1978, *18,* 201–206.

Kahn, R., Goldfarb, A., Pollack, M., & Peck, A. Brief objective measures for determination of mental status in the aged. *American Journal of Psychiatry,* 1960, *117,* 326–328.

Kiesler, D. J. A scale for the rating of congruence. In C. Rogers (Ed.), *The therapeutic relationship and its impact.* Madison: University of Wisconsin Press, 1967.

Knight, B. Psychotherapy and behavior change with the non-institutionalized aged. *International Journal of Aging and Human Development,* 1979, *3,* 221–236.

Kramer, M., Taube, G., & Redick, R. Patterns of use of psychiatric facilities by the aged: Past, present, and future. In C. Eisdorfer & M. P. Lawton (Eds.), *The psychology of adult development and aging.* Washington, D. C.: American Psychological Association, 1973.

Kuypers, J. A., & Bengston, V. L. Competence and social breakdown: A social-psychological view of aging. *Human Development,* 1973, *16,* 37–49.

Larson, M. Descriptive account of group treatment of older people by a caseworker. *Journal of Geriatric Psychiatry,* 1970, *3,* 231–240.

Lewinsohn, P. Clinical and theoretical aspects of depression. In K. Calhoun, H. Adams, & K. Mitchell (Eds.), *Innovative treatment methods of psychopathology.* New York: Wiley, 1974.

Lewinsohn, P., Biglan, A., & Zeiss, A. Behavioral treatment of depression. In P. Davidson (Ed.), *The behavioral management of anxiety, depression and pain.* New York: Brunner/Mazel, 1976.

Lewinsohn, P., & Graf, M. Pleasant activities and depression. *Journal of Consulting and Clinical Psychology,* 1973, *41,* 261-268.

Lewinsohn, P., & Libet, J. Pleasant events, activity schedules, and depression. *Journal of Abnormal Psychology,* 1972, *79,* 291-295.

Lewinsohn, P., Weinstein, M., & Alper, T. A behavioral approach to the group treatment of depressed persons: A methodological contribution. *Journal of Clinical Psychology,* 1970, *26,* 1525-1532.

Lewinsohn, P., Weinstein, M., & Shaw, D. Depression: A clinical research approach. In R. Rubin & C. Franks (Eds.), *Advances in behavior therapy.* New York: Academic Press, 1969.

Libet, J., & Lewinsohn, P. Concept of social skill with special reference to the behavior of depressed persons. *Journal of Consulting and Clinical Psychology,* 1973, *40,* 304-312.

Liederman, P. C., Green, R., & Liederman, V. R. Outpatient group therapy with geriatric patients. *Geriatrics,* 1967, *22,* 148-153.

Lowenthal, M. F., & Berkman, R. L. *Aging and mental disorder.* San Francisco: Jossey-Bass, 1967.

Luborsky, L., Singer, B., & Luborsky, L. Comparative studies of psychotherapies. *Archives of General Psychiatry,* 1975, *32,* 995-1008.

MacPhillamy, D. J., & Lewinsohn, P. Depression as a function of levels of desired and obtained pleasure. *Journal of Abnormal Psychology,* 1974, *83,* 651-657.

Marshall, K. A. Empathy, genuineness, and regard: Determinants of successful therapy with schizophrenics? A critical review. *Psychotherapy: Theory, Research and Practice,* 1977, *14,* 57-64.

McCall, R. B., & Appelbaum, M. I. Bias in the analysis of repeated-measures designs: Some alternative approaches. *Child Development,* 1973, *44,* 401-415.

McNair, D. Self-rating scales for assessing psychopathology in the elderly. In A. Raskin & L. Jarvik (Eds.), *Psychiatric symptoms and cognitive loss in the elderly.* New York: Hemisphere, 1979.

Munoz, R. *Cognitive therapy in the outpatient treatment of depression.* Unpublished doctoral dissertation, University of Oregon, 1977.

O'Leary, K. D., & Borkovec, T. D. Conceptual, methodological, and ethical problems of placebo groups in psychotherapy research. *American Psychologist,* 1978, *33,* 821-830.

Padfield, M. The comparative effects of two counseling approaches on the intensity of depression among rural women of low socioeconomic status. *Journal of Counseling Psychology,* 1976, *23,* 209-214.

Parloff, M., Waskow, I., & Wolfe, B. Research on therapist variables in relation to process and outcome. In S. Garfield & A. Bergin (Eds.), *Handbook of psychotherapy and behavior change* (2nd ed.). New York: Wiley, 1978.

Pfeiffer, E. Psychopathology and social pathology. In J. E. Birren & K. W. Schaie (Eds.), *Handbook of the psychology of aging.* New York: Van Nostrand Reinhold, 1977.

Prkachin, K., Craig, K., Papageorgis, D., & Reith, G. Nonverbal communication deficits and response to performance feedback in depression. *Journal of Abnormal Psychology,* 1977, *86,* 224–234.

Rebok, G. W., & Hoyer, W. The functional context of elderly behavior. *Gerontologist,* 1977, *17,* 27–34.

Rechtschaffen, A. Psychotherapy with geriatric patients: A review of the literature. *Journal of Gerontology,* 1959, *14,* 73–86.

Rehm, L. P. A self-control model of depression. *Behavior Therapy,* 1977, *8,* 787–804.

Richards, W. S., & Thorpe, G. L. Behavioral approaches to the problems of later life. In M. Storandt, I. Siegler, & M. F. Elias (Eds.), *The clinical psychology of aging.* New York: Plenum, 1978.

Robinson, J. C., & Lewinsohn, P. Behavior modification of speech characteristics in a chronically depressed man. *Behavior Therapy,* 1973, *4,* 150–152.

Rogers, C. *Client-centered therapy.* Boston: Houghton-Mifflin, 1951.

Rogers, C. (Ed.). *The therapeutic relationship and its impact.* Madison: University of Wisconsin Press, 1967.

Roth, D. Suggestions for behavioral group therapy of depression. In D. Upper & S. Ross (Eds.), *Behavioral Group Therapy, 1980: An Annual Review.* Champaign, Ill.: Research Press, 1980.

Rowland, K., & Haynes, S. A sexual enrichment program for elderly couples. *Journal of Sex & Marital Therapy,* 1978, *4,* 91–113.

Salzman, C., & Shader, R. Clinical evaluation of depression in the elderly. In A. Raskin & L. Jarvik (Eds.), *Psychiatric symptoms and cognitive loss in the elderly.* New York: Hemisphere, 1979.

Schinke, S. P., & Rose, S. D. Interpersonal skill training in groups. *Journal of Counseling Psychology,* 1976, *23,* 442–448.

Seligman, M. E. P. Depression and learned helplessness. In R. Friedman & M. Katz (Eds.), *The psychology of depression: Contemporary theory and research.* New York: Wiley, 1974.

Seligman, M. E. P. *Helplessness: On depression, development and death.* San Francisco: Freeman, 1975.

Shaw, B. F. Comparison of cognitive therapy and behavior therapy in the treatment of depression. *Journal of Consulting and Clinical Psychology,* 1977, *45,* 543–551.

Siegel, S. *Nonparametric statistics for the behavioral sciences.* New York: McGraw-Hill, 1956.

Sloane, R., Staples, F., Cristol, A., Yorkston, N., & Whipple, K. *Psychotherapy versus behavioral therapy.* Cambridge, Mass.: Harvard University Press, 1975.

Taylor, F., & Marshall, W. Experimental analysis of a cognitive-behavioral therapy for depression. *Cognitive Therapy and Research,* 1977, *1,* 59–72.

Thurstone, L. L., & Thurstone, T. G. *SRA Primary Mental Abilities Test.* Chicago: Science Research Associates, 1948.

Truax, C. B. A scale for the rating of accurate empathy. In C. Rogers (Ed.), *The therapeutic relationship and its impact.* Madison: University of Wisconsin Press, 1967.

Truax, C. B., & Mitchell, K. M. Research on certain therapist interpersonal skills in relation to process and outcome. In A. Bergin & S. Garfield (Eds.), *Handbook of psychotherapy and behavior change.* New York: Wiley, 1971.

Webb, E. J., Campbell, D. T., Schwartz, R. D., & Sechrest, L. *Unobtrusive measures: Nonreactive research in the social sciences.* Chicago: Rand McNally, 1966.

Youngren, M. *The functional relationship of depression and problematic interpersonal behavior.* Unpublished doctoral dissertation, University of Oregon, 1977.

Zeiss, A. *Interpersonal behavior problems of the depressed.* Unpublished doctoral dissertation, University of Oregon, 1977.

Zeiss, A., Lewinsohn, P., & Munoz, R. Nonspecific improvement effects in depression using interpersonal skills training, pleasant activity schedules, or cognitive training. *Journal of Consulting and Clinical Psychology,* 1979, *47,* 427–439.

Zung, W. W. A self-rating depression scale. *Archives of General Psychiatry,* 1965, *12,* 63–70.

Chapter 10

The Effectiveness of Group-Administered Relaxation Training as an Adjunctive Therapy for Essential Hypertension

D. Michael Rice
P. Scott Lawrence

Abstract

With the increase in the incidence of essential hypertension, a trend toward self-control techniques has emerged, especially since pharmaceutical agents may produce undesirable side effects. The present study was designed to assess the effects of group-administered progressive relaxation training on heart rate, muscle tension, and blood pressure, enabling not only testing of the procedure for blood pressure reduction, but also concomitant changes on other physiological measures. The physiological measures were taken before treatment and 2–3 days following treatment for all subjects while they were resting, doing pencil-and-paper mazes (a fine-motor task), or holding a weight (a gross-motor task). This procedure allowed for the assessment of generalization of treatment results both outside of the treatment setting and while engaged in activities other than rest. Sixteen subjects (eight males and eight females who had been diagnosed as having essential hypertension and were on medication) were randomly assigned to each of two groups. One group of eight received relaxation training, while the other participated in discussions of their disorder and served as a hypertensive control group during the study. Four males and four females with normal blood pressures were also used as a normotensive comparison group. Results indicated that the treatment group achieved significantly greater reductions in diastolic blood pressure compared to the control group. No significant posttreatment differences were found between the two hypertensive groups on the heart rate, systolic blood pressure, or muscle tension measures. The differences in reduction between the two hypertensive groups were evident across the generalization tasks. Thus, group-administered relaxation training holds potential as an adjunctive treatment for essential hypertension. The training procedures per se and process factors operating within the groups are viewed as facilitating treatment effectiveness.

Self-control techniques utilized as therapy for patients with essential hypertension have received considerable attention in recent years. Research has demonstrated that individuals may be trained to control their own arterial blood pressure without use of medication (Benson, 1975; Blanchard & Young, 1974; Fey & Lindholm, 1978; Schwartz, 1973; Shapiro, Gershon, Gershon, & Stern, 1969; Shoemaker & Tasto, 1975; Byassee, Note 1). Research investigating the effectiveness of these procedures appears to fall into two categories of therapy: biofeedback and relaxation training.

Biofeedback techniques offer improved methods for providing an individual with feedback or information about specific physiological processes that enable her to control many functions that once were regarded as "automatic, involuntary, or reflexive" (e.g., heart rate, blood pressure, or brain waves) (Byassee, Note 1). Preliminary positive results have been found for essential hypertension, cardiac arrhythmias, migraine and tension headaches, and abnormal EEG (Schwartz, 1973). Several studies providing patients with auditory or visual feedback indicate patients can be taught to reduce blood pressure readings (Fey & Lindholm, 1975; Fidel, 1975; Shapiro et al., 1969). Fey and Lindholm found a progressive relaxation plus blood pressure biofeedback group achieved greater systolic blood pressure reductions than either a progressive relaxation alone group or a control relaxation procedure plus blood pressure biofeedback group. Heart rate and diastolic blood pressure reductions were found in all three groups, with the groups trained in progressive relaxation demonstrating the greatest reductions.

Lowering of blood pressure has been associated with progressive muscular relaxation (Jacobson, 1939) and hypnotically suggested relaxation (Paul, 1969). Individually administered relaxation training procedures have been shown to be beneficial in producing clinically significant reductions in blood pressure (Shoemaker & Tasto, 1975.)

Several researchers have utilized relaxation training in groups as a technique to enhance the efficiency of the systematic desensitization procedure by treating several subjects at once (Ihli & Garlington, 1969; Kondas, 1967; Lazarus, 1961; Paul & Shannon, 1966). Group relaxation techniques were compared by Byassee, Farr, and Meyer (Note 2) in the treatment of essential hypertensive patients. Self-relaxation, autogenic relaxation, and progressive relaxation were all found to produce reductions in systolic blood pressure. Relaxation training also has been shown to be more beneficial than nonspecific therapy or medication alone (Taylor, Farquhar, Nelson, & Agras, 1977).

There are many advantages to the use of group-administered relaxation training. It is more cost-effective to treat several patients simultaneously rather than individually, and training may be more effective since patients have the opportunity to model others who demonstrate appropriate tensing and relaxing phases while learning the technique. The group setting also allows for reinforcement through discussion of feelings and provides a context for patients to interact with one another.

THE PRESENT STUDY

This study was designed to evaluate the effectiveness of relaxation training as an adjunctive therapy when administered simultaneously to a group of eight hypertensive subjects. In addition to studying the effects of the training in terms of blood pressure, concomitant changes in EMG and heart rate and the effects of simple tasks on the physiological responses of subjects were examined. Acquisition of EMG data from subjects offered an indication of the level of relaxation as defined by reduction of muscle tension.

Few researchers have used electromyographic physiological measures to verify decreased muscle relaxation when relaxation is used either exclusively or as part of systematic desensitization with hypertensives. Jacobson (1939) reported a relationship between blood pressure and reduced electromyographic data from various muscle groups. Paul (1969) and Paul and Trimble (1970) also reported physiological data in their studies dealing with relaxation training. Paul reported that relaxation training effected greater reduction in muscle tension (EMG), heart rate, respiratory rate, and anxiety differential (a measure of subjective tension and distress) when compared both to a control group and a hypnotic suggestion group. Paul and Trimble found "live" relaxation training superior to recorded relaxation training, both in the magnitude and extent of physiological change.

Most studies using relaxation training or systematic desensitization have relied upon self-report or subjective measures of relaxation as the sole criterion that relaxation has occurred. However, Paul and Trimble (1970) and Sammons (1975) found that decreases in physiological measures and increased reports of relaxation by the subject do not always correspond. Often subjects, although having an increased EMG, report feelings of increased relaxation (Sammons, 1975). These data make self-report measures of relaxation unreliable, although they have often been used in relaxation procedures.

Group relaxation has been shown to have results comparable to individual relaxation training effects in reducing tension. Studies to date have not looked at the physiological effects of group relaxation training;

all have relied on subjective reports. Only two studies have investigated group relaxation training with essential hypertensives (Taylor et al., 1977; Byassee et al., Note 2). Although significant reductions in blood pressure were reported, blood pressure was the only physiological measure taken.

As opposed to assessing the generalization of any effects of relaxation training to the "natural environment," the current study focused on generalization to specific laboratory situations. Subjects were required to return after four sessions of treatment for posttreatment measures, which were taken while they sat quietly for 5 minutes and then while they performed two tasks, each lasting 5 minutes. One task (mazes) involved use of the lower arm muscles (fine-motor movement), and the other involved full arm tension from holding a weight. Physiological measures were taken during the tasks prior to training, and after four sessions of training. Data were collected 2 to 3 days following the last training session.

This was the first study to look at the effects of group relaxation training on various tasks where multiple physiological measures were taken simultaneously. The purpose of this design was to look at the generalization of the treatment effects to each physiological measure in three situations: physiological changes during a task, the physiological responses of hypertensive individuals, and the responses of normotensive individuals.

METHOD

Subjects

Eight persons diagnosed as having essential hypertension by a physician were administered group relaxation training as an adjunct to pharmacological therapy. Eight subjects with essential hypertension, who were also on medication for their disorder, served as a comparison hypertensive control group for the treatment period. Both the treatment group and the hypertensive control group included four males and four females. Eight subjects were also chosen to serve as a normotensive comparison group, having diastolic blood pressures not exceeding 90 mmHg at any point during the pretest session. Subjects ranged in age from 27 to 56 years, and were selected from their response to a newspaper article offering the relaxation training to individuals with essential hypertension but no other physical disorders. Each subject was required to be under the care of a physician, to be on medication for his condition, and to have been on the same medication and dosage for at least 1 month prior to entering the study.

The upper limits of normal blood pressure levels are usually defined arbitrarily; no consensus has been reached. However, once resting blood pressure levels rise above some arbitrary limit—140/90, for example—the physician suspects essential hypertension, especially if the levels remain above this limit on repeated measurement (Weiner, 1979). Many writers accept a lower limit of 140 mmHg systolic and 90 mmHg diastolic (Geiger & Scotch, 1963; Gressell, 1949), which was the limit used in this study.

Mean pretreatment blood pressures are presented in Table 10.1 (page 233). Each subject's blood pressures varied less than 4 mmHg when taken several times with the subject in a seated, resting position prior to the pretest. While the mean diastolic blood pressure readings for hypertensive subjects in this study were just within the range considered hypertensive (i.e., over 90 mmHg diastolic on multiple readings), the subjects were demonstrating elevated blood pressure readings despite receiving pharmaceutical treatment. Thus, all subjects placed within the treatment or hypertensive control groups demonstrated blood pressure readings that, under the conditions assessed in this study, continued to fall above the normotensive range.

Apparatus and Treatment Setting

The relaxation training procedure was presented to the patients in a comfortable conference room within the psychology department of a large southern university. Heart rate and electromyogram were recorded using a 2-channel Grass Model 79 polygraph. Blood pressure was recorded with an electronic blood pressure cuff, Sears Model 262–12350.

The relaxation training instructions were those used by Sammons (1975) and consisted of a modified Jacobson-Wolpe version.[1] Three tasks were utilized to assess the extent and generalization of the relaxation training: Task 1 required the subject simply to sit quietly for 5 minutes; Task 2 was a paper-and-pencil task, WISC-R mazes (Wechsler, 1974), with the mazes being completed by the subject during a 5-minute period; Task 3 required the subject to hold a 6.5 × 6.6 × 9.5 centimeter object (a standard 6-volt battery) weighing 646 grams for a 5-minute period.

Procedure

Subjects participated in one pretreatment session, four treatment sessions, and one posttreatment session. Once a subject had been chosen as a possible participant, she was seen for an initial session at the laboratory by an experimenter. At that time, the experimenter discussed the rationale of the research and the client was scheduled for all following visits. A

---

[1] A detailed manual of the relaxation training instructions can be obtained from the first author at the Psychology Department, The University of North Carolina at Greensboro.

brief history pertaining to the subject's disorder was obtained, including medication status, length of time since onset, and medication side effects. The 16 hypertensive subjects were match-paired according to sex, after which one member of each pair was randomly selected for either the treatment group or hypertensive control group, while the 8 normotensives were matched with the other groups according to sex. Pretreatment physiological readings were also obtained.

During each recording session (pre- and post-), each subject was asked to remain relaxed for approximately a 10-minute habituation period, during which time the instruments were calibrated. The subject then began Task 1, 2, or 3, depending on a randomly assigned sequence. Measures were taken at intervals of 0–60 seconds and 240–300 seconds during the 5 minutes. There was a 2-minute rest period between each task situation. After the 2-minute rest, the next task in the subject's sequence began, and data were recorded during the same intervals of the 5-minute period. Two minutes following the last task in the sequence, data were recorded for 1 minute. The subject was then disconnected from all recording devices and asked if she had experienced any discomfort or had any comments about the session.

After the pretreatment measures were taken individually, each subject was scheduled to return as a member of the group to which she had been assigned. Each subject in the treatment group was scheduled for all four sessions of the treatment during the pretreatment session. Following the first relaxation training session, the subjects were asked how they felt about the session and if they had any questions. They were reminded of the scheduled time of the next session, and the events of upcoming sessions were briefly discussed. Subjects also were instructed to practice relaxation for two 5-minute periods each day prior to the late-afternoon sessions. The following two treatment sessions were similar except the treatment rationale was abbreviated and the relaxation training instructions only covered tensing and relaxing each muscle group once. The last treatment session included only relaxing statements, without going through each muscle group. At the end of the last treatment session, each subject scheduled a time to return to the laboratory for a posttreatment session. At that time, the same procedure was followed as during the pretreatment session.

The hypertensive control group also had four visits to the examiner. During the sessions, the examiner assumed the role of a reflective listener, and attempted to involve the subjects in conversations pertaining to their health status. They were encouraged to comment on events in their lifestyle that they felt might be stressful. Research information and other ideas on the possible role of stress in hypertension were presented by the examiner in the first two sessions. During subsequent sessions, other risk factors of cardiovascular diseases, such as cigarette smoking and lack of exercise, were discussed. No comments were made during any of the sessions to suggest that an individual subject should change anything in her lifestyle. After four visits with the examiner for the group sessions, all subjects were scheduled to return to the laboratory for a posttreatment evaluation. At that time, all dependent measures over the three situations were repeated.

Four dependent measures were taken in this study, and the data collection procedures were identical across all experimental conditions. Physiological measures included an electromyogram, heart rate, and systolic and diastolic blood pressure. Muscle tension (EMG) was recorded from the trapezius muscle group with the electrode pair placed 6 centimeters below the palpated spinous process of the seventh cervical vertebra and 2 centimeters to the right of the midline (for a right-handed subject). The EMG data were reported in mean microvolts per minute ($\mu v/m$). Heart rate was recorded from the radial artery of the wrist and was reported in beats per minute (b/m). Blood pressure was measured with an electronic inflatable blood pressure cuff and was reported in millimeters of mercury (mmHg). All recordings were averaged over 1-minute recording intervals.

Interobserver Agreement

Data collection involved two components: (a) quantifying trace recordings for EMG and heart rate for each 1-minute recording interval, and (b) reliably reading and recording blood pressure information for each subject while he was involved in a particular task. A total of 288 observations were used in the final data analysis. From these, 24 observations (8.3% of the total) were chosen randomly for checking of interobserver agreement on each dependent variable. For these 24 observations, trace recordings were scored by different individuals on two separate occasions. Blood pressure measurements were also recorded by two different people at the same time. Pearson product-moment correlation coefficients then were calculated from data for each dependent variable. Correlation coefficients were .99 for systolic blood pressure, electromyogram data, and heart rate. The correlation coefficient for diastolic blood pressure was .93.

RESULTS

The data were analyzed via analysis of covariance (ANCOVA), in order to adjust statistically for differences existing among subjects before the experimental manipulation (Keppel, 1973). This procedure also served to account for initial differences between the treatment groups and to increase the power of the analysis in reducing the within-group variability (Huck & McLean, 1975). Newman-Keuls post hoc tests were performed on each significant effect on a given dependent variable.

Diastolic Blood Pressure

The diastolic blood pressure ANCOVA yielded a significant main effect for groups, $F(2, 17) = 4.11$, $p < .05$. Adjusted cell means for diastolic blood pressures summed across all groups are provided in Table 10.1. Post hoc analyses indicated the treatment and control groups differed significantly on the posttest after statistical adjustment for within- and between-group differences. The hypertensive control group's mean diastolic blood pressure measures were significantly higher than the treatment group's across all conditions ($p < .01$), while the diastolic blood pressures of the normotensive subjects were found to be significantly lower ($p < .01$) than the treatment group and the hypertensive control group subjects' values. Table 10.1 includes the adjusted cell means for all dependent variables as well as the original pretest means and difference scores between pre- and posttest means prior to adjustments by the ANCOVA procedure. The treatment group was found to reduce 3.75 mmHg from the pretest to the posttest on the original means, while the hypertensive control group achieved average reductions of 2.0 mmHg. The normotensive group achieved a lesser reduction of 0.86 mmHg. Figure 10.1 illustrates that improvement was not specific to a particular task. When the pretest differences were statistically controlled, the adjusted posttest means indicated a significantly greater reduction in blood pressure for the treatment group compared to the hypertensive control group.

A significant main effect was also found for sex, $F(1, 17) = 4.50$, $p < .05$. The diastolic blood pressure readings for males were found to be on the average 5.92 mmHg higher than females for the posttest sessions.

The analysis of covariance also yielded a significant main effect for task, $F(2, 35) = 5.08$, $p < .01$. The diastolic blood pressure readings on the posttest were significantly higher ($p < .01$) on the weight task (adjusted mean = 84.93) and maze task (adjusted mean = 84.78) than on the resting task (adjusted mean = 82.32).

Systolic Blood Pressure

The systolic blood pressure ANCOVA yielded a significant main effect for the interval during which the blood pressure was recorded (the first or the second), $F(1, 17) = 12.16$, $p < .01$. The interval main effect cannot be accurately discussed except with reference to the significant Task × Interval interaction, $F(2, 35) = 5.39$, $p < .01$. Newman-Keuls comparisons indicated systolic blood pressures to be significantly higher ($p < .05$) at the second interval of the weight task compared with the second interval of the rest task. Also, systolic blood pressures were found to increase significantly from the first to the second interval of the weight task ($p < .01$).

Table 10.1
Pretest, Mean Difference Scores, and Adjusted Cell Means
for Each Dependent Variable[a]

	DIASTOLIC BLOOD PRESSURE		
	Treatment	Control	Normotensives
Pretest	91.04	96.14	71.52
Difference Scores	3.75	2.06	0.86
Adjusted Cell Means	87.09*	93.69	71.25

	SYSTOLIC BLOOD PRESSURE		
	Treatment	Control	Normotensives
Pretest	126.46	143.25	112.10
Difference Scores	4.30	8.50	4.12
Adjusted Cell Means	122.39	130.18	112.32

	EMG		
	Treatment	Control	Normotensives
Pretest	53.81	57.22	80.63
Difference Scores	7.31	.22	20.44
Adjusted Cell Means	47.40	61.19	58.75

	HEART RATE		
	Treatment	Control	Normotensives
Pretest	81.27	75.52	70.85
Difference Scores	6.29	3.13	2.39
Adjusted Cell Means	73.32	72.50	70.00

[a]Cell Means are adjusted by the ANCOVA procedure with pretest scores as covariate.

$*p < .01$

Figure 10.1. Diastolic blood pressures for groups and tasks using adjusted cell means.

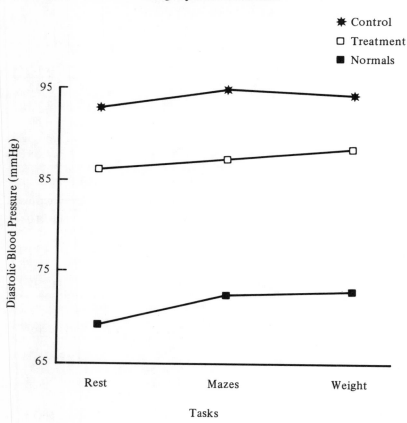

EMG

A significant main effect for task was found by analysis of covariance of the EMG data, $F(2, 35) = 14.78$, $p < .001$. Newman-Keuls post hoc analysis indicated all three means were significantly different from one another ($p < .01$). EMG measures were found to be lowest on the resting task, intermediate on the maze task, and highest on the weight task. No other interaction or main effect was significant for the EMG dependent variable.

Heart Rate

Analysis of covariance performed on the heart rate data indicated a significant Task $\times$ Interval $\times$ Group interaction, $F(4, 35) = 2.65$, $p < .05$.

Newman-Keuls post hoc analysis indicated the hypertensive control group had significantly higher ($p < .05$) heart rates than the normotensive group at the second interval of the resting task.

DISCUSSION

The first purpose of this experiment was to evaluate the effectiveness of group-administered progressive relaxation training as an adjunctive therapy for essential hypertension. The treatment group produced significantly lower diastolic blood pressure readings than the hypertensive control group at the posttest recording session. The normotensive group was significantly lower than both hypertensive groups, which was not surprising since by definition the normotensive group had lower diastolic blood pressures. No treatment effects were demonstrated for the other dependent variables. Thus, the treatment group was able to achieve significantly greater reductions in diastolic blood pressure than the hypertensive control or normotensive group, indicating the therapy was effective. Similar changes did not appear on other physiological measures, although one typically would expect concomitant changes in systolic blood pressure, heart rate, and muscle tension due to the reduction in overall physiological arousal brought about by the relaxation training.

The second purpose of the experiment was to assess the generalization of effects obtained from relaxation. On what is considered to be the most important dependent variable, diastolic blood pressure, the treatment group demonstrated greater reductions than the hypertensive control group across all tasks presented following treatment. Thus, there is some evidence for the generalization of blood pressure reductions to the other tasks used in this experiment.

The third purpose of this experiment was to investigate the reduction of blood pressure concomitant with reduction in EMG. Muscle tension levels indicated by EMG recordings during the three tasks were significantly different, with the rest phase producing the lowest levels of tension, the fine-motor task intermediate levels, and the weight task the highest levels. The EMG levels were predicted to be at the prementioned values, due to the muscle tension requirements of each task. A significant difference in EMG levels was not found between the experimental groups or between the pre- and posttest sessions. Thus, it could be hypothesized that the reductions in blood pressure, which were significantly greater in the treatment group than in the hypertensive control group, were brought about by some aspect of relaxation training unrelated to muscle tension. Also, reduction in muscle tension may not be necessary for generally improved diastolic blood pressure levels. Reductions in diastolic blood pressure were demonstrated for the treatment group and generalized across tasks requiring varying levels of tension. Also, the treatment group was the only group that demonstrated reductions in diastolic blood pressure on the weight task; this task required the highest muscle tension levels.

This study also serves as an example of the useful features of control-group studies. Subjects were assigned to different conditions randomly, allowing group differences at posttesting to be attributed to treatment and not to group characteristics. Use of the "discussion group" allowed for some control over factors such as attention to the disorder, group interaction, and expectancy as competing explanations of treatment effects (Rose, 1979).

Group training seems to be a cost-effective manner of providing several individuals with therapy at one time, and has some features that may help many clients. For instance, individuals within therapy groups tend to score more alike after treatment than individuals in other groups under the same treatment conditions (Rose, 1979). Such reductions in variability are assumed to be a result of the common experience shared by the group members. Rose (1979) points out that "the more interactive the group treatment, the more likely it is that group members will affect one another's learning" (p. 74). In this study, subjects within both groups were observed to interact freely prior to and following each treatment session. Subjects were able to identify with other patients with the same presenting problem, and to see that they were not unique in having such a disorder. The groups also afforded an atmosphere of emotional and interpersonal support, particularly since each member was trying to gain some self-control over her problem. It is possible that discussions pertaining to use of relaxation as a stress management technique were facilitated by modeling between members. Finally, the group-training sessions set up a situation whereby group members reinforced each other's expectancy of improvement as a result of participation in the training.

Some discussion should also be directed to the clinical significance of the relaxation procedure utilized in this experiment. Several subjects in both hypertensive groups achieved reductions in blood pressure readings. Three subjects within the treatment group brought their blood pressure into the average range (i.e., average readings below 90 mmHg), as compared with only one subject in the hypertensive control group. It is hypothesized that simply focusing on one's illness by discussing "illness factors" may have brought about beneficial results to subjects within the hypertensive control group.

The present study was found to support the findings of Taylor et al. (1977), in which a "relaxation plus medical treatment" group achieved a significantly greater reduction in systolic blood pressure compared to the "medical treatment only" group. The difference between the "relaxation" and "medical treatment only" groups for diastolic blood pressure readings was nearly significant. Also, all subjects within the relaxation group demonstrated reductions in diastolic blood pressure. Thus, the findings of the present study tend to be in general agreement with those of Taylor, except that a significant difference between groups on the systolic blood pressure readings was not found in the present study.

Another major difference between this study and that of Taylor et al. (1977) is that between-group differences were established after summing blood pressure readings across tasks such as mazes and holding a weight, in order to assess generalization of the treatment effects. Generalization has not been previously assessed in an experiment involving a non-pharmaceutical therapeutic technique as an adjunct treatment for essential hypertension.

This study supports the premise that short-term relaxation training provided in a small group situation is effective in reducing diastolic blood pressure, and indicates that treatment effects generalize across tasks requiring varying muscle tension requirements. The fact that there was no significant EMG treatment effect may indicate that other physiological mechanisms are operative in addition to the muscle-related reduction in peripheral resistance hypothesized in relaxation. For instance, it is possible that the effects of relaxation were not simply added to those of the medication, but that relaxation enhanced the physiological effects of the medication. Since several subjects improved significantly in both the treatment and hypertensive control groups, group process variables may have also played a part.

Although this study attempted to assess generalization of the treatment effects from relaxation training, there were certain limitations. First, the study was a short-term outcome study which did not address the issue of maintenance or persistence of treatment effects over time. It is possible that treatment effects diminished rapidly after training. Taylor et al. (1977), for example, found no significant treatment effects at a 6-month follow-up. Subjects might have benefited from longer amounts of practice or specific generalization training in order to bring about significant levels of generalization to situations outside of the treatment setting. Second, though the treatment effects generalized across the resting, maze, and weight tasks, generalization was not tested on tasks requiring gross-motor activities such as walking or changes in body orientation. Third, the only fine-motor task assessed was a simple maze task. Treatment effects may or may not have generalized to more detailed fine-motor activities.

It is suggested that future research be a series of single-subject experiments which first test for changes in blood pressure following relaxation training. Tests for generalization of the results to various tasks might then be conducted. Generalization tasks might gradually include more "real life" tasks such as typing, lifting heavy objects, or walking. Enhanced generalization might also be "built in" to the relaxation procedure by the gradual introduction of increased motor and cognitive activity.

With the controlling mechanisms for blood pressure being extremely complex, especially pertaining to the etiology of hypertension, psychologists may make their most significant contributions by studying what procedures are most beneficial to each patient. It does not at this point seem reasonable to assume that all patients with essential hypertension would respond to the same non-pharmaceutical or pharmaceutical therapy. There are currently many forms of medication available that attack blood pressure regulation in different ways. Similarly, patients may respond to different forms of self-regulatory techniques such as relaxation training, biofeedback instruction, autogenic training, or even meditation with the end result of reduced blood pressure.

Once several subjects are identified as responsive to a particular type of self-regulatory training, more homogeneous groups could be composed. For example, separate groups of subjects could be established for biofeedback training, meditation, and other forms of treatment. Additional research may focus upon evaluating different methods for differentiating subjects who might respond best within certain groups. Comparisons should then be made between "tailored intervention" approaches versus training within heterogeneous groups.

REFERENCE NOTES

1. Byassee, J. E. *Self-control interventions for essential hypertension.* Unpublished manuscript, April 1976. (Available from James E. Byassee, Ph.D., Halifax County Mental Health Center, Roanoke Rapids, N.C.).
2. Byassee, J. E., Farr, S. P., & Meyer, R. G. *Progressive relaxation and autogenic training in the group treatment of essential hypertension.* Unpublished manuscript, Fall 1976. (Available from James E. Byassee, Ph.D., Halifax County Mental Health Center, Roanoke Rapids, N.C.).

REFERENCES

Benson, H. *The relaxation response.* New York: Morrow, 1975.
Blanchard, E. B., & Young, L. D. Clinical applications of biofeedback training, a review of evidence. *Archives of General Psychiatry,* 1974, *30,* 573–588.
Fey, S. G., & Lindholm, E. Systolic blood pressure and heart rate changes during three sessions involving biofeedback or no biofeedback. *Psychophysiology,* 1975, *12,* 513–519.
Fey, S. G., & Lindholm, E. Biofeedback and progressive relaxation: Effects on systolic and diastolic blood pressure and heart rate. *Psychophysiology,* 1978, *15,* 239–247.

Fidel, E. A. The effectiveness of biofeedback and relaxation procedures in reducing high blood pressure (Doctoral dissertation, Texas Tech University, 1975). *Dissertation Abstracts International*, 1975, *36*, 3035B. (University Microfilms No. 75-26,838)

Geiger, H. J., & Scotch, N. A. Epidemiology of essential hypertension: Review and special attention to psychologic and socio-cultural factors I. Biologic mechanisms and descriptive epidemiology. *Journal of Chronic Disabilities*, 1963, *16*, 1151-1181.

Gressell, G. C. Personality factors in arterial hypertension. *Journal of the American Medical Association*, 1949, *140*, 60-72.

Huck, S. W., & McLean, R. A. Using a repeated measures ANOVA to analyze the data from a pretest-posttest design: A potentially confusing task. *Psychological Bulletin*, 1975, *82*, 511-518.

Ihli, K. L., & Garlington, W. K. A comparison of group vs. individual desensitization of test anxiety. *Behaviour Research and Therapy*, 1969, *7*, 207-209.

Jacobson, E. Variation of blood pressure with skeletal muscle tension and relaxation. *Annals of Internal Medicine*, 1939, *12*, 1194-1212.

Keppel, G. *Design and analysis: A researcher's handbook*. Englewood Cliffs, N.J.: Prentice-Hall, 1973.

Kondas, O. Reduction of examination anxiety and "stage-fright" by group desensitization and relaxation. *Behaviour Research and Therapy*, 1967, *5*, 275-281.

Lazarus, A. A. Group therapy of phobic disorders by systematic desensitization. *Journal of Abnormal and Social Psychology*, 1961, *63*, 504-510.

Paul, G. L. Physiological effects of relaxation training and hypnotic suggestion. *Journal of Abnormal Psychology*, 1969, *74*, 425-437.

Paul, G. L., & Shannon, D. T. Treatment of anxiety through systematic desensitization in therapy groups. *Journal of Abnormal Psychology*, 1966, *71*, 124-135.

Paul, G. L., & Trimble, R. W. Recorded vs. "live" relaxation training and hypnotic suggestion: Comparative effectiveness for reducing physiological arousal and inhibiting stress response. *Behavior Therapy*, 1970, *1*, 285-302.

Rose, S. *Group therapy: A behavioral approach*. Englewood Cliffs, N.J.: Prentice-Hall, 1979.

Sammons, R. A. Effects of subjects' expectancy of experimenter's involvement on live and taped relaxation training (Doctoral dissertation, University of North Carolina at Greensboro, 1974). *Dissertation Abstracts International*, 1975, *35*, 6111B. (University Microfilms No. 75-13,716)

Schwartz, G. Biofeedback as therapy: Some theoretical and practical issues. *American Psychologist*, 1973, *28*, 666-673.

Shapiro, D., Gershon, B., Gershon, E., & Stern, M. Effects of feedback and reinforcement on the control of human systolic blood pressure. *Science*, 1969, *163*, 588-590.

Shoemaker, J. E., & Tasto, D. L. The effects of muscle relaxation on blood pressure of essential hypertensives. *Behaviour Research and Therapy,* 1975, *13,* 29–43.

Taylor, C. B., Farquhar, J. W., Nelson, E., & Agras, S. Relaxation therapy and high blood pressure. *Archives of General Psychiatry,* 1977, *34,* 339–342.

Wechsler, D. *Wechsler Intelligence Scale for Children–Revised.* New York: The Psychological Corporation, 1974.

Weiner, H. *Psychobiology of Essential Hypertension.* New York: Elsevier North Holland, Inc., 1979.

Chapter 11

Behavioral Group Therapy with Psychiatric Outpatients: A Controlled Study

Ian R. H. Falloon

Abstract

A controlled outcome study of behavioral group therapy methods suggested that group-centered group discussion is an effective treatment for psychiatric outpatients with severe interpersonal deficits. The addition of overt modeling and role rehearsal appeared to further enhance the outcome, but not significantly. However, the addition of a highly structured homework procedure showed more substantial benefits for those who completed this task. Furthermore, the benefits of homework were sustained over a period of up to 2 years, whereas the advantages associated with role rehearsal were less evident with time. Patients with diagnoses of social phobia, depressive neurosis, and sexual deviance showed good results, while substance abusers and schizophrenics were less successful and tended to drop out. Nonspecific variables, such as attraction for the group and its leaders or expectation of improvement, were considered to have been associated with treatment outcome. In addition, factors associated with social support in the home environment may have affected outcome and were probably related to the rate of attrition.

Group psychotherapy has evolved as a major therapeutic intervention for individuals with deficits in social competence (Battegay, 1977). The development of this treatment modality has been achieved with minimal empirical guidelines. The therapeutic ingredients of groups are still considered by many to be essentially social phenomena inaccessible to psychological evaluation. Considerable theoretical interest in the structural aspects of groups and styles of leadership has not resulted in rigorous studies to support the hypotheses generated through this discussion. Although the complexity of group interaction is daunting to the behavioral researcher, the careful examination of specific group treatment procedures and their effects on outcome goals may lead to a better understanding of the curative potential of this modality.

Social skills training is a behavior therapy method that often employs the small group setting for the development of interpersonal competence (Goldstein, 1973; Liberman, King, DeRisi, & McCann, 1975). Several specific components derived from psychodrama and social learning paradigms are employed. These include: role-playing of social interactions that group members find difficult in their daily lives; modeling by the therapist and other group members of alternative ways of handling these interpersonal situations; specific performance feedback and social reinforcement; and the completion of homework tasks between sessions. With its specific emphasis on interpersonal interaction, social skills training presents the group psychotherapy researcher with a clearly defined structure in which to work.

Over the past decade, a number of studies of behavioral group therapy have specifically aimed at enhancing interpersonal and social performance of psychiatric inpatients (Booraem & Flowers, 1972; Doty, 1975; Gutride, Goldstein, & Hunter, 1973; Lomont, Gilner, Spector, & Skinner, 1969) and outpatients (Field & Test, 1975; Percell, Berwick, & Biegel, 1974). The results of these studies suggest that behavioral group therapy that employs role rehearsal, modeling, and specified homework assignments, in addition to problem-solving discussion, facilitates changes in the social interaction of group members in their everyday lives. However, questions remain as to whether this method confers advantages over more traditional group therapy methods that rely mainly on structured group discussion. A controlled study was conducted by the author at the Maudsley Hospital in London to explore the following issues:

1. Does the addition of role rehearsal and modeling to goal-directed group discussion enhance the effects of behavioral group therapy in changing the interpersonal functioning of psychiatric outpatients?
2. Does the addition of a structured homework program further increase effectiveness?
3. Are these effects sustained at follow-up?

In addition to studying the impact of various therapeutic interventions on the treatment outcome, an attempt was made to examine aspects of group process in a behavioral group. Cohesiveness, or attraction of members to the group, is considered to play a central role in determining the outcome of group therapy (Bednar & Lawlis, 1971; Yalom, 1970). Liberman (1971) demonstrated the effectiveness of operant conditioning techniques in increasing group cohesiveness and showed that this was associated with symptomatic improvement. It was hypothesized that behavioral group therapy that included role rehearsal and modeling would promote inter-personal contact during therapy sessions and would foster greater group cohesiveness than an almost identical discussion approach. Furthermore, in keeping with earlier published reports (Clark & Cuthbert, 1965; Kapp, Gleser, Brissenden, Emerson, Wingt, & Kashdan, 1964; Liberman, 1971; Yalom & Rand, 1966), it was postulated that the level of group cohesiveness would show a positive association with outcome.

METHOD

This study aimed at evaluating the effectiveness of behavioral group therapy methods in changing a broad range of social and related functions in psychiatric outpatients. After an extensive pretreatment assessment, patients were randomly assigned to one of three conditions: (a) goal-directed group discussion and a control daily homework program (D); (b) goal-directed group discussion and a control daily homework program plus role rehearsal and modeling of social role behavior (R); and (c) goal-directed group discussion plus role rehearsal and modeling plus an experimental structured daily homework program (E).

Treatment was conducted over ten 75-minute sessions at weekly inter-vals in small groups (6–10 subjects each), with subsequent follow-up at a mean of 16 months. Each group had two co-leaders (one male, one female) who shared the task of leading the group discussions. Figure 11.1 shows the experimental design.

Subjects

The patients who entered this study were psychiatric patients attending the Maudsley Hospital Outpatient Clinic for treatment of difficulties in social functioning. Because the indications for behavioral group therapy had not been established, it was considered important to include a wide range of patients, but those with organic mental disorders or presently receiving intensive psychotherapy (either dynamic or behavioral) were excluded. Selection was otherwise based exclusively on the ability of the screening therapist to elicit 10 target social situations in which the patient reported experiencing moderate to severe anxiety or inadequacy, e.g., "starting a conversation with a girl I find attractive" or "being put down by a person at work." Patients who were already on stable medication

Figure 11.1. Experimental design.

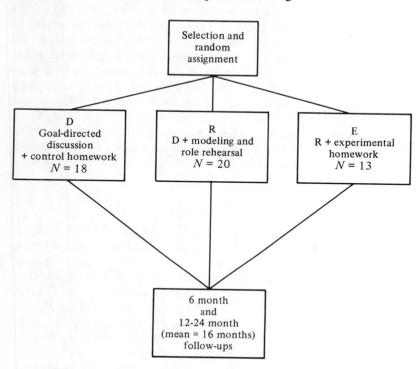

continued this at the same dosage throughout the 10-week group treatment. No patients were started on medication during the study.

In all, 104 patients were considered for treatment. Only 6 were not accepted, all of whom had highly circumscribed social problems, usually social phobias; 22 others refused our offer of treatment. Of the 76 who began treatment, 56 completed the 10 sessions. During the treatment period 5 others were excluded from the statistical analysis: 1 was diagnosed as having progressive cerebral degeneration and 4 others received additional psychotherapy outside the study. Table 11.1 shows the characteristics of the patients who started and finished treatment.

Group Leaders

Three pairs of group leaders were selected. The male leaders consisted of a psychiatrist and two psychiatric nurse-therapists, all trained behavior therapists. The female leaders were three experienced occupational therapists. All leaders were experienced in group therapies and had been leaders of skills training groups. Each male-female pair conducted one group in each of the three conditions (D, R, and E).

Table 11.1
Patient Characteristics

	Began Treatment $N = 76$	Ended Treatment $N = 51*$	Dropouts $N = 16$
Age (years)	26.8	28.2	23.5
Sex			
Male	55	34	13
Female	21	17	3
Marital Status			
Married	11	10	1
Single	64	41	14
Divorced	1	0	1
Job Status			
Employed	50	34	7
Unemployed	26	17	9
Diagnosis			
Social phobia	25	18	5
Personality disorder	18	12	3
Depression	13	10	1
Schizophrenia	6	4	2
Sexual deviance	4	4	0
Substance abuse	7	2	5
Obsessive-compulsive disorder	3	1	0
Problem Duration (years)	11.3	11.9	5.4

*Five patients were withdrawn from the study when they ceased to meet entry criteria; four were withdrawn when their group was postponed.

Two pilot groups were conducted to train leaders and, in addition, 20 hours were spent training the leaders in the research procedures, including specific methods for dealing with anticipated difficulties in the group process. Leaders took turns role-playing these situations with their colleagues, in order to improve the effectiveness of their interventions.

A training manual was prepared with detailed instructions and session-by-session therapist guidelines for discussion and role-rehearsal groups (Falloon, Lindley, & McDonald, 1974).

Assessment

Outcome evaluation was based on assessment 1 week before and after treatment and at 6 and 12–24 month (mean of 16 month) follow-up.

Target problems. These consisted of 10 individually specified, difficult interpersonal situations chosen by the patient in an interview. Each situation was rated for reported *anxiety and avoidance, functional incapacity* resulting from incompetent performance, and *frequency* of performance. These target problems covered many social contexts, e.g., conversations (with friends or the opposite sex, in groups, with older people, new acquaintances, or bosses), expressing feelings (affection, criticism, anger, compliments), social functions (parties, clubs, lectures, evening classes), sexual situations (asking for dates, initiating physical contact, handling intimate sexual situations), work situations (interviewing, approaching the boss, asking advice, being checked upon), or community situations (eating in restaurants, shopping, being stared at, taking public transportation). Ratings were made by the patient and by an assessor blind to the treatment condition.

Social anxiety. An inventory of social situations was rated for self-reported anxiety and avoidance, and measured generalization of anxiety reduction from the individualized target problems to broader social areas.

Social leisure activity. Twenty-three common social leisure activities were rated for the frequency of performance. This rating measured the generalization of the increased performance of the target problems to other social activities.

Self-image. The concept "myself as I am now" was rated on nine semantic differential bipolar scales, including attractive/unattractive, unsure/confident, relaxed/tense, friendly/hostile, shy/bold, coping/not coping, interesting/boring, assertive/nonassertive, and poised/awkward.

Mood. Scales for self-rating tension/anxiety and unhappiness were administered.

Social role functioning. In a structured interview an independent assessor rated work, social, and general adjustment on a shortened version of the Structured and Scaled Interview to Assess Maladjustment (SSIAM) (Gurland, Yorkston, Stone, Frank, & Fleiss, 1972). A rating of "expressiveness" was obtained by extracting items relating to the expression of positive and negative feelings.

Process Measures

At the end of every session, each patient rated his attraction to the *male leader,* the *female leader,* and the *group as a whole.* These ratings were placed in a sealed ballot box and patients were told that this box would not be opened until they had completed treatment in order to foster valid ratings.

Treatment Conditions

In an attempt to match the content of the sessions across groups, each session was structured around a selected issue. These topics were selected from an analysis of the most common target problems. The topics of the sessions were arranged in a graded hierarchy of social difficulty, starting with basic conversation skills and progressing to more complex situations such as work, groups, friendships, and sexual relationships. A handout that provided basic information on the topic of the next session was distributed a week in advance. Coping rather than mastery was encouraged, with emphasis on attainment of competence rather than excellence, and on performance of social tasks outside rather than during the sessions. Each group had individual *weekly* homework assignments plus either control or experimental *daily* homework.

Discussion groups (D). Each session began with all group members reporting their performance on an individual weekly homework assignment they had attempted. The group was prompted to provide praise and encouragement and to discuss alternative solutions where difficulties had been encountered. The main topic of the session was then introduced by the co-leaders. Patients were invited to describe specific related interpersonal encounters in which they experienced difficulty and, with the help of the group, to discuss alternative, more effective social behavior.

Leaders prompted and praised constructive, relevant discussion and mutual help. They avoided providing direct advice themselves until suggestions from other group members had been exhausted. Specific techniques such as relaxation, successive approximation, self-control, and "coping" self-verbalization were discussed, but overt practice or modeling was avoided during sessions. Patients who attempted to disrupt the group discussion were paid minimal attention and were prompted to remain task-oriented.

At the end of the discussion, each member set a goal to perform a specific social interaction that she found difficult for weekly homework, usually a target problem. Group members and leaders prompted realistic goal-setting. Members were encouraged to meet outside the sessions to provide specific support for their weekly homework tasks. Absent members were contacted by other group members, provided with a summary of the group discussion (as well as the handouts), and encouraged to attend the next session.

The following is a transcript of part of a discussion group session:

Eve:	I have a problem when I have to go with my husband to dinner parties.
Male leader:	What kind of difficulty do you have?
Eve:	I just get very nervous and I tell my husband I don't want to go. Sometimes I get a headache or feel . . .
Tom:	What does your husband say?
Eve:	He understands, I think. He says he'll go on his own and it'll be all right.
Tom:	No. What I mean is, does he know that it bothers you?

Female leader:	That's a good question.
Jill:	Yeah. Have you told him about this, you, your anxiety?
Eve:	No. I feel too embarrassed. It's silly, isn't it?
Male leader:	Do other people think this is a silly matter?
Tom:	No. I certainly don't. I used to feel like that, especially if I didn't know the people very well.
Female leader:	You felt nervous about going to dinner parties?
Tom:	Yeah. But I don't worry much now. I never get invited! (Laughs) No, I'm only joking.
Male leader:	Perhaps you could tell Eve how you learned to cope with this problem.
Tom:	I don't know really. I imagine I got used to it and stopped worrying.
Joe:	What time does the group finish today?
Male leader:	Was there anything you can remember doing to overcome your fear, Tom?
Tom:	Not really. I just forced myself, I suppose. Yeah.
Male leader:	How did you do that?
Tom:	I just decided I was going to go to dinners and places like that, and that was it.
Male leader:	So you made a decision that you would go regardless?
Tom:	Yes.
Female leader:	Forcing yourself to face up to any situation that makes you anxious is a good method of learning to cope with anxiety. Have you tried that, Eve?
Eve:	Sometimes I do that, but I get frightened that I'll start screaming in the middle of the dinner and my husband will lose his job.
Joe:	What does your husband do?
Eve:	He's an architect.
Female leader:	Joe, what would you do if you got very anxious at an important dinner party?
Joe:	I'd take a stiff whiskey. (Laughter)
Female leader:	That's another suggestion. A way to relax. Sarah, have you got any suggestions?
Sarah:	I can't think of anything. What about relaxation?
Tom:	(Addressing female leader) Sue, she could do some relaxation exercises or yoga or something before she went out.
Eve:	I tried once but it didn't work.
Male leader:	Well, Eve, we've got one or two ideas to help you get through these dinner parties. Tom suggested you go

no matter how bad you feel. Jill suggested talking to your husband. Joe suggested having a whiskey, and Tom suggested doing relaxation exercises or yoga. Has anyone got any other suggestions? Any strategies that have worked for us when we have had to do something that frightens us?

Role rehearsal groups (R). The main content of these group sessions was introduced with role-played modeling by the leaders of two or three brief social interactions that were target problems for most members. After this demonstration, group members rehearsed these interaction sequences with the leaders coaching. Constructive feedback was given about the behavior observed and, when appropriate, about the associated feelings, thoughts, fantasies, and physiological states evoked during the role rehearsal. Competent and comfortable performance was shaped by reinforcement from leaders and group members. In all other respects, the role-rehearsal groups closely resembled the discussion groups, with identical topics, handouts, weekly and daily homework procedures, and goal-setting.

The following is a transcript of part of a modeling and role-rehearsal session:

Male leader:	What are some other difficulties you have at work?
Penny:	I don't like to ask for time off. My boss is pretty strict about that. What do you think I should do?
Male leader:	I'm pleased you brought that problem up, Penny.
Female leader:	How many other people have difficulty asking their boss for time off?
George:	I do.
Pat:	I do, too.
Female leader:	This seems a common problem for our group. Penny, Pat, and George all have difficulty asking for time off, so let's all practice ways of improving our skills in this area. But first, Bill and I will give a demonstration. I'll try to be Bill's boss. He works in an office and he wants to take some time off his work. (Both get out of their seats. Bill, the male leader, goes out the door. The female leader sits as if working at a desk. Bill knocks on the door.)
Female leader:	Come in!
Bill:	Ms. Edwards, have you got a minute?
Female leader:	What do you want, Bill?
Bill:	I would like to take a couple of hours off tomorrow morning to go to the doctor.

Female leader:	Tomorrow, that's Wednesday. That's not a very good time for you to be away.
Bill:	It was the only time I could get, Ms. Edwards. I'd be happy to stay late to make up my time.
Female leader:	O.K.
Male leader:	(Out of role; laughing) She's tough. I didn't think I'd make it!
Female leader:	What did you notice about the way Bill did that?
Sam:	I don't think he should have offered to stay late.
George:	Nor do I.
Female leader:	What did he do that you liked, George?
George:	Well, he looked you in the eye. And, ah, he came right to the point and said what he wanted. I never do that.
Female leader:	So he looked at me and asked exactly what he wanted.
George:	Yeah.
Pat:	He was firm with her and wouldn't be put off.
Male leader:	How did I do that?
Pat:	I don't know.
Male leader:	Penny?
Penny:	Ah, he told her that he had to go then. I suppose . . .
Female leader:	And he spoke in a loud, firm voice. O.K. Now we want each of you to pair off and take turns at being the boss and the employee and ask for time off. We will give each of you some coaching. O.K. I will help you two (speaking to Pat and George). Who's going to be the boss first?
George:	Oh, I will.
Female leader:	What's your boss like, Pat?
Pat:	It's a woman. She's very difficult to talk to, and she always gets mad when anybody asks her anything.
Female leader:	She sounds pretty tough.
Pat:	Yeah.
Female leader:	Can you be tough like Pat's boss?
George:	I'll give it a try. (In role) What do you want, Miss Stewart?
Pat:	Oh, I was just going to ask you if you would mind if I took tomorrow off to go to the dentist.
George:	You mean the whole day?
Pat:	Well, yes.
George:	That's ridiculous. What's he going to do? Pull them all out?
Pat:	No.

George:	If you will work extra hours, I'll consider it.
Pat:	Yes. I'll try.
George:	O.K. You can go.
Female leader:	That's good. You came right to the point, Pat, and you spoke very clearly. How did that feel?
Pat:	Terrible. I didn't know what to say.
Female leader:	What were you saying to yourself when he told you the request was ridiculous?
Pat:	My mind was blank. I wished I'd never asked. My boss is just like that—always making people feel small.
George:	I wasn't being serious.
Female leader:	Can we try that again? And this time I'd like you to speak in a firm voice that sounds as if you really must go to the dentist.
Pat:	All right. Mrs. Baker, I have to go to the dentist tomorrow. I have a bad toothache, and it's the only appointment, so I'd appreciate it if you could let me take the day off.
George:	The whole day? Don't you think you could come in in the afternoon?
Pat:	Yes. I could come in after the appointment, I suppose.
Female leader:	That was better. You spoke in a much firmer voice and sounded much more determined to get the time off. How did that seem to you?
Pat:	Well, O.K., I suppose. Do you think I should go in after the appointment?
Female leader:	George, how did Pat come across to you?
George:	She seemed more confident. But I wouldn't go back to work after the dentist. Just say you'll make up the hours.

Experimental homework groups (E). The sessions in this condition were identical to role-rehearsal groups; however, in addition to the weekly homework task assigned at the end of each session, patients carried out structured daily homework. Patients were asked to record daily on a worksheet (see Figure 11.2) the frequency with which they performed their 10 target problem behaviors and the difficulty they experienced. These completed social tasks earned self-scored points that were based on the patients' own ratings of difficulty. The daily total of points was exchanged for self-selected reinforcers such as food, hobbies, or television.

This rather complex self-controlled program was supervised on a daily basis by a significant other (a friend, relative, or workmate) who was selected by the patient. Significant others were provided with a written guide to

Figure 11.2. Example of Daily Activities Record.

DAILY ACTIVITIES RECORD

Name Joe Bloggs   Date 12 September, 1980

Daily Tasks	Value Points	How Often Done	Total Points
1. Talking to neighbor for 5 mins	2	1 ②3 4 5 6 7 8 9 10	4
2. Talking to secretary for 5 mins	5	1 2 ③4 5 6 7 8 9 10	15
3. Asking boss a question	5	1 ②3 4 5 6 7 8 9 10	10
4. Going for a drink with workmates	6	1 ②3 4 5 6 7 8 9 10	12
5. Making a phone call	5	①2 3 4 5 6 7 8 9 10	5
6. Asking personal advice	8	1 2 3 4 5 6 7 8 9 10	–
7. Asking girl for date	8	1 2 3 4 5 6 7 8 9 10	–
8. Holding girl's hand	8	1 2 3 4 5 6 7 8 9 10	–
9. Going to a dance/disco	6	1 2 3 4 5 6 7 8 9 10	–
10. Going to night class/lecture	4	1 2 3 4 5 6 7 8 9 10	–
Any other difficult situations you were able to cope with–			
11. Telling a person at work he made me angry			10
12.			
		Total	56

252

Privileges	Points	Number of Times	Total
1. Watching TV for 30 mins	20	2	40
2. Eating piece of cake	15	1	15
3. Having extra cup of tea	10		
4. Going to a movie	20		
5. Reading magazines for 15 mins	5		
		Total	55

Checker's comment   *Trying hard. A bit unhappy after work. Enjoyed watching TV.*

Mary Bloggs, mother

the homework program and were invited to discuss difficulties with the group leaders at any time. The significant others were instructed to provide support and encouragement for patients from day to day. Group leaders reviewed the daily records and recorded weekly totals on a group chart.

Control homework. In order to control for the effects of daily record-keeping, all patients in D and R groups were asked to compile a daily record of the frequency with which they engaged in self-selected "enjoyable events." They were similarly instructed to select a significant other who provided day-to-day feedback on their mood and support for their partici-pation in the program. The differences between the experimental patients' homework and that of the control patients are summarized in Table 11.2.

Table 11.2
Components of Experimental vs. Control Homework

Event	Control	Experimental
Weekly Social Task	+	+
Reinforcement From Group for Efforts	+	+
Daily Record of Pleasant Events	+	
Daily Contact With Significant Other	+	+
Daily Record of Social Target Problems		+
Self-Reinforcement for Daily Performance		+
Reinforcement From Significant Other for Daily Performance		+

RESULTS

Overall Improvement

Fifty-one patients completed the group therapy program and continued to fulfill the selection criteria. At the 6-month follow-up, 50 completed further assessment, and 44 (86%) completed assessments during the second year of follow-up.

All patients showed improvement on at least several measures. An analy-sis of variance on pre-post measures showed highly significant improvement on all measures ($p < .0001$ - $p < .0002$). This improvement was sustained at 6-month and 16-month follow-up.

Role Rehearsal vs. Discussion

There was a consistent but small advantage for role rehearsal in 11 of the 12 outcome measures. A multivariate analysis of variance of the combined outcome measures demonstrated a near-significant trend favoring role rehearsal over discussion ($p < .08$). In order to explore this trend in greater detail, repeated measures analyses of covariance were conducted with pre-treatment measures as the covariates. (Please note that for these measures, the lower the score is, the greater the improvement.) There were no significant differences between the two treatment conditions on pre-treatment measures.

Target ratings. Substantial improvement in the 10 individualized target problems was noted for almost every patient after treatment. As well as a reduction in anxiety in these situations, patients reported entering these situations more frequently (see Figure 11.3). Surprisingly, there was no significant advantage for role rehearsal on these specific targets. However, both groups attempted to enter target situations as weekly homework assignments, and this may have been a more crucial change factor than role rehearsal and modeling in the sessions.

Generalization measures. There was evidence for significant generalization of the subjects' social anxiety reduction to situations not specifically dealt with in the sessions. Contrary to expectations, slightly greater generalization was noted in the discussion condition at the end of treatment (see Figure 11.3). This may have resulted from an emphasis on *general* strategies for dealing with social difficulties in the discussion groups, while role rehearsal focused on highly *specific* situations. Increased participation in social interaction was more prominent in the role-rehearsal groups and approached significance ($p < .09$).

Social functioning. Improved social functioning resulted from the behavioral group therapy. The work status of role-rehearsal patients improved considerably during treatment. Five of six patients who were not employed before treatment had obtained steady work at the end of treatment. The majority of those already working reported progress in their jobs and improved interpersonal relationships with workmates and supervisors. Discussion group patients reported less improvement, but two out of five unemployed obtained work. However, rehearsal was not significantly superior to discussion on the work or the social adjustment measures (see Figure 11.4). While some patients became more open, made new friends, contacted old friends, and felt increased confidence in their social interaction, others still approached social contacts with considerable trepidation at the end of treatment. However, whereas prior to treatment they had not even considered entering social relationships, they were now attempting to form friendships with others.

The SSIAM interview items relating to expression of positive and negative feelings towards family, friends, and work contacts (see Figure 11.5) improved significantly more after role rehearsal than after discussion ($p < .04$). In several cases, this improvement led to problems in family

**Figure 11.3. Rehearsal and modeling vs. discussion comparisons
in target and generalization measures for pre- and
posttreatment and 6-month follow-up.**

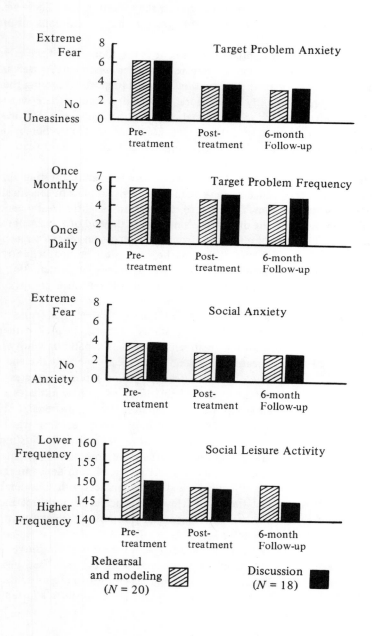

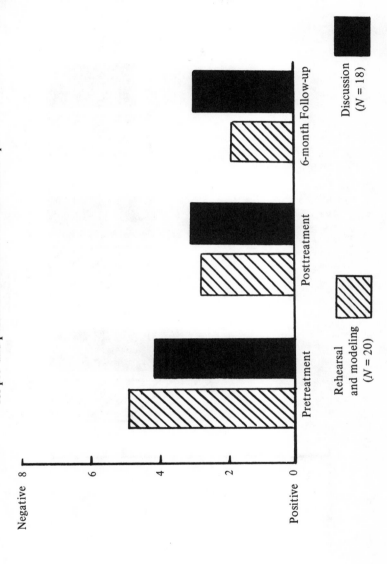

Figure 11.4. Rehearsal and modeling *vs.* discussion comparisons of mean work adjustment ratings (five scales) for pre- and posttreatment and 6-month follow-up.

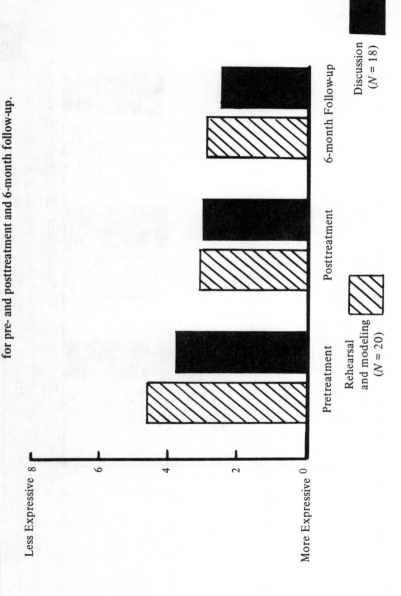

Figure 11.5. Rehearsal and modeling vs. discussion comparisons of mean expressiveness (assertiveness) ratings for pre- and posttreatment and 6-month follow-up.

relationships. As single patients became more assertive with their parents and began to go out with friends, some parents attempted to dissuade them. One girl's father accused her of sexual misconduct when visiting middle-aged neighbors. A 23-year-old patient's mother phoned the hospital in tears when he had not returned home half an hour after the end of a treatment session. He was out practicing initiating conversations with two fellow group members. The elderly mother of a 35-year-old man discouraged him from participating in the treatment or from expanding his social contacts. He told her he wanted to become more independent. During treatment he partially succeeded and attended most sessions. At a follow-up visit it became clear that his mother had reasserted her control when she accused two research workers of trying to take him away from her when she needed him at home to take the place of her husband who had died some years ago.

Three patients complained that pre-existing marital difficulties had been made worse; two were women whose husbands resented their increased social competence; both declined offers of marital therapy and managed to resolve these conflicts successfully with their husbands.

Increased social competence and heterosexual contact uncovered difficulties with sexual behavior in several patients. Specific family, marital, and sexual problems were handled in one or two brief directive individual sessions during the follow-up period. Improved ability of patients to discuss their feelings in an open manner was thought to contribute to the ease with which most of these difficulties were resolved.

As might have been expected, there was little change on the scale of general personality adjustment with either treatment condition, although there was a non-significant trend for role rehearsal to result in more improvement than discussion. Several patients reported considerable change and felt that they could now feel confident in dealing with a variety of life stresses, and that they had become stronger personalities.

Self-image and mood. Most patients developed a more positive self-image and improved mood after treatment. Only two patients recorded small decrements in their self-image ratings after treatment. The anxiety-management techniques trained in the role-rehearsal groups probably accounted for the slight superiority of this condition in reducing persistent tension and anxiety.

In summary, although role rehearsal produced a trend toward greater change than discussion on almost every rating, this superiority attained statistical significance on only one measure: the expressiveness (or assertiveness) scale. The trend suggested by the multivariate analysis would not appear to result from substantial superiority of role rehearsal on one or two independent variables, but rather from a consistent pattern of greater improvement across most variables.

Overall levels of improvement were sustained on all measures 6 and 16 months after treatment; however, differences between the two treatment conditions became increasingly blurred over time.

Effect of Systematic Daily Homework

It had been hoped that 20 randomly assigned patients would complete treatment in the role-rehearsal plus experimental homework condition. However, the rather complex task that this modality entailed reduced compliance levels substantially. A further complication was the removal of one group from the data analysis in this condition when a spate of public transport strikes forced the postponement of the group. Thus, of the 13 patients who completed attendance in this condition, 7 completed all aspects of their experimental homework as instructed. Surprisingly, this level of compliance was similar to that of patients completing the control homework. Eleven out of 20 role-rehearsal and 10 out of 18 discussion patients completed the control program.

To control for factors that may have led patients to cooperate with homework, such as a tendency to compliance or contact with significant others, the outcome of those patients who completed all aspects of experimental homework was compared with that of patients who completed all aspects of the control procedure. The experimental homework condition was superior on 11 out of 12 outcome measures (see Figure 11.6). These differences reached the 5% level on repeated measures analysis of variance for Unhappiness ($p <.02$) and Target Problem Frequency ($p <.05$), and approached significance for Self-image ($p <.10$). In contrast to the weakening of the effects of role rehearsal at follow-up, experimental homework appeared to stabilize, and, in some patients, to facilitate improvement after treatment. By the 6-month follow-up, the gains after treatment were even more significantly in favor of the experimental modality. Significant differences were evident for Target Problem Anxiety ($p < .02$), Target Problem Frequency ($p < .05$), Self-image ($p < .02$), and Unhappiness ($p < .05$), and approached significance for Social Anxiety ($p < .08$).

At long-term follow-up the superiority of the experimental condition was maintained, but somewhat reduced, so that only Target Problem Anxiety ($p <.05$) reached significance, while Target Problem Frequency and Unhappiness approached significance ($p <.10$). Social leisure activities had decreased in both conditions at long-term follow-up. This was difficult to account for, although one possible explanation was that this follow-up was carried out during winter months when social leisure activity was probably reduced in the general population. If this was the case, a similar reduction in activity would have been expected in the combined role-rehearsal and discussion populations. This reduction was not very evident. However, longitudinal measures of social activity may be expected to show substantial seasonal fluctuation.

Figure 11.6. Experimental vs. control homework comparisons of target, self-image, and unhappiness measures for pre- and posttreatment and 6-month follow-up.

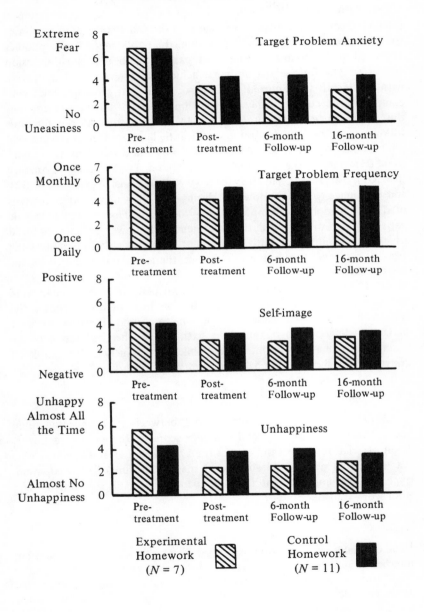

INTRAPERSONAL VARIABLES AND OUTCOME

Diagnosis

The three main diagnostic subgroups (social phobia, inadequate personality disorder, and depressive neurosis) showed similar good responses to treatment, with improvement sustained at follow-up. Social phobics improved their self-image more than patients with neurotic depression (p <.02). The four sexual deviants included in the study all improved, with no recidivism reported at follow-up. The four schizophrenics who completed the course made significant improvement with treatment, but this improvement was poorly sustained at follow-up. At the 6-month follow-up, schizophrenics showed significantly less improvement than social phobics on Target Problem Anxiety (p <.05) and Social Leisure Activity (p <.05), and at the 16-month follow-up on Target Problem Anxiety (p <.01), Target Problem Frequency (p <.05), Social Anxiety (p <.02), and Self-image (p <.01). However, during the follow-up period no relapses of florid schizophrenic symptomatology occurred. The two schizophrenic patients who dropped out during treatment both showed evidence of florid psychotic symptoms at initial assessment, but were able to complete the arduous assessment procedures, and were, therefore, not excluded on the basis of their mental state.

Only two of the seven alcohol- or drug-dependent patients completed the course. All except one took alcohol or drugs before attending the sessions in spite of the leaders' instructions to abstain. The one abstinent patient made good progress until the sixth session when he began drinking again and broke a leg when hit by a car while drunk. The two who completed group therapy showed minimal improvement.

Other Intrapersonal Variables

Multiple correlations were performed between 19 sociodemographic and pretreatment variables[1] and 7 change scores at the end of treatment. Eight correlations were significant at the 5% level or better. Good outcome was associated with initial absence of medication, unskilled occupation, expectancy of improvement, lower frequency of social leisure activity, and poor work adjustment.

---

[1] These variables were the following: age, sex, marital status, living situation, number of siblings, class, work status, occupation, educational attainment, IQ, duration of disability, medication, pretreatment expectancy, social anxiety, social leisure activity, self-image, work, social adjustment, and general adjustment.

Outcome also was affected by interpersonal and group variables, such as the development of the group and attraction toward the group or leader.

INTERPERSONAL AND GROUP VARIABLES AND OUTCOME

Development of the Groups

Session One was tense in all groups. Several subjects failed to attend. Two had panic attacks en route and returned home, but managed to attend subsequent sessions. Discussion groups focused on how much nonverbal expression, like posture and eye contact, affected interpersonal communication. Anxiety-management techniques were discussed. Role-rehearsal groups demonstrated and practiced postures characteristic of common mood states, learned how to discriminate affective expression through postural cues, and assisted one another in sitting and standing in a relaxed, receptive, and confident manner.

Session Two remained tense, particularly in discussion groups. In role-rehearsal groups subjects appeared more relaxed and reported success in the homework assignments they had set at the end of the first session. Some reported improved mood had resulted from posture change, others noted a greater awareness of nonverbal expression in others. The topic of nonverbal communication was continued with discussion and practice of facial expression and hand gestures.

Session Three was less buoyant in most groups. Several patients reported that treatment was not helping, and that they felt angry toward the leaders. The vocal expression of feelings through tone, pitch, and volume was discussed and practiced. Raising their voices in anger was very difficult for many patients. Nine subjects dropped out (65% of total dropouts) at this stage.

During Sessions Four through Seven, major improvement occurred. The skills discussed or rehearsed included meeting people, handling authority, having job interviews, expressing positive and negative feelings, and interacting in a variety of group situations. Patients in both types of groups were encouraged to meet together between sessions to practice the skills they had learned. Some groups met after the sessions at nearby pubs, coffee shops, or group members' homes. The majority of homework assignments were successfully attempted, but half the patients reported difficulty in gaining the assistance of relatives or friends to help them.

Session Eight proved difficult for role-rehearsal groups. Practicing initiating friendly contact with a stranger was difficult to role-play with group members they already knew well. They contrasted the difficulties they still had in real life with their ease when performing in the group. Some members reported overt symptoms of depression.

In Session Nine, with the group's agreement beforehand, a 10-minute sex-education film was shown to role-rehearsal patients to be informative as well as to facilitate discussion for the many subjects with sexual difficulties. Most patients remained too inhibited to discuss their sexual problems or anxieties freely in a group, but later individually remarked on the value of the film. The discussion group discussed sexual behavior without seeing the film.

Session Ten finished optimistically, with patients reporting improvement in social skills and self-confidence. A few commented on their difficulties in transferring improved social interaction in the group to similar situations in real life. This comment was less prominent among discussion patients, who themselves advocated the use of role rehearsal to improve the training program. By the end of the treatment, one-third of the patients reported only minimal difficulties in social interaction. The remainder reported improvement in at least some areas of social function.

Several single patients who were living at home complained of parents' dissuading them from going out with friends. Less severe problems in attaining independence from overpossessive family ties were not uncommon, but many subjects successfully increased their social autonomy. This increase generally led to improved family and marital interaction.

Modeling of negative behavior occurred in all three conditions. Some role-rehearsal patients refused to participate in role-playing; others interrupted sessions with derogatory remarks about groups, the leaders, and themselves. Group leaders prompted constructive criticism wherever possible, and attempted to guide members making off-target comments back to the topic under consideration.

Group Attraction

Considerable consistency in the pattern of group development in the nine groups was reflected in the mean ratings of attraction for the group as a whole after each session. The attraction of patients to the group tended to increase from session to session. The mean attraction to the group was significantly greater in role-rehearsal than discussion groups (see Table 11.3).

The trend toward progressively greater attraction for the group was interrupted at two points in each of the completed 10-session courses. The first dip occurred at the third and fourth sessions and coincided with the period when negative feelings, mainly anger, were expressed toward the leaders and the group structure. Often this hostility was covert and was expressed as reduced participation and failure to attempt homework assignments, but at other times overt hostility was expressed. One patient told a male leader that he reminded him of his father and that he always became upset with persons in authority. A second period when attraction for the group declined was around the eighth session, when negative feelings, this time predominantly unhappiness and fear, were expressed. Patients reported feeling that, although they felt comfortable and competent in the group, the world outside had not changed but had remained a threatening place. This feeling appeared linked to the approaching end of treatment. At these two critical points the majority of dropouts left.

Leader Attraction

Mean attraction to leaders was greater for patients in the role-rehearsal groups than for patients in the discussion groups (see Table 11.3). There was no difference in attraction to leaders on the basis of sex. In all groups, subjects were initially attracted more to the leaders than to the group, but in the role-rehearsal groups, attraction for the group caught up within three or four sessions and remained similar to attraction to the leaders. In discussion groups, attraction to the group did not at any point approach attraction to the leaders. For the male discussion leader, attraction was significantly greater than for the group ($p < .02$), while the superiority of attraction toward the female leader approached significance ($p < .10$).

Table 11.3
Comparison of Mean Postsession Attraction Measures
in Role-Rehearsal and Discussion Conditions

Attraction Rating	Role Rehearsal $N = 33$	Discussion $N = 18$
Group	6.59*	5.55
Male Leader	7.04**	5.93
Female Leader	6.19**	5.77

$*p < .05$
$**p < .01$

Dropouts

Sixteen patients (21%) of those starting the 10-week course either dropped out or failed to attend at least six sessions. They showed less attraction to the group and leaders than those completing the training. In order to control for increased attraction with time, the mean attraction ratings obtained after the sessions each dropout attended were compared with the combined mean ratings of fellow group members who completed the course. A two-tailed Mann-Whitney U-test revealed significant differences on all three measures (see Table 11.4).

Dropouts were mainly single, unemployed males who tended to be more socially anxious ($p <.10$) and to have more general psychiatric symptoms ($p <.05$) than completers. The reasons they gave for dropping out were that the group did not suit them, they were too anxious, or that their problems seemed different from those of the others. Four subjects gave rapid improvement as their reason for premature termination. There was evidence for

Table 11.4
Comparison of Postsession Attraction Measures of Dropouts with the Mean Ratings of Those Who Completed the Group

Attraction Rating	Dropouts $N = 16$	Completers $N = 16$
Group	3.78	5.77*
Male Leader	4.23	6.28*
Female Leader	4.22	6.12*

*$p <.05$

such improvement in three of the four. A further feature of dropouts was the lack of a supportive significant other. Whereas 3 out of 39 subjects (8%) with an involved friend or family member dropped out, 13 out of 37 (35%) without this environmental support discontinued treatment. This difference was significant at the .01 level. Despite differences in attraction, there was no difference in the dropout rate in the two types of groups. In the one role-rehearsal group that was postponed after four sessions, attraction of members was similar to that of other role-rehearsal groups up to that point.

Correlation Between Attraction and Change

The three attraction measures were correlated with seven change measures using Pearson's product-moment coefficient (see Table 11.5). Significant positive correlations were found between improved self-image and attraction for the leaders ($p <.01$) and the group ($p <.05$). Reduction of Target Problem Anxiety was associated with attraction for the leaders ($p <.01$).

DISCUSSION

Substantial improvements in social functioning were recorded after 10 sessions of behavioral group therapy that focused directly on the interpersonal communication skills of a population of psychiatric outpatients. Many patients who had unsuccessfully sought help for their social difficulties

Table 11.5
Correlation Between Mean Postsession Attraction Ratings
and Outcome Change Measures

Change Rating	Attraction Ratings		
	Male Leader	*Female Leader*	*Group*
Target Problem Anxiety	.41**	.35**	.26
Target Problem Frequency	.05	.08	.08
Self-image	.38**	.37**	.33*
Social Anxiety	.26	.19	.15
Social Leisure Activity	.05	.08	.08
Work Adjustment	.06	.06	.04
Social Adjustment	.06	.13	.15

$*p < .05$
$**p < .01$

through dynamic group and individual psychotherapy methods improved markedly with this approach. Moreover, the impact of changes in social functioning remained evident during the second year of follow-up. Although no quantitative rating of mental status was included in the assessment, the two mood scales suggest that, at least in this area, improved social functioning was associated with a reduction in psychopathology. Medication and all other psychiatric treatment were held constant throughout the treatment program, so that these changes were probably attributable to the treatment. It was notable that very few patients, including those who dropped out, deteriorated during treatment.

Because this study did not include no-treatment or nonspecific treatment conditions, it was not possible to conclude that the specific focus on social behavior was essential to the changes observed. It is possible that nonspecific factors such as therapist attention, enthusiasm, patient expectations, and group support may have been responsible for part of the variance. The significance of these variables will be explored later in this chapter. However, the main thrust of this research was to explore the relative contributions of several components frequently employed in behavioral group therapy— goal-directed discussion, role rehearsal, modeling, and structured homework—in the facilitation of change in social behavior.

Effectiveness of Role Rehearsal and Modeling

The results suggested that role rehearsal plus overt modeling of specific social behavior sequences is more effective than small group discussion about similar behavior. It is postulated that role rehearsal and modeling contributed an anxiety-reducing practice effect that facilitated patients' entry into social and interpersonal situations they had previously avoided. Marzillier, Lambert, and Kellett (1976) noted a similar increase in the frequency of social behavior after a course of individual social skills training. The constraints of the group setting prevented extensive training of individuals who completely lacked a repertoire of social skills to handle a given situation. However, the majority of patients in this study possessed an adequate repertoire of skills, but were inhibited from using them appropriately by anxiety or lack of confidence. The group method appeared particularly useful for them, whereas those with a limited range of communication skills may have benefited more from intensive individual treatment.

The separate effects of modeling and role rehearsal were not evaluated in this study. The modeling served to introduce each new role-rehearsal experience and appeared to facilitate subsequent role rehearsal during the session. Employed in this manner, it is doubtful that it contributed substantially to treatment outcome. Modeling by other patients and demonstration of alternative methods of handling difficult social situations may have helped some patients expand their repertoire of responses. While it was not feasible to observe each patient's behavioral performance on his 10 target problems before and after treatment, a videotaped assessment of conversation skill—a target problem for most individuals—was carried out on a subsample. A rater who did not know the treatments given to the patients, or whether the videotaped sequence had been recorded before or after treatment, rated improved conversation skill after therapy in 15 of the 16 patients and significant improvement for the subgroup overall. Role rehearsal produced no greater improvement in conversation skill than discussion. Although the numbers were small ($R = 12; D = 4$), this finding was consistent with the results of other workers using similar assessment methods (Argyle, Bryant, & Trower, 1974; Marzillier et al., 1976). However, unlike discussion patients, role-rehearsal patients did project a significantly improved social image during their conversations. These results suggest that a behavioral assessment of conversation skill that gives equal emphasis to each of the varied elements of nonverbal and verbal communication (e.g., eye contact, voice volume, or content) may not adequately reflect the behavioral changes that indicate increased confidence and poise. Further work in social psychology directed toward elucidating the relative importance of each of the elements of nonverbal and verbal communication may assist the clinician, who may then be able to concentrate on those deficits that lead to the greatest functional impairment. In the assessment of conversation skill used in this study, all components of communication skills were accorded equal importance. However, the weightings given to elements of communication are undoubtedly situation-specific and may vary substantially. For example, the importance of eye contact will be more significant in a face-to-face conversation than when talking on a telephone, and physical contact will be more important when initiating sexual contact than when discussing a problem with a supervisor. Thus, it is difficult to consider interpersonal skills as a single entity with one optimal training approach. Future research may examine the training of specific skills, e.g., conversations, dating, or work relations, in populations with clearly specified deficits.

Though a multivariate analysis supported the trend in favor of role rehearsal and modeling, it was clear that the discussion group was an effective treatment method in its own right. The hypothesized advantage of the role-rehearsal treatment may have been reduced in this study for three reasons. First, the strict control of within-sessions content reduced the amount of personalized practice and coaching of target behaviors that was possible. Second, it was unavoidable that patients in the discussion groups also practiced the social behavior concerned with interaction in the group treatment setting, such as expressing opinions and feelings, asking and responding to questions, discussing personal problems in a group, listening attentively, and giving compliments to others. Many of these behaviors were target problems for patients. Thus, it is not surprising that cohesive group discussion proved a useful vehicle for improving them. Third, in all groups social tasks related to target problems were set by patients and completed between sessions, with discussion and coaching at the beginning of each session. This focus on real-life progress was considered a major factor in facilitating real-life change. It was evident that the discussion group was much more than a mere control for nonspecific variables. It appears to be a very useful treatment method, restricted only in the mode by which issues are presented. A substantial amount of useful problem solving was carried out in the supportive group discussions. Thus, the significance that can be attached to the slight but consistent superiority of role rehearsal may be greater than if it had been compared with a placebo control.

Considerable effort was made to control for variables that may have biased the results. Allocation to treatment conditions was random; therapists led a group in each condition; blind assessments were made wherever possible; and a carefully prescribed guide for every session was provided. Despite these controls, what evidence was there of independent variables that may have accounted for the superiority of role rehearsal? Random assignment produced groups that were closely matched for age, sex, duration of disability, and other sociodemographic variables. There were no significant differences between the pretreatment assessments on any dependent measures. The patient's expectations of improvement, which were significantly correlated with successful outcome, were similar in both conditions.

Despite efforts to make all groups as cohesive as possible, greater cohesion and attraction to the group and the leaders developed in role-rehearsal groups. Increased attraction to the group correlated positively with several outcome measures, and significantly with self-image, suggesting the value of a cohesive group experience in increasing patients' self-esteem. Leader attraction correlated significantly with a reduction in specific anxieties as well as self-image. (Attraction to the group leaders was the same for all leaders, with no distinction between male or female leaders.) It may be hypothesized that an important mediating variable in the effectiveness of role rehearsal was the greater levels of interpersonal attraction in those groups. It was not possible in this study to determine whether the role rehearsal and modeling was responsible for more positive feelings than discussion, or whether the increased attraction was the result of some other factor.

The patients were invited to discuss their feelings about their treatment at the completion of the course. There was some consensus that the clear focus on overcoming specific interpersonal difficulties and the awareness that other people shared these difficulties were major factors mediating change. Most models of group therapy stress the value of shared experiences, but may prove more effective where a more specific focus is placed on overcoming interpersonal communication deficits and learning problem-solving skills. To this end, role rehearsal and modeling may be usefully employed in addition to more traditional group-centered discussion.

It might be argued that group development is disrupted by the use of a directive approach, and that group tensions would build up and lead to the breakdown of the treatment process and a high dropout rate. While a pattern of group development similar to that described in psychoanalytic group therapy was observed in all groups studied, there was no evidence that the structure imposed on the groups inhibited the therapeutic process or accounted for dropouts. Attrition was surprisingly low, especially when one considers that many patients selected for treatment were often extremely fearful of group situations. There was no screening to exclude patients considered unsuitable for group therapy, and the groups were selected on a random basis. It was noted that dropouts occurred predominantly at two points in the group development. The attraction ratings indicated that these two points corresponded to sessions where low mean scores of group cohesion and leader attraction were recorded in each of the completed groups. It seemed important that the therapists allowed some time for expression of negative feelings during these low points, which were clearly felt by all the participants. A structured therapy program is not a substitute for basic therapeutic skill, and time spent in discussing here-and-now tension within the group provided excellent opportunity for dealing with the appropriate communication of feelings. However, care was taken to avoid an exclusive focus on within-group issues at the expense of dealing with similar problems in the home environment. Role rehearsal and modeling, rather than inhibiting the group process, may have enhanced it through the opportunities it gave for less verbal members to express themselves. Liberman (1970) suggests that the expression of positive feelings in a group is possibly more crucial than expression of negative feelings. There appeared to be more positive statements made in role rehearsal than in discussion groups. Unfortunately, no measurement of the content of group interaction was made to verify this impression.

There was no reduction in the dropout rate associated with role rehearsal, despite the higher attraction ratings in the role rehearsal groups and the low attraction for the group among dropouts. Two factors have been considered to lower dropout rates in group therapy: careful group selection and detailed briefing on group procedures and expectations prior to treatment (Bednar, West, Evensen, Lanier, & Melnick, 1974). The research design of this study hampered the selection process, although homogeneity was achieved through the selection of only those patients with widespread moderate-severe social difficulties. A handout was given to all patients prior to the start of treatment, providing information on the nature of the group sessions and a rationale for the specific interventions employed. A similar handout was provided a week before each session, so that patients were prepared for the next session. Most patients reported that they read these sheets, and several invited their significant others to read them as well. There was no evidence that these procedures reduced the number of dropouts. However, the involvement of a significant other did reduce attrition. Further studies of behavioral groups may specifically explore this finding and other strategies aimed at improving attendance.

Effects of Structured Homework

Patients who completed daily homework assignments relevant to their target problems under the guidance of a significant other showed a much superior outcome to those who completed a control homework task that was unrelated to social difficulties. This effect continued at follow-up. Recording of daily events, contact with a significant other, and compliance were controlled. Improvement is thus shown to emanate not merely by the patient's being compliant, but by what she actually does as a result of being compliant. This superiority may be attributed to the specific focus of the homework on targeted social behavior on a daily basis, as well as the self-administered tangible reinforcement and social approval and support from selected persons in the home environment, and to a lesser extent from other group members.

Only half the patients cooperated with the homework program, a result unlikely to have been due to the complexity of the program alone, because the simpler control homework was completed by a similar proportion of patients. A common problem was contracting the assistance of a significant other. In pilot work this problem had proved less difficult when the friend or relative was interviewed before treatment. Such a procedure would seem worthy of further study. The importance of assuring a supportive environment in which the patient can practice and develop a more effective repertoire of skills appears crucial. Very often patients with social deficits live with parents who either show similar deficits or who actively discourage the patient from performing the skills she has learned. Unless such families are closely involved in the entire program, the lack of support for patients' attempts to increase their social competence is likely to lead to a rapid return to pretreatment levels of function once the treatment course has been completed. This pattern was noted in those patients who returned to unsupportive and sometimes hostile environments. Similar deterioration has been noted in schizophrenic and depressed patients returning to unsupportive families (Vaughn & Leff, 1976).

However, many patients had left home and were living alone in London. For them the behavioral group offered an opportunity to make the social contacts they found so difficult in their small apartments. It was very difficult to find a significant other in the home environment to help them with their homework. Although patients were encouraged to meet with one another in twos or threes to carry out homework tasks outside the group, relatively few managed to do so. The extent to which this occurred seemed to depend on the proximity of patients' homes, the adequacy of public transport, and patients' financial resources. Patients attended the groups from all over London and the Home Counties (often taking up to 2 hours to travel to the sessions). Few had cars and most had only limited finances, so that meetings apart from those managed immediately after sessions were limited.

It was difficult to recommend suitable venues where patients could seek suitable company in their own neighborhoods, e.g., clubs, discos, or meetings, although several excellent guidebooks on London activities were available. Ideally, all group members would come from a discrete neighborhood where the mutual support developed in the group could be usefully deployed in informal meetings between sessions.

A promising development in student analogue research termed "practice dating" might be of help to the patient who lacks a close associate (Christensen & Arkowitz, 1974). Students with difficulties in forming heterosexual relationships are randomly paired, then instructed to arrange "practice dates." After each date they discuss their performance with a therapist, who provides feedback, coaching, and instructions. After practice dating, college students have shown a lasting increase in social interaction with persons of both sexes. The value of a similar approach in less competent psychiatric patients remains untested. Role-rehearsal sessions could be combined with real-life practice with group members who might be trained to coach one another in the real-life setting.

Problems in the Assessment of Social Behavior

Social and interpersonal communication behavior is extremely complex. Assessment of this process is, therefore, very difficult. Although elegant descriptions of the nonverbal and verbal components of social interaction are available, there is little evidence of the validity of these components as predictors of social competence. Many individuals who function at a very effective level of social competence show deficits in communication skills, while others with adequate communication behavior prove ineffectual in their social functioning. Thus, the strong emphasis of many behavioral investigators on assessment of the components of communication behavior may not correlate with more functional measures of social role performance.

In this study, outcome was measured on a multilevel battery that included measures of social functioning, mood, self-image, and specific target difficulties. An analysis of specific communication behavior that employed an extended conversation format was videotaped and rated blindly. Although lack of resources prevented many patients from completing this behavioral assessment before and after treatment, those who did showed that the behavioral group therapy had indeed produced positive changes in communication behaviors. These observational measures correlated significantly with the other outcome measures ($r = .46-.63$), suggesting that communication behavior and social role functioning are associated. Because of the small numbers involved, it was not possible to demonstrate any differences between the discussion and role-rehearsal methods; however, there was some suggestion that subtle positive changes in the perception of the patient by others occurred in the role-rehearsal condition that were less evident in discussion patients. Further work in this area is indicated to validate many hypotheses concerning the relative significance of nonverbal and verbal components of behavior and the increase in social skills noted by observers after behavioral group therapy.

The frequency with which weekly homework assignment tasks were completed was not measured. Measurement of this, while lacking experimental rigor, may be a readily available measurement of progress in clinical treatment programs. Patients sometimes can be asked to provide tangible evidence of completed assignments, e.g., a cinema ticket, a purchase or receipt from a supermarket, or a library card (Liberman et al., 1975). However, when the tasks involve interpersonal situations, such as initiating conversations or giving and receiving affection, it is difficult to obtain such validation. Ratings by close contacts may be useful in these instances. Another method of assessing change in the natural environment involves training patients to rate reliably the performance of one another (Falloon, 1980). In the latter instance, patients complete their homework assignments in pairs and provide assessments of behavior in the real-life environment.

Prognostic Factors

A wide range of patients entered this study. Patients who suffered from substance abuse showed a high dropout rate. They all used alcohol or illicit drugs to cope with their social anxieties, and often attended sessions at least partially intoxicated. Attempts to persuade them to reduce or stop their substance abuse while participating in the groups proved unsuccessful in all cases, although two patients managed to complete at least half the course using minimal amounts of nonprescribed preparations. Those doing further work with these patients will need to examine their drug-taking behavior closely and to find ways to restructure their coping skills, so that taking drugs is not the major method for dealing with social and interpersonal stress. The ever-increasing use of minor tranquilizers (particularly the benzo-diazepines for reducing a wide range of everyday stresses, including in large part interpersonal anxiety) suggests that behavioral group therapy interventions that focus on anxiety reduction may be very useful alternatives to this problem of near-epidemic proportions.

Schizophrenic patients in remission had improved as much as other diagnostic groups by the end of treatment. However, in contrast to the other diagnostic subgroups, the schizophrenics seemed unable to sustain their improvement at follow-up. The importance of long-term follow-up is illustrated by this finding and must cast doubt on the conclusions of studies of social skills training such as Goldsmith and McFall (1975) where, though half the subjects were schizophrenic, there was no detailed follow-up after the end of treatment.

It is possible that schizophrenics may derive lasting changes from training of longer duration that is followed by additional "booster" sessions throughout the follow-up. In addition, all the schizophrenics had prominent family conflict and were unable to obtain assistance from family members with the daily homework program. It is possible that this lack of environmental support for improvements in social behavior led to a rapid fall of gains when reinforcement obtained through the group was no longer available.

Prescribed medication was associated with a significantly poorer outcome, but this may merely reflect the presence of more severe psychopathology. Patients with social phobia, inadequate personality disorder, and neurotic depression all responded well to treatment, though depressives improved less in their self-image. The latter complained that, although they were able to change their behavior, they experienced little sense of achievement or satisfaction from their interpersonal endeavors. Improvements in self-esteem may be assisted by groups that place greater emphasis on cognitive factors, such as the use of positive or coping self-statements and self-reinforcement procedures similar to those employed by Beck, Rush, Shaw, and Emery (1979).

Good outcome correlated significantly with high initial expectations of treatment, unskilled occupation and poor work adjustment, and a low rate of social leisure activity before treatment. Age, sex, marital status, intelligence, and length of disability did not affect outcome, but men tended to drop out more frequently than women. This approach, therefore, appeared to meet the needs of a broad group of psychiatric outpatients who were motivated to change their social role functioning, many of whom were considered unsuitable for dynamic group therapy. The excess attrition rate for men who started treatment appeared to be associated with two factors. First, all the substance abusers and schizophrenics in the study were male; second, few of the male dropouts received support from significant others. Both of these variables were associated with attrition.

CONCLUSIONS

The results of this study suggest that behavioral group therapy may be an effective treatment method for outpatients with a wide range of social and interpersonal difficulties. Substantial, though incomplete, improvement was noted in patients with neurotic conditions and personality disorders. Schizophrenics in remission showed some short-lived gains and may require treatment of longer duration to produce stable changes. Substance abusers appeared to benefit minimally. Role rehearsal and therapist modeling appeared to facilitate treatment outcome and to enhance group cohesion. A structured homework procedure showed additional benefits for those who completed it. Perhaps greater attention might be usefully focused on homework procedures that enhance generalization of social performance in the natural setting.

Despite the highly structured format of the behavioral group, it was apparent that nonspecific group process variables were operating. An improved understanding of these factors may lead to more effective therapy and to a reduction in the attrition rate from group therapies.

REFERENCES

Argyle, M., Bryant, B., & Trower, P. Social skills training and psychotherapy. *Psychological Medicine*, 1974, *4*, 435–443.

Battegay, R. Characteristics and new trends in group psychotherapy. *Acta Psychiatrica Scandinavica*, 1977, *56*, 21–31.

Beck, A. T., Rush, A. J., Shaw, B. F., & Emery, G. *Cognitive therapy of depression.* New York: Academic Press, 1979.

Bednar, R. L., & Lawlis, G. F. Empirical research in group psychotherapy. In A. E. Bergin & S. L. Garfield (Eds.), *Handbook of psychotherapy and behavior change.* New York: Wiley, 1971.

Bednar, R. L., West, C., Evensen, P., Lanier, D., & Melnick, J. Empirical guidelines for group therapy: Pretraining, cohesion, and modeling. *Journal of Applied Behavioral Science, 1974, 10,* 149-162.

Booraem, C. D., & Flowers, J. V. Reduction of anxiety and personal space as a function of assertion training with severely disturbed neuro-psychiatric inpatients. *Psychological Reports, 1972, 30,* 923-929.

Christensen, A., & Arkowitz, H. Preliminary report on practice dating and feedback as treatment for college dating problems. *Journal of Counseling Psychology,* 1974, *21,* 92-95.

Clark, J. B., & Cuthbert, S. A. Mutually therapeutic perception and self-awareness in a therapy group. *Journal of Applied Behavioral Science,* 1965, *1,* 180-194.

Doty, D. W. Role playing and incentives in the modification of the social interaction of chronic psychiatric patients. *Journal of Consulting and Clinical Psychology,* 1975, *43,* 676-682.

Falloon, I. R. H. Psychiatric patients as raters of social behavior. *Journal of Behavior Therapy and Experimental Psychiatry,* 1980, *11,* 215-217.

Falloon, I. R. H., Lindley, P., & McDonald, R. *Social training: A manual.* London: Maudsley Hospital, 1974.

Field, G. D., & Test, M. A. Group assertive training for severely disturbed patients. *Journal of Behavior Therapy and Experimental Psychiatry,* 1975, *6,* 135-137.

Goldsmith, J. B., & McFall, R. M. Development and evaluation of an inter-personal skill-training program for psychiatric inpatients. *Journal of Abnormal Psychology,* 1975, *84,* 51-58.

Goldstein, A. P. *Structured learning therapy: Toward a psychotherapy for the poor.* New York: Academic Press, 1973.

Gurland, B. J., Yorkston, N. J., Stone, H. R., Frank, J. D., & Fleiss, J. L. The Structured and Scaled Interview to Assess Maladjustment (SSIAM): Description, rationale, and development. *Archives of General Psychiatry,* 1972, *27,* 259-264.

Gutride, M. E., Goldstein, A. P., & Hunter, G. F. The use of modeling and role playing to increase social interaction among asocial psychiatric patients. *Journal of Consulting and Clinical Psychology,* 1973, *40,* 408-415.

Kapp, F., Gleser, A., Brissenden, A., Emerson, R., Wingt, J., & Kashdan, G. Group participation and self-perceived personality change. *Journal of Nervous and Mental Disease,* 1964, *139,* 255-265.

Liberman, R. P. A behavioral approach to group dynamics. *Behavior Therapy,* 1970, *1,* 312-327.

Liberman, R. P. Behavioral group therapy: A controlled clinical study. *British Journal of Psychiatry,* 1971, *119,* 535-544.

Liberman, R. P., King, L. W., DeRisi, W. J., & McCann, M. *Personal effectiveness*. Champaign, Ill.: Research Press, 1975.

Lomont, J. F., Gilner, F. H., Spector, N. J., & Skinner, K. K. Group assertion training and group insight therapies. *Psychological Reports*, 1969, *25*, 463-470.

Marzillier, J. S., Lambert, C., & Kellett, J. A controlled evaluation of systematic desensitisation and social skills training for socially inadequate psychiatric patients. *Behaviour Research and Therapy*, 1976, *14*, 225-238.

Percell, L. P., Berwick, P. T., & Biegel, A. The effects of assertive training on self-concept and anxiety. *Archives of General Psychiatry*, 1974, *31*, 502-504.

Vaughn, C. E., & Leff, J. P. The influence of family and social factors on the course of psychiatric illness: A comparison of schizophrenic and depressed neurotic patients. *British Journal of Psychiatry*, 1976, *129*, 125-137.

Yalom, I. D. *The theory and practice of group psychotherapy*. New York: Basic Books, 1970.

Yalom, I. D., & Rand, K. Compatibility and cohesiveness in therapy groups. *Archives of General Psychiatry*, 1966, *15*, 267-275.

Chapter 12

Group Behavior Therapy for the Treatment of Obesity: Issues and Suggestions

Maxwell R. Knauss
D. Balfour Jeffrey

Abstract

This chapter examines clinical issues that arise when behavioral treatment packages for weight reduction are implemented with a group therapy modality. The design is intended to assist therapists in planning, running, and evaluating the efficacy of time-limited, problem-focused weight-reduction groups. Clinical issues are explored and suggestions are offered with regard to therapist preparation, therapist attitudes toward obesity, common questions asked by obese clients, group interaction, and client attrition. Tables and figures, including a topic agenda for treatment sessions, weekly weight-reduction therapist guidelines, a posttreatment questionnaire, a physician's approval form, and a weight reduction contract, are provided to facilitate behavioral group treatment planning. *

*This chapter is based on a therapist treatment manual developed for the first author's doctoral dissertation (Knauss, 1980), under the direction of the second author. The authors wish to thank Jim Wahlberg and Julia Stroud, who reviewed an earlier draft of this article and whose comments and suggestions were incorporated in the final revision. Reprints of this chapter and other information related to the behavioral management of obesity may be obtained from D. Balfour Jeffrey, Department of Psychology, University of Montana, Missoula, Montana 59812.

Obesity is an extremely prevalent problem in the United States. Its incidence has been estimated at between 20% and 30% in the general population, which means that 40 to 80 million Americans are obese (Abramson, 1977a; U. S. Public Health Service, 1967). Losing weight has been a national preoccupation for many years. Currently Americans spend an astonishing 10 billion dollars a year on a vast array of dietary foods, as well as weight-reduction medications, devices, books, and programs (U. S. Department of Health, Education, and Welfare, Note 1).

Behavioral techniques developed to treat this problem are designed to systematically retrain eating, exercise, emotional, and coping habits. The efficacy of these behavioral techniques has been demonstrated through a number of well-controlled clinical outcome studies (Chapman & Jeffrey, 1978; Hagen, 1974; Hall, Hall, DeBoer, & O'Kulitch, 1977; Harris, 1969; Harris & Hallbauer, 1973; Jeffrey, 1974; Jeffrey & Christensen, 1975; Mahoney, 1974; Mahoney, Moura, & Wade, 1973; Wollersheim, 1970, 1977). Stunkard and Mahoney (1976) have concluded that behavioral techniques "have been shown to be superior to all other treatment modalities for managing mild to moderate obesity" (p. 54). Although behavioral approaches appear promising at this time, further research and development is needed. The current efficacy and the potential for further development of behavior therapy techniques in this area is becoming increasingly recognized by both health professionals and the general public. Weight Watchers and other lay dieting clubs have also incorporated behavioral techniques.

In the majority of reported clinical outcome studies, treatment packages are implemented in group treatment sessions. Kingsley and Wilson (1977) designed a study to evaluate the effectiveness of individual versus group treatment modalities. This study compared individual and group behavior therapy with a social pressure group (similar to a Take Off Pounds Sensibly group). While the individual and group behavioral treatments did not significantly differ from each other in terms of posttreatment weight loss, they were both superior to the social pressure group. At a long-term follow-up, the behavioral group treatment showed better maintenance than did the individual behavioral treatment. On the basis of these results, Kingsley and Wilson suggest that group behavior therapy might be the ideal treatment modality for obesity because group pressure and cohesion serve as powerful motivating influences upon members to adhere to behavioral weight-reduction strategies.

With the increasing recognition of the efficacy of behavioral group therapy in the treatment of obesity, both psychotherapists and other health care professionals are becoming more and more involved in conducting behavioral weight-reduction groups. In contrast to the numerous research studies published in this area, relatively little attention has been focused upon the practical clinical issues involved in implementing behavioral treatment packages utilizing the group therapy modality (see Rose, 1977). The purpose of this chapter, then, is to discuss practical issues we have found important in conducting weight-reduction groups and to present suggestions for leading these groups based upon our clinical and research experience. This chapter will focus upon the characteristics of effective group leadership and optimal group interaction rather than emphasizing or describing specific behavioral treatment techniques. See Jeffrey and Knauss (in press) for a detailed analysis of the etiologies, assessments, and treatments of obesity. Treatment issues and suggestions are divided into sections covering therapist preparation, therapist attitudes toward obesity, common questions asked by obese clients, group interaction, and client attrition.

THERAPIST PREPARATION

Obviously it is necessary for therapists to have an adequate understanding of the nature of the problem they are attempting to treat, if they are to maximize the possibility of a successful outcome. Obesity is currently regarded as a complex multifaceted disorder with hereditary, metabolic, nutritional, behavioral, and social components (Jeffrey & Knauss, in press; Leon & Roth, 1977; Rodin, 1977). Within the last 10 years there has been an enormous amount of research published on obesity. Several recent reviews and books have summarized research on the etiology and treatment of obesity: Abramson (1977b); Bellack (1977); Foreyt (1977); Jeffrey and Knauss (in press); Leon (1976); Leon and Roth (1977); Rodin (1977); Stunkard and Mahoney (1976); and Williams, Martin, and Foreyt (1976).

After acquiring this necessary background, weight-reduction therapists must prepare for the specific type of group they plan to offer. This preparation involves, first of all, making a number of practical decisions: (a) the number of clients who will be allowed to participate, (b) client entrance requirements, (c) the number and length of group sessions, (d) the agenda for each of these sessions, and (e) homework assignments between group meetings. Several authors have discussed specific behavioral treatment techniques, as well as other practical matters involved in implementing behavioral weight-reduction programs (Abramson, 1977a; Christensen, Jeffrey, & Pappas, 1977; Foreyt, 1977; Jeffrey, 1976; Williams et al., 1976).

Comprehensive group behavior therapy involves assessment, treatment, and maintenance phases (see Table 12.1). Each phase of therapy involves certain materials as an integral part of the behavioral techniques employed. Necessary assessment materials include questionnaires assessing readiness to begin, motivation to participate in treatment, and current eating and activity habits. Self-monitoring forms are also employed during the assessment period to obtain baselines on caloric intake, caloric expenditure, affective states associated with eating, and times and situations during which eating occurs. During the treatment phases of therapy, self-monitoring forms that detail caloric intake and expenditure, diet and exercise plans, lists of calories contained in specific foods, didactic material containing a rationale and description of the behavioral techniques utilized, and other treatment materials will be needed. The maintenance phase of therapy requires material describing behavioral strategies to promote maintenance of weight loss and charts or forms needed to implement these strategies.

Booster sessions, that is, follow-up group meetings after formal treatment is completed, have been investigated as a maintenance-enhancing strategy (Kingsley & Wilson, 1977). The rationale is that these meetings provide members support and reinforcement to continue implementing their behavioral self-management programs. While treatments employing booster sessions have not demonstrated statistically superior weight loss or maintenance to treatments without booster sessions, it appears that therapeutic contact meets important needs for clients and may help to maintain their motivation to make necessary lifestyle changes (Knauss, Jeffrey, & Knauss, Note 2). Weight-reduction therapists may therefore choose to schedule booster sessions at 3 or 4 week intervals. We have employed a non-structured format emphasizing review of individual progress, utilization of behavioral treatment techniques, and group problem-solving and role-playing activities to generate solutions to problems encountered since the previous group meeting.

Prior to the initial group meeting, therapists should select and prepare treatment materials, which can be gathered from a number of sources and collated, prepared, and reproduced by the weight therapists. An alternative is to use a currently available book as a textbook for the group members. Jeffrey and Katz's (1977) *Take It Off and Keep It Off: A Behavioral Approach to Weight Loss and Healthy Living* presents a comprehensive, multifaceted self-management weight-reduction program based upon the most promising research currently available, written in a style that the lay person can understand. It is self-contained, in that it includes all information and materials necessary to implement a complete self-management weight-reduction program.

The present authors have used the Jeffrey and Katz (1977) book as a client textbook in a number of weight-reduction groups. A typical agenda for a 12-session treatment group employing this book is contained in Table 12.1. The sessions are divided into assessment, treatment, and maintenance phases. The topic for each weekly group session is presented along with the relevant book chapter(s), suggested readings, and homework assignments.

Table 12.2 contains an example of weekly session guidelines developed and refined as a result of our experience in conducting weight-reduction groups. These guidelines correlate with Table 12.1 and provide outlines for 12 weekly, 90-minute group therapy sessions organized around the behavioral treatment package contained in the Jeffrey and Katz (1977) book. While we have found this 12-session schedule to suit our purposes, it can be varied to meet the needs of particular clients and weight-reduction therapists.

Another type of preparation becomes important when two therapists work together to co-lead a weight-reduction group. Since group behavior therapy for obesity is a structured treatment, co-therapists can insure that they will function together effectively by devising a schedule of activities for each group meeting, from which leadership responsibilities for these activities can be assigned. For instance, one therapist might review the weekly homework assignment with group members at the beginning of the meeting, and later in the session the other therapist might introduce a new concept or treatment technique. We have found that this type of co-therapist preparation and session scheduling is most easily accomplished during weekly review/planning meetings. During these meetings the co-therapists review audio- or videotapes of the previous session and share feedback about each other's therapeutic behavior and the group interaction. On the basis of this review and the preestablished topic for the next treatment session, the therapists then develop a schedule for that session. This schedule contains topics and activities that will be covered, the amount of time allotted for each, and which therapist will lead the particular activity. The purpose of this type of preparation is to insure that the co-therapists work together as effectively as possible to maximize the treatment impact of the behavioral package. The weekly session guidelines in Table 12.2 are designed to assist weight-reduction therapists in planning group sessions and coordinating leadership responsibilities.

Collecting posttreatment feedback from group members provides data necessary for weight therapists to improve their therapeutic skills. Figure 12.1 provides a posttreatment questionnaire that elicits feedback regarding the frequency of use of various self-management techniques and the adequacy with which each of the weight-reduction therapists performed various leadership functions, along with suggestions for improving the group treatment program.

THERAPIST ATTITUDES TOWARD OBESITY

The treatment of obesity represents a relatively new function for psychotherapists, and some therapists may harbor incorrect and potentially

Table 12.1
Topic Agenda for Group Treatment Sessions

Phase of Treatment	Session	Topic	Homework Assignment
Assessment	1	Introduction	*Read* Chapters 1, 2, and 3. *Complete* Tables 3–1 through 3–5.
	2	Assessment of Readiness to Lose Weight	*Read* Chapters 4 and 5. *Complete* Table 4–4; keep Eating Record for 1 week.
	3	Setting Realistic Goals and Beginning to Diet	*Choose* diet (i.e., food exchange or "common sense"); begin dieting; hand in self-monitoring forms.
	4	Caloric Reduction and Dieting	*Read* Chapter 6. *Complete* exercises.
	5	Physical Activity I	*Complete* Planned Physical Activities chart; hand in a record of the week's physical activities using the Physical Activity Diary form.
	6	Physical Activity II	*Read* Chapter 7. *Complete* exercises.
Treatment	7	Eliciting Support from Significant Others I	Ask a significant other who hinders weight loss efforts to change; reinforce a significant other who helps.

8	Eliciting Support from Significant Others II	*Read* Chapter 8. *Complete* Tables 8–1 and 8–2.
9	Developing Effective Food Management Habits	*Read* Chapter 9. *Complete* exercises.
10	Learning to Cope With Feelings I	Begin implementing "nonweighty" alternatives for coping with feelings.
11	Learning to Cope With Feelings II	*Read* Chapter 10. *Complete* exercises.
12	Reaching Long-Range Goals	*Read* Chapter 11.
Maintenance	Booster Sessions (Optional)	

Table 12.2
Weight-Reduction Therapists' Weekly Session Guidelines

Session 1: Introduction
1. Weigh-in and collection of fees (35 minutes)
   a) Weigh-in
   b) Collection of fees, deposits, and signing of contracts
   c) Collection of Physician Approval Forms
2. Program introduction (30 minutes)
   a) Weight-therapists' introduction
   b) Group introduction exercise
   c) Sharing of personal expectations for the program
3. Therapist overview of behavioral weight-reduction program (15 minutes)
   a) Energy-balance model, emphasizing that negative balance promotes weight loss
   b) Self-observation and self-monitoring of behavior
   c) Realistic goal setting
   d) Rearranging the environment
   e) Using graded practice to learn new behavior
   f) Using self-reward instead of self-punishment
   g) Building commitment for permanent lifestyle change
4. Discussion of weekly topics (distribute copies of *Take It Off and Keep It Off*) (10 minutes)
5. Homework: Read Chapters 1, 2, and 3, and complete Tables 3–1 through 3–5

Session 2: Assessment of Readiness to Lose Weight
1. Weigh-in and collection of late Physician Approval Forms (10 minutes)
2. Discussion of assessment exercises (30 minutes)
   a) Your Reasons for Losing Weight (Table 3–1)
   b) Sources of Reinforcement for Maintaining Your Present Weight (Table 3–2)
3. Discussion of assessment exercises (25 minutes)
   a) Weight Gain and Loss History (Table 3–3)
   b) Significant Others List (Table 3–4)
4. Therapist overview of importance of realistic goal setting (15 minutes)
   a) Emphasis on habit change rather than weight loss
   b) Importance of self-reward for habit change rather than self-punishment for failure
   c) Influence of goal setting on probability of success
   d) "One step at a time"—setting of small, concrete, realistic goals
5. Homework: Read Chapters 4 and 5, and complete Table 4–4. After use of Eating Record (Table 3–6) explained, record eating behavior for 1 week using Eating Record.
   Hand in: Eating Record

Session 3: Setting Realistic Goals and Beginning to Diet
1. Weigh-in and collection of homework (Eating Record) (10 minutes)
2. Discussion of self-monitoring of eating (20 minutes)
   a) When people eat most
   b) Eating as a means of coping with anxiety, boredom, anger, etc.
   c) Other problematic situations members have become aware of
3. Discussion of each person's weight loss goals and whether they are realistic (25 minutes)
   a) Short-term
   b) Long-term
   c) Time frame
4. Continued discussion of goals and discussion of Reward Menus (Table 4-4) (15 minutes)
5. Therapist overview of Food Exchange diet and "Common Sense" diet (20 minutes)
   a) "Common Sense" diet
   b) Food Exchange diet
      1) Food groups
      2) How to use the forms
      3) Choosing the caloric level best for each member
6. Homework: Choose diet (i.e., Food Exchange or "Common Sense" diet), begin dieting, and hand in self-monitoring forms (i.e., Food Exchange chart or Eating Diary for "Common Sense" diet).

Session 4: Caloric Reduction and Dieting
1. Weigh-in and collection of homework (Self-monitoring first week of diet) (10 minutes)
2. Individual update on each member's first week's dieting efforts (keep it brief), noting problems to return to and reinforcing positive habit change (20 minutes)
3. Group problem solving for problems encountered during first week of dieting (60 minutes)
4. Homework: Read Chapter 6 and complete exercises

Session 5: Physical Activity I
1. Weigh-in (10 minutes)
2. Individual update on "solutions" from last week's group problem solving and any new difficulties, reinforcing habit change (20 minutes)
3. Therapist presentation of importance of exercise (5 minutes)
   a) Burns calories and contributes to negative energy balance
   b) Reduces appetite
   c) Improves general physical condition and health
   d) Contributes to feelings of psychological and physical well-being
   e) Social benefits—creates opportunities to make new friendships
   f) Societal benefits—saves energy

Table 12.2 *(continued)*

4. Discussion of Physical Activity Review (Table 3–5) and kinds of activities that can be included in a personal activities program (25 minutes)
5. Design of a personal activities program, completing Planned Physical Activities (Table 6–4) chart (30 minutes)
6. Homework: After use of Physical Activity Diary (p. 318) explained, record 1 week's physical activity using Physical Activity Diary. Complete Planned Physical Activities chart if unfinished.
   Hand in: Physical Activity Diary

Session 6: Physical Activity II
1. Weigh-in and collection of homework (Physical Activities Diary) (10 minutes)
2. Individual update on first week of physical activities program, noting problems and reinforcing members' efforts (20 minutes)
3. Group problem solving for problems encountered in physical activities program (60 minutes)
4. Homework: Read Chapter 7 and complete exercises

Session 7: Eliciting Support from Significant Others I
1. Weigh-in (10 minutes)
2. Individual update on "solutions" from last week's group problem solving (20 minutes)
3. Discussion of how significant others help or hinder weight-loss efforts (20 minutes)
   a) Discuss Tables 3–4 and 7–1
   b) Note common themes or problems
4. Modification of behavior of people who hinder weight-loss efforts (40 minutes)
   a) Deciding what changes to make—discussion of Tables 7–2 and 7–3
   b) How to accomplish changes
      1) Group problem solving
      2) Role-playing and assertion-training
   c) Importance of reinforcing helpful others
   d) "Buddy System"—exchanging phone numbers, so members can call each other for support
5. Homework: Approach one significant other who hinders your weight-loss efforts and ask him to change. Reinforce one significant other who helps your weight-loss efforts.

Session 8: Eliciting Support from Significant Others II
1. Weigh-in (10 minutes)
2. Individual update and discussion of reinforcement of significant others who help and of attempts to ask hindering others to change (20 minutes)
   a) Identify successes and reinforce
   b) Note difficulties

3. Group problem solving for problems resulting from asking a significant other to change (60 minutes)
   a) Identify what went wrong, generate new solutions, etc.
   b) Role-play new responses
4. Homework: Read Chapter 8 and complete Tables 8–1 and 8–2

Session 9: Developing Effective Food Management Habits
1. Weigh-in (10 minutes)
2. Individual update on "solutions" from last week's group problem solving (20 minutes)
3. Therapist presentation of importance of situational control (10 minutes)
   a) Stimulus control of eating behavior
   b) Chaining of behavior—eating as the last behavior in a long chain
   c) Stimulus control in buying, storing, preparing, serving, eating, and cleaning up food
4. Discussion of how to manage food and choose food-management habits to change (50 minutes)
   a) Discuss Tables 8–1 and 8–2
   b) Note common problems
   c) Use group problem solving to develop solutions
5. Homework: Read Chapter 9 and complete exercises

Session 10: Learning to Cope With Feelings I
1. Weigh-in (10 minutes)
2. Individual update on progress in changing food-management behaviors (20 minutes)
3. Discussion of how feelings influence eating
   a) Discuss Table 9–1
   b) Note common emotional eating problems
4. Discussion of "nonweighty" alternatives to eating (45 minutes)
   a) Discuss Table 9–2
   b) Use group problem solving to help members generate new alternatives for coping
5. Homework: Begin to implement "nonweighty" alternatives for coping with feelings

Session 11: Learning to Cope With Feelings II
1. Weigh-in (10 minutes)
2. Individual update on attempts to handle feelings in "nonweighty" fashions (20 minutes)
3. Group problem solving for identified problems (60 minutes)
4. Homework: Read Chapter 10 and complete exercises

Session 12: Reaching Long-Range Goals
1. Weigh-in and collection of homework (exercises) (10 minutes)
2. Individual update (20 minutes)
3. Discussion of Problem Situations (Table 10–3) (20 minutes)
4. Administration of posttreatment questionnaire (35 minutes)

Table 12.2 *(continued)*

5. Distribution of refund checks, reminding subjects of dates of booster sessions and follow-ups (5 minutes)
6. Homework: Read Chapter 11

Booster Sessions
1. Weigh-in (10 minutes)
2. Individual update (20 minutes)
3. Group discussion and problem solving (60 minutes)
   a) Encourage "buddy system" support
   b) Reinforce progress and appropriate habit change
   c) Generate solutions to problems encountered since previous meeting

Figure 12.1. Posttreatment Questionnaire.

POSTTREATMENT QUESTIONNAIRE

Name_____ Sex: M F
Age _____ Birthdate _____
Address _____
Home Phone _____ Office Phone _____

At the end of each weight-reduction group, we conduct an evaluation to assess how the program has gone and to find ways to improve it the next time we offer it. Filling in this questionnaire will help us in this endeavor.

Thank you.

I. DIRECTIONS: Evaluate *how frequently* you used each of the weight loss techniques during the treatment program. Select the number from the scale that best approximates your answer and place it in the blank to the left of each item.

	Never	Once a Month	Twice a Month	Once a Week	Once a Day
	1	2	3	4	5

_____ 1. Setting realistic goals

_____ 2. Recording your food intake

_____ 3. Rewarding yourself for success rather than punishing yourself for failure

_____ 4. Using the Food Exchange diet

_____ 5. Using the "Common Sense" diet or another diet

_____   6. Recording your physical activity level

_____   7. Engaging in a physical activity program

_____   8. Identifying people who hinder your weight loss efforts and asking them to change their behavior

_____   9. Reinforcing people who support your dieting efforts

_____   10. Using relaxation training procedures

_____   11. Managing food effectively

_____   12. Focusing on lifestyle change rather than simple dieting

_____   13. Monitoring your weight

_____   14. Using problem-solving procedures to cope with negative feelings, difficult eating situations, or other problems

_____   15. Using techniques to cope with "weight plateaus"

_____   16. Employing weight maintenance strategies (e.g., doing something immediately if you gain weight)

II. DIRECTIONS: Rate the ability of each group leader in *performing the following treatment functions*. Select the number from the scale below that approximates your answer and place it in the blank to the left of each item.

Poor	Unsatisfactory	Average	Good	Excellent
1	2	3	4	5

A. Name _____

_____   1. Ability to generate positive weight loss expectations, optimism, and enthusiasm for success

_____   2. Ability to relate to individual participants in a warm, friendly, and personal manner

_____   3. Ability to create cohesiveness, solidarity, and unity among group members

_____   4. Ability to present information in a clear, concise, and direct manner

_____   5. Ability to demonstrate concern and caring for each individual's difficulties in losing weight, and for each participant's ultimate success in the program

_____   6. Ability to promote active participation from every group member

_____   7. Flexibility to discuss important related personal issues

_____   8. Overall ability as a group leader

          9. General comments regarding the abilities of_____
_____ as a group leader _____
_____
_____
_____

Figure 12.1 *(continued)*

B. Name _____

_____ 1. Ability to generate positive weight loss expectation, optimism, and enthusiasm for success

_____ 2. Ability to relate to individual participants in a warm, friendly, and personal manner

_____ 3. Ability to create cohesiveness, solidarity, and unity among group members

_____ 4. Ability to present information in a clear, concise, and direct manner

_____ 5. Ability to demonstrate concern and caring for each individual's difficulties in losing weight, and for each participant's ultimate success in the program

_____ 6. Ability to promote active participation from every group member

_____ 7. Flexibility to discuss important related personal issues

_____ 8. Overall ability as a group leader

9. General comments regarding the abilities of_____
_____ as a group leader _____

III. We would welcome your evaluative comments on the Weight Reduction Program in order to help us in planning for the future. Please orient your comments toward:

A. Aspects of the program that were most beneficial_____

B. Components of the program that could be eliminated _____

C. Changes you would recommend in future Weight Reduction Programs__

IV. Have you reached your overall weight loss goal?   Yes _____ No _____
(check one)

If not, how much more weight do you have to lose in order to reach your goal? _____ pounds

destructive attitudes concerning obesity. In their preparation to lead a weight-reduction group, it is important for therapists to survey their own attitudes regarding obesity, just as it is important to become acquainted with the most recent literature on the etiology and treatment of the disorder. The therapists' attitudes will influence the manner in which they interact with group members, and may be conveyed implicitly even when not directly disclosed. Certain attitudes may lead therapists to behave in ways that diminish their personal effectiveness as well as the effectiveness of the self-management program. It is imperative that prospective weight-reduction therapists become aware of their attitudes toward obesity and validate them against current research evidence. Potentially destructive and biased attitudes can then be replaced with informed, constructive ones.

Several attitudes may reduce a group leader's effectiveness. One is that obesity represents an insignificant problem. Therapists may view the condition as less distressing or debilitating than the problems with which they typically deal. Obesity may be perceived as less challenging than other behavioral and emotional problems though, ironically, obesity may be as recalcitrant as any problem the therapist attempts to treat. The therapist who strongly believes that obesity is insignificant and that her time is better spent treating "real" emotional and behavioral problems should not become a weight-reduction therapist. Her involvement probably would not benefit, and might be detrimental to, obese clients. Such an attitude is unfortunate, as there are tremendous medical and psychological problems associated with and resulting from obesity.

Another negative belief is that obesity is largely a medical or nutritional problem and should therefore be treated by physicians or nutritionists. Although there are certainly nutritional and metabolic components in obesity, they are by no means the sole causal factors. We have led a number of groups that have included several obese nutritionists as clients. Obviously even individuals who have an extensive knowledge of nutrition sometimes are unable to lose weight and maintain that weight loss.

When obesity is regarded as being primarily a nutritional or medical disorder, many psychotherapists feel inadequately prepared and are therefore reluctant to lead weight-reduction groups. Such an attitude might lead to a lack of confidence which could be detrimental to treatment efficacy. However, when obesity is regarded as a complex multidetermined disorder which is significantly influenced by eating, exercise, and emotional and coping habits, it can be seen that psychotherapists are in an excellent position to help obese clients. Psychotherapists can use their expertise in the area of behavior change to help obese clients make the lifestyle changes necessary to lose weight and maintain the weight loss. In addition, therapists can make their therapy a learning experience by eliciting information from clients who are well versed in nutritional matters.

The belief that obesity is the result of moral weakness or lack of will power is a potentially destructive belief. Although few psychotherapists would regard other psychological problems as resulting from moral weakness or lack of will power, many regard obesity and other addictive behaviors as such. They may not even be aware of holding this attitude, which is represented by the view that obesity is the individual's fault because he does not take the time to exercise regularly or to eat properly. The causal attribution is that the individual is solely responsible for the problem because he does not choose to pursue a simple solution, such as not eating so much; he must be either ignorant, lazy, or lacking in will power. This type of dispositional attribution may lead the therapist to interact with the obese client in a smug or condescending manner. The therapist may subtly and unknowingly convey the message, "I am thin and you could be, too, if you would only try a little harder."

The majority of obese people make similar self-attributions regarding their obesity and view it as being the consequence of personal failure. This results in guilt, self-reproach, and low self-esteem. The individual comes to believe that he lacks an essential attribute for success (i.e., will power) and that he has little control over gaining more of that attribute. Most people believe that they either are or are not endowed with will power. It is small wonder that depression often accompanies obesity. The attribution of the cause of the problem to lack of will power serves only to immobilize the client. Failure at previous weight loss attempts supports this attribution and gives the client little hope that he will actually succeed at the present attempt. If the therapist also views obesity as resulting from a lack of will power, she reaffirms the client's pessimism and immobilization.

While the client may not be able to gain more will power, he can alter his behavior through the application of environmental and self-modification procedures. To motivate the client to make the necessary lifestyle changes, it is very important that the therapist help the client reconstrue his problems in a more constructive manner. Behavioral approaches to treating obesity are based upon a model in which obesity is conceptualized as a complex problem with many causes. Research evidence implicates environmental, psychological, and metabolic etiological factors. Thus the individual is not held solely responsible for the problem, which helps reduce feelings of guilt. At the same time, the client is told to assume responsibility for the solution to the problem and become actively involved in treatment. He is provided with a comprehensive, structured behavioral program to help in making the necessary environmental and self-modifications. The focus of the program is always positive, in that it is based upon self-reward for habit change rather than self-punishment for failure to change.

COMMON QUESTIONS ASKED BY OBESE CLIENTS

There are typical questions a weight therapist may be asked during initial group sessions. Some of these questions will be discussed here because the manner in which they are handled has important implications for the quality of group interaction. Generally, questions should be responded to as honestly as possible and in a manner that enhances the client's motivation and group cohesiveness.

A common question is whether or not the therapist has ever been obese and has had to lose weight. Many obese clients seem to prefer being treated by a therapist who has personally overcome obesity. This preference may be based upon the belief that only therapists who have experienced obesity are truly able to understand the clients' problems. Also, it may be assumed that the therapist who was obese and managed to reduce might have some special knowledge to share with the clients which will also help them to succeed.

If the therapist has a history of obesity and successful weight loss, disclosing some of the details of this experience at appropriate times during treatment can enhance group cohesion. The therapist can make use of his own background to illustrate certain points or model certain attitudes. The therapist who has never been obese must openly disclose this when questioned. He should be prepared to discuss with the group the reasons behind his interest in treating obesity. The belief that only a formerly obese weight-therapist can treat obese clients effectively should be directly and thoroughly addressed.

Typically, the client who questions the therapist about his weight history is usually concerned about the therapist's sensitivity to and understanding of this problem as well as the therapist's commitment to helping clients find a solution. We have attempted to address both of these issues by stating: "Psychotherapists are frequently successful at treating, through the application of scientifically derived principles, a wide variety of problems that they have not personally experienced. The important issue is not whether we or other therapists have been overweight, but whether we understand the problem of obesity and are sensitive to the feelings and concerns of the overweight person. We must also be committed to working with the person who is trying to lose weight. A previously overweight person is not necessarily sensitive and concerned about people who are trying to lose weight now. We have an understanding of the complexity of this problem and the difficulties people have in losing weight, but we are always open to learning more about it. We are committed to working with people who are trying to lose weight and to helping them succeed." Most clients are receptive to this response and value the therapists' honesty and willingness to address their concerns directly.

A second question that is frequently raised during the initial session concerns the weight-reduction therapist's training and experience in general and his experience as a weight-group therapist in particular. It is the therapist's ethical responsibility to describe accurately both his training and experience in conducting psychotherapy, as well as weight-reduction groups, so that the obese individual can make an informed decision regarding whether or not to enter therapy. If this is the therapist's first weight-reduction group, this matter should be discussed and the training function of the program should be explained. In our treatment program two therapists run each group, and new therapists are paired with partners who have had previous experience. This arrangement allows for the training of new group leaders without sacrificing the treatment efficacy of the program.

A third type of question involves the completion of assessment instruments, homework exercises, and self-monitoring forms. Although we attempt to keep paper work to a minimum, clients may ask why they are required to fill out so many forms. It should be explained that the self-monitoring forms and other assessment devices serve both treatment and research functions. Many are designed to provide feedback and to increase the clients' awareness of various behaviors that are integral components of the self-management procedures. When data are being collected for research purposes, it should be explained to clients that completion of self-monitoring and assessment forms not only benefits them directly, but can also lead to program improvements that will benefit others who participate in similar programs in the future. Of course, they must fully understand how the data will be used and give their permission for its use.

GROUP INTERACTION

There are several potential advantages of group therapy over other modes of implementation of a self-management package. The first and most apparent advantage of group therapy is that it allows a more efficient use of the therapists' time than does individual therapy. The second is that involvement in a group can serve to motivate clients to attend group sessions, as well as to implement self-management procedures between sessions. From client feedback and program evaluations, we find that attending group sessions is often rated as a very important aspect of the treatment program. There appears to be a reciprocal influence in that good attendance also seems to enhance feelings of solidarity and thus improves the quality of group interaction. The reinforcement that clients receive from the therapists and other group members seems to be an important factor in sustaining the clients' commitment and keeping them in therapy. The third advantage of group therapy is that it offers a greater opportunity for clients to learn new behaviors via observational learning, modeling, role-playing, and group problem solving. Clients have an opportunity to engage in much vicarious learning by observing the methods other clients employ in solving problems similar to their own. The entire group can be used in creative problem solving for either an individual problem or a shared one. This type of exercise is also beneficial in helping all involved clients improve their problem-solving skills. Group members can be utilized to play additional parts in role-play exercises, which give the client an opportunity to practice new behaviors and to receive feedback from other members before he tries to implement them in the natural environment. These procedures not only lead to the acquisition of new behaviors, but also inculcate the notion that a client's particular problems are not unique, which contributes to greater group cohesiveness and a more open discussion of problems.

Behavior therapy groups are generally problem-focused. Group inter-action should concentrate on obesity, issues related to it, and the lifestyle changes necessary to modify it permanently. These include changes in eating, exercise, and emotional coping habits. The format of behavioral group meetings is structured in that there are generally designated topics, assigned readings, and homework exercises for each week. While awareness and shar-ing of feelings are encouraged, these are not encounter or confrontation groups, and both the techniques utilized and the focus of the interaction are quite different. Increased awareness of feelings and behaviors is considered a prerequisite for habit change. Such an awareness is seen as necessary but not sufficient to create habit change and is thus considered a means to the goal of the treatment program rather than an end in itself. Therefore, therapists should not allow members to coerce or pressure other members to reveal things they are not ready to disclose. There should be an effort to create a warm atmosphere and encouragement toward group support and mutual reinforcement.

Didactic and Group Process Interaction

There are two basic types of interaction that occur in behavioral weight reduction groups—didactic interaction and group process interaction. Didac-tic interaction involves conveying factual material, giving assignments, or explaining exercises. The success of didactic interaction depends solely on the therapist's preparation, familiarity with the material, and ability to communicate the material in a manner that group members can understand. While one therapist is imparting this type of information, a co-therapist can play a central role by assessing the group members' reactions for later discussion. She should note any cues that indicate agreement, disagreement, or failure to understand the material. These cues can then be incorporated into the subsequent discussion. For example, a possible opening might be, "Joan, while Max was talking about _____ , you smiled and nodded. I was wondering if you have experienced similar events that you would like to share with the group?" Group process interaction involves group members' sharing feelings and experiences with each other, engaging in group problem solving, or role-playing problem solutions. During this type of interaction, the therapist assumes a role of guidance and facilitation rather than one of didactic interaction.

An effective group leader must be proficient at working in both modes and must be able to make comfortable transitions between the two modes. While there is usually some didactic presentation by the therapists during each group meeting, the majority of the time within most sessions is typically spent in group process activities.

Group Cohesiveness

Weight therapists need to be aware of the importance of group cohesiveness for productive group therapy and must strive to establish and maintain this cohesion. Group cohesiveness refers to the quality of interaction that occurs when each member feels that he belongs in the group, that he is accepted by the other members, and that he has something of value both to contribute and to receive from the group (Flowers, 1979; Rose, 1977). Although group cohesiveness is difficult to define precisely and to assess objectively, it is nonetheless a very important principle. It is generally assessed subjectively by the therapist, based upon the general level of participation, involvement, and reinforcement for contributions. A cohesive group is one in which every member has a chance to participate and in which members actively interact with each other.

The development of group cohesiveness begins with the initial group meeting in which clients become acquainted with each other. The therapists can get the interaction started by welcoming members to the program, introducing themselves, and discussing their interest and experience in leading weight groups. To facilitate the acquaintance of group members, the therapists might employ a structured introduction exercise. One that we have found effective involves having clients turn to the individual next to them, introduce themselves, and spend 5 minutes getting to know each other. The clients then introduce the person with whom they became acquainted to the rest of the group. This exercise tends to work well because it reduces the task of getting to know a group of strangers to the more manageable task of getting to know one other person. Since it takes time for group members to learn each other's names, it is a good idea to go around the group and have members reintroduce themselves during the first few meetings.

The places in the room where the therapists sit can have a significant effect upon group interaction. If the therapists sit next to each other, the group may focus their attention on them, thus inhibiting group process. The goal in group process interactions is to get group members talking and sharing with each other rather than with the therapists. Therapists should discourage having communication constantly directed toward themselves by encouraging members to talk to one another. To do this, the therapists must know when to be quiet, and they must not insist upon being the center of attention throughout the entire session. Domination of group interaction by the therapists inhibits group process and discourages group cohesion.

Throughout the treatment sessions, therapists should do everything possible to encourage group sharing. It is important to create a warm, supportive atmosphere where clients can feel accepted and good about themselves. The therapists should always make an attempt to involve everyone in the interaction. They can do this by creating openings for group members to share experiences and feelings. For instance, if one individual shares a particular experience, the therapist can give other members a chance to share by asking, "Has anyone else had a similar experience?"

Therapists can encourage contributions from group members by reinforcement, most directly through straightforward acknowledgement. For instance, the therapist might respond to a client's communication by saying, "That is an important point." Clarification, summarization, and reflection also demonstrate that the therapist is listening and understanding, and all three are indirectly reinforcing for the client. Therapists can also reinforce group members' contributions by referring back to previous communications in order to illustrate a current point, demonstrating that what had been said was important enough to be remembered. For instance, the therapist might say, "This is related to something that Joan shared with us a moment ago." In a sense, the therapist is modeling behaviors that she hopes group members will adopt by eventually beginning to reinforce each other for their contributions. The degree to which group members reinforce each other probably reflects the level to which group cohesiveness has been developed.

In many groups there are one or more individuals who are quiet, shy, or have difficulty expressing themselves. It is important for the therapist to draw these people into the group interaction. If they are not involved, they may feel ignored or alienated and thus may decide not to return for future sessions. Since some clients will not take advantage of the openings created by the therapist, she can draw this type of client into the interaction by directing a question to him. The question must be carefully phrased to give the client a chance to contribute without being put on the spot. Another method of involving the shy client is for the therapist to approach him and start a conversation before or after the session, thus bringing the shy client into contact with other group members seeking out the therapist at those times. A similar strategy is for the therapist to sit next to the shy person during the meeting. Another technique that we have found useful is to allow each client 2 or 3 minutes at the beginning of a session to share his progress over the past week. Here, the shy client does not feel singled out and the information he imparts can be used to direct the conversation toward him during the subsequent discussion.

Domination of the group by an overly talkative group member can also have negative effects. Therapists must constantly monitor the group interaction to prevent it from being dominated by a single client. If a client is dominating the group, the therapist must take the responsibility for terminating that individual's communication as tactfully as possible and giving other clients a chance to speak. For example, if a group member has been dominating the group interaction with a lengthy description of the numerous ways in which his wife sabotages his weight-loss attempts and is about to begin a similar description of his parents' behavior, the therapist must intervene, perhaps saying, "John has been sharing with us some of the ways in which a significant other hinders his weight-reduction efforts. Have any of the rest of you had similar experiences?" If an individual repeatedly monopolizes the group, the therapist should talk to that person alone after a group session is completed.

Group Composition

In a problem-focused group, it is important that all of the members share a similar problem. If a client is currently experiencing a more severe or distressing problem than obesity (e.g., depression or marital disharmony), then involvement in a behavioral weight-reduction group may not be the most suitable treatment program. It is recommended that weight therapists complete some type of initial screening before admitting clients to a group, to insure that group placement is appropriate. However, even when clients are prescreened, weight therapists should remain alert for disclosure of problems that the program is not designed to treat. For instance, rapid weight gain can be a result of depression. If a depressed client is identified, an appropriate referral should be made so that the client can receive the type of treatment required. This is not to say that any client exhibiting other emotional or behavioral problems should automatically be prohibited from joining a weight-reduction group. Often this type of group involvement can be an excellent adjunct to individual therapy aimed at treating other problems. The client with co-existing problems should be allowed to continue participating in the weight-reduction group as long as the therapists judge that she can benefit from the participation, and as long as her participation does not diminish the effectiveness of the treatment program for other group members.

Occasionally a client may have an underlying medical problem that significantly contributes to his weight problem, or that would be exacerbated by alterations in diet and exercise patterns. To rule out these possibilities, it is advisable to require all clients to obtain a physician's approval before entering a weight-reduction group. Figure 12.2 contains a Physician Approval Form to be used for this purpose. If a client does have significant obesity-related medical problems, the weight therapist must make a decision either to exclude him from participation or to work with his physician to develop an individualized program to meet his special needs.

Figure 12.2. Physician Approval Form.

PHYSICIAN APPROVAL FORM

Dear Doctor _____:

Beginning this month, we will be initiating a behavioral weight-control program through the_____ . Our treatment program is complex and multifaceted, and is composed of behavioral procedures that emphasize gradual weight loss by modifying eating habits, increasing physical activity, and developing lifestyles that are more conducive to healthy living.

Your signature on this form indicates that you have no medical reservations concerning

_____ 's
(Patient's Name)

participation in this weight-control program. It also indicates that in your opinion the above-named patient can safely lose up to_____ pounds. Please indicate any special dietary and exercise requirements or restrictions:

_____
_____
_____

If you have any questions concerning the treatment program, please contact us at _____ .
(Organization and Telephone Number)

Thank you for your time and cooperation.
Sincerely yours,

(Sign Name and Title of Weight-Reduction Therapist)

Physician's Signature _____
Address _____ Telephone _____

CLIENT ATTRITION

Attrition rates ranging as high as 83% have been reported in the experimental literature on the treatment of obesity (Hagen, Foreyt, & Durham, 1976). Attrition rates of such magnitude are disastrous for the researcher because they render data uninterpretable. Thus, high attrition rates are a major methodological problem in obesity outcome research (Jeffrey, 1976). High attrition also presents a problem in clinical practice because it either prevents group cohesion from developing or destroys whatever cohesion already exists. When the attrition rate in a group is high, not only is group cohesion destroyed but the remaining members' motivation to attend sessions and their commitment to treatment also seem to diminish. Presently, three methods of reducing client attrition can be suggested: (a) prescreening clients, (b) making attendance mandatory, and (c) requiring a monetary deposit that is refundable contingent upon session attendance.

Prescreening Clients

Prescreening clients involves assessing current readiness, motivation, and commitment to making lifestyle changes necessary to lose weight and to maintain the weight loss permanently. This type of assessment can be completed by utilizing self-report questions or exercises such as those described by Christensen et al. (1977) or Jeffrey and Katz (1977). The prescreening session also provides a good opportunity to give prospective clients an overview of the behavioral treatment program so that they are able to make an informed decision as to whether it appears to be the type of program in which they would like to become involved. If prescreening indicates that a client is not motivated or that her current life situation is not conducive to making the necessary lifestyle changes, she should be dissuaded from entering the treatment program at that time. Clients are advised to postpone entry into a behavioral weight-reduction group until they are sufficiently ready, rather than entering a group when they are not and consequently dropping out of treatment.

Mandatory Attendance

Mandatory attendance is a necessary requirement in most problem-focused treatment groups because what occurs in one session is usually a prerequisite for the activities of the next session. In the prescreening session, it should be emphasized that once individuals enter a group they have a responsibility to themselves, as well as to the other group members, to attend all meetings. Weight therapists can explain that any member's absence from a group session diminishes the quality of the session for the other members because those absent are unable to contribute to the interaction. During the course of a 16-session treatment program, a client may have a legitimate, unavoidable reason for an occasional absence; in such a case she is instructed to call before the next regular group meeting time to schedule an individual make-up session. During this session, one of the weight therapists weighs the client in, reviews material covered during the missed group session with her, and gives her the weekly homework assignment.

Monetary Deposit

Requiring clients to leave a monetary deposit with the therapists at the beginning of treatment, to be refunded contingent upon session attendance, is another method of reducing attrition. In a study evaluating the effectiveness of this strategy, Hagen et al. (1976) compared $20 deposit, $5 deposit, and no deposit conditions. It was found that the $20 deposit significantly reduced attrition as compared to the other two conditions. When utilizing a deposit, a contract must be drawn up at the beginning of treatment, specifying the terms of the refund. Figure 12.3 contains a sample contract which details a deposit and incentive payback schedule aimed at insuring session attendance and reducing premature termination from treatment. It should also be clearly explained to the clients that their deposits will be refunded based upon session attendance and *not* upon weight loss. Weight therapists must strongly encourage clients to attend group sessions whether or not they lose weight.

SUMMARY

This chapter has focused on the clinical and practical issues that arise when behavioral weight-reduction techniques are implemented within a group-treatment modality. We have discussed treatment issues and have offered suggestions regarding therapist preparation, therapist attitudes toward obesity, common questions asked by obese clients, group interaction, and client attrition. Hopefully, this discussion will assist in orienting beginning weight therapists to some of the important issues involved in leading behavioral weight-reduction groups. The suggestions were presented to help therapists prepare to lead such groups as effectively as possible, but should also be relevant to researchers who must train weight therapists in order to implement behavioral treatment conditions within their studies.

While we have concerned ourselves with the implementation of behavioral weight-reduction techniques rather than upon the techniques themselves, it should not be concluded that behavioral techniques are viewed as less important. A growing body of research is demonstrating that behavioral techniques hold the most promise for treating the complex disorder known as obesity. Our emphasis upon implementation issues is

Figure 12.3. Weight Reduction Contract.

WEIGHT REDUCTION CONTRACT

I do hereby promise to attempt to lose weight by using the procedures described in *Take It Off and Keep It Off* and during my group sessions. I further agree to attend 12 group treatment sessions. (If follow-up weigh-ins are being conducted, the dates should be specified here.) To participate in the program, I will pay a _____ fee to cover the costs for
(specify amount)
the book and materials. Furthermore, I agree to leave a _____
refundable deposit with the program.   (specify amount)

I understand that the refunds of this deposit will be used to help maintain my motivation to effect lifestyle changes necessary for permanent weight loss. Therefore, I agreed to the following incentive system and payback schedule:

1) A total of _____ will be refunded for attending all group
(specify amount)
sessions *and* completing all homework assignments. For each group session I attend and submit a copy of that week's homework assignment, I will receive _____. This refund *does not* depend
(specify amount)
upon weight loss, but upon attendance and completion of homework assignments. In the event that I cannot attend a group session, I will telephone my group leader at least 24 hours in advance at _____
(telephone
_____ and schedule a make-up session. If I attend the make-up
number)
session, I will not lose my weekly refund. However, if I fail to complete the homework assignment *or* miss a session, I will lose _____
(specify amount)
of my deposit. For missing two sessions I lose _____ , etc.
(specify amount)
A check containing the entire amount of my refunded deposit will be presented at the last session on _____ . I realize that I *must*
(specify date)
attend the last group session to receive my refund.

2) (If the weight-reduction therapists decide to conduct follow-up weigh-ins and cover the attendance with the deposit, the terms should be specified here. For instance: _____ will be refunded for
(specify amount)
attending each follow-up weigh-in. They will be scheduled on _____
(specify
____ and _____ . These refunds also are *not* contingent upon
date)   (specify date)
losing weight, but upon weighing in and completing a follow-up questionnaire.)

3) All nonrefunded money will be donated to _____
_____
(Name of Non-Profit Program) .

I, _____ , have read the above contract and
       (Print Name)
agree to its conditions.

        Applicant _____
                    (Signature)

        Date _____

The weight-reduction therapist has read the above contract and agrees to
fulfill his or her part of the contract.

        Weight-Reduction Therapist _____
                               (Signature)

        Date _____

based on the belief that the manner in which behavioral techniques are
implemented exerts a powerful influence upon their effectiveness. Further
refinement and validation of the behavioral weight-reduction techniques
that comprise current treatment packages will occur as component analysis
studies are completed. As obesity research progresses, the impact of implementation variables upon treatment outcome will also be subjected to
systematic investigation. Only with continued research will the development
of a safe, effective, and permanent treatment for this disorder be achieved.

REFERENCE NOTES

1. U. S. Department of Health, Education, and Welfare. *Facts from FDA*
   (Publication No. (FDA) 73-2036). Rockville, Md.: U. S. Department of
   Health, Education, and Welfare, 1973.
2. Knauss, M. R., Jeffrey, D. B., & Knauss, C. S. *Scheduling of therapeutic
   contact in a behavioral weight reduction program.* Paper presented at the
   meeting of the American Psychological Association, Montreal, September
   1980.

REFERENCES

Abramson, E. E. (Ed.). *Behavioral approaches to weight control.* New York:
Springer, 1977. (a)

Abramson, E. E. Behavioral approaches to weight control: An updated
review. *Behaviour Research and Therapy,* 1977, *15,* 355-363. (b)

Bellack, A. S. Behavioral treatment for obesity: Appraisal and recommendations. In M. Hersen, R. M. Eisler, & P. M. Miller (Eds.), *Progress in
behavior modification* (Vol. 4). New York: Academic, 1977.

Chapman, S. L., & Jeffrey, D. B. Situational management standard setting,
and self-reward in a behavior modification weight loss program. *Journal
of Consulting and Clinical Psychology,* 1978, *46,* 1588-1589.

Christensen, E. R., Jeffrey, D. B., & Pappas, J. P. A therapist manual for a behavior modification weight reduction program. In E. E. Abramson (Ed.), *Behavioral approaches to weight control.* New York: Springer, 1977.

Flowers, J. V. Behavioral analysis of group therapy and a model for behavioral group therapy. In D. Upper and S. M. Ross (Eds.), *Behavioral group therapy, 1979: An annual review.* Champaign, Ill.: Research Press, 1979.

Foreyt, J. P. (Ed.). *Behavioral treatments of obesity.* New York: Pergamon, 1977.

Hagen, R. L. Group therapy versus bibliotherapy in weight reduction. *Behavior Therapy,* 1974, *5,* 222–234.

Hagen, R. L., Foreyt, J. P., & Durham, T. W. The dropout problem: Reducing attrition in obesity research. *Behavior Therapy,* 1976, *7,* 463–471.

Hall, S. M., Hall, R. G., DeBoer, G., & O'Kulitch, P. Self and external management compared with psychotherapy in the control of obesity. *Behavior Research and Therapy,* 1977, *15,* 89–95.

Harris, M. B. Self-directed program for weight control: A pilot study. *Journal of Abnormal Psychology,* 1969, *74,* 263–270.

Harris, M. B., & Hallbauer, E. S. Self-directed weight control through eating and exercise. *Behaviour Research and Therapy,* 1973, *11,* 523–529.

Jeffrey, D. B. A comparison of the effects of external control and self-control on the modification and maintenance of weight. *Journal of Abnormal Psychology,* 1974, *83,* 404–410.

Jeffrey, D. B. Behavioral management of obesity. In W. E. Craighead, A. E. Kazdin, and M. J. Mahoney (Eds.), *Behavior modification: Principles, issues, and applications.* Boston: Houghton-Mifflin, 1976.

Jeffrey, D. B., & Christensen, E. R. Effect of behavior therapy vs. "will power" in the management of obesity. *Journal of Psychology,* 1975, *90,* 303–311.

Jeffrey, D. B.. & Katz, R. C. *Take it off and keep it off: A behavioral program for weight loss and healthy living.* New York: Prentice-Hall, 1977.

Jeffrey, D. B., & Knauss, M. R. The etiologies, assessments, and treatments of obesity. In S. N. Haynes & L. Gannon (Eds.), *Psychosomatic disorders: A psychophysiological approach to etiology and treatment.* New York: Gardner Press, in press.

Kingsley, R. G., & Wilson, G. T. Behavior therapy for obesity: A comparative investigation of long-term efficacy. *Journal of Consulting and Clinical Psychology,* 1977, *45,* 288–298.

Knauss, M. R. *The effects of scheduling of therapeutic contact upon weight loss and maintenance in a behavioral weight reduction program.* Unpublished doctoral dissertation, University of Montana, 1980.

Leon, G. R. Current directions in the treatment of obesity. *Psychological Bulletin,* 1976, *83,* 557–578.

Leon, G. R., & Roth, L. Obesity: Psychological causes, correlations, and speculations. *Psychological Bulletin,* 1977, *84,* 117–139.

Mahoney, M. J. Self-reward and self-monitoring techniques for weight control. *Behavior Therapy,* 1974, *5,* 48–57.

Mahoney, M. J., Moura, N., & Wade, T. The relative efficacy of self-reward, self-punishment, and self-monitoring techniques for weight loss. *Journal of Consulting and Clinical Psychology,* 1973, *40,* 404–407.

Rodin, J. Bidirectional influences of emotionality, stimulus responsivity, and metabolic events in obesity. In J. Maser and M. E. P. Seligman (Eds.), *Psychopathology: Experimental models.* San Francisco: Freeman, 1977.

Rose, S. D. *Group therapy: A behavioral approach.* Englewood Cliffs, N. J.: Prentice-Hall, 1977.

Stunkard, A. J., & Mahoney, M. J. Behavioral treatment of the eating disorders. In H. Leitenberg (Ed.), *Handbook of behavior modification.* New York: Appleton-Century-Crofts, 1976.

U. S. Public Health Service. *Obesity and health* (Publication No. 1485). Washington, D. C.: U. S. Government Printing Office, 1967.

Williams, B. J., Martin, S., & Foreyt, J. P. (Eds.), *Obesity: Behavioral approaches to dietary management.* New York: Brunner/Mazel, 1976.

Wollersheim, J. P. Effectiveness of group therapy based upon learning principles in the treatment of overweight women. *Journal of Abnormal Psychology,* 1970, *76,* 462–474.

Wollersheim, J. P. Follow-up of behavioral group therapy for obesity. *Behavior Therapy,* 1977, *8,* 996–998.

Chapter 13

Long-Term Follow-Up of Couples' Treatment of Obesity

Carol Landau Heckerman
Robert E. Zitter

Abstract

A 3-year follow-up of subjects treated for obesity included 19 female and male subjects. Subjects who had participated in couples' training reported a mean weight loss of 31.5 pounds. Subjects with noncooperative spouses attended a standard behavioral group alone and had a mean weight loss of 11.8 pounds. Subjects who had cooperative spouses but also attended a behavioral group alone lost an average of 10.1 pounds. Due to small sample size, there were no significant differences between groups. A review of other studies of couples' training suggests that this treatment technique has not produced consistent long-term results. The authors suggest several clinical research issues that should be explored, including improvements in the assessment of marital interaction for its effects on treatment and weight loss.

*The authors would like to thank Kelly D. Brownell for his assistance and encouragement.

309

Couples' treatment is one of the most recent developments in the behavioral treatment of obesity. The interest in the involvement of the spouse in treatment was brought about by at least two factors. First, researchers have been looking for ways to improve the long-term efficacy of the behavioral treatment for obesity. Although behavioral therapy has been demonstrated to be the most effective treatment approach for obesity, weight losses tend to be moderate and variable, and maintenance remains a dilemma. In addition, several authors have suggested that the role of the spouse is a significant factor. Mahoney and Mahoney (1976) reported a correlation between weight loss and family support as defined by family cooperation, encouragement, and attendance of family as well as subject. Stuart and Davis (1972) reported that husbands of wives in a weight-control program were more likely than their wives to offer food to their spouses and to initiate food-relevant conversations. The husbands were also more likely to criticize rather than to praise eating behaviors. These reports are consistent with those in the area of compliance with general medical regimens, such as the study by Heinzelmann and Bagley (1970), where adherence of male participants to an exercise program was positively correlated with the support of their wives.

Jacobson (Note 1) described three theoretical rationales for involving the spouse in behavioral treatment programs. First, a spouse may reinforce over-eating and/or inactivity and thus may lead his mate to the development of obesity. Second, even if the spouse were not involved in the etiology of obesity, he might be involved in the maintenance of the overweight person's lifestyle. Finally, a systems approach would suggest that the overeating and inactivity habits serve a function in the marriage. Couples' treatment would be necessary in the first two situations in order to change the spouse's pattern of reinforcing maladaptive eating and exercising behavior. The systems viewpoint would predict that couples' treatment is necessary in order to determine how the obesity fits into the marriage and how it reflects other problems. Once identified, marital therapy could address these issues.

Theoretically, a psychoanalytic viewpoint can apply here also. This perspective would suggest that the overweight client and/or the spouse have unresolved conflicts regarding oral needs. Following this rationale, parallel individual psychotherapy or psychoanalytically oriented marital therapy could identify, address, and resolve these intrapsychic conflicts.

A potential benefit of couples' training for the treatment of obesity is the group support for the couple as a unit, as well as for the obese individual. One of the early anecdotal comments concerning the behavioral group treatment of obesity was the high morale and support experienced by group members. The couples' approach enhances this aspect. In couples' group treatment, the spouse of the obese person can share questions, concerns, and sources of frustration. Furthermore, the group can address issues pertinent to the two individuals as a couple, such as social events and family pressures, which can affect eating behavior. Thus, the benefits of group dynamics can assist the overweight person, the spouse, and the two individuals as a couple.

Over the past 5 years, there have been at least six studies that have evaluated spouse involvement in the treatment of obesity. Rosenthal (1975) found that female subjects whose husbands were included in a weight-loss program lost more weight than those whose treatment did not include their husbands. She also reported that partial involvement, where the husbands attended only the first four meetings of the program, was as effective as full participation. Full participation in her study included attendance at all meetings, contingency contracting, and working together as a team on behavior changes. The mean weight losses in the full husband involvement ($N = 10$), partial husband involvement ($N = 10$), and no husband involvement ($N = 6$) were 10, 10, and 6 pounds, respectively.

In a recent study by Brownell, Heckerman, Westlake, Hayes, and Monti (1978), 29 subjects (19 females and 10 males) were treated in a 10-week behavioral group program followed by monthly sessions for 6 months. In the Cooperative Spouse, Couples' Training condition, subjects and spouses were fully involved in the treatment. Husbands and wives, seen in a group of nine couples, received treatment manuals, monitored their own and their spouses' eating behavior, and worked together on changing eating behaviors. In a second condition—Cooperative Spouse, Subject Alone—the spouse of the obese person was willing to become involved in treatment but the subject attended the group alone. The Noncooperative Spouse, Subject Alone condition included subjects whose spouses had refused to participate in the program, and who also attended the group alone. In this study, it was found that the Cooperative Spouse, Couples' Training condition was more effective than the other two conditions in producing significant weight loss at 3-month and 6-month follow-ups. When analyses of covariance were used to control for the sex and initial weight of the subjects, the same results were found. The results were impressive clinically, with weight losses of almost 30 pounds for the Cooperative Spouse, Couples' Training group, 19.4 pounds for the Cooperative Spouse, Subject Alone group, and 15.1 pounds for the Noncooperative Spouse, Subject Alone group.

Other studies have provided mixed results. Saccone and Israel (1978), in a recent study of 48 females and 1 male subject, reported that reinforcement by a significant other for behavior change, such as cutting down on snacks, was more effective at producing and maintaining weight loss than (a) monetary reinforcement by the therapist for either weight loss or behavior change, (b) monetary reinforcement by a significant other for weight loss, and (c) a standard behavioral program without monetary reinforcement. The mean weight loss of the Reinforcement by Significant Other for Behavior Change condition was 13 pounds at the end of treatment, as compared to mean weight losses of approximately 6 pounds for the other conditions. At a 3-month follow-up, the weight losses were 15 pounds and 7 pounds, respectively. Thus, the type of spouse involvement appeared to be an important consideration.

O'Neill, Curry, Hirsch, Riddle, Taylor, Malcolm, and Sexauer (1979) analyzed data concerning both spouse involvement and the sex of the subject. They found no effect for spouse involvement for weight loss at posttreatment or at follow-up. In this study spouses were encouraged to provide support to the subject and to discuss their responses to the spouse's weight loss. This study also found, as do most studies, that males lose more weight and maintain the weight losses better than females.

Pearce, LeBow, and Orchard (Note 2) reported a study in which subjects were randomly assigned to one of four conditions: a behavioral couples' training group, a behavioral treatment program for the subjects alone, a nonbehavioral treatment group, and a delayed treatment control group. Results at posttreatment indicated a superiority of both behavioral groups over the control groups, but there were no differences between the couples' training and the behavioral group for subjects alone. However, follow-up periods of 3, 6, 9, and 12 months revealed that couples' training was significantly more effective than the individual behavioral group. Weight losses for the couples' group were 16.5 and 18.19 pounds at the 6- and 12-month follow-ups, respectively.

Zitter (1979) compared full, partial, and minimal spouse involvement in a study of 38 females. In the Full Participation condition, subjects and spouses met every week, monitored their own behavior changes, and reinforced each other for change. In the Partial Participation condition, spouses attended only the first and last meetings, but spouses worked together outside of the group on behavior change, and data were brought in every week. In the Minimal Participation condition, the spouses attended the first and last meetings, but there was no monitoring or reinforcement for behavior change. The mean number of pounds lost were 12.02, 13.21, and 14.07 in the Full Participation, Partial Participation, and Minimal Participation conditions, respectively. No differences were found between groups on any weight-loss measure at posttreatment or follow-up.

Finally, Brownell (Note 3) reported that a replication of his 1978 study with a larger sample size did not yield the same results.

In summary, on the positive side we have Rosenthal (1975), Brownell et al. (1978), Saccone and Israel (1978), and Pearce, LeBow, and Orchard (Note 2); on the negative side we have O'Neill et al. (1979), Zitter (1979), and Brownell (Note 3). Thus, the issue of spouse involvement is promising, but it is still open to further investigation. Since the dramatic results of the Brownell et al. (1978) study have not been replicated, we cannot conclude that couples' treatment is *the* answer.

An additional question with respect to couples' treatment is long-term maintenance. The hope of involving a significant person in the obese person's environment was that the new eating habits and weight loss would be maintained over a long period of time. Yet none of the studies we have reported here had follow-up periods longer than 1 year. The purpose of the present study was to examine the long-term maintenance of weight loss for subjects involved in couples' treatment.

METHOD

Subjects

Subjects were 13 females and 6 males who had been treated in an earlier program (Brownell et al., 1978). Of the 10 subjects who could not be reached or who refused to participate in the follow-up, three were from the Cooperative Spouse, Couples' Training group; one was from the Cooperative Spouse, Subject Alone group; and five were from the Noncooperative Spouse, Subject Alone group.

Procedure

Subjects were contacted by phone 3 years after the conclusion of the first study and were requested to attend a brief session during which they would be weighed. The subjects reported their weight over the phone and were later weighed by the senior author or by a research assistant under the supervision of the senior author.

RESULTS

Results indicate that the mean number of pounds lost after 3 years was 31.5 for the Cooperative Spouse, Couples' Training group (1 male, 5 females), 10.1 for the Cooperative Spouse, Subject Alone group (4 males, 3 females), and 11.8 for the Noncooperative Spouse, Subject Alone group (1 male, 5 females). Due to the small sample size, these results were not significantly different using pounds lost, percentage weight change, or the weight-reduction quotient.

DISCUSSION

The weight losses of subjects from the couples' treatment group after 3 years are impressive. The mean weight loss of 31.5 pounds is inflated by the tremendous weight loss of one subject, but all six of the subjects in the couples' treatment group maintained a weight loss of at least 17 pounds. The lack of statistical significance reflects large variability of weight losses and a small sample size. Thus, there is a need for replication, particularly in light of the three studies noted which did not demonstrate a positive effect for couples' treatment. In addition, several clinical research issues should be examined.

Nature of Spouse Involvement

All of the studies noted that involved the spouses of the overweight person can be described as behavioral. They all emphasized social learning principles. However, the studies differed as to the amount of structure of the involvement. For example, in the Brownell et al. (1978) study, subjects and spouses were instructed to reinforce such specific behaviors as eating in one location only. On the other hand, the O'Neill et al. (1979) report is not clear on the specificity of spouse support. Similarly, the use of written versus verbal instruction requires greater attention. Studies such as Zitter's (1979) more detailed examination of spouse involvement should be encouraged.

Habit Change vs. Weight Loss

All of the studies emphasized that the spouse or significant other reinforced habit change rather than weight loss. Yet the results and discussion tended to emphasize weight loss. Brownell et al. (1978) reported that the Couples' Training group had significantly higher behavior change scores as measured by daily logs than the subjects in the other two groups. This issue is not addressed in all studies, which, unfortunately, is a common pattern in the area of obesity treatment. As Saccone and Israel (1978) reported, reinforcing habit change leads to greater weight loss than reinforcing weight loss. Yet, we must remember to examine the specific habit changes over follow-up periods. Given the difficulty in gaining subjects' compliance, this is a more difficult but necessary task.

Marital Satisfaction and Weight Loss

A final and thought-provoking issue is the relationship between marital satisfaction, weight loss, and treatment. Four studies have addressed the marital relationship issue.

Rosenthal (1975) did not evaluate marital satisfaction, but she did ask subjects to evaluate the important components of their program. That rated highest by the couples was working together as a team. Rated as least helpful were the husband's recording of his supportive behaviors and the husband's learning to use behavioral procedures. These results might suggest that the nonspecific factors of treatment were the most important. It is noteworthy that none of the studies reviewed thus far have included a group where the subjects and spouses attended a nonbehavioral group.

In the Brownell et al. (1978) paper, the authors used the Family Environment Scale (Moos, 1974) and found no difference between the treatment groups, nor any predictors of weight loss. In the analysis of the logs of the spouse and the subject, the authors reported a high correlation between the subject's and spouse's records of the *spouse's* eating behavior but not the *subject's* eating behavior. This suggests greater difficulty in measuring the behavior of the identified "problem" member of the couple.

Zitter (1979) did the most complete marital assessment of his subjects, using the Locke-Wallace Marital Adjustment Scale (Locke & Wallace, 1959), the Primary Communications Inventory (Navran, 1967), and the Areas of Change Questionnaire (Weiss & Buckler, Note 4). He found the total sample mean score on the Locke-Wallace to be 113.4, which fell in the range of adjusted couples but slightly below the mean of the adjusted sample reported by Locke and Wallace (1959). Zitter found no significant differences between cooperative and noncooperative couples nor any correlation between marital adjustment levels, pretreatment weight, or weight loss during treatment.

Black, Ewart, and Black (Note 5) reported a study of 31 subjects (10 males, 21 females) who requested treatment for obesity at the Stanford Heart Disease Prevention Program. Using the Locke-Wallace Marital Adjustment Scale, the Areas of Change Questionnaire, and the Ability and Performance Rating, which assessed subjects' and spouses' beliefs and expectations, they obtained different results. They found that 40% of the couples fell into the distressed category by any one of the inventories. The authors commented, however, that the couples seemed happier from a clinical point of view than couples requesting marital therapy. The best predictor of outcome proved to be the Ability and Performance Rating. In the *nondistressed* couples, the spouse's statement that he could perform the required behavior changes was correlated with all three outcome measures —the weight loss in pounds, percentage weight change, and weight reduction quotient.

None of the studies found a change in the marital relationship during the time of treatment. Clearly, we need to do more research in this area. What are some of the issues in the assessment of marital relationships and weight programs? First, the studies that have looked at the relationship used self-report measures, which can be affected by subjects' tendency to give socially desirable answers and by the demand characteristics of the situation. Subjects who come to a weight-loss program may not be open about their marital problems, or may even be afraid that they will be excluded from treatment if marital problems are detected. Two anecdotes illustrate this point. In one single-subject study (Heckerman & Zitter, Note 6), the couple refused to fill out marital inventories. The authors were concerned that there would be other difficulties with compliance to the program, or that perhaps marital problems might exist and would interfere with therapy. This was not the case. There were few compliance problems, and if marital problems existed, they did not interfere with the program. On the other hand, Zitter (1979) found that one woman who dropped out of his study because of an impending divorce had *not* scored in the distressed range on the marital satisfaction measures!

It would also make sense to use a wider range of assessment modalities. In addition to self-report questionnaires, observational techniques using either audio- or videotapes for recording would be useful in obtaining more direct measures of marital functioning. For example, tape recordings of mealtime interactions, such as those discussed by Stuart and Davis (1972), could provide a better assessment of family eating patterns. Assessment accuracy could be improved if the couple were instructed to try to interact in as typical a fashion as possible. In the Stuart and Davis (1972) data, the wives were participating in a weight-control program, and may have been more conscious of their behavior and therefore less likely to behave normally. The differences found between the spouse's and the subject's food interactions may have been artificially large.

An additional area of inquiry is the nature of the noncooperative spouse. It is important to report accurately why a spouse was not cooperative. Did the spouse actually refuse, or did the subject state that the spouse refused? Were there baby-sitting problems? Was the spouse embarrassed, angry, or detached? Was the spouse overweight? It would appear that the group of noncooperative spouses is quite heterogeneous and the reasons for their lack of cooperation should be described in greater detail.

Theoretical Considerations

Finally, the various theoretical rationales for couples' treatment can be examined empirically. For example, even though early reviews of the literature did not show that obese subjects were more conflicted or psychopathological than non-obese subjects (Stuart & Davis, 1972), this psychodynamic perspective could be reexamined using both obese subjects and spouses. Such assessment instruments as the MMPI, or even projective tests, could be included.

Perhaps of greater clinical significance would be more detailed examinations of the use of systems and behavioral approaches in treatment. The report of Black et al. (Note 5) indicating that 40% of their couples were distressed suggests that marital satisfaction may indeed be an issue. If marital dissatisfaction is found, the perceived relationship between marital conflict and obesity would be of further interest. Given the sensitive nature of this material, perhaps more extensive clinical interviews would be necessary. The demand characteristics of most behavioral groups might not elicit this material; systematic interviews, however, could be included.

Finally, more detailed accounts of both eating *and* exercising behavior could enhance the behavioral approach. Baseline self-monitoring and spouse monitoring could be used to assess the specific areas of dysfunctional behavior. This approach could involve single-subject as well as group designs (Heckerman & Zitter, Note 6), and it would be important to assess and attempt to change the activity level—the often overlooked variable.

Thus, it can be seen that the use of couples' treatment has made a positive contribution to the behavioral group treatment of obesity, but that further replication with attention to theoretical perspectives is needed.

REFERENCE NOTES

1. Jacobson, N. *A discussion of couples treatment of clinical problems.* Panel presentation at the meeting of the Association for the Advancement of Behavior Therapy, San Francisco, December 1979.
2. Pearce, J. W., LeBow, M. D., & Orchard, J. *The role of spouse involvement in the behavioral treatment of obese women.* Paper presented at the meeting of the Canadian Psychological Association, Quebec City, Quebec, June 15, 1979.
3. Brownell, K. D. *Maintenance of weight loss through behavior training of spouses.* Paper presented at the annual meeting of the American Psychological Association, New York, September 1979.
4. Weiss, R. L., & Buckler, G. R. *Areas of change.* Unpublished manuscript, University of Oregon, 1975.
5. Black, D. R., Ewart, C. K., & Black, J. K. *The role of relationship adjustment in the treatment of obesity.* Paper presented at the annual meeting of the American Psychological Association, New York, September 1979.
6. Heckerman, C. L., & Zitter, R. B. *Spouse monitoring and reinforcement in the treatment of obesity.* Paper presented at the meeting of the Association for the Advancement of Behavior Therapy, San Francisco, December 1979.

REFERENCES

Brownell, K. D., Heckerman, C. L., Westlake, R. J., Hayes, S. C., & Monti, P. M. The effects of couples' training and partner cooperativeness in the behavioral treatment of obesity. *Behaviour Research and Therapy,* 1978, *16*, 323-333.

Heinzelmann, F., & Bagley, R. W. Response to physical activity programs and their effects on health behavior. *Public Health Reports,* 1970, *85*, 905-911.

Locke, H. S., & Wallace, K. M. Short-term marital adjustment and prediction tests: Their reliability and validity. *Journal of Marriage and Family Living,* 1959, *21,* 251–255.

Mahoney, M. J., & Mahoney, K. Treatment of obesity: A clinical exploration. In B. J. Williams, S. Martin, & J. P. Foreyt (Eds.), *Obesity: Behavioral approaches to dietary management.* New York: Brunner/Mazel, 1976.

Moos, R. *Family Environment Scale, Preliminary Manual.* Palo Alto, Calif.: Consulting Psychologists Press, 1974.

Navran, L. Communication and adjustment in marriage. *Family Process,* 1967, *6,* 173–184.

O'Neill, P. M., Curry, H. S., Hirsch, F. A., Riddle, F. E., Taylor, C. I., Malcolm, R. J., & Sexauer, J. D. Effect of sex of subject and spouse involvement on weight loss in a behavioral treatment program: A retrospective investigation. *Addictive Behaviors,* 1979, *4,* 1–11.

Rosenthal, B. *The role of a significant other in the behavioral treatment of overweight women.* Unpublished dissertation, University of Connecticut, 1975.

Saccone, A. J., & Israel, A. C. Effects of experimenter versus significant other-controlled reinforcement and choice of target behavior on weight loss. *Behavior Therapy,* 1978, *9,* 271–278.

Stuart, R. B., & Davis, B. *Slim chance in a fat world: Behavioral control of overeating.* Champaign, Ill.: Research Press, 1972.

Zitter, R. *Spouse involvement in a behavioral weight loss program.* Unpublished dissertation, West Virginia University, 1979.

SUBJECT INDEX

Ability and Performance Rating,
315
Accurate empathy, 195, 200
Achievement Place, 155, 156, 161
Adolescent Self-Expression Scale,
81, 90, 91, 95–96, table 5.1
(p. 98), 102
Adult Self-Expression Scale (ASES),
41, 53, table 3.2 (p. 55), 56,
tables 3.4 and 3.5 (p. 57)
Areas of Change Questionnaire, 315
Assertion skills, table 1.1 (p. 10)
Assertion training
in cognitive behavior therapy,
43, 48–50, 54
in a large group format, 28–29,
37
learning principles incorporated
into, 16
for sex offenders, as treatment,
169–170
studies, 8
Assessment
of client improvement, 168
nonverbal, 174, 180–181
role-playing as method of, 31,
87–88, 123, 130–131,
172–174
of social behavior, problems in,
273–274
of social skills deficits in juvenile
delinquents, 105, 116–125
"Attack therapy", 154
Attrition
in obesity treatment groups,
302–303, fig. 12.3 (p. 304)

in social skills training groups,
270–271

Barrett-Lennard Relationship Inventory, 200, 204
Beck Depression Inventory (BDI),
41, 51, 53, table 3.2 (p. 55),
56, tables 3.4 and 3.5 (p. 57),
58, 59, 199, 208, fig. 9.1
(p. 209)
Behavioral Assertion Test (BAT),
13, 172–174
Behavioral logs, use of, 48
Behavioral rehearsal, 16, 82, 129
Behavior Role-play Test (BRT), 81,
87–88, 90, 91, 96, table 5.1
(p. 98), 100, 101
Biofeedback, in the treatment of
hypertension, 226

Client-centered therapy, 168,
194–195
Cognitive behavior therapy
description of, 42
pregroup interview in, 61–62
problem-solving module in,
60–61
studies, 50–51
three-module system of, 43–50
Cognitive Distortion Vignettes
(CDV), 199
Cognitive restructuring (CR), 43,
47–48, 54
Cohesiveness, 242–243, 270,
298–300
Congruence (genuineness), 195, 200

Contracts, weight-reduction, 303,
    fig. 12.3 (pp. 304–305)
Conversational skills, 8, 9, table 1.1
    (p. 11), 13, 15

Daily Activities Record, 251, fig.
    11.2 (pp. 252–253)
Dating anxiety, 5
Dating initiation skills, 8, table 1.1
    (p. 11)
Deep muscle relaxation (DMR),
    45–46
Depressives
    behavioral vs. supportive ap-
        proach to treatment of,
        202–203, 213–217
    elderly
        behavior therapy with,
            191–192
        studies of, 188–189
    younger, behavior therapy with,
        190–191
Didactic interaction, 297–298
Directive competence, 200
Dysfunctional Attitude Scale
    (DAS), 60, 199

Electromyographic recording
    (EMG), 227, 229, 231, 235,
    237
Enthusiasm, 200
Expectancies, effects on treatment
    of, 62

Face-Hand Test, 197
Family conference report cards,
    157, fig. 7.1 (p. 158), 158
Family Environment Scale, 315
Feedback
    between co-therapists, 283
    on efficacy of treatment, by
        clients, 167–168, 283
    to elderly depressives, in group
        therapy, 202
    giving, as therapist role in
        assertion training, 49

in job interview training, 16–17
interpersonal, 154
peer-group, in treatment of
    juvenile delinquency,
    154–155, 164–165
on skill components, by
    adjudicated youths, 121
in social skills training, 6, 82,
    129, 242, 249
videotape used for, 157

Gambrill and Richey Assertion
    Scales, 31, tables 2.1 and 2.2
    (p. 33), 34, 35, 171, 175,
    176, 180
Group process interaction, 297–298
Group therapy
    advantages of, over self-manage-
        ment packages, 296–297
    effectiveness of, for the elderly,
        192–193, 213

Hamilton Rating Scale for
    Depression (HRS-D), 41, 54,
    table 3.3 (p. 56), 56, 58
Hollingshead Two-Factor Index of
    Social Class, table 3.1 (p. 52)
Homework assignments
    in behavioral group therapy, 242
    in cognitive restructuring, 47
    for elderly depressives, in group
        therapy, 202
    in obesity treatment, 282, table
        12.1 (pp. 284–285), table
        12.2 (pp. 286–290), 296,
        303, fig. 12.3 (p. 304)
    in social skills training, 273
        for adjudicated youths, 135,
            136, 146–147
        for psychiatric outpatients,
            242, fig. 11.1 (p. 244),
            247, 249, 251–254,
            260, fig. 11.6 (p. 261),
            271–273
Hopkins Symptom Checklist
    (SCL-90), 199

Hypertension, studies of relaxation training for, 226–227

Instruction, in social skills training, 6
Interpersonal Events Schedule (IES), 199, 208

Job interview skills, 5, 8, table 1.1 (pp. 10–11), 13, 16–17
Juvenile delinquency
  control of groups undergoing treatment for, 104–105, 143–150
  generality of group training approach to, 150–151
  groups as a treatment modality for, 103–104
  intervention approaches for, 84–86
  maintenance of maladaptive behaviors in, 83–84
  obtaining cooperation for treatment of, 149–150
  peer-group feedback in treatment of, 164–165
  social skills deficits related to, 105, 114, 116–125

Leadership ability of therapists, 67–68, 74–76, 129–130
Locke-Wallace Marital Adjustment Scale, 315

Mental retardation, 4–5
Mental Status Questionnaire, 197
Methodological problems, 34–36, 169, 193–195
Minnesota Multiphasic Personality Inventory (MMPI), 197, 199, fig. 9.1 (p. 209), 316
Modeling, 6, 16, 46, 86–87, 129, 242, 243, 267–271

NASA game, 32, tables 2.1 and 2.2 (p. 33), 172, 176, 180

Negative feedback
  in controlling youths in social skills training groups, 144–145
  skill components of, fig. 6.1 (p. 121)
Nowicki-Strickland Locus of Control Scale (NSLCS), 81, 83, 90, 91, 96–97, table 5.1 (p. 98)

Obesity
  attrition reduction in groups treated for, 302–303, fig. 12.3 (p. 304)
  booster sessions in treatment of, 282
  couples' treatment of, theoretical rationales for, 310, 316–317
  habit changes vs. weight loss in treatment of, 314
  marital satisfaction, in relation to success of treatment of, 314–317
  physician approval form for treatment of, 279, 301, fig. 12.2 (p. 301)
  posttreatment questionnaire used with treatment of, 279, 283, fig. 12.1 (pp. 290–293)
  psychoanalytic view of, 310
  questions asked during treatment of, 295–296
  screening of clients being treated for, 300–301, 302
  session topic agenda for treatment of, 279, 282, table 12.1 (pp. 284–285)
  spouse involvement in treatment of, 311–313, 314
  studies on, 280–281, 310–313, 314–317
    behavioral, 280
    couples', 311–317

Obesity *(continued)*
  therapist attitudes toward, 283,
    293–295
  therapist preparation for treat-
    ment of, 279, 281–283
  weekly session guidelines for
    therapist treatment of,
    279, 283, table 12.2
    (pp. 286–290)

Peer-criticism skills training, 157–
    160
  behavior specification interview
    as part of, 156–157
Peer reporting, 155, 157–160, 161,
    fig. 7.4 (p. 162), 164
Performance anxiety, 6–7, 20, 36–
    37, 82
Piers-Harris Children's Self-Concept
    Scale (PHCSCS), 81, 90–91,
    96, table 5.1 (p. 98)
Pleasant Events Schedule (PES),
    171–172, 175, 176, 180
Practice, 6, 157
Primary Communications Inven-
    tory, 315
Primary Mental Abilities Test
    (PMA), table 9.1 (p. 198)
Problem behaviors, of adjudicated
    youths in group therapy, 97,
    100–101, 143–147
Problem-solving training, 60–61,
    86, 92–95, 101

Rathus Assertiveness Schedule, 31,
    32, tables 2.1 and 2.2 (p. 33),
    34, 35, 171, 175, 176, 180
Reinforcement Survey Schedule,
    218
Reinforcing consequences, in social
    skills training, 6
Relationship factors, in treatment
    outcome, 193–195
Relationship Happiness Scale, 31,
    tables 2.1 and 2.2 (p. 33), 34,
    35

Relaxation training, 43, 45–47, 54,
    226–228, 235–238
Role-playing (role-rehearsal)
  in assertion training, 29, 30, 32,
    34, 36, 37, 49
  as assessment method, 31, 87–
    88, 123, 130–131, 172–
    174
  in social skills training, 17, 22,
    242, 272–273
    for adjudicated youths,
      129, 146
    for psychiatric outpatients,
      242–243, 249–251,
      267–271

Schizophrenics, 4–5, 262, 274, 275
Self-appraisal, 20–21
Self-report delinquency scale, 135
Self-report inventories, 14, 35, 227
Sensitivity, 70–71
  definition of, 70
  measurements of, 71–74
  and therapist leadership, 75–76
Social competence, definition of,
    116
Social skills
  acquisition of, 4–7
  checklists for, 119–120, 122–
    125
  components of, 121
  definition of, 4
Social skills training
  active treatment components
    of, 14–17
  assessment of clients' compe-
    tency prior to, 12–14
  behavioral definition of goal
    responses in, 8–12
  evaluation of, in applied settings,
    21–22
  generalization of, 18–21, 147–
    149, 164, 179, 255
  procedural issues in, 17–21
  purpose and aim of, 7–8
  studies, 82, 114–115, 242

State-Trait Anxiety Inventory
(STAI), 41, 51, 53, table
3.2 (p. 55), 56, tables 3.4 and
3.5 (p. 57)
Structured and Scaled Interview to
Assess Maladjustment
(SSIAM), 246, 255
Subjective Units of Discomfort
Scale (SUDS), 45
Subject variables and treatment
outcome, 196, 217–218,
274–275

Systematic desensitization, 226, 227

Videotapes, use of
for assessment, 160, 172–174
in skills training, 48, 49, 86–87,
92–93, 157–159, 174

WISER Way, 93–94, 102–103

Zung Self-Rating Depression Scale
(SDS), 199, 208, fig. 9.1
(p. 209)

AUTHOR INDEX

Abramson, E.E., 280, 281
Agras, S., 226
Alexander, J.F., 85
Alper, B.S., 154
Alper, T., 191
Anderson, S.C., 168
Appelbaum, M.I., 205
Argyle, M., 268
Arkowitz, H., 11, 59, 272
Ayala, H.E., 165
Azrin, N.H., 31

Bach, G.R., 154
Baer, D.M., 149, 157
Bagley, R.W., 310
Bandura, A., 5, 58, 87, 93, 114,
    214
Barlow, D., 22
Barrett-Lennard, G.T., 200, 204
Bastien, S., 91
Battegay, R., 241
Bean, L.L., 52
Beck, A.T., 42, 50, 51, 53, 54, 60,
    82, 191, 199, 275
Bednar, R.L., 192, 216, 243, 271
Bellack, A.S., 4, 5, 8, 18, 281
Bellucci, J.E., 91
Bender, M., 197
Bengston, V.L., 196
Bennis, W.G., 154
Benson, H., 45, 226
Berenson, B.G., 168
Berger, L., 193
Berger, M., 192, 193, 214
Bergin, A., 194
Berkman, R.L., 189

Berler, E.S., 9
Berlew, D.E., 154
Berwick, P.T., 242
Beuhler, R.E., 84
Biegel, A., 28, 242
Biglan, A., 197
Black, D., 114, 315, 316
Black, J.K., 315
Blanchard, E.B., 5, 226
Blaney, P., 190
Blocksma, D.D., 168
Blom, G.E., 85
Blumberg, A., 164
Blumenthal, M.D., 189
Bodner, G.E., 32, 172
Bond, F.T., 84
Booraem, C.D., 30, 32, 36, 68, 75,
    169, 170, 171, 172, 242
Borkovec, T.D., 215
Bornstein, M.R., 8
Bowers, K.S., 84
Brancale, R., 170
Braukmann, C.J., 8, 11, 84, 118,
    161, 165
Brendtro, L.K., 154
Briar, S., 114
Brissenden, A., 243
Britton, G., 170
Brockway, B.S., 82
Broder, P.K., 135, 150
Brown, L., 170
Brown, T.R., 75
Brownell, K.D., 311, 312, 313,
    314, 315
Bryan, J.H., 28
Bryant, B., 268

Buckler, G.R., 315
Bunker, B.B., 154
Burkhard, J., 82
Burnside, I., 213
Butler, R., 188, 189
Byassee, J.E., 226, 228

Callner, D.A., 8
Calmas, W., 170
Cameron, R., 20
Camp, B.W., 85
Campbell, D., 191
Campbell, D.T., 21, 169, 216
Carkhuff, R.R., 167, 168
Carney, L.P., 115
Cartwright, M.H., 62
Cautela, J.R., 192, 218
Cavior, N., 154
Chapman, S.L., 280
Christensen, A., 272
Christensen, E.R., 280, 281, 302
Chu, F.D., 28
Claiborne, M., 9, 10
Clark, J.B., 243
Clark, J.P., 114
Coghlan, D.J., 41
Cohen, M., 170
Cohn, G.M., 189
Cohn, Y., 114
Coleman, E., 170
Cone, J.D., 14
Cooper, C.G., 28, 29
Corby, N., 169
Cotler, S., 170
Covi, L., 199
Cowen, E.L., 28
Coyne, J.C., 190, 217
Craig, K., 190
Cristol, A., 194
Cumming, E., 196
Cummings, N.A., 59
Curran, J.P., 4, 5, 6, 8, 18, 59
Curry, H.S., 312
Cuthbert, S.A., 243

Davis, B., 310, 316
Davison, G.C., 62, 170

Day, M., 67
DeBoer, G., 280
De Lange, J.M., 82, 88
DeLo, J.S., 91
DeRisi, W.J., 242
Derogatis, L.R., 199
Deutsch, R.M., 154
Dies, R.D., 67
Donahoe, C.P., Jr., 82
Doty, D.W., 242
Dressel, M.E., 9, 10
Durham, T.W., 302
D'Zurilla, T.J., 42, 60, 82, 86, 88,
    93, 116, 117

Eber, H., 169
Ebersole, G.O., 68, 71
Edelstein, B.A., 8, 10, 114
Edwards, N., 169
Eisdorfer, C., 28, 189, 213
Eisler, R.M., 5, 8, 9, 10, 13, 19, 86,
    172, 174, 180
Eitzen, D.A., 118
Elder, J.P., 114
Ellis, A., 42, 47, 54, 82, 170
Emerson, R., 243
Emery, G., 50, 275
Empey, L.T., 154, 155
Erbaugh, J., 199
Esty, J.E., 67
Evensen, P., 271
Ewart, C.K., 315

Falloon, I.R.H., 245, 274
Farquhar, J.W., 226
Farr, S.P., 226
Fay, G., 85, 93
Fazio, A., 50
Feldman, G., 154
Fey, S.G., 226
Fidel, E.A., 226
Field, G.D., 242
Finch, A.J., Jr., 83
Fink, M., 197
Fisher, R.H., 164
Fitts, H., 18

Fixsen, D.L., 8, 11, 82, 84, 85,
114, 118, 154, 155, 161, 165
Flannery, R.B., 192
Fleiss, J.L., 246
Flowers, J.V., 28, 29, 30, 32, 36,
37, 68, 75, 169, 170, 171,
172, 242
Fodor, I.E., 83, 84
Follette, W., 59
Foreyt, J.P., 281, 302
Foy, D.W., 8
Frangia, G.W., 168
Frank, J.D., 7, 8, 194, 246
Fredericksen, L.W., 8, 18
Freedman, B.J., 82, 83, 84, 117,
118
Friedman, P.H., 86
Furman, W., 8, 11, 13
Furniss, J.M., 84

Gaitz, C.M., 189
Galassi, J.P., 16, 53, 85, 91
Galassi, M.D., 16, 85, 91
Gallagher, D., 199
Gambrill, E.D., 31, 171
Ganzer, V.J., 82, 84, 86, 87, 114
Garlington, W.K., 226
Gauthier, J., 192
Gay, M., 53
Geiger, H.J., 229
Geller, M.I., 8, 11, 67
Gershaw, H.J., 155
Gershon, B., 226
Gershon, E., 226
Gerst, M., 93
Giffin, K., 154
Gilbert, F.S., 6, 8
Gilchrist, L., 85, 93
Gilner, F.H., 242
Gioe, V.J., 50
Glasgow, R.E., 11, 59
Glass, D., 191
Glatzer, H., 67
Glazeski, R.C., 9, 10
Gleser, A., 243
Glick, B., 155

Golann, S.E., 28
Goldberg, H., 154
Goldberg, I.D., 59
Goldfarb, A., 197
Goldfried, A.P., 10
Goldfried, M.R., 10, 42, 60, 62, 82,
86, 88, 93, 116, 117
Goldman, N., 114
Goldman, R.D., 29, 37
Goldsmith, J.B., 82, 274
Goldstein, A.P., 62, 155, 242
Golembiewski, R.T., 164
Goodman, J., 84, 85
Gordon, S.B., 14
Gorsuch, R.L., 53
Gottesman, L.E., 189, 213
Graf, M., 190
Green, D.R., 85, 115
Green, M.A., 193
Green, R., 197
Gressell, G.C., 229
Grieger, R., 42
Gross, S.Z., 114
Grusec, J.E., 93
Guerra, J., 28, 30, 36, 170
Gurland, B., 189, 246
Gutride, M.E., 242

Haber, L., 193, 213
Hagen, R.L., 280, 302, 303
Hall, R.G., 280
Hall, S.M., 280
Hallbauer, E.S., 280
Hamilton, M., 54
Hammen, C., 191, 199
Harper, R., 47
Harris, D.B., 90, 96
Harris, D.E., 75
Harris, M.B., 280
Hartford, M., 216
Hathaway, S.R., 197
Hathorn, S., 8
Hauserman, N., 84
Hawkins, R.P., 14
Hayes, S.C., 311
Haynes, S., 216

Hazel, J.S., 148, 150
Heckerman, C.L., 311, 316, 317
Heinzelmann, F., 310, 316
Herbert, F., 85
Hersen, M., 4, 5, 8, 9, 10, 18, 22, 86, 114, 172
Hersko, M., 85
Hines, P., 11
Hirsch, F.A., 312
Hogan, J.L., 164
Hollandsworth, J.C., 9, 10, 14, 16, 53
Hollon, S.D., 50, 51, 58
Hoyer, W., 192
Huck, S.W., 231
Hunter, G.F., 242

Ihli, K.L., 226
Ingersoll, B., 193
Israel, A.C., 311, 312, 314

Jacobs, A., 153
Jacobs, M., 154
Jacobson, E., 45, 51, 54, 226, 227
Jacobson, N., 310
Jakubowski, P., 47, 51, 54, 82
Jarvis, P.E., 67
Jeffery, R.W., 93
Jeffrey, D.B., 280, 281, 282, 283, 302
Jenkins, J.O., 8
Jersild, A., 91
Jones, R., 31

Kagan, J., 83
Kahn, R., 197
Kanter, S.S., 67
Kaplan, R.M., 169
Kapp, F., 243
Kashdan, G., 243
Kastenbaum, R., 218
Katz, R.C., 282, 302
Kaul, J.T., 192, 216
Kazdin, A.E., 14, 47, 155
Keane, T.M., 20
Keefe, F.J., 14
Keefe, T., 164

Keilitz, I., 150
Keller, O.J., 154
Kellett, J., 268
Kelly, J.A., 5, 8, 9, 10, 11, 13, 14, 15, 16, 18, 20, 21
Kendall, P.C., 84
Kennedy, T.D., 82
Keppel, G., 231
Kern, J.M., 20
Kiesler, D.J., 200
Kifer, R.E., 85, 115, 118, 165
King, L.W., 28, 242
Kingsley, R.G., 280, 282
Kirigin, K.A., 165
Kirkley, B.G., 20
Klein, N.C., 85
Klerman, G.L., 54
Knauss, C.S., 282
Knauss, M.R., 279, 281, 282
Knight, B., 192
Kogan, N., 83
Kondas, O., 226
Kopel, S.A., 14
Kovacs, M., 50
Kramer, J.A., 5
Kramer, M., 188
Krantz, G., 59
Krantz, S., 199
Kuehn, F., 148
Kuypers, J.A., 196

Lakin, M., 67
Lambert, C., 268
Lambert, M., 194
Lamier, D., 271
Lamparski, D., 5
Lange, A.J., 7, 47, 51, 54, 82
Larson, M., 193, 213
Laughlin, C., 8, 9, 10
Laventure, R., 170
Lawlis, G.F., 243
Laws, D.R., 82, 169
Lazarus, A.A., 45, 91, 169, 226
LeBow, M.D., 312
Lefcourt, H.M., 83
Lefeber, J.A., 84
Leff, J.P., 272

Leiderman, P.H., 68, 71
Leon, G.R., 281
Levenson, A.I., 28
Levin, S., 67
Levine, M., 154
Lewis, M.A., 85, 115, 188, 189
Liberman, R.P., 28, 242, 243, 271
Libet, J., 171, 190
Lichtenstein, E., 11
Lieberman, M.A., 67
Liederman, P.C., 193, 213
Liederman, V.R., 193
Limentain, D., 67
Lindholm, E., 226
Lindley, P., 245
Lindquist, C.U., 5
Linehan, M.M., 10
Lipman, R.S., 199
Liss-Levinson, N., 170
Litrownik, A.J., 169
Little, V.L., 84
Litz, M.C., 16, 85
Locke, B.Z., 59
Locke, H.S., 315
Lomont, J.F., 242
Lott, L.A., Jr., 85
Lowenthal, M.F., 189
Lubeck, S.G., 154
Luborsky, L., 194, 215
Lushene, R.E., 53

McCall, R.B., 205
McCann, M., 242
McCarthy, D.J., 91
MacDonald, M.L., 5, 8
McDonald, R., 245
McFall, R.M., 8, 29, 82, 86, 171, 174, 274
McGarvey, W., 199
McGovern, K., 11, 82
McGovern, T., 170
McGrath, R.A., 5
McKinley, J.C., 197
McLean, R.A., 231
MacLennon, B.W., 85
McNair, D., 199
MacPhillamy, D.J., 171, 190

Mahoney, K., 310
Mahoney, M.J., 87, 280, 281, 310
Maiuro, R.D., 85, 93
Malcolm, R.J., 312
Maloney, D.M., 85
Mansfield, L., 192
Marshall, K.A., 192, 195
Marshall, W.L., 50, 191
Marston, A.R., 8, 29, 171, 174
Martin, S., 281
Martinson, W.D., 5
Martorano, R.D., 16
Marzillier, J.S., 268
Matarazzo, J., 68, 75, 167, 168, 169
Meichenbaum, D., 20, 42, 82, 84, 85, 87
Melnick, J., 5, 8, 13, 16, 271
Mendelson, M., 199
Menlove, F.L., 93
Meyer, R.G., 226
Miller, J.S., 84
Miller, P.M., 5, 8, 9, 10, 86, 172
Minkin, B.L., 8, 11, 84, 114, 118, 161
Minkin, N., 8, 9, 11, 84, 114, 118, 161
Mirels, H.L., 85
Mischel, W., 5, 14
Mitchell, K.M., 195
Mock, J.E., 199
Montgomery, L.E., 83
Monti, P.M., 311
Moos, R.H., 155, 315
Morris, N.E., 50
Morrison, B.J., 164
Moser, A.J., 85
Moura, N., 280
Munoz, R.F., 58, 191, 200, 214
Murphy, P., 193
Myers, J.K., 52

Narick, M.M., 114
Naster, B.J., 31
Navran, L., 315
Nelson, E., 226
Nelson, W.M., III, 84

Nickell, M.A., 82, 84
Nietzel, M.T., 16
Nivid, J., 171
Nowicki, S., Jr., 83, 91, 97
Nunnally, J.C., 169

O'Kulitch, P., 280
O'Leary, K.D., 82, 215
Ollendick, T.H., 114
O'Neill, P.M., 312, 314
Ora, J.P., 168
Orchard, J., 312
Ostrom, T.M., 85

Padfield, M., 191
Papageorgis, D., 190
Pappas, J.P., 281
Parloff, M., 196
Parsons, B.V., 85
Patterson, G.R., 84
Patterson, J.N., 20
Patterson, J.T., 8, 9, 10, 11
Patterson, R.L., 82, 84
Patton, B.R., 154
Paul, G.L., 226, 227
Paykel, E.S., 54
Pearce, J.W., 312
Pearson, L., 83
Peck, A., 197
Percell, L.P., 242
Pfeiffer, E., 188, 189
Phillips, E.A., 82, 155
Phillips, E.L., 8, 11, 28, 82, 84, 85,
    114, 115, 118, 154, 155,
    161, 165
Phillips, J., 8, 18
Piaget, G.W., 168
Piers, E.V., 90, 96
Piliavin, I., 114
Pinkston, S., 8
Platt, J.J., 42
Pollack, M., 197
Porter, E.H., Jr., 168
Prkachin, K., 190
Prusoff, B.A., 54

Quarterman, E.E., 189

Rabow, J., 155
Rashbaum-Selig, M., 85
Rathus, S.A., 16, 31, 171
Rebok, G.W., 192
Rechtschaffen, A., 189
Redick, R., 188
Rehm, L.P., 191
Reisinger, J.J., 168
Reiss, A., 114
Reith, G., 190
Rhyne, L.D., 5
Rich, A.R., 170
Richards, W.S., 191, 192
Richey, C.A., 31, 171
Riddle, F.E., 312
Rimm, D.C., 82
Risley, T.R., 157
Roberts, J., 28
Robin, A., 85
Robinson, J.C., 191
Rodin, J., 281
Rogers, C., 194
Rose, S.D., 82, 148, 192, 214, 236,
    281, 298
Rosen, J.C., 59
Rosenblood, L.K., 85
Rosenthal, B., 311, 312, 314
Rosenthal, L., 82
Ross, R.R., 84
Ross, S.M., 8
Roth, D., 217
Roth, L., 281
Rotter, J.B., 83, 91
Rowland, K., 216
Rush, A.J., 50, 51, 58, 275

Saccone, A.J., 311, 312, 314
Salzman, C., 213
Sammons, R., 227, 229
Sank, L.I., 41, 43, 47
Sarason, I.G., 82, 84, 86, 87, 114
Sarbinetta, T., 83
Schein, E.H., 154
Schinke, S.P., 214
Schlundt, D.G., 82
Schmickley, V.G., 50
Schneider, M., 85

Schroeder, H.E., 170
Schumaker, J.B., 148, 150
Schwartz, D.A., 28
Schwartz, G., 226
Schwartz, R.D., 216
Scotch, N., 229
Seacat, G.F., 68, 75
Sechrest, L., 28, 216
Seghorn, T., 170
Seligman, M.E.P., 59, 83, 191
Serber, M., 82, 169, 170
Serna, L., 150
Sexauer, J.D., 312
Shader, R., 213
Shaffer, C.S., 41, 43, 47
Shaffer, M., 190
Shannon, D.T., 226
Shapiro, D., 226
Shapiro, J., 41
Shaw, B.F., 50, 51, 58, 191, 214,
    216, 275
Shaw, D., 191
Sheldon-Wildgen, J., 148, 150
Sherman, J.A., 148, 155
Sherman, M., 155
Shipley, C., 50
Shoemaker, J.E., 226
Shure, M., 85
Siegel, S., 204
Silverman, A., 193
Simon, S.J., 8, 11
Singer, B., 194
Skinner, K.K., 242
Skrzypek, G.J., 83
Sloane, R., 194, 214, 215, 217
Small, I., 68, 75
Smith, M.J., 48
Spector, N.J., 242
Spielberger, C.D., 53
Spivack, G., 42, 60, 85
Sprafkin, R.P., 155
Stain, K.B., 83
Stanley, J.C., 21, 169
Staples, F., 194
Steele, C.M., 85
Steele, F.I., 154
Stern, M., 226

Stevens, J., 9
Stevenson, I., 169
Stocker, R.B., 8
Stokes, T.F., 149
Stone, H.R., 246
Stotsky, B., 189, 213
Strickland, B.R., 83, 91, 97
Stuart, R.B., 85, 310, 316
Stunkard, A.J., 280
Swift, M.S., 242
Sykes, R.E., 114

Talkington, J., 200
Tapper, B., 169, 171
Tasto, D.L., 226
Taube, G., 188
Taylor, C.B., 226, 228, 236
Taylor, C.I., 312
Taylor, F.G., 50
Taylor, S., 191, 193
Test, M.A., 242
Thompson, L.W., 199
Thorpe, G.L., 191, 192
Thurman, C., 5, 8, 11
Thurstone, L.L., 198
Thurstone, T.G., 198
Timbers, B.J., 8, 11, 84, 118, 161
Timbers, G.D., 8, 11, 84, 118, 161
Tinsley, D., 170
Toch, H., 114
Trimble, R.W., 227
Trotter, S., 28
Trower, P., 268
Truax, C.B., 167, 168, 195, 200
Trupin, E.L., 85, 93
Turner, S.M., 18
Twentyman, C.T., 4, 8, 18, 29, 82,
    86

Urey, J.R., 5, 8, 9, 10, 11, 13, 15,
    16
U. S. Department of Health,
    Education and Welfare, 280
U. S. Public Health Service, 280

Van Doorninck, W.J., 85
Vaughan, C.E., 272

Vorrath, H.H., 154
Vygotsky, L.S., 84

Wade, T., 280
Walder, E., 154
Wallace, K.M., 315
Walters, R.H., 5, 114
Ward, C.H., 199
Waskow, I., 196
Watkins, J.T., 50, 51, 54, 58
Webb, E.J., 216
Wechsler, D., 229
Weiner, H., 229
Weinstein, M., 191
Weiss, R.L., 315
Weissman, A.N., 60, 199
Welch, L., 83
Werder, P., 82, 84
Werner, J.S., 114, 115
West, C., 271
Westlake, R.J., 311
Whipple, K., 194
Whitaker, D.S., 67
Whiteley, J.M., 28, 29
Whittaker, J.K., 154, 164
Wiens, A.N., 59
Wildman, B.G., 5, 8, 9, 11
Wile, D.B., 67
Wilkinson, M.D., 83
Williams, B.J., 281

Wilson, G.T., 8, 82, 170, 280, 282
Wingt, J., 243
Wolf, M.M., 8, 82, 84, 85, 114,
     118, 119, 155, 157, 161, 165
Wolfe, B., 196
Wolfe, J., 82
Wollersheim, J.P., 280
Wolpe, J., 36, 45, 91, 169, 170,
     171
Wyden, P., 154

Yalom, I.D., 7, 8, 62, 68, 71, 243
Yong, J.N., 85
Yorkston, N., 194, 246
Young, E.R., 82
Young, L.D., 226
Youngren, M., 191, 199, 200, 201

Zaremba, B.A., 150
Zax, M., 28
Zeiss, A.M., 58, 191, 197, 199,
     200, 214, 216
Zelinski, E., 199
Zerface, J.P., 5
Zimering, R.T., 4, 18
Zimmerman, J., 135
Zitter, R.B., 312, 314, 315, 316,
     317
Zung, W.W., 199